The Theory of Oligopoly with Multi-Product Firms

2nd Revised and Enlarged Edition

Springer
Berlin
Heidelberg
New York
Barcelona
Hongkong
London
Milan
Paris
Singapore
Tokyo

Koji Okuguchi · Ferenc Szidarovszky

The Theory of Oligopoly with Multi-Product Firms

Second, Revised
and Enlarged Edition

With 9 Figures

Springer

[redacted]

Professor Dr. Koji Okuguchi
Gifu Shotokugakuen University
Department of Economics and Information
Nakauzura
Gifu-shi, Gifu-ken 500-8288, Japan

Professor Dr. Ferenc Szidarovszky
University of Arizona
Systems and Industrial Engineering Department
PO Box 210020
Tucson, AZ 85721-1120, USA

The first edition was published in 1990 under the same title as Lecture Notes in Economics and Mathematical Systems, vol. 342.

ISBN 3-540-65779-7 Springer-Verlag Berlin Heidelberg New York

Cataloging-in-Publication Data applied for
Die Deutsche Bibliothek - CIP-Einheitsaufnahme
Okuguchi, Koji:
The theory of oligopoly with multi-product firms /
Koji Okuguchi; Ferenc Szidarovsky. - 2., rev. and enl. ed. -
Berlin; Heidelberg; New York; Barcelona; Hongkong; London; Milan; Paris;
Singapore; Tokyo : Springer, 1999
ISBN 3-540-65779-7

Hardcover design: Erich Kirchner, Heidelberg
SPIN 10725547 42/2202-5 4 3 2 1 0 - Printed on acid-free paper

[redacted]

Preface

In the mid 1960's both authors undertook independent works in oligopoly and game theory. However, it was not until 1983 that they formally met. Since then, they have continued meeting either in Budapest or Tokyo. Their collaboration has resulted in numerous publications as well as in this work.

Essentially, this book has two origins. First, it originated in previous results, either published or circulated in mimeograph form. Finely sifting their results, the authors constructed a concise reinterpretation of their achievement to date. However, this unifying process led to the second origin. Reconsideration, particularly in this comprehensive approach, generated new results. This was especially true in the analysis of the existence, uniqueness and global stability of the Cournot-Nash equilibrium for oligopoly with multi-product firms, and for several modified Cournot and related models.

This book should be ideal for graduate students in economics or mathematics. However, as the authors have firmly grounded their ideas in the formal language of mathematics, the student should possess some background in calculus, linear algebra, and ordinary differential and difference equations. Additionally, the book should be useful to researchers in oligopoly and game theory as well as to mathematically oriented economists. The methodology developed for analyzing the existence and stability of oligopoly equilibrium should prove useful also in theoretical analysis of other economic models.

We are both very grateful to Professor Wilhelm Krelle for his careful review and helpful suggestions. In addition, Koji Okuguchi wishes to thank Professors W. Krelle, D. Bös and R. Selten for arranging his stay at the Institut für Gesellschafts-und Wirtschaftswissenschaften, Universität Bonn. It was here that some important results were obtained. He is also indebted to Takeshi Yamazaki, whose help was instrumental in obtaining some of the results in this book. Ferenc Szidarovszky is indebted to the Department of Mathematical Sciences at the University of Texas at El Paso and to the Department of Systems and Industrial Engineering at the University of Arizona. Both of these institutions offered ideal working conditions during his visiting professorships and from 1990 during his tenure. Additionally, Szidarovszky thanks Professor J. Szép of the University of Economics in Budapest, for his help during various stages of research. His special thanks go to his former and current graduate students, Jerome Yen, Ling Shen, and Weiye Li for their participation in the research that has led to this book. Both authors thank Éva Németh and Genine Robbins for their efficient and accurate secretarial work.

Finally, this book is a revised version of the earlier one which appeared in 1990 under the same title as No. 342 in *Lecture Notes in Economics and Mathematical Systems* (Springer-Verlag). In the process of revision, we have deleted many parts from the earlier version and tried to include as many new results as possible on the problems which are now actively being discussed on the frontier of economic research.

Table of Contents

1 Introduction

Since the appearance of the classic book by Cournot in 1838, increasing attention has been given to oligopoly, especially after the revival of interest in game theory in the past few decades. Oligopoly is a state of industry where a small number of firms produce homogeneous goods or close substitutes competitively.

Many models consider this situation as a static noncooperative game, which is not repeated in time. In these models the central problem is to find sufficient conditions which guarantee the existence and uniqueness of the so called Cournot or Cournot-Nash equilibrium. This concept will be defined and examined in Chapters 2 and 3.

The static models do not describe the real economic situations properly since the firms produce and sell goods on the market repeatedly over time. This fact implies that dynamic models which are able to describe and analyze the dynamic behavior of firms are more appropriate. These models can be divided into two main types. In the first type the time scale is assumed discrete, and in the second continuous. In both types of models no time lag is assumed between producing and selling the goods. At any time period the profit of each firm depends not only on its outputs but also on the outputs of all other firms which are unknown to the firms when they make their production decisions. Hence at each time, each firm must form expectations on other firms' most likely outputs.

Cournot examined this situation under discrete time scale and assumed that in each period each firm believed that all its rivals' outputs would remain the same as in the preceding period. This simplifying assumption has been modified and generalized by several economists for oligopoly with or without product differentiation and with single product firms. In this book, we will introduce and examine the most popular generalization of Cournot's model, which is known as adaptive expectation. As an example of another type of expectation we will briefly discuss extrapolative expectations as well.

The development of this book is as follows. After discussing static models in Chapters 2 and 3, dynamic models with discrete time scale will be discussed in Chapter 4. In Section 4.1 expectations à la Cournot will be analyzed and adaptive expectations will be discussed in Section 4.2. A special sequential adjustment process under expectations à la Cournot will be introduced in Section 4.3, and extrapolative expectations will be discussed in Section 4.4. The remaining part of Chapter 4 will be devoted to special problems such as those involving market saturation or production adjustment costs in the dynamic models or assuming nonoptimal output selections by the firms, as well as to modifed oligopoly models such as rent-seeking, labor-managed oligopolies, and oligopsonies. Models under continuous time scales will be examined in Chapter 5, where the continuous counterparts of the discrete models will be discussed. In this chapter Cournot, and both adaptive and extrapolative expectations will be first examined, and in the second part the case of nonoptimal output selections, the presence of production adjustment costs and modified models such as rent-seeking, labor-managed oligopolies, and oligopsonies will be analyzed. In Chapter 6 special nonlinear models will be discussed. In the first two sections quadratic models will be introduced, and in Sections 6.3 ad 6.4 the general nonlinear case will be presented. Some applications of the oligopoly theory will be introduced in Chapter 7. We will consider the effect of taxation and multiple markets, and particular applications will be discussed in water resources, international fishery, and networks. In Section 7.7, the controllability of dynamic oligopolies will be briefly considered. At the end of each chapter we will give a short literature review with directions for further readings.

Finally, we mention that all of our models are formulated in partial equilibrium model framework in the sense that oligopoly is analyzed without considering its impacts on other industries and/or those from other industries. In our models, however, multi-product firms are explicitly introduced. All theoretical results so far obtained by other economists on oligopoly without product differentiation as well as on oligopoly with product differentiation but with single product firms will emerge as special cases of our general results.

2 Oligopoly Games and Their Extensions

In this chapter several versions of the oligopoly game are introduced. The most simple model, the classical oligopoly game, will be first described and then its extensions will be analyzed.

2.1 The Cournot Model

Consider a market in which N firms produce a homogeneous good to sell at a unit price which depends on the total output of the industry. The economic interpretation of this property will be analyzed later in Section 2.3. Assume that each firm faces a cost of production which depends only on the output of the firm itself. If L_k denotes the production capacity of firm k, then it can decide about its own output x_k, which therefore should satisfy the inequality $0 \le x_k \le L_k$. Thus, the set of strategies of firm k is given by the closed bounded interval $[0, L_k]$. Let p and C_k $(k = 1, 2, ..., N)$ denote the unit price function and cost function of firm k. This market situation can be modelled as an N-person game where the set of strategies of player (firm) k is the interval $X_k = [0, L_k]$, and its payoff function (profit), can be formulated as

$$\varphi_k(x_1, x_2, ..., x_N) = x_k p\left(\sum_{l=1}^{N} x_l\right) - C_k(x_k). \tag{2.1.1}$$

The *Cournot oligopoly* is an N-person noncooperative game defined by sets X_k of strategies and payoff functions φ_k $(i = 1, 2, ..., N)$. By using the *strategic form* notations (see *e.g.*, Friedman, 1986) of N-person games, Cournot oligopoly may be denoted by $\Gamma = \{N;\ X_1, ..., X_N;\ \varphi_1, ..., \varphi_N\}$.

The solution of the Cournot oligopoly is the *Nash-Cournot equilibrium point* which can be defined as follows:

Definition 2.1.1. A vector $\mathbf{x}^* = (x_1^*, ..., x_N^*)$ is called *Nash-Cournot equilibrium point* of game Γ, if for $k = 1, 2, ..., N$,

(a) $x_k^* \in X_k$;

(b) For arbitrary $x_k \in X_k$,

$$\varphi_k\left(x_1^*,\dots,x_{k-1}^*,x_k^*,x_{k+1}^*,\dots,x_N^*\right) \ge \varphi_k\left(x_1^*,\dots,x_{k-1}^*,x_k,x_{k+1}^*,\dots,x_N^*\right). \tag{2.1.2}$$

In other words, the Nash-Cournot equilibrium point is an N-tuple of strategies for which each player maximizes his own payoff with respect to his own strategy selection, given the strategy choices of all other players. That is, no player can increase his payoff by changing his strategy unilaterally.

Some authors refer to the above equilibrium point as an equilibrium in *pure strategies*. Since in this book no *mixed* (*i.e.* probabilistic) strategies will be considered, equilibria will mean only pure strategy equilibria.

A Cournot oligopoly does not necessarily have an equilibrium point. The following example shows a duopoly (2-person game) in which no equilibrium point exists.

Example 2.1.1. Select N=2, and define $X_1 = X_2 = \left[0, \frac{1}{2}\right]$. Set

$$s = x_1 + x_2,$$
$$p(s) = 1 - s$$
$$C_k(x_k) = \begin{cases} 10x_k + 5 & \text{if} \quad 0 < x_k \le \frac{1}{2} \\ 10, & \text{if} \quad x_k = 0 \end{cases} \qquad (k = 1,2).$$

Let (x_1^*, x_2^*) be an equilibrium point, if there exists any. Assume first that $x_1^* > 0$. Then

$$\begin{aligned}\varphi_1(x_1, x_2^*) &= x_1(1 - x_1 - x_2^*) - 10x_1 - 5 \\ &= -x_1^2 - (9x_1 + x_1x_2^* + 5), \qquad (x_1 > 0)\end{aligned}$$

and

$$\frac{\partial \varphi_1}{\partial x_1}(x_1, x_2^*) = -2x_1 - 9 - x_2^* < 0.$$

Consequently for any x_1, such that $x_1^* - x_1$ is sufficiently small positive number,

$$\varphi_1(x_1, x_2^*) > \varphi_1(x_1^*, x_2^*),$$

hence (x_1^*, x_2^*) is not an equilibrium point. Assume next that $x_1^* = 0$. Then

$$\varphi_1(0, x_2^*) = -10,$$

but

$$\lim_{x_1 \to +0} \varphi_1(x_1, x_2^*) = 0 \bullet p(s^*) - 5 = -5 > \varphi_1(0, x_2^*).$$

Hence for sufficiently small $x_1 > 0$, $\varphi_1(x_1, x_2^*) > \varphi_1(x_1^*, x_2^*)$. Thus, (x_1^*, x_2^*) is not an equilibrium point. We note that a similar example is presented in Okuguchi (1976).

Even in cases when equilibrium point exists the uniqueness of the equilibrium point is not generally true. This is illustrated next.

Example 2.1.2. Select N=2, and $X_1 = X_2 = [0, 1.5]$. Define $C_1(x_1) = 0.5x_1$, $C_2(x_2) = 0.5x_2$ and

$$p(s) = \begin{cases} 1.75 - 0.5s, & \text{if} \quad 0 \le s \le 1.5 \\ 2.5 - s & \text{if} \quad 1.5 \le s \le 2.5 \\ 0, & \text{if} \quad s \ge 2.5 \,. \end{cases}$$

Then we can show that any arbitrary point (x_1^*, x_2^*) from the set

$$X^* = \{(x_1, x_2) | 0.5 \le x_1 \le 1, \quad 0.5 \le x_2 \le 1, \quad x_1 + x_2 = 1.5\}$$

is an equilibrium point. Let $x_1^* + x_2^* = 1.5$, then

$$\frac{\partial}{\partial x_1} \varphi_1(x_1^* - 0, x_2^*) = p'(1.5 - 0) \bullet x_1^* + p(1.5) - C_1'(x_1^* - 0)$$
$$= -0.5x_1^* + 1 - 0.5 = 0.5(1 - x_1^*) \ge 0,$$

and

$$\frac{\partial}{\partial x_1} \varphi_1(x_1^* + 0, x_2^*) = p'(1.5 + 0) \bullet x_1^* + p(1.5) - C_1'(x_1^* - 0)$$
$$= -1 \bullet x_1^* + 1 - 0.5 = 0.5 - x_1^* \le 0.$$

Note that φ_1 is concave in x_1 for fixed values of x_2 such that $x_1 + x_2 \le 2.5$. Therefore x_1^* gives maximal profit for firm 1 among all outputs x_1 such that $x_1 + x_2^* \le 2.5$. Assume next that $x_1 + x_2^* > 2.5$. Then

$$\varphi_1(x_1, x_2^*) = x_1 p(x_1 + x_2^*) - C_1(x_1) < -C_1(x_1) < -C_1(x_1^*) < x_1^* p(x_1^* + x_2^*) - C_1(x_1^*) = \varphi_1(x_1^*, x_2^*),$$

since $x_1 > x_1^*$. Hence x_1^* is optimal among all feasible outputs. One may similarly verify that x_2^* gives the maximal profit for firm 2 with fixed value of x_1^*. Thus (x_1^*, x_2^*) is an equilibrium point.

The model in the above formulation assumes that all necessary inputs for production are available even for the maximal possible total output $\sum_{k=1}^{N} L_k$ of the industry. A generalization of the above model can be formulated by assuming that necessary inputs are available for producing only up to a certain quantity ξ of the total output of the industry. This alternative assumption implies that all strategy vectors $\mathbf{x} = (x_1, ..., x_N)$ must satisfy the condition

$$\sum_{k=1}^{N} x_k \le \xi. \tag{2.1.3}$$

That is, the set of all feasible strategy vectors is

$$X = \left\{ \mathbf{x} \middle| \mathbf{x} = (x_1, ..., x_N) \in R^N,\ 0 \le x_k \le L_k (\forall k),\ \sum_{k=1}^{N} x_k \le \xi \right\}.$$

In general, X is only a subset of the Cartesian product of the individual strategy sets X_k. The strategic form of this game is given by specifying the number N of players, the individual sets X_k of strategies, the feasible set X of the simultaneous strategies, and the payoff functions φ_k. Using the strategic form notation we may write

$$\Gamma = \{N;\ X_1, ..., X_N;\ X;\ \varphi_1, ..., \varphi_N\}. \tag{2.1.4}$$

In cases when X is the Cartesian product of the strategy sets $X_1, ..., X_N$, there is no need to specify set X. Consequently, the specification of set X is not needed, as it was shown in the case of the original formulations given at the beginning of this section. Games in which the set of the simultaneous strategy vectors is restricted to a subset of the Cartesian product of the strategy sets are sometimes called *pseudogames* (see for example, Friedman, 1986).

The solution, that is the equilibrium point of pseudogames, is defined analogously to Definition 2.1.1 as

Definition 2.1.2. A vector $\mathbf{x}^* = (x_1^*, ..., x_N^*)$ is called an equilibrium point of pseudogame Γ if

(a) $\mathbf{x}^* \in X$;

(b) For arbitrary k and x_k such that vector $\mathbf{x} = \left(x_1^*, ..., x_{k-1}^*, x_k, x_{k+1}^*, ..., x_N^*\right) \in X$ we have

$$\varphi_k\left(\mathbf{x}^*\right) \geq \varphi_k(\mathbf{x}).$$

The only difference between the definitions of equilibrium points in the classical oligopoly game and the corresponding pseudogame is the additional condition that both vectors, $\mathbf{x}^*$ and $\mathbf{x}$ in Definition 2.1.2, belong to the restricted set X of simultaneous strategies.

2.2 Models with Product Differentiation

Consider a market with N producers of differentiated product. Because of product differentiation it is assumed that the unit price p_k of the product of firm k $(k = 1, 2, ..., N)$ depends on the production levels x_l of each of the firms. That is, $p_k = p_k\left(x_1, x_2, ..., x_N\right)$. If C_k denotes the cost function of firm k, then the payoff function of player (firm) k can be formulated as

$$\varphi_k\left(x_1, ..., x_N\right) = x_k p_k\left(x_1, ..., x_N\right) - C_k\left(x_k\right). \tag{2.2.1}$$

Let L_k denote the capacity limit of firm k, then the set of strategies for player k is given by the closed interval $X_k = \left[0, L_k\right]$. If no limitation is assumed on the inputs necessary for production, then the *oligopoly game*, $\Gamma = \left\{N;\ X_1, ..., X_N;\ \varphi_1, ..., \varphi_N\right\}$, with *product differentiation* is obtained.

The solution of this game is defined by the equilibrium points, which can be formulated in the same way as was done for the classical oligopoly game in Definition 2.1.1.

The corresponding pseudogame may be similarly formulated. Assume that the available sources are sufficient only for production plans $\mathbf{x} = \left(x_1, ..., x_N\right)$ belonging to a subset X of the Cartesian product $X_1 \times X_2 \times ... \times X_N$ of the strategy sets. Here only those output vectors $\mathbf{x} = \left(x_1, ..., x_N\right)$ which satisfy the additional relation, $\mathbf{x} \in X$, are feasible. The resulting pseudogame then can be denoted as

$$\Gamma = \left\{N;\ X_1, ..., X_N;\ X;\ \varphi_1, ..., \varphi_N\right\}.$$

The equilibrium point of this pseudogame can be defined analogously to Definition 2.1.2.

In the above two models it was assumed that the firms decide on their production levels. These models are called *quantity setting or quantity adjusting* oligopoly models. Similar models can be formulated on the basis of the assumption that the firms make decisions on the unit prices of the products which they produce. These models are called *price setting or price adjusting* oligopoly models. A price setting oligopoly model with product differentiation can be formulated as follows.

Let N again be the number of firms and assume that they produce differentiated products. Because of product differentiation the demand function facing firm k $(1 \le k \le N)$ is a function of the prices of all N firms. That is, $d_k(p_1,\dots,p_N)$ is the demand on the market for product k, where $p_1,\dots,p_N$ denote the market prices of all firms. This property will be analyzed in detail in the next section. If C_k denotes the cost function of firm k, then the payoff function (profit) of firm k can be given as

$$\pi_k(p_1,\dots,p_N) = p_k d_k(p_1,\dots,p_N) - C_k(d_k(p_1,\dots,p_N)). \tag{2.2.2}$$

The set of strategies of firm k is again a closed interval $I_k = [0, \overline{P}_k]$, where $\overline{P}_k$ is the possible highest price of product k. Thus, the resulting game is $\Gamma = \{N;\ I_1,\dots,I_N;\ \pi_1,\dots,\pi_N\}$. In many applications we may assume reasonably that $\overline{P}_k$ is finite. The equilibrium point of this price adjusting model can be defined analogously to Definition 2.1.1.

Finally, we remark that many authors refer to quantity and price adjusting models as *Cournot* and *Bertrand* oligopolies, respectively. Similarly to Example 2.1.1, one may easily construct a price adjusting duopoly which has no equilibrium point. Similarly to Example 2.1.2, it is also easy to construct a price adjusting duopoly which has infinitely many equilibrium points.

2.3 Multiproduct Models

Consider again a market with N producers, but now assume that each of them produces M kinds of products. If $x_k^{(m)}$ $(1 \le k \le N,\ 1 \le m \le M)$ denotes the production level of firm k of product m, then the strategy of firm k is characterized by the output vector $\mathbf{x}_k = (x_k^{(1)},\dots,x_k^{(M)})$. Let the cost function of firm k be denoted by $C_k(\mathbf{x}_k)$. It is also assumed that the unit price p_m of product m depends on the total output vector

$$\mathbf{s} = \left(\sum_{k=1}^{N} x_k^{(1)}, \ldots, \sum_{k=1}^{N} x_k^{(M)} \right)$$

of the industry. The economic interpretation of this property may be given as follows (see Vives, 1984).

In our economy, we have N firms, each one producing M kinds of products, and a continuum of consumers of the same type with utility functions $U(\mathbf{s})$. The representative consumer maximizes $U(\mathbf{s}) - \mathbf{p}^T\mathbf{s}$, where $\mathbf{p}$ is the price vector and $\mathbf{s} \geq \mathbf{0}$. Let P denote the set of possible price vectors $\left(P \subseteq R_+^M\right)$, and assume that for all $\mathbf{p} \in P$, function $U(\mathbf{s}) - \mathbf{p}^T\mathbf{s}$ has a unique maximizer $\mathbf{d}(\mathbf{p})$. Function $\mathbf{d}(\mathbf{p})$ is called the *demand function.* If $\mathbf{d}$ is invertable then $\mathbf{p} = \mathbf{d}^{-1}(\mathbf{s})$ gives the market *price vector.*

As a special case assume that

$$U(\mathbf{s}) = \mathbf{s}^T\mathbf{Q}\mathbf{s} + \mathbf{b}^T\mathbf{s} + c,$$

where $\mathbf{Q} + \mathbf{Q}^T$ is a negative definite constant matrix, $\mathbf{b}$ is a constant vector and c is a scalar. Assuming that $\mathbf{d}(\mathbf{p})$ is an interior point of R_+^M simple differentiation shows that

$$\left(\mathbf{Q} + \mathbf{Q}^T\right)\mathbf{d}(\mathbf{p}) + \mathbf{b} - \mathbf{p} = \mathbf{0}.$$

That is,

$$\mathbf{d}(\mathbf{p}) = \left(\mathbf{Q} + \mathbf{Q}^T\right)^{-1}\mathbf{p} - \left(\mathbf{Q} + \mathbf{Q}^T\right)^{-1}\mathbf{b},$$

and

$$\mathbf{p}(\mathbf{s}) = \mathbf{d}^{-1}(\mathbf{s}) = \left(\mathbf{Q} + \mathbf{Q}^T\right)\mathbf{s} + \mathbf{b}.$$

Introduce matrix $\mathbf{A} = \mathbf{Q} + \mathbf{Q}^T$ which is symmetric. Hence, $\mathbf{p}(\mathbf{s}) = \mathbf{A}\mathbf{s} + \mathbf{b}$. However this property does not hold in cases when the output of some firms is used by other firms as inputs in their production processes.

By using the above notation the profit function of firm k is formulated as

$$\varphi_k(\mathbf{x}_1, \ldots, \mathbf{x}_N) = \sum_{m=1}^{M} x_k^{(m)} p_m(\mathbf{s}) - C_k(\mathbf{x}_k) = \mathbf{x}_k^T\mathbf{p}(\mathbf{s}) - C_k(\mathbf{x}_k), \tag{2.3.1}$$

where $\mathbf{p} = (p_1, \ldots, p_M)^T$. If X_k denotes the set of all feasible output vectors for firm k $(k = 1, 2, \ldots, N)$, then an N-person game $\Gamma = \{N;\ X_1, \ldots, X_N;\ \varphi_1, \ldots, \varphi_N\}$ is defined as the *multiproduct oligopoly* game. Set X_k is assumed to be a subset of R_+^M and it does not necessarily equal the Cartesian product of one dimensional intervals $\left[0, L_k^{(m)}\right]$, where $L_k^{(m)}$ denotes the capacity limit of firm k from product m. This more general assumption on the strategy sets X_k is more realistic since the same limited inputs may be used to produce several kinds of products which make the production levels of different products dependent on each other.

This model can be further extended by assuming that the demands for different products are not independent. In this case a pseudogame can be defined in which it is assumed that the total output vector $\mathbf{s} = \sum_{k=1}^{N} \mathbf{x}_k$ should satisfy the additional assumption that $\mathbf{s} \in D$, where $D \subseteq R_+^M$ is the *demand set* of the market. The resulting pseudogame can be then denoted by $\Gamma = \{N;\ X_1, \dots, X_N;\ X;\ \varphi_1, \dots, \varphi_N\}$, where $X = \left\{ \mathbf{x} \middle| \mathbf{x} = (\mathbf{x}_1, \dots, \mathbf{x}_N),\quad \mathbf{x}_k \in X_k\ (\forall k),\ \sum_{k=1}^{N} \mathbf{x}_k \in D \right\}$.

Finally, we remark that on the basis if Examples 2.1.1 and 2.1.2 one may easily construct a multiproduct duopoly which has no equilibrium point and also one which has infinitely many equilibrium points.

2.4 Group Equilibrium Problems

Consider again the same firms and the same market situation given in the previous section, but assume now that the firms form coalitions and the objective of each firm is to maximize the profit of the coalition to which it belongs. Mathematically, each coalition is a subset G_i of $\mathbf{N} = \{1, 2, \dots, N\}$. If the number of coalitions is denoted by K, then the following assumptions are made:

(a) For $i = 1, 2, \dots, K,\quad G_i \subseteq \mathbf{N}$;

(b) For $i \neq j,\quad G_i \cap G_j = \phi$;

(c) $G_1 \cup G_2 \cup \dots \cup G_K = \mathbf{N}$;

(d) The set S_i of strategies for coalition G_i $(i = 1, 2, \dots, K)$ is the Cartesian product of the strategy sets of the firms belonging to G_i. That is,

$$S_i = \underset{j \in G_i}{\times} X_j ;$$

(e) The payoff function of each coalition G_i equals the sum of the payoff functions of the firms from G_i. That is, with $\mathbf{s} = \sum_{k=1}^{N} \mathbf{x}_k$

$$\psi_i(\mathbf{x}_1,...,\mathbf{x}_N) = \sum_{j \in G_i} \left(\mathbf{x}_j^T \mathbf{p}(\mathbf{s}) - C_j(\mathbf{x}_j)\right) \quad (1 \le i \le K). \tag{2.4.1}$$

Assumption (a) means that the coalitions are formed by only the original firms. By assumption (b), these coalitions are mutually exclusive, and assumption (c) means that the union of the coalitions equals the set of all firms. In other words, each firm belongs to exactly one coalition. Assumption (d) implies that no further restriction is made on the strategy sets because of coalition formation and assumption (e) means that the overall profit of any coalition equals the sum of the profits of the firms from that coalition. So no additional cost of profit occurs simply because of coalition formation.

In this resulting K-person game the coalitions are the players with strategy sets S_i and payoff functions ψ_i. Therefore this new game can be denoted as $\Gamma = \{K;\ S_1,...,S_K;\ \psi_1,...,\psi_K\}$.

We shall next introduce a reduction principle which permits us to reduce the equilibrium problem of this *group equilibrium problem* to a certain multiproduct oligopoly game. This methodology is based on the solution of the following nonlinear optimization problem:

$$\begin{array}{ll} \text{minimize} & \sum_{j \in G_i} C_j(\mathbf{x}_j) \\ \text{subject to} & \mathbf{x}_j \in X_j \quad (j \in G_i) \\ & \sum_{j \in G_i} \mathbf{x}_j = \mathbf{s}_i \end{array} \tag{2.4.2}$$

for i=1,2,...,K, where $\mathbf{s}_i$ is a parameter from the set

$$T_i = \left\{ \mathbf{t} \middle| \mathbf{t} \in R_+^M,\ \mathbf{t} = \sum_{j \in G_i} \mathbf{x}_j \text{ with } \mathbf{x}_j \in X_j \right\}.$$

This minimization problem has to be solved for every value $\mathbf{s}_i \in T_i$. Let $Q_i(\mathbf{s}_i)$ denote the optimal objective function value. Define the following multiproduct oligopoly game: $\Gamma' = \{K;\ T_1,...,T_K;\ \tau_1,...,\tau_K\}$, where

$$\tau_i(\mathbf{s}_1,...,\mathbf{s}_K) = \mathbf{s}_i^T \mathbf{p}\left(\sum_{l=1}^{K} \mathbf{s}_l\right) - Q_i(\mathbf{s}_i). \tag{2.4.3}$$

Note that in (2.4.3) function Q_i gives the optimally allocated cost among the firms within coalition G_i. This reduction principle can be formulated as

Theorem 2.4.1 Games Γ and Γ' are equivalent in the following sense:

(a) If $(\mathbf{x}_1^*,\ldots,\mathbf{x}_N^*)$ is an equilibrium point of game Γ, then with $\mathbf{s}_i^* = \sum_{j\in G_i} \mathbf{x}_j^*$, vector $(\mathbf{s}_1^*,\ldots,\mathbf{s}_K^*)$ is an equilibrium point of game Γ';

(b) If $(\mathbf{s}_1^*,\ldots,\mathbf{s}_K^*)$ is an equilibrium point of game Γ', and the optimal solutions of problem (2.4.2) with i=1,2,...,K and fixed values of $\mathbf{s}_1^*,\mathbf{s}_2^*,\ldots,\mathbf{s}_K^*$ are $(\mathbf{x}_j^*)_{j\in G_1},\ldots,(\mathbf{x}_j^*)_{j\in G_K}$, then $(\mathbf{x}_1^*,\ldots,\mathbf{x}_N^*)$ is an equilibrium point of game Γ.

It is also worthwhile to mention that certain analytic properties of cost functions C_k are also inherited by functions Q_i as the following theorem asserts.

Theorem 2.4.2 Assume that set X_k is convex for all k.

(a) If functions C_k $(1 \le k \le N)$ are continuous on X_k, then functions Q_i $(1 \le i \le K)$ are also continuous on T_i;

(b) If functions C_k $(1 \le k \le N)$ are convex on X_k, then functions Q_i $(1 \le i \le K)$ are also convex on T_i;

(c) If functions C_k $(1 \le k \le N)$ are increasing in each component of $\mathbf{x}_k$ on X_k, then functions Q_i $(1 \le i \le K)$ are also increasing in each component of $\mathbf{s}_i$ on T_i.

We omit the proof of this theorem since it is a simple consequence of the theory of convex programming (see *e.g.*, Simmons, 1975, for fundamental principles).

This reduction principle implies that the group equilibrium concept of multiproduct oligopoly games is not of essential importance and therefore in further chapters it will not be discussed.

2.5 Rent Seeking Models

Let N denote the number of agents. If x_i is the expenditure of agent i $(1 \le i \le N)$ on the rent seeking activity and $f_i(x_i)$ is his production function for lotteries, then the probability for winning the rent is given as

$$p_i = \frac{f_i(x_i)}{\sum_{j=1}^{N} f_j(x_j)}. \tag{2.5.1}$$

If the rent is normalized to be 1, then the expected net rent of agent i can be expressed in the following way:

$$\varphi_i(x_1,\ldots,x_N) = p_i - x_i = \frac{f_i(x_i)}{\sum_{j=1}^{N} f_j(x_j)} - x_i\ . \tag{2.5.2}$$

Here we assume that $f_i(0)=0$ and $f_i(x_i)>0$ as $x_i>0$ for all i, and if $x_1 = x_2 = \ldots = x_N = 0$, then φ_i is defined to be equal to zero for all i.

Introduce the notation $y_i = f_i(x_i)$ $\left(y_i \in [0, f_i(\infty))\right)$, then the net rent of agent i can be reformulated as

$$\pi_i(y_1,\ldots,y_n) = \frac{y_i}{\sum_{j=1}^{N} y_j} - g_i(y_i), \tag{2.5.3}$$

where $g_i = f_i^{-1}$. It is realistic to assume that the production functions f_i are strictly increasing, so f_i^{-1} is well defined for all i. Notice that the payoff functions (2.5.3) coincide with the payoff functions of the single-product oligopoly game without product differentiation by introducing the notation

$$s = \sum_{j=1}^{N} y_j, \quad p(s) = \frac{1}{s}, \text{ and } C_i(y_i) = g_i(y_i).$$

Hence this game is mathematically equivalent to the classical oligopoly game, therefore all results to be proved later in this book for single product oligopolies without product differentiation can be automatically applied to rent seeking models. However, the unbounded strategy sets and the payoff function (2.5.3) do not satisfy the conditions of the existence theorems to be presented later in this book, therefore the existence and uniqueness of the equilibrium points of rent seeking models need to be discussed in a separate section.

2.6 Labor-Managed Oligopoly

Let N denote again the number of firms, and assume first that they produce the same product. Let x_k be the output of firm k and let $p\left(\sum_{l=1}^{N} x_l\right)$ be the unit price. Let w be the competitive wage rate and c_k firm k's fixed cost. If l_k is the amount of labor of firm k, the inverse production function is $l_k = h_k(x_k)$. The profit of firm k per unit labor is given as

$$\varphi_k(x_1,\ldots,x_N) = \left\{x_k p\left(\sum_{l=1}^{N} x_l\right) - wh_k(x_k) - c_k\right\} \Big/ h_k(x_k) \tag{2.6.1}$$

for k=1,2,...,N. If we assume again that the set of feasible strategies of firm k is given by the closest bounded interval $[0, L_k]$, then an N-person game is formulated.

This model can be easily extended to the cases of product differentiation and multiproduct firms. In the case of product differentiation, let $p_k(x_1,\ldots,x_N)$ denote the price function of the kth firm, therefore the payoff function per unit labor of this firm can now be given as follows:

$$\varphi_k(x_1,\ldots,x_N) = \{x_k p_k(x_1,\ldots,x_N) - wh_k(x_k) - c_k\} / h_k(x_k). \tag{2.6.2}$$

In the case of multiproduct firms, let $\mathbf{x}_k = \left(x_k^{(1)},\ldots,x_k^{(M)}\right)$ denote the output vector of firm k, similarly to multiproduct oligopolies discussed earlier in Section 2.3. If p_m is the price function of product m and $\mathbf{p} = (p_1,\ldots,p_M)^T$, then the profit function per unit labor of firm k is formulated as

$$\varphi_k(\mathbf{x}_1,\ldots,\mathbf{x}_N) = \left\{\mathbf{x}_k^T \mathbf{p}\left(\sum_{l=1}^{N} \mathbf{x}_l\right) - wh_k(\mathbf{x}_k) - c_k\right\} \Big/ h_k(\mathbf{x}_k). \tag{2.6.3}$$

Here $h_k(\mathbf{x}_k)$ denotes the amount of labor needed to produce output $\mathbf{x}_k$ by firm k.

2.7 Oligopsony

It is assumed now that N firms are oligopolistic in the product market and at the same time oligopsonists in the factor market. All firms are assumed to produce

M kind of products with the help of labor and capital. As in the case of multiproduct oligopolies, let $\mathbf{x}_k = \left(x_k^{(1)}, \ldots, x_k^{(M)}\right)$ denote the output vector of firm k, and let L_k and K_k denote the labor and capital use of firm k, respectively. We do not assume optimal usage of these factors of production, therefore the feasible set for $\mathbf{x}_k$ with any pair (L_k, K_k) is $X_k(L_k, K_k) \subseteq R_+^M$ with the additional property that $\mathbf{x}_k \in X_k(L_k, K_k)$ and $\mathbf{0} \le \mathbf{z}_k \le \mathbf{x}_k$ imply that $\mathbf{z}_k \in X_k(L_k, K_k)$. If $\mathbf{p}\left(\sum_{l=1}^N x_l\right)$ is the price vector, w and r are the wage rate and rental of capital which are assumed to depend on the total labor $\sum_{l=1}^N L_l$ and total capital $\sum_{l=1}^N K_l$, respectively, then the profit of firm k can be expressed as follows:

$$\varphi_k(\mathbf{x}_1, L_1, K_1, \ldots, \mathbf{x}_N, L_N, K_N) = \mathbf{x}_k^T \mathbf{p}\left(\sum_{l=1}^N \mathbf{x}_l\right) - L_k w\left(\sum_{l=1}^N L_l\right) - K_k r\left(\sum_{l=1}^N K_l\right). \quad (2.7.1)$$

Here we assume that labor and capital are available with some limitation. We therefore assume that the total labor and capital use belongs to a two-dimensional feasible resource-set $X_s \subseteq R_+^2$ such that $(L, K) \in X_s$ and $(0,0) \le (L', K') \le (L, K)$ imply that $(L', K') \in X_s$.

The above model defines an N-person pseudogame, where the firms are the players, the strategy of each firm is an (M+2)-dimensional vector $\mathbf{u}_k = (\mathbf{x}_k, L_k, K_k)$ with feasible strategy set

$$S_k = \left\{\mathbf{u}_k = (\mathbf{x}_k, L_k, K_k) \middle| (L_k, K_k) \in X_s, \mathbf{x}_k \in X_k(L_k, K_k)\right\} \quad (2.7.2)$$

with the additional condition that

$$\left(\sum_{l=1}^N L_l, \sum_{l=1}^N K_l\right) \in X_s. \quad (2.7.3)$$

The payoff function of firm k $(1 \le k \le N)$ is given by equation (2.7.1). The equilibrium of this pseudogame can be defined similarly to Definition 2.1.2.

2.8 Two-Stage and Multi-Stage Oligopolies

Any firm in perfectly or imperfectly competitive situation engages in productive activity over several time periods. It is quite common to assume that in two- or multi-stage oligopolies the cost function of each firm at any time period t $(t \geq 2)$ depends not only on its most current output but also on its previous output or on the industry total output of the previous time period. This assumption is based on the facts that the productivity of labor of any firm in an industry may increase if production is repeated over time as well as the inputs necessary for the industry's production may be supplied more cheaply in later periods because of economies of scale in the input producing industry. On the other hand, increase in the output of the industry in any time period increases the total demand for the input, leading to its higher price. In other cases, expansion of an industry in any time period may induce the industry to devote its effort to educate its labor more systematically, leading to higher labor productivity.

For the sake of simplicity, consider only one product and two time periods. If N denotes the number of firms and x_{1k} and x_{2k} are the outputs of firm k in time periods 1 and 2, respectively, then the profit of this firm in period 1 is given as

$$\varphi_{1k} = x_{1k} p\left(\sum_{l=1}^{N} x_{1l}\right) - C_{1k}(x_{1k}), \tag{2.8.1}$$

where p is the price function and C_{1k} is the cost function of firm k in time period 1. The profit of the same firm in period 2 has the similar form:

$$\varphi_{2k} = x_{2k} p\left(\sum_{l=1}^{N} x_{2l}\right) - C_{2k}\left(x_{2k}, \sum_{l=1}^{N} x_{1l}\right). \tag{2.8.2}$$

So the total profit of firm k is the following:

$$\varphi_{1k} + \varphi_{2k} = x_{1k} p\left(\sum_{l=1}^{N} x_{1l}\right) + x_{2k} p\left(\sum_{l=1}^{N} x_{2l}\right) - C_{1k}(x_{1k}) - C_{2k}\left(x_{2k}, \sum_{l=1}^{N} x_{1l}\right). \tag{2.8.3}$$

The strategy of each firm is a vector (x_{1k}, x_{2k}) when both components belong to interval $[0, L_k]$ (L_k being the capacity limit of firm k). The payoff function of firm k is given by relation (2.8.3). The equilibrium point of the resulting N-person game can be defined analogously to the cases discussed earlier in this chapter.

A T-period extension of the above model can be given as follows. Let x_{tk} be the output of firm k in period t $(1 \leq k \leq N,\ \ 1 \leq t \leq T)$, p the price function, and C_{tk} the cost function of firm k in period t. Therefore the strategy of each firm is a vector $\mathbf{x}_k = (x_{1k}, x_{2k}, \ldots, x_{Tk})$ with $x_{tk} \in [0, L_{tk}]$ (L_{tk} being the capacity limit of firm k in period t), and the total profit of firm k is formulated as

$$\varphi_k(\mathbf{x}_1,\ldots,\mathbf{x}_N)=x_{1k}p\left(\sum_{l=1}^{N}x_{1l}\right)-C_k(x_{1k})+\sum_{t=2}^{T}\left\{x_{tk}p\left(\sum_{l=1}^{N}x_{tl}\right)-C_{tk}\left(x_{tk},\sum_{\tau=1}^{t-1}\sum_{l=1}^{N}x_{\tau l}\right)\right\}. \tag{2.8.4}$$

Notice that in the above models we always assumed that the cost in any later time-period depends on the total output of the industry up to that time period.

2.9 A Hierarchical Model

In this section a special hierarchical model will be introduced. This model is a sequential Stackelberg oligopoly and is based on the assumption that the firms choose outputs sequentially. Let p be the price function and C_k the cost function of firm k $(1 \le k \le N)$. At time period t=1, only the first firm is assumed to be in the market, so

$$\varphi_1(x_1)=x_1p(x_0^*+x_1)-C_1(x_1), \tag{2.9.1}$$

where x_0^* is the total production level of firms not belonging to the oligopoly. In this model, for the sake of simplicity, we assume that x_0^* is kept constant. At time period t=2, the second firm selects output based on his payoff function

$$\varphi_2(x_1,x_2)=x_2p(x_0^*+x_1+x_2)-C_2(x_2). \tag{2.9.2}$$

At each later time period $t=k$ $(k \ge 2)$, firm k decides on his output level, and his payoff is given as

$$\varphi_k(x_1,\ldots,x_k)=x_kp(x_0^*+x_1+x_2+\ldots+x_k)-C_k(x_k). \tag{2.9.3}$$

If we assume that at each time period the entering firm maximizes his payoff function given the output of all firms which entered the market earlier, then the output of the firms are determined in the following way:

$$x_k^*=\arg\max\left\{x_kp(x_0^*+x_1^*+\ldots+x_{k-1}^*+x_k)-C_k(x_k)\right\} \quad x_k\in[0,L_k] \tag{2.9.4}$$

where $L_1,\ldots,L_N$ denote the capacity limits of the firms.

2.10 Supplementary Notes and Discussions

2.1 The classical model (2.1.1) was first formulated by Cournot (1838). The equilibrium concept (2.1.2) for two-person, zero-sum games was first introduced by von Neumann (1928). His saddle-point theory was followed by von Neumann and Morgenstern (1944). The reader may consult Rives (1975) on the early history of game theory. The classical oligopoly game is discussed by many authors. The important references are Okuguchi (1976), Friedman (1977, 1981, 1986), Friedman and Hoggatt (1980), and Szidarovszky, Gershon and Duckstein (1986).

The extensions of games to pseudogames are discussed in Szép and Forgó (1985), and Friedman (1986). An early result is due to Debreu (1952).

The application of the classical oligopoly game to natural resources management is discussed in Bogárdi and Szidarovszky (1976). In that paper comparisons of different group equilibrium problems are outlined.

2.2 Models with product differentiations are discussed by Hadar (1966), Krelle (1976), Okuguchi (1976), and Friedman (1986).

The comparison of Bertrand and Cournot oligopolies is presented in Okuguchi (1984), Vives (1984) and Cheng (1985).

2.3 Multiproduct oligopoly models were first formulated by Selten (1970) and Szidarovszky (1978) for quantity strategies and by Eichhorn (1971a,b) for price strategies. See also Krelle (1976) and Funke (1985).

2.4 Group equilibrium problems were first analyzed by Szidarovszky (1975, 1978), and an existence theorem has been extended to group equilibrium problems by Szidarovszky and Yakowitz (1982). The reduction principle is discussed in details in Szidarovszky (1978).

2.5 Rent-seeking games were introduced by Tullock (1980). The existence and uniqueness of the pure Nash equilibrium was first examined by Pérez-Castrillo and Verdier (1992), and a general existence result was proved by Okuguchi (1995), however in this paper identical production functions were assumed. This result was later extended to the nonsymmetric case by Szidarovszky and Okuguchi (1997a).

2.6 The seminal work of Ward (1958) can be considered the first to have discussed labor-managed oligopolies. Hill and Waterson (1983) have formulated profit-maximizing and labor-managed Cournot oligopolies without product differentiation and with identical cost functions, and compared the long-run equilibrium numbers for the two oligopolies. Neary (1984) has extended their result for the nonsymmetric case. Okuguchi (1991) has derived a general existence and uniqueness theorem with asymmetric cost functions. Comparative statics for profit maximizing and labor-managed Cournot oligopolies are presented in Okuguchi (1993).

2.7 Cournot oligopoly involving oligopsony has been first introduced by Okuguchi (1996a) and Chiarella and Okuguchi (1996). Okuguchi (1996a) has proved the existence of a unique Cournot equilibrium which is the fixed point of a function involving only the industry output. Chiarella and Okuguchi (1996) have analyzed a dynamic duopoly involving oligopsony. A more general existence theorem of a Cournot equilibrium is proved in Szidarovszky and Okuguchi (1996).

2.8 The model introduced in this section is the straightforward extension of the two-stage model of Okuguchi and Yamazaki (1996) to any number of stages. In their original work, Okuguchi and Yamazaki (1996) have shown the existence of a unique subgame-perfect equilibrium under certain concavity and differentiability conditions.

2.9 Bertrand and hierarchical Stackelberg oligopolies with product differentiation were examined and the equilibrium prices were compared by Okuguchi and Yamazaki (1994). The model presented here is the Cournot counterpart of their model.

3 Existence and Uniqueness Results

In this chapter the existence of the Nash-Cournot equilibrium point in the multiproduct oligopoly game will be first investigated. Then on the basis of the general results special cases will be examined. These include models with product differentiation and the classical Cournot model. In the second part of this chapter modified oligopoly models such as rent seeking games, labor-managed oligopolies, and oligopsonies will be discussed.

3.1 Existence Results for Multiproduct Oligopoly

Consider now the *multiproduct oligopoly* game where N is the number of the firms and M is the number of products. Let $\mathbf{x}_k = \left(x_k^{(1)},\dots,x_k^{(M)}\right)^T$ denote the output of firm k, where $x_k^{(m)}$ is the output of firm k of product m. The total output of all firms is then given as $\mathbf{s} = \sum_{k=1}^{N} \mathbf{x}_k$. The price function (or inverse demand function) $\mathbf{p}$ is assumed to be nonnegative and dependent on $\mathbf{s}$. The cost function C_k of firm k is assumed to depend only on the output $\mathbf{x}_k$ of firm k. Thus, the profit of firm k can be expressed as:

$$\varphi_k(\mathbf{x}_1,\dots,\mathbf{x}_N) = \mathbf{x}_k^T\mathbf{p}(\mathbf{s}) - C_k(\mathbf{x}_k). \tag{3.1.1}$$

Let X_k denote the set of all feasible output vectors for firm k, then X_k can be considered the set of strategies of firm k. Assume that the following conditions hold:

(A) X_k is a closed, convex, bounded set in R_+^M such that $\mathbf{x}_k \in X_k$ and $\mathbf{0} \le \mathbf{t}_k \le \mathbf{x}_k$ imply that $\mathbf{t}_k \in X_k$;

(B) There exists a convex, closed set S in R_+^M such that $S \ne \{\mathbf{0}\}$, $\mathbf{p}(\mathbf{s}) = \mathbf{0}$ if $\mathbf{s} \notin S$, furthermore $\mathbf{s} \in S$ and $\mathbf{0} \le \mathbf{t} \le \mathbf{s}$ imply that $\mathbf{t} \in S$;

(C) For all k, function C_k is strictly increasing in each component $x_k^{(m)}$ and it is continuous on X_k;

(D) For all k, function φ_k is continuous on $\times_{k=1}^{N} X_k$ and is concave in $\mathbf{x}_k$ with any fixed $\mathbf{x}_l \in X_l (l \neq k)$ in the set

$$X^* = \left\{ (\mathbf{x}_1, ..., \mathbf{x}_N) \middle| \mathbf{x}_k \in X_k \quad (k = 1, ..., N), \ \sum_{k=1}^{N} \mathbf{x}_k \in S \right\}.$$

The main result of this section is the following.

Theorem 3.1.1. Under assumptions (A) - (D) the multiproduct oligopoly game has at least one Nash-Cournot equilibrium point.

Proof. First we prove that no equilibrium point exists in $\left(\times_{k=1}^{N} X_k \right) \setminus X^*$. Assume contrary to the assertion that $\mathbf{x}^* = (\mathbf{x}_1^*, ..., \mathbf{x}_N^*) \notin X^*$. Then $\mathbf{p}(\mathbf{s}^*) = \mathbf{0}$, where $\mathbf{s}^* = \sum_{k=1}^{N} \mathbf{x}_k^*$. Since $S \neq \{\mathbf{0}\}$, vector $\mathbf{x}^*$ has at least one positive element, which is denoted by $x_{k_0}^{(m_0)^*}$. The assumption that S is closed implies that there exists a value $\left(0 < x_{k_0}^{(m_0)} < x_{k_0}^{(m_0)^*} \right)$ such that

$$\mathbf{x}_{k_0} = \left(x_{k_0}^{(1)^*}, ..., x_{k_0}^{(m_0-1)^*}, x_{k_0}^{(m_0)}, x_{k_0}^{(m_0+1)^*}, ..., x_{k_0}^{(M)^*} \right) \in X_{k_0}$$

and

$$\mathbf{x} = \left(\mathbf{x}_1^*, ..., \mathbf{x}_{k_0-1}^*, \mathbf{x}_{k_0}, \mathbf{x}_{k_0+1}^*, ..., \mathbf{x}_N^* \right) \notin X^*.$$

This vector satisfies the relation

$$\varphi_{k_0}(\mathbf{x}) = \mathbf{x}_{k_0}^T \mathbf{p}\left(\sum_{k \neq k_0} \mathbf{x}_k^* + \mathbf{x}_{k_0} \right) - C_{k_0}(\mathbf{x}_{k_0}) = -C_{k_0}(\mathbf{x}_{k_0}) > -C_{k_0}(\mathbf{x}_{k_0}^*) = \mathbf{x}_{k_0}^{*T} \mathbf{p}\left(\sum_{k=1}^{N} \mathbf{x}_k^* \right) - C_{k_0}(\mathbf{x}_{k_0}^*) = \varphi_{k_0}(\mathbf{x}^*),$$

which contradicts the assumption that $\mathbf{x}^*$ is an equilibrium point.

Consider now the pseudogame with the additional constraint that the total output vector $\mathbf{s}$ of all firms must belong to set S. Let Γ and Γ^* denote the original game and the pseudogame, respectively. The above arguments imply that any equilibrium point of game Γ is necessarily an equilibrium point of game Γ^*.

We shall next prove that any equilibrium point of game Γ^* is an equilibrium point of game Γ as well.

Assume that $\mathbf{x}^* = (\mathbf{x}_1^*,...,\mathbf{x}_N^*)$ is an equilibrium point of game Γ^*. Let firm k be any firm $(1 \le k \le N)$, and let $\mathbf{x}_k \in X_k$ be arbitrary. Define $\mathbf{x} = (\mathbf{x}_1^*,...,\mathbf{x}_{k-1}^*,\mathbf{x}_k,\mathbf{x}_{k+1}^*,...,\mathbf{x}_N^*)$. If $\mathbf{x} \in X^*$, then $\varphi_k(\mathbf{x}^*) \ge \varphi_k(\mathbf{x})$, since in this case $\mathbf{x}$ is a feasible simultaneous strategy vector for game Γ. If $\mathbf{x} \notin X^*$, then

$$\varphi_k(\mathbf{x}) = -C_k(\mathbf{x}_k) \le -C_k(\mathbf{0}) = \varphi_k(\overline{\mathbf{x}}),$$

where $\overline{\mathbf{x}} = (\mathbf{x}_1^*,...,\mathbf{x}_{k-1}^*,\mathbf{0},\mathbf{x}_{k+1}^*,...,\mathbf{x}_N^*) \in X^*$, and therefore $\varphi_k(\overline{\mathbf{x}}) \le \varphi_k(\mathbf{x}^*)$. Consequently, $\varphi_k(\mathbf{x}) \le \varphi_k(\mathbf{x}^*)$, which proves that $\mathbf{x}^*$ is an equilibrium point of game Γ.

Finally we note that game Γ^* satisfies the conditions for the generalized Nikaido-Isoda theorem (Szép and Forgó, 1985), and hence it has at least one equilibrium point which is also an equilibrium point for game Γ. □

The concavity of functions φ_k on the set X^* is an assumption which cannot be easily verified in most cases. The following lemma will imply a sufficient condition for the concavity of function φ_k in its kth variable. First a definition is presented.

Definition 3.1.1. A function $\mathbf{f}: D \mapsto R^M$ (where $D \subseteq R^M$) is called *monotone* if for all $\mathbf{x},\mathbf{y} \in D$

$$(\mathbf{x}-\mathbf{y})^T(\mathbf{f}(\mathbf{x})-\mathbf{f}(\mathbf{y})) \ge 0. \tag{3.1.2}$$

Function $\mathbf{f}$ is called *strictly monotone* if strict inequality holds in (3.1.2) for all $\mathbf{x} \neq \mathbf{y}$.

Lemma 3.1.1. Let function $\mathbf{f}$ be defined on a convex set $D \subseteq R_+^M$. Assume that -$\mathbf{f}$ is monotone on D and each component of $\mathbf{f}$ is concave on D. Then function $g(\mathbf{x}) = \mathbf{x}^T\mathbf{f}(\mathbf{x})$ is concave on D.

Proof. Let $\alpha, \beta \ge 0$ such that $\alpha + \beta = 1$, and let $\mathbf{x},\mathbf{y} \in D$. Then by multiplying relation (3.1.2) by $\alpha\beta$ we have

$$\alpha\beta\mathbf{x}^T\mathbf{f}(\mathbf{y}) + \alpha\beta\mathbf{y}^T\mathbf{f}(\mathbf{x}) \ge \alpha\beta\mathbf{x}^T\mathbf{f}(\mathbf{x}) + \alpha\beta\mathbf{y}^T\mathbf{f}(\mathbf{y}),$$

which implies

$$(\alpha\mathbf{x} + \beta\mathbf{y})^T(\alpha\mathbf{f}(\mathbf{x}) + \beta\mathbf{f}(\mathbf{y})) \ge \alpha\mathbf{x}^T\mathbf{f}(\mathbf{x}) + \beta\mathbf{y}^T\mathbf{f}(\mathbf{y}). \tag{3.1.3}$$

Since each component of function **f** is concave,

$$\mathbf{f}(\alpha\mathbf{x}+\beta\mathbf{y}) \geq \alpha\mathbf{f}(\mathbf{x})+\beta\mathbf{f}(\mathbf{y}).$$

From inequality (3.1.3) we conclude that for all $\mathbf{x} \in D$,

$$(\alpha\mathbf{x}+\beta\mathbf{y})^T\mathbf{f}(\alpha\mathbf{x}+\beta\mathbf{y}) \geq \alpha\mathbf{x}^T\mathbf{f}(\mathbf{x})+\beta\mathbf{y}^T\mathbf{f}(\mathbf{y}).$$

That is,

$$g(\alpha\mathbf{x}+\beta\mathbf{y}) \geq \alpha g(\mathbf{x})+\beta g(\mathbf{y}),$$

which proves the assertion. □

Remark. A practical characterization of monotone functions given in Ortega and Rheinboldt (1970) is as follows:

Let D be an open, convex set and let **f** be continuously differentiable on D. Then -**f** is monotone if and only if matrix $\mathbf{J}(\mathbf{x})+\mathbf{J}(\mathbf{x})^T$ is negative semidefinite for all $\mathbf{x} \in D$, where $\mathbf{J}(\mathbf{x})$ is the Jacobian of **f**. That is, $\mathbf{u}^T\left(\mathbf{J}(\mathbf{x})+\mathbf{J}(\mathbf{x})^T\right)\mathbf{u} \leq 0$ for all $\mathbf{u} \in R^M$.

On the basis of Lemma 3.1.1 we shall prove the following result.

Theorem 3.1.2. Assume that conditions (A), (B) and (C) hold, furthermore function **p** is continuous and -**p** is monotone on S. If each component of function **p** is concave on S and functions C_k are convex on $X_k (k = 1,2,...,N)$, then the multiproduct oligopoly game has at least one equilibrium point.

Proof. Lemma 3.1.1 implies that profit functions φ_k are concave in $\mathbf{x}_k$. From the assumptions of the theorem we conclude that functions φ_k are continuous. Therefore the generalized Nikaido-Isoda theorem implies that pseudogame Γ^* (introduced in the proof of Theorem 3.1.1) has at least one equilibrium point. The proof of Theorem 3.1.1 also implies that this is an equilibrium point of game Γ as well. □

Corollary. The Remark which has been made after proving Lemma 3.1.1 implies that the monotonicity of -**p** can be replaced by the assumption that $\mathbf{J}(\mathbf{x})+\mathbf{J}(\mathbf{x})^T$ is negative semidefinite, where $\mathbf{J}(\mathbf{x})$ is the Jacobian of **p**. Let $J_{ij}(\mathbf{x})$ denote the (i,j) element of matrix $\mathbf{J}(\mathbf{x})$. Assume that

$$J_{jj}(\mathbf{x}) < 0, \quad \left|J_{jj}(\mathbf{x})\right| \geq \sum_{i \neq j}\left|J_{ji}(\mathbf{x})\right| \text{ and } \left|J_{jj}(\mathbf{x})\right| \geq \sum_{i \neq j}\left|J_{ji}(\mathbf{x})\right|. \tag{3.1.4}$$

Then the Gerschgorin Circle Theorem (Szidarovszky and Yakowitz, 1978) implies that all eigenvalues of matrix $\mathbf{J}(\mathbf{x})+\mathbf{J}(\mathbf{x})^T$ are nonpositive, hence matrix $\mathbf{J}(\mathbf{x})+\mathbf{J}(\mathbf{x})^T$ is negative semidefinite. Consequently, function -**p** is monotone. In many applications it is easy to show that relations (3.1.4) hold.

The uniqueness of the equilibrium point under the assumptions of Theorems 3.1.1 and 3.1.2 is not generally true. In Example 2.1.2 we introduced a single-product duopoly which has infinitely many equilibrium points and satisfies the conditions of Theorems 3.1.1 and 3.1.2 with N=2 and M=1.

The oligopoly model with *product differentiation* and with single product firms will be next analyzed. In this case M=N, furthermore

$$x_k^{(m)} = \begin{cases} x_k & \text{if } k = m \\ 0 & \text{otherwise.} \end{cases}$$

Hence all theorems which were proven for multiproduct oligopoly games can be applied without any limitations. The conditions must now be rewritten in the following form:

(A') X_k is a closed interval $[0, L_k]$, where L_k denotes the capacity limit of firm k;

(B') There exists a convex, closed set S in R_+^M such that $S \neq \{\mathbf{0}\}$, $\mathbf{p}(x_1,\dots,x_N) = \mathbf{0}$ for $(x_1,\dots,x_N) \notin S$, furthermore $\mathbf{x} \in S$ and $\mathbf{0} \le \mathbf{t} \le \mathbf{s}$ imply that $\mathbf{t} \in S$;

(C') Functions C_k are strictly increasing and continuous on X_k;

(D') Function φ_k is continuous on $\times_{k=1}^{N} X_k$ and is concave in x_k with fixed x_l $(l \neq k)$ in the set $X^* = S \cap \times_{k=1}^{N} X_k$.

Similarly to Theorem 3.1.1 we can prove the following existence result.

Theorem 3.1.3. Under assumptions (A') - (D') the oligopoly model with product differentiation and with single product firms has at least one equilibrium point.

Note that in this case the assumption that function -**p** is monotone can be replaced by the more simple assumption that the unit price function p_k of product k is decreasing in x_k. Consequently, we have the following:

Theorem 3.1.4. Assume that conditions (A'), (B') and (C') hold; furthermore function **p** is continuous and each component p_k of **p** is decreasing in its own variable x_k and is concave on S. If in addition, function C_k is convex on

X_k $(k=1,2,\dots,N)$, then the oligopoly game with product differentiation and with single product firms has at least one equilibrium point.

We can also verify that the uniqueness of the equilibrium point does not follow from the conditions of Theorems 3.1.3 and 3.1.4. In Example 2.1.2 we introduced a single-product duopoly with infinitely many equilibrium points. That special game satisfies all conditions of Theorems 3.1.3 and 3.1.4 with $N=M=2$, $p_1 \equiv p_2 \equiv p$ (where p is the price function in Example 2.1.2), and the same cost functions.

3.2 Relation of Equilibrium Problems to Fixed Point and Nonlinear Complementarity Problems

In this section the relations of the equilibrium problem of oligopoly games to other problem areas in applied mathematics will be outlined.

Consider now the multiproduct oligopoly game defined in Section 2.3 with sets X_k of strategies, set X of simultaneous strategies, and price and cost functions $\mathbf{p}$ and C_k, respectively. Our fixed point concept is based on the principle of *best reply mappings*, which can be defined as follows.

Definition 3.2.1. The best reply mapping for player k is a point-to-set mapping from X to X_k such that for all $\mathbf{x}=(\mathbf{x}_1,\dots,\mathbf{x}_N)\in X$,

$$\mathbf{r}_k(\mathbf{x})=\{\mathbf{t}_k \mid \mathbf{t}_k \in X_k,\ \varphi_k(\mathbf{x}_1,\dots,\mathbf{x}_{k-1},\mathbf{t}_k,\mathbf{x}_{k+1},\dots,\mathbf{x}_N)=\max \varphi_k(\mathbf{x}_1,\dots,\mathbf{x}_{k-1},\tau_k,\mathbf{x}_{k+1},\dots,\mathbf{x}_N)\},\tag{3.2.1}$$

where the maximum is taken for all $\tau_k \in X_k$ such that

$$(\mathbf{x}_1,\dots,\mathbf{x}_{k-1},\tau_k,\mathbf{x}_{k+1},\dots,\mathbf{x}_N)\in X.$$

Thus $\mathbf{r}_k(\mathbf{x})$ gives the best strategy choice(s) of firm k to the strategy combination $\mathbf{x}$. That is, $\mathbf{r}_k(\mathbf{x})$ gives the best strategy choice to the strategy selections $\mathbf{x}_i (i\neq k)$ of the other players.

Definition 3.2.2. The best reply mapping is a point-to-set mapping from X to X associating each strategy combination $\mathbf{x}\in X$ with all vectors $\mathbf{t}\in X$ such that $\mathbf{t}=(\mathbf{t}_1,\dots,\mathbf{t}_N)$ and $\mathbf{t}_k \in \mathbf{r}_k(\mathbf{x})$ $(k=1,2,\dots,N)$.

The definition of equilibrium points implies the following result.

Theorem 3.2.1. Vector $\mathbf{x}^* \in X$ is an equilibrium point of the multiproduct oligopoly game if and only if $\mathbf{x}^* \in \mathbf{r}(\mathbf{x}^*)$. That is, $\mathbf{x}^*$ is an equilibrium if and only if it is a fixed point of mapping **r**.

Remark. Note that the dimension of this fixed point problem is *MN* since each strategy vector $\mathbf{x}_k$ is *M* dimensional. In the case of the oligopoly game a drastic reduction in the dimension of the fixed point problem can be achieved. This reduction is discussed next. For k=1,2,...,N and all $\mathbf{t}_k, \mathbf{x}_k \in X_k$ and $\mathbf{s} \in D$ (where D is the demand set of the market introduced in Section 2.3) define

$$\psi_k(\mathbf{t}_k, \mathbf{x}_k, \mathbf{s}) = \mathbf{t}_k^T \mathbf{p}(\mathbf{s} - \mathbf{x}_k + \mathbf{t}_k) - C_k(\mathbf{t}_k), \tag{3.2.2}$$

where ψ_k gives the profit of firm k after changing its strategy $\mathbf{x}_k$ to $\mathbf{t}_k$ by assuming that the total output of the industry is s. For all $\mathbf{s} \in D$ define

$$\overline{X}_k(\mathbf{s}) = \left\{ \mathbf{x}_k \middle| \mathbf{x}_k \in X_k, \psi_k(\mathbf{x}_k, \mathbf{x}_k, \mathbf{s}) = \max_{\substack{\mathbf{t}_k \in X_k \\ \mathbf{s} - \mathbf{x}_k + \mathbf{t}_k \in D}} \psi_k(\mathbf{t}_k, \mathbf{x}_k, \mathbf{s}) \right\} \tag{3.2.3}$$

and finally let

$$\overline{X}(\mathbf{s}) = \left\{ \mathbf{u} \middle| \mathbf{u} = \sum_{k=1}^{N} \mathbf{x}_k, \mathbf{x}_k \in \overline{X}_k(\mathbf{s}), \ l = 1,2,\ldots,N \right\}. \tag{3.2.4}$$

Then the following result holds:

Theorem 3.2.2. A vector $\mathbf{x}^* = (\mathbf{x}_1^*, \ldots, \mathbf{x}_N^*) \in X$ is an equilibrium point of the multiproduct oligopoly game if and only if for $\mathbf{s}^* = \sum_{k=1}^{N} \mathbf{x}_k^*$, $\mathbf{s}^* \in \overline{X}(\mathbf{s}^*)$ and $\mathbf{x}_k^* \in \overline{X}_k(\mathbf{s}^*)$ $(k = 1,2,\ldots,N)$.

Remark 1. Note that the dimension of the point-to-set mapping $\overline{X}$ is only M, which makes the computation of the equilibrium point possible. In the special case of M=1 the computation of the equilibrium point is actually based on the numerical solution of the one dimensional fixed point problem $s \in \overline{X}(s)$, as it will be discussed in detail later in Section 3.3.

Remark 2. An alternative proof for Theorem 3.1.1 can be given by applying fixed point theorems for the above fixed point problem.

An application of the fixed point problem of the best reply mapping to the uniqueness of the equilibrium point will be next presented. Before stating our main uniqueness theorem, two definitions are introduced.

Definition 3.2.3. A point-to-set mapping $\mathbf{R}$ from X to X is called strictly monotone if $\mathbf{x}_1, \mathbf{x}_2 \in X, \mathbf{x}_1 \neq \mathbf{x}_2, \mathbf{y}_1 \in \mathbf{R}(\mathbf{x}_1)$, and $\mathbf{y}_2 \in \mathbf{R}(\mathbf{x}_2)$ then

$$(\mathbf{x}_1 - \mathbf{x}_2)^T (\mathbf{y}_1 - \mathbf{y}_2) > 0. \tag{3.2.5}$$

Note that if $\mathbf{R}$ is a one dimensional point-to-point mapping, then (3.2.5) means that $\mathbf{R}$ is strictly increasing. Notice that strict monotonicity of point-to-set mappings is defined here in the same way as we defined strictly monotone functions (see Definition 3.1.1) earlier.

Definition 3.2.4. A point-to-point mapping $\mathbf{R}$ from X to X is called a contraction if there exists a constant $0 \le \varepsilon < 1$ such that for all $\mathbf{x}_1, \mathbf{x}_2 \in X$,

$$\|\mathbf{R}(\mathbf{x}_1) - \mathbf{R}(\mathbf{x}_2)\| \le \varepsilon \|\mathbf{x}_1 - \mathbf{x}_2\|, \tag{3.2.6}$$

where $\|\bullet\|$ is an arbitrary vector norm.

Our main uniqueness theorem can be formulated as follows.

Theorem 3.2.3. Assume that at least one of the following conditions hold:

(a) Mapping $\mathbf{x}$-$\mathbf{r}(\mathbf{x})$ is strictly monotone;
(b) Mapping $\mathbf{r}(\mathbf{x})$-$\mathbf{x}$ is strictly monotone;
and
(c) Mapping $\mathbf{r}(\mathbf{x})$ is point-to-point and contraction.

Then the equilibrium point is unique, if it exists.

Proof. Assume that $\mathbf{x}_1^*$ and $\mathbf{x}_2^*$ are two different equilibrium points. Then $\mathbf{x}_1^* \in \mathbf{r}(\mathbf{x}_1^*)$ and $\mathbf{x}_2^* \in \mathbf{r}(\mathbf{x}_2^*)$. That is, $\mathbf{0} \in \mathbf{R}(\mathbf{x}_1^*)$ and $\mathbf{0} \in \mathbf{R}(\mathbf{x}_2^*)$, where $\mathbf{R}(\mathbf{x}) = \mathbf{r}(\mathbf{x}) - \mathbf{x}$. If condition (a) or (b) holds then we may select $\mathbf{y}_1 - \mathbf{y}_2 = \mathbf{0}$ $\left(\in \mathbf{R}(\mathbf{x}_k^*),\ k = 1,2\right)$, and in this case

$$(\mathbf{x}_1^* - \mathbf{x}_2^*)^T (\mathbf{y}_1 - \mathbf{y}_2) = 0,$$

which contradicts assumption (3.2.5).

Assume next that condition (c) holds, then $\mathbf{r}(\mathbf{x}_1^*) = \mathbf{x}_1^*$ and $\mathbf{r}(\mathbf{x}_2^*) = \mathbf{x}_2^*$, and therefore

$$\|\mathbf{r}(\mathbf{x}_1^*) - \mathbf{r}(\mathbf{x}_2^*)\| = \|\mathbf{x}_1^* - \mathbf{x}_2^*\| \neq 0,$$

which contradicts (3.2.6). □

Corollary. Assume next that $\mathbf{r}(\mathbf{x})$ is a point-to-point mapping. Then obviously the equilibrium point is unique if $\mathbf{R}(\mathbf{x})$ is one-to-one (that is, $\mathbf{R}(\mathbf{x}^{(1)}) = \mathbf{R}(\mathbf{x}^{(2)})$ implies that $\mathbf{x}^{(1)} = \mathbf{x}^{(2)}$), where $\mathbf{R}(\mathbf{x})=\mathbf{r}(\mathbf{x})-\mathbf{x}$. In the mathematical literature there are several well known conditions which guarantee that function $\mathbf{R}(\mathbf{x})$ is one-to-one, or in other words, univalent. Assuming continuous differentiability of $\mathbf{R}(\mathbf{x})$ the most frequently applied conditions are:

(i) All leading principal minors of the Jacobian $\mathbf{J}_\mathbf{R}(\mathbf{x})$ of $\mathbf{R}(\mathbf{x})$ are positive ($\mathbf{J}_\mathbf{R}(\mathbf{x})$ is then called a *P*-matrix);
(ii) All leading principal minors of the Jacobian $\mathbf{J}_\mathbf{R}(\mathbf{x})$ of $\mathbf{R}(\mathbf{x})$ are negative ($\mathbf{J}_\mathbf{R}(\mathbf{x})$ is then called a *N*-matrix);
(iii) Matrix $\mathbf{J}_R(\mathbf{x}) + \mathbf{J}_R(\mathbf{x})^T$ is negative (or positive) semidefinite, and between any points $\mathbf{x}^{(1)} \neq \mathbf{x}^{(2)}$ there is a point $\mathbf{x}^{(0)}$ such that $\mathbf{J}_\mathbf{R}(\mathbf{x}^{(0)}) + \mathbf{J}_\mathbf{R}(\mathbf{x}^{(0)})^T$ is a negative (or positive) definite.

For the proof of (i) see Gale and Nikaido (1965); for the proof of (ii) see Inada (1971). It is known (see Ortega and Rheinboldt, 1970), that condition (iii) implies that $-\mathbf{R}(\mathbf{x})$ (or $\mathbf{R}(\mathbf{x})$) is strictly monotone and this implies that $\mathbf{R}(\mathbf{x})$ is one-to-one. A stronger version of (iii) is:

(iii') Matrix $\mathbf{J}_\mathbf{R}(\mathbf{x}) + \mathbf{J}_\mathbf{R}(\mathbf{x})^T$ is negative (or positive) definite for all $\mathbf{x}$.

If $\mathbf{J}_\mathbf{r}(\mathbf{x})$ denotes the Jacobian of $\mathbf{r}(\mathbf{x})$, then $\mathbf{J}_\mathbf{R}(\mathbf{x}) = \mathbf{J}_\mathbf{r}(\mathbf{x}) - \mathbf{I}$. Consequently (iii') is equivalent to the assumption that

(iii") All eigenvalues of $\mathbf{J}_r(\mathbf{x}) + \mathbf{J}_\mathbf{r}(\mathbf{x})^T$ are less (or greater) than 2.

The relation of equilibrium problems to *nonlinear complementarity problems* will next be examined. Consider again the multiproduct oligopoly game discussed in Section 2.3, and assume that the following conditions hold:

(α) All assumptions of Theorem 3.1.1 are satisfied;

(β) For all k, $X_k = [0, L_k^{(1)}] \times \ldots \times [0, L_k^{(M)}]$, where $L_k^{(m)}$ gives the capacity limit of firm k of product m;

(γ) $S = \left\{ \mathbf{s} | \mathbf{s} = \sum_{k=1}^{N} \mathbf{x}_k, \mathbf{x}_k \in X_k, \; k = 1,2,\ldots,N \right\}$;

(δ) Functions $\mathbf{p}$ and C_k are differentiable (k=1,...,N).

Assumptions (α) and (γ) imply that all payoff functions φ_k are continuous on X and concave in $\mathbf{x}_k$ for fixed values of $\mathbf{x}_l$ ($l \neq k$). Assumption (β) means that sets X_k of strategies are the Cartesian products of one dimensional intervals.

Let $\mathbf{x}^* = (\mathbf{x}_1^*, \ldots, \mathbf{x}_N^*)$ be an equilibrium point. Then for all k, $\mathbf{x}_k^*$ maximizes the function $\varphi_k(\mathbf{x}_1^*, \ldots, \mathbf{x}_{k-1}^*, \mathbf{x}_k, \mathbf{x}_{k+1}^*, \ldots, \mathbf{x}_N^*)$ in X_k. Consequently, $\mathbf{x}^*$ is an equilibrium point if and only if $\mathbf{x} = \mathbf{x}^*$ satisfies relations

$$\frac{\partial \varphi_k(\mathbf{x})}{\partial x_k^{(m)}} \begin{cases} \leq 0 \text{ if } x_k^{(m)} = 0 \\ = 0 \text{ if } 0 < x_k^{(m)} < L_k^{(m)} \\ \geq 0 \text{ if } x_k^{(m)} = L_k^{(m)} \end{cases} \tag{3.2.7}$$

for m=1,2,...,M. By introducing the slack variables

$$z_k^{(m)} = \begin{cases} = 0 \text{ if } x_k^{(m)} > 0 \\ \geq 0 \text{ if } x_k^{(m)} = 0, \end{cases}$$

$$v_k^{(m)} = \begin{cases} = 0 \text{ if } x_k^{(m)} < L_k^{(m)} \\ \geq 0 \text{ if } x_k^{(m)} = L_k^{(m)}, \end{cases}$$

and

$$w_k^{(m)} = L_k^{(m)} - x_k^{(m)},$$

relation (3.2.7) can be rewritten as

$$\frac{\partial \varphi_k(\mathbf{x})}{\partial x_k^{(m)}} - v_k^{(m)} + z_k^{(m)} = 0, \tag{3.2.8}$$

and the definitions of the slack variables imply that

$$\begin{aligned} z_k^{(m)} x_k^{(m)} &= 0, \\ v_k^{(m)} w_k^{(m)} &= 0. \end{aligned} \tag{3.2.9}$$

We may therefore summarize relations (3.2.8) and (3.2.9) as

$$\begin{aligned}
&\nabla_{\mathbf{x}_k}\varphi_k(\mathbf{x}) - \mathbf{v}_k + \mathbf{z}_k = 0 \\
&\mathbf{z}_k^T\mathbf{x}_k = \mathbf{v}_k^T\mathbf{w}_k = 0 \qquad\qquad (3.2.10)\\
&\mathbf{z}_k, \mathbf{x}_k, \mathbf{v}_k, \mathbf{w}_k \geq \mathbf{0},
\end{aligned}$$

where $\nabla_{\mathbf{x}_k}$ is the notation of the gradient operator with respect to $\mathbf{x}_k$. We will rewrite these relations as a nonlinear complementarity problem.

Introduce the notation

$$\mathbf{v} = \begin{bmatrix} \mathbf{v}_1 \\ \mathbf{v}_2 \\ \vdots \\ \mathbf{v}_N \end{bmatrix}, \mathbf{L} = \begin{bmatrix} \mathbf{L}_1 \\ \mathbf{L}_2 \\ \vdots \\ \mathbf{L}_N \end{bmatrix}, \nabla\varphi(\mathbf{x}) = \begin{bmatrix} \nabla_{\mathbf{x}_1}\varphi_1(\mathbf{x}) \\ \nabla_{\mathbf{x}_2}\varphi_2(\mathbf{x}) \\ \vdots \\ \nabla_{\mathbf{x}_N}\varphi_N(\mathbf{x}) \end{bmatrix},$$

$$\mathbf{t} = \begin{bmatrix} \mathbf{x} \\ \mathbf{v} \end{bmatrix}, \text{ and } \mathbf{h}(\mathbf{t}) = \begin{bmatrix} -\nabla\varphi(\mathbf{x}) + \mathbf{v} \\ \mathbf{L} - \mathbf{x} \end{bmatrix}, \qquad (3.2.11)$$

then equations (3.2.10) are equivalent to the nonlinear complementarity problem

$$\begin{aligned}
&\mathbf{t}^T\mathbf{h}(\mathbf{t}) = 0 \qquad\qquad (3.2.12)\\
&\mathbf{t} \geq \mathbf{0},\ \mathbf{h}(\mathbf{t}) \geq \mathbf{0}.
\end{aligned}$$

Thus we have proved the following result.

Theorem 3.2.4. Under conditions $(\alpha)-(\delta)$, a vector $\mathbf{x}^*$ is an equilibrium point of the multiproduct oligopoly game if and only if there exists nonnegative vector $\mathbf{v}^*$ such that $\mathbf{x}^*$ and $\mathbf{v}^*$ solve the nonlinear complementarity problem.

Remark 1. Assume that φ_k is nonconcave in $\mathbf{x}_k$, but all other conditions hold. Then any equilibrium (if exists) necessarily satisfies relations (3.2.7), therefore it is a solution of the nonlinear complementarity problem (3.2.12). However, problem (3.2.12) may have solutions which are not equilibrium points.

Remark 2. There are existence results for the solutions of nonlinear complementarity problems (see Karamardian, 1969), which could also be used to prove Theorem 3.1.1. The uniqueness of the equilibrium of multiproduct oligopolies can be examined based on the uniqueness of the solutions of nonlinear complementarity problems. For example, it is easy to prove that if $\mathbf{h}(\mathbf{t})$ is strictly monotone, then problem (3.2.12) must not have two solutions. In contrary, assume that $\mathbf{t}$ and $\bar{\mathbf{t}}$ $(\mathbf{t} \neq \bar{\mathbf{t}})$ are both solutions. Then

$$0 < (\mathbf{t}-\bar{\mathbf{t}})^T(\mathbf{h}(\mathbf{t})-\mathbf{h}(\bar{\mathbf{t}})) = \mathbf{t}^T\mathbf{h}(\mathbf{t}) - \bar{\mathbf{t}}^T\mathbf{h}(\mathbf{t}) - \mathbf{t}^T\mathbf{h}(\bar{\mathbf{t}}) + \bar{\mathbf{t}}^T\mathbf{h}(\bar{\mathbf{t}}^T) = -\bar{\mathbf{t}}^T\mathbf{h}(\mathbf{t}) - \mathbf{t}^T\mathbf{h}(\bar{\mathbf{t}}) \leq 0,$$

which is an obvious contradiction.

Corollary. Assume that for all k, m and $\mathbf{x} \in X_1 \times X_2 \times \ldots \times X_N$,

$$\frac{\partial \varphi_k\left(x_1^{(1)},\ldots,x_k^{(m-1)},0,x_k^{(m+1)},\ldots,x_N^{(M)}\right)}{\partial x_k^{(m)}} > 0 \tag{3.2.13}$$

and

$$\frac{\partial \varphi_k\left(x_1^{(1)},\ldots,x_k^{(m-1)},L_k^{(m)},x_k^{(m+1)},\ldots,x_N^{(M)}\right)}{\partial x_k^{(m)}} < 0, \tag{3.2.14}$$

and conditions $(\alpha)-(\delta)$ hold. Then there is at least one equilibrium point and all equilibrium points are interior points of $X_1 \times X_2 \times \ldots \times X_N$.

Proof. This assertion is a consequence of Theorem 3.1.1 and relation (3.2.7).

□

Assume now that the conditions of Theorem 3.2.4 are satisfied and (3.2.13) and (3.2.14) hold. Then any equilibrium point $\mathbf{x}$ satisfies relations (3.2.10) with $\mathbf{v}_k = \mathbf{z}_k = 0$. That is,

$$\nabla_{\mathbf{x}_k}\varphi_k(\mathbf{x}) = \mathbf{0} \quad (k = 1,2,\ldots,N).$$

By using the special form of the profit functions, these equations are equivalent to the following:

$$\mathbf{g}_k(\mathbf{x}) \equiv \mathbf{J}_p\left(\sum_{l=1}^{N}\mathbf{x}_l\right)^T \mathbf{x}_k + \mathbf{p}\left(\sum_{l=1}^{N}\mathbf{x}_l\right) - \nabla_{\mathbf{x}_k}C_k(\mathbf{x}_k) = \mathbf{0} \quad (k = 1,2,\ldots,N),$$

where $\mathbf{J}_p(\mathbf{s})$ is the Jacobian of $\mathbf{p}(\mathbf{s})$. Introduce the notation

$$\mathbf{g}(\mathbf{x}) = \begin{bmatrix} \mathbf{g}_1(\mathbf{x}) \\ \mathbf{g}_2(\mathbf{x}) \\ \vdots \\ \mathbf{g}_N(\mathbf{x}) \end{bmatrix}. \tag{3.2.15}$$

The above derivations imply the following uniqueness result: If the conditions of Theorem 3.2.4 and relations (3.2.13) and (3.2.14) hold, and in addition, function $\mathbf{g}(\mathbf{x})$ is one-to-one, then the equilibrium point of the multiproduct oligopoly game is unique.

Remark. Sufficient conditions which guarantee that a function is one-to-one have been discussed earlier in this section, and can be applied to function $\mathbf{g}$ to prove the uniqueness of the equilibrium point.

3.3 Uniqueness and Properties of Equilibria in the Classical Game

The classical oligopoly game is a single-product oligopoly without product differentiation which can be derived from the multiproduct case by letting m=1. In this special case functions p and C_k are both real valued functions of real variables s and x_k, respectively. Sets X_k and S are subsets of the real line. Hence conditions (A) - (D) of Theorem 3.1.1 can be reformulated as follows:

(A") The set X_k of feasible outputs of firm k (k=1,...,N) is a closed interval $[0,L_k]$ where L_k is the capacity limit of firm k;
(B") There exists a $\xi > 0$ such that $p(s) = 0$ for $s \geq \xi$;
(C") Function C_k is strictly increasing and continuous on X_k;
(D") Function φ_k is continuous on $\bigtimes_{k=1}^{N}[0, L_k]$ and is concave in x_k with any fixed $x_l \in X_l \ (l \neq k)$ in the set

$$X^* = \left\{ (x_1, \dots, x_N) \middle| x_k \in X_k \quad (k = 1, \dots, N), \ \sum_{k=1}^{N} x_k \leq \xi \right\}.$$

Then Theorem 3.1.1 simplifies as follows.

Theorem 3.3.1. Under assumptions (A") - (D") the classical oligopoly game has at least one equilibrium point.

Observe next that function $-p$ is monotone if and only if p is decreasing. Hence Theorem 3.1.2 can now be restated as

Theorem 3.3.2. Assume that conditions (A"), (B") and (C") hold. Assume furthermore that function p is continuous and decreasing in $[0,\xi]$. If p is concave on $[0,\xi]$ and all functions C_k are convex on $[0,L_k]$ (k=1,...,N), then the classical oligopoly game has at least one equilibrium point.

The proof of Theorem 3.1.2 is based on the generalized Nikaido-Isoda Theorem, which does not provide a computational procedure for finding the equilibria, and does not provide any information on the structure of the set of all equilibrium points.

In the following part of this section a new constructive proof of Theorem 3.3.2 will be presented in order to introduce computer methods for finding the equilibria and also to characterize the set of all equilibrium points.

For any $\delta > 0$ and real function g, define the forward and backward divided differences as

$$g_\delta^+(x) = \frac{1}{\delta}\left(g(x+\delta) - g(x)\right)$$

and

$$g_\delta^-(x) = \frac{1}{\delta}\left(g(x) - g(x-\delta)\right).$$

In terms of these divided differences, we define functions $\phi_{j\,\delta}^+$ and $\phi_{j\,\delta}^-$ to be

$$\phi_{j\,\delta}^+(s,t) = p(s+\delta) + tp_\delta^+(s) - C_{j\,\delta}^+(t)$$

and

$$\phi_{j\,\delta}^-(s,t) = p(s-\delta) + tp_\delta^-(s) - C_{j\,\delta}^-(t).$$

We list below several inequalities concerning divided differences of a concave function $g(x)$. These properties will be referred to frequently in later developments.

For any $\delta, \Delta > 0$,

$$g_\delta^-(x) \geq g_\Delta^+(x). \tag{3.3.1}$$

If $\delta > \Delta > 0$,

$$g_\delta^-(x) \geq g_\Delta^-(x), \tag{3.3.2}$$

and

$$g_\delta^+(x) \leq g_\Delta^+(x). \tag{3.3.3}$$

Finally, if $x_1 > x_2$ and δ is positive,

$$g_\delta^-(x_1) \leq g_\delta^-(x_2)$$

and

$$g_\delta^+(x_1) \leq g_\delta^+(x_2).$$

Moreover, all of the inequalities (3.3.1) through (3.3.3) are strict if $g(x)$ is strictly concave. These properties are simple consequences of the concavity of function g. The details are left to the reader who will also be able to use the above properties to conclude that

1. $\phi_{j\ \delta}^-$ and $\phi_{j\ \delta}^+$ are both decreasing functions of t;
2. $\phi_{j\ \delta}^-$ and $\phi_{j\ \delta}^+$ are both decreasing functions of s;
3. $\phi_{j\ \delta}^+$ decreases with increasing δ;
4. $\phi_{j\ \delta}^-$ increases with increasing δ;
5. If p is strictly monotonic or if C_j is strictly convex, then the monotonicities asserted by 3. and 4. are strict;
6. For all s,t and positive δ, Δ,

$$\phi_{j\ \delta}^-(s,t) \geq \phi_{j\ \Delta}^+(s,t). \tag{3.3.4}$$

For each s in $[0,\xi]$ and for each j=1,2,...,N, we define set $\overline{X}_j(s)$ by the three conditions below:

$$\begin{aligned}
&\text{(i)} \quad 0 \in \overline{X}_j(s) \text{ if } \phi_{j\ \delta}^+(s,0) \leq 0, \text{ all } \delta > 0,\\
&\text{(ii)} \quad L_j \in \overline{X}_j(s) \text{ if } \phi_{j\ \delta}^-(s,L_j) \geq 0, \text{ all } \delta > 0,\\
&\text{(iii)} \quad \text{if } 0 < t < L_j, t \in \overline{X}_j(s) \text{ if } \phi_{j\ \delta}^-(s,t) \geq 0 \geq \phi_{j\ \Delta}^+(s,t) \text{ for all } \delta, \Delta > 0.
\end{aligned} \tag{3.3.5}$$

It will turn out that $\overline{X}_j(s)$ is the set of the best strategies for player j if the output of the industry is s. Some properties of sets $\overline{X}_j(s)$ are given by the following statements. Note first that $\overline{X}_j(s)$ is the same as mapping (3.2.3) for M=1.

Lemma 3.3.1. For each $s \in [0,\xi]$,

(a) $\overline{X}_j(s)$ is not empty and is a (possibly degenerate) closed interval $[\alpha_j(s), \beta_j(s)]$.

(b) Assume furthermore that either p is strictly decreasing or that C_j is strictly convex. If $s_1 < s_2$ and $t_k \in \overline{X}(s_k)$, $k = 1,2$, then $t_1 \geq t_2$. The inequality is strict if p is strictly monotonic.

(c) $t^* \in \overline{X}_j(s)$ if and only if t^* maximizes $\psi_j(t) = \phi_j(s - t^* + t, t) = tp(s - t^* + t) - C_j(t)$.

Proof. (a) Towards showing that $\overline{X}_j(s)$ is not empty, we define

$$t_0 = \sup\left\{t \middle| \phi_{j\,\delta}^-(s,t) \geq 0 \text{ for all } \delta > 0\right\}. \tag{3.3.6}$$

If the set defined in (3.3.6) is empty, then (3.3.4) implies that $\varphi_{j\,\Delta}^+(s,t) < 0$ for all $t, \Delta > 0$. The continuity of functions p and C_j implies that $0 \in \overline{X}_j(s)$. Assume that t_0 exists, then $\varphi_{j\,\delta}^-(s, t_0) \geq 0$ for all $\delta > 0$, which follows again from the continuity of p and C_j. Therefore if $t_0 = L_j$, then $t_0 \in \overline{X}_j(s)$. Otherwise $0 < t_0 < L_j$. We shall now prove that t_0 satisfies case (iii) of (3.3.5). In contrary to this assertion assume that $\varphi_{j\,\Delta}^+(s, t_0) > 0$ for some $\Delta > 0$. The continuity of $\varphi_{j\,\Delta}^+$ in t implies that for a small $u > 0$, $\varphi_{j\,\Delta}^+(s, t_0 + u) > 0$. Therefore from (3.3.4) we conclude that $\varphi_{j\,\delta}^-(s, t_0 + u) > 0$ for all $\delta > 0$, which contradicts the definition of t_0.

Statement (b) is vital to later developments and therefore we present its verification in detail.

Suppose in contrary to the assertion that $t_1 < t_2$. Define $Q = \phi_{j\,\delta}^+(s_1, t_1) - \phi_{j\,\delta}^-(s_2, t_2)$. By virtue of the definitions (3.3.5) of $\overline{X}_j(s)$, $\phi_{j\,\delta}^+(s_1, t_1) \leq 0$ and $\phi_{j\,\Delta}^-(s_2, t_2) \geq 0$, and so for all $\delta, \Delta \geq 0$,

$$Q \leq 0. \tag{3.3.7}$$

We will show that the hypothesis that $t_2 > t_1$ leads to values δ and Δ which contradict (3.3.7). Note that Q is expressed as

$$Q = \left[p(s_1 + \delta) - p(s_2 - \Delta)\right] + \left[t_1 p_\delta^+(s_1) - t_2 p_\Delta^-(s_2)\right] + \left[-C_{j\,\delta}^+(t_1) + C_{j\,\Delta}^-(t_2)\right].$$

Our objective is now to demonstrate that each of the bracketed terms in nonnegative for small enough δ and $\Delta = \delta$ with at least one term being positive. Let us refer to these bracketed terms as T_1, T_2, and T_3, respectively. Since p is decreasing, if $\delta + \Delta < s_2 - s_1$, then T_1 is nonnegative and in fact is positive if p is strictly decreasing. For $\delta < s_2 - s_1$ and $\Delta = \delta$,

$$p_\delta^+(s_1) \geq p_\delta^+(s_2 - \delta) = p_\delta^-(s_2),$$

so

$$T_2 \geq (t_1 - t_2)p_\delta^-(s_2).$$

Under the hypothesis that $t_2 > t_1$, both factors on the right side are nonpositive. The term $p_\delta^-(s_2)$ is nonpositive because p is decreasing.

Finally, if $\delta < t_2 - t_1$, using the notation $g(t) = -C_j(t)$ and the monotonicity of $g_\delta^+(t)$, we have

$$g_\delta^+(t_1) - g_\delta^-(t_2) \geq g_\delta^+(t_2 - \delta) - g_\delta^-(t_2) = 0.$$

If C_j is strictly convex, the monotonicity is strict and T_3 is therefore positive.

To demonstrate statement (c), the reader may verify that 0 maximizes $\psi(t)$ if and only if $\Psi(0) \geq \Psi(\delta)$, that is, if and only if

$$-C_j(0) - [\delta p(s+\delta) - C_j(\delta)] \geq 0.$$

It is easy to see that this is equivalent to condition (i) of (3.3.5), and thus $0 \in \overline{X}_j(s)$. Similarly, in other cases $t*$maximizes $\psi(t)$ if and only if condition (ii) holds if $t^* = L_j$, and (iii) holds for $0 < t^* < L_j$. □

Lemma 3.3.2. If the price function p is differentiable and $p' < 0$, then for each $s \in [0, \xi]$ and for each $j = 1, 2, \ldots, N$, $X_j(s)$ is a singleton set; that is, in the notation of part (a) of Lemma 3.3.1,

$$\alpha_j(s) = \beta_j(s), \quad 1 \leq j \leq N.$$

Proof. We will show that under the conditions of the lemma, if $t_1 < t_2$, then for sufficiently small δ,

$$\phi_{j\,\delta}^+(s, t_1) > \phi_{j\,\delta}^-(s, t_2), \qquad (3.3.8)$$

which implies that t_1 and t_2 cannot both belong to $\overline{X}_j(s)$.

Toward demonstrating (3.3.8) note that

$$\phi_{j\delta}^{+}(s,t_1)-\phi_{j\delta}^{-}(s,t_2)=p(s+\delta)-p(s-\delta)+t_1\big(p(s+\delta)-p(s)\big)/\delta$$
$$-t_2\big(p(s)-p(s-\delta)\big)/\delta-C_{j\delta}^{+}(t_1)+C_{j\delta}^{-}(t_2).$$

Since $C_j(x)$ is convex, $C_{j\delta}^{-}(x)$ is increasing in x. Consequently, if $\delta<t_2-t_1$, we have

$$C_{j\delta}^{-}(t_2)-C_{j\delta}^{+}(t_1)=C_{j\delta}^{-}(t_2)-C_{j\delta}^{-}(t_1+\delta)\geq 0,$$

and therefore

$$\phi_{j\delta}^{+}(s,t_1)-\phi_{j\delta}^{-}(s,t_2)\geq (t_1-t_2)p'(s)+0(\delta).$$

Finally, inequality (3.3.8) follows from the assumption that $p'<0$ and the fact that $\phi_{j\delta}^{+}(s,t)$ increases and $\phi_{j\delta}^{-}(s,t)$ decreases as δ converges to 0. □

Corollary. The assertion of the lemma also holds if the derivative of p exists and the cost functions are all strictly convex.

We now state the main result of this section.

Theorem 3.3.3. Assume that all conditions of Theorem 3.3.2 hold and either the unit price function p is strictly decreasing or all the cost functions C_j are strictly convex. Let X^* denote the set of Cournot equilibrium points. Then

(1) X^* is a polyhedron;
(2) The total output s^* is the same for every equilibrium point;
and
(3) If p' exists, and either $p'(s)$ is negative or the C_j's are strictly convex, then the equilibrium point is unique.

Proof. We first demonstrate (2). Suppose s is the total output. Then from part (c) of Lemma 3.3.1, $\bar{\mathbf{x}}=\bar{\mathbf{x}}(s)$ is an equilibrium vector only if for each coordinate j, $\bar{x}_j(s)\in\bar{X}_j(s)$. From part (b), if $s_1<s_2$,

$$\bar{x}_j(s_1)\geq\bar{x}_j(s_2),\ \ 1\leq j\leq N. \tag{3.3.9}$$

But for s_1 and s_2 both to be total outputs we require that $\sum_{j=1}^{N}\bar{x}_j(s_1)=s_1$ and $\sum_{j=1}^{N}\bar{x}_j(s_2)=s_2$. Thus (3.3.9) implies a contradiction to $s_1<s_2$ and the total output must therefore be the same for all equilibrium points. Let s^*

denote the unique production level at any equilibrium point. Then from (a) of Lemma 3.3.1 it is clear that X^* can be represented as

$$X^* = \left\{ \mathbf{x} \middle| x_j \in \left[\alpha_j(s), \beta_j(s)\right] \text{ and } \sum_{i=1}^{N} x_i = s^* \right\}, \tag{3.3.10}$$

which is obviously a polyhedron. Under the differentiability assumption, Lemma 3.3.2 and its corollary imply that each of the intervals in (3.3.10) is a singleton, and thus X^* is also a singleton. □

Remark. The assertion of the theorem is very interesting since the set of the equilibrium points is a polyhedron even if the game is nonlinear. The uniqueness of the equilibrium is not true in general under the conditions of Theorem 3.3.3. See for example, the duopoly of Example 2.1.2. It satisfies all of the conditions of Theorem 3.3.3 and nevertheless has infinitely many equilibrium points.

3.4 Linear Oligopoly Models

In this section a special multiproduct oligopoly game will be analyzed. Assume that the price function and all cost functions are linear

$$\mathbf{p}(\mathbf{s}) = \mathbf{A}\mathbf{s} + \mathbf{b}, \quad C_k(\mathbf{x}_k) = \mathbf{b}_k^T \mathbf{x}_k + c_k \quad (k = 1, 2, \ldots, N).$$

In Section 2.3 we presented economic reasons why this form of the price function is realistic. Assume that the following conditions hold:

(A) The set X_k of feasible outputs of firm k is

$$X_k = \left[0, L_k^{(1)}\right] \times \ldots \times \left[0, L_k^{(M)}\right],$$

where $L_k^{(m)}$ denotes its capacity of product m;

(B) The set X of simultaneous strategies of the firms equals $X_1 \times X_2 \times \ldots \times X_N$.

The main purpose of this section is to demonstrate the relation between the equilibrium problem of this linear multiproduct oligopoly game and a certain quadratic programming problem.

Let $\mathbf{x}^* = (\mathbf{x}_1^*, \ldots, \mathbf{x}_N^*)$ denote an equilibrium point. Then for all k, x_k^* maximizes the function

$$\varphi_k\left(\mathbf{x}_1^*,\ldots,\mathbf{x}_{k-1}^*,\mathbf{x}_k,\mathbf{x}_{k+1}^*,\ldots,\mathbf{x}_N^*\right)=\mathbf{x}_k^T\left(\mathbf{A}\mathbf{x}_k+\mathbf{A}\sum_{l\neq k}^{N}\mathbf{x}_l^*+\mathbf{b}\right)-\left(\mathbf{b}_k^T\mathbf{x}_k+c_k\right).$$

Since each component $x_k^{(m)}$ of $\mathbf{x}_k$ is between 0 and $L_k^{(m)}$, the first order conditions for optimality imply

$$\frac{\partial\varphi_k\left(\mathbf{x}^*\right)}{\partial x_k^{(m)}}\begin{cases}\leq 0 \text{ if } x_k^{(m)*}=0\\ \geq 0 \text{ if } x_k^{(m)*}=L_k^{(m)}\\ =0 \text{ if } 0<x_k^{(m)*}<L_k^{(m)}.\end{cases} \tag{3.4.1}$$

Introduce the slack variables (as in Section 3.2)

$$w_k^{(m)}=L_k^{(m)}-x_k^{(m)},\ z_k^{(m)}\begin{cases}=0 \text{ if } x^{(m)*}>0\\ \geq 0 \text{ otherwise},\end{cases}$$

and

$$v_k^{(m)}=\begin{cases}=0 \text{ if } x^{(m)*}<L_k^{(m)}\\ \geq 0 \text{ otherwise}.\end{cases}$$

Then for all k and m,

$$\frac{\partial\varphi_k\left(\mathbf{x}^*\right)}{\partial x_k^{(m)}}-v_k^{(m)}+z_k^{(m)}=0,$$

that is, with $\mathbf{v}_k=\left(v_k^{(m)}\right)_{m=1}^{M}$, $\mathbf{z}_k=\left(z_k^{(m)}\right)_{m=1}^{M}$,

$$\nabla_{\mathbf{x}_k}\varphi_k\left(\mathbf{x}^*\right)-\mathbf{v}_k+\mathbf{z}_k=0. \tag{3.4.2}$$

Using the special forms of $\mathbf{p}(\mathbf{s})$ and $C_k(\mathbf{x}_k)$,

$$\left(\mathbf{A}+\mathbf{A}^T\right)\mathbf{x}_k^*+\mathbf{A}\sum_{l\neq k}\mathbf{x}_l^*+\mathbf{b}-\mathbf{b}_k-\mathbf{v}_k+\mathbf{z}_k=\mathbf{0} \text{ for } k=1,2,\ldots,N.$$

Introduce the notation

$$\mathbf{Q} = \begin{bmatrix} \mathbf{A}+\mathbf{A}^T & \mathbf{A} & \cdots & \mathbf{A} \\ \mathbf{A} & \mathbf{A}+\mathbf{A}^T & \cdots & \mathbf{A} \\ \vdots & \vdots & & \vdots \\ \mathbf{A} & \mathbf{A} & & \mathbf{A}+\mathbf{A}^T \end{bmatrix}, \mathbf{b}^{(0)} = \begin{bmatrix} \mathbf{b} \\ \mathbf{b} \\ \vdots \\ \mathbf{b} \end{bmatrix}, \mathbf{b}^{(1)} = \begin{bmatrix} \mathbf{b}_1 \\ \mathbf{b}_2 \\ \vdots \\ \mathbf{b}_N \end{bmatrix},$$

$$\mathbf{v} = \begin{bmatrix} \mathbf{v}_1 \\ \mathbf{v}_2 \\ \vdots \\ \mathbf{v}_N \end{bmatrix}, \mathbf{w} = \begin{bmatrix} \mathbf{w}_1 \\ \mathbf{w}_2 \\ \vdots \\ \mathbf{w}_N \end{bmatrix}, \mathbf{L} = \begin{bmatrix} \mathbf{L}_1 \\ \mathbf{L}_2 \\ \vdots \\ \mathbf{L}_N \end{bmatrix},$$

where $\mathbf{w}_k = \left(w_k^{(m)}\right)_{m=1}^{M}$, $\mathbf{L}_k = \left(L_k^{(m)}\right)_{m=1}^{M}$. Then the above relations reduce to

$$\begin{aligned} &\mathbf{Qx}^* + \mathbf{b}^{(0)} - \mathbf{b}^{(1)} - \mathbf{v} + \mathbf{z} = \mathbf{0} \\ &\mathbf{x} + \mathbf{w} = \mathbf{L} \\ &\mathbf{x}^T\mathbf{z} = \mathbf{v}^T\mathbf{w} = 0, \\ &\mathbf{x}, \mathbf{v}, \mathbf{z}, \mathbf{w} \geq \mathbf{0}, \end{aligned} \tag{3.4.3}$$

where the last three relations are implied by the definitions of the slack variables. Thus the following result has been verified:

Theorem 3.4.1. Let $\mathbf{x}^*$ be an equilibrium point of the linear multiproduct oligopoly game. Then $\mathbf{x}^*$ satisfies relations (3.4.3) with some vectors $\mathbf{v}$, $\mathbf{w}$ and $\mathbf{z}$.

Assume next that

(C) Matrix $\mathbf{A} + \mathbf{A}^T$ is negative semidefinite.

This condition is satisfied, for example, if matrices $\mathbf{A}$ and $\mathbf{A}^T$ are strictly diagonally dominant. Under assumptions (A) - (C), payoff function φ_k is continuous, and concave in $\mathbf{x}_k$. Thus a vector $\mathbf{x}^*$ is an equilibrium point if and only if it maximizes function

$$\varphi_k\left(\mathbf{x}_1^*, \ldots, \mathbf{x}_{k-1}^*, \mathbf{x}_k, \mathbf{x}_{k+1}^*, \ldots, \mathbf{x}_N^*\right),$$

and in this case the first order conditions (3.4.1) are sufficient and necessary. We have seen that (3.4.1) is equivalent to relations (3.4.3), and hence we have the following result.

Theorem 3.4.2. Assume that conditions (A) - (C) hold. A vector $\mathbf{x}^*$ is an equilibrium point of the linear multiproduct oligopoly game if and only if it satisfies relations (3.4.3) with some vectors **v**, **w**, and **z**.

Observe next that the Kuhn-Tucker conditions (see Hadley, 1964) of the quadratic programming problem

$$\begin{array}{ll} \text{maximize} & \frac{1}{2}\mathbf{x}^T\mathbf{Q}\mathbf{x} + \left(\mathbf{b}^{(0)} - \mathbf{b}^{(1)}\right)^T\mathbf{x} \\ \text{subject to} & \mathbf{0} \le \mathbf{x} \le \mathbf{L} \end{array} \tag{3.4.4}$$

coincide with relations (3.4.3). Thus we have the following

Theorem 3.4.3. Assume that conditions (A) - (C) hold. Then if $\mathbf{x}^*$ is an equilibrium point, it is an optimal solution of problem (3.4.4); if $\mathbf{x}^*$ is an optimal solution of problem (3.4.4), then it is an equilibrium point of the linear multiproduct oligopoly game.

Proof. For the complete proof of the Theorem we have to verify that under assumptions (A) - (C), the objective function of (3.4.4) is concave. That is, matrix $\mathbf{Q}+\mathbf{Q}^T$ is negative semidefinite. In this case the Kuhn-Tucker conditions are necessary and sufficient. Consider the quadratic form of matrix $\mathbf{Q}+\mathbf{Q}^T$:

$$2\sum_{k=1}^{N}\mathbf{u}_k^T\left(\mathbf{A}+\mathbf{A}^T\right)\mathbf{u}_k + \sum_{k=1}^{N}\sum_{l\neq k}\mathbf{u}_k^T\left(\mathbf{A}+\mathbf{A}^T\right)\mathbf{u}_l = -\sum_{k=1}^{N}\left(\mathbf{D}\mathbf{u}_k\right)^T\left(\mathbf{D}\mathbf{u}_k\right) - \left(\sum_{k=1}^{N}\mathbf{D}\mathbf{u}_k\right)^T\left(\sum_{l=1}^{N}\mathbf{D}\mathbf{u}_l\right) \le 0,$$

where **D** is determined so that $\mathbf{D}^T\mathbf{D} = -\left(\mathbf{A}+\mathbf{A}^T\right)$. The existence of matrix **D** is verified for example, in Szidarovszky and Yakowitz (1978). □

Remark. In proving Theorem 5.1.2 (Section 5.1) a more general method will be introduced to prove that under assumption (C), matrix $\mathbf{Q}+\mathbf{Q}^T$ is negative semidefinite.

Corollary. Assume that

(C') Matrix $\mathbf{A}+\mathbf{A}^T$ is negative definite.

Then the equilibrium point of the linear multiproduct oligopoly game is unique and coincides with the unique optimal solution of problem (3.4.4).

Proof. It is sufficient to mention that under assumption (C'), problem (3.4.4) has a strictly concave objective function, and therefore there is a unique solution.

□

3.5 Numerical Methods for Finding Cournot-Nash Equilibria

In this section numerical methods will be presented which enable us to determine the Cournot-Nash equilibria.

Theorem 3.2.1 has reduced the equilibrium problem to the fixed-point problem of a point-to-set mapping. Similarly, Theorem 3.2.2 presented a different fixed-point problem, the dimension of which is usually smaller than that of the fixed-point problem given in Theorem 3.2.1. In the case of both fixed-point problems standard methods can be used for finding the fixed points. Such methods are described for example in Scarf (1973). In the special case, when the best reply mapping $\mathbf{r}(\mathbf{x})$ (see Definition 3.2.2) is one-to-one and a contraction, then standard iteration techniques are available (see for example, Szidarovszky and Yakowitz, 1978).

In Section 3.2 we introduced a nonlinear complementarity problem and proved in Theorem 3.2.4 that it is equivalent to the Cournot-Nash equilibrium problem. Hence any method for finding the solutions of nonlinear complementarity problems can be applied for determining the equilibrium points of multiproduct oligopoly games. A comprehensive summary of such methods is given for example in Karamardian (1969). A large class of these methods formulate the problem as a variational inequality of the form

$$\mathbf{f}^T(\mathbf{x})(\mathbf{y}-\mathbf{x}) \geq 0 \text{ for all } \mathbf{y} \in K, \tag{3.5.1}$$

where $\mathbf{f}: K \mapsto R^p$, K being a convex subset in R^p. One of the most frequently used methods for solving problem (3.5.1) is the following, which is called the *diagonalization method.* Construct first a function $\mathbf{G}(\mathbf{x},\mathbf{y}): K \times K \mapsto R^p$ with properties:

(i) $\mathbf{G}(\mathbf{x},\mathbf{x}) = \mathbf{f}(\mathbf{x}) \quad (\forall \mathbf{x} \in K)$;

(ii) For all $\mathbf{x},\mathbf{y} \in K$, the Jacobian $\mathbf{G}_x(\mathbf{x},\mathbf{y})$ of $\mathbf{G}$ with respect to $\mathbf{x}$ is symmetric and positive definite.

Then apply the following iteration process. Select first an initial approximation $\mathbf{x}^{(0)} \in K$, and then solve in each step t (t=1,2,...) the variational inequality

$$\mathbf{G}^T\left(\mathbf{x}^{(t)},\mathbf{x}^{(t-1)}\right)\left(\mathbf{x}-\mathbf{x}^{(t)}\right) \geq 0 \text{ for all } \mathbf{x} \in K. \tag{3.5.2}$$

It can be proven that under certain conditions $\mathbf{x}^{(t)}$ converges to the solution of (3.5.1). If one selects function $\mathbf{G}(\mathbf{x},\mathbf{y}) = \left(G_1(\mathbf{x},\mathbf{y}),\dots,G_N(\mathbf{x},\mathbf{y})\right)$, where

$$G_k(\mathbf{x},\mathbf{y}) = C_k(x_k) - p(x_k + Y_k) - x_k p'(x_k + Y_k)$$

for the classical Cournot market (M=1) with $Y_k = \sum_{l \neq k} y_l$, then (3.5.2) can be reduced to the optimization problem

$$\text{maximize } x_k p\left(x_k + \sum_{l \neq k} x_l^{(t-1)}\right) - C_k(x_k) \quad (k = 1,2,...,N). \tag{3.5.3}$$

Note that this sequential optimization method is identical to the dynamic oligopoly model with discrete time scales and Cournot expectation which will be discussed in Sections 4.1. and 6.3. Note also that all other dynamic models to be discussed in Chapters 4, 5 and 6 are also applicable for determining equilibria, when the state transition equation is viewed as iteration equation.

The existence theorems of Section 3.3 imply a simple iteration procedure for finding the equilibrium point in a single product oligopoly market. Assume now, in addition to the assumptions of Theorem 3.3.3, that functions p and C_j are all differentiable, and p'<0. In this special case sets $\overline{X}_j(s)$ (defined in (3.3.5)) can be redefined as

$$\overline{X}_j(s) = \begin{cases} 0, \text{ if } p(s) - C'_j(0) \leq 0 \\ L_j, \text{ if } L_j p'(s) + p(s) - C'_j(L_j) \geq 0 \\ 0 < t < L_j, \text{ if } tp'(s) + p(s) - C'_j(t) = 0. \end{cases} \tag{3.5.4}$$

Set $\overline{X}_j(s)$ consists of one point as the consequence of Lemma 3.3.2. Consequently, $\overline{X}_j(s)$ is a function of s and Lemma 3.3.1 implies that this function is decreasing for all j. The sum s^* of the equilibrium strategies x_j^* is therefore the unique solution of equation

$$\sum_{j=1}^{N} \overline{X}_j(s) - s = 0. \tag{3.5.5}$$

Observe that at s=0 the left hand side of this equation is nonnegative since all $\overline{X}_j(s)$ values are nonnegative. For $s = \xi$ and all j, $\overline{X}_j(s)$=0. Therefore the left hand side of equation (3.5.5) is negative. Consequently, there is a unique root, s^*, in $[0, \xi)$, and the equilibrium strategies are

$$x_j^* = \overline{X}_j(s^*), \quad j = 1,2,...,N.$$

It is worthwhile to mention that equation (3.5.5) can be solved by standard methods of numerical analysis, such as the bisection or secant method. For further details see for example Chapter 5 of Yakowitz and Szidarovszky (1986).

If a multiproduct (or classical) oligopoly market is linear, then Theorems 3.4.2 and 3.4.3 are applicable in determining equilibria. In applying Theorem 3.4.2 the nonnegative solution of system (3.4.3) must be determined. In applying Theorem 3.4.3 the convex quadratic programming problem (3.4.4) should be solved. For both types of problems standard techniques are also available (see for example, Hadley, 1964).

Before concluding this section, a simple algorithm will be introduced to solve the classical oligopoly game under the assumption that functions p and C_j (j=1,2,...,N) are linear. Denote

$$p(s) = as + b, \quad C_j(x_j) = A_j x_j + B_j \quad (j = 1,2,...,N),$$

and if the conditions of Theorem 3.3.3 hold, then

$$a < 0, \quad A_j > 0 \quad (j = 1,2,...,N).$$

Without losing generality we may assume that

$$A_1 \le A_2 \le ... \le A_{N-1} \le A_N,$$

since we can number the firms in any arbitrary order. In this special case (3.5.4) implies that

$$\overline{X}_j(s) = \begin{cases} 0, \text{ if } as + b - A_j \le 0 \\ L_j, \text{ if } L_j a + as + b - A_j \ge 0 \\ 0 < t < L_j, \text{ if } ta + as + b - A_j = 0. \end{cases} \tag{3.5.6}$$

For j=1,2,...,N define

$$u_j = \frac{A_j - b}{a} \text{ and } v_j = \frac{A_j - b - L_j a}{a} = u_j - L_j, \tag{3.5.7}$$

then

$$u_1 \ge u_2 \ge ... \ge u_{N-1} \ge u_N,$$

and for all j,

$u_j > v_j$.

Relations (3.5.7) imply that

$$\overline{X}_j(s) = \begin{cases} 0, \text{ if } s \geq u_j \\ L_j, \text{ if } s \leq v_j \\ u_j - s, \text{ if } v_j < s < u_j . \end{cases}$$

Using the above notations the algorithm is as follows:

Step 1. Let $w_1, w_2, ..., w_{2N+2}$ denote the elements of the set $\{0, u_1, u_2, ..., u_N, v_1, v_2, ..., v_N, \xi\}$ in increasing order.

Set k:=1.

Step 2. Define

$$I(k) = \{j | w_k \geq u_j\}$$

and

$$J(k) = \{j | w_k \leq v_j\}.$$

Set

$$x_j = \begin{cases} 0, & \text{if } j \in I(k) \\ L_j, & \text{if } j \in J(k) \\ u_j - w_k, & \text{if } j \notin I(k) \cup J(k). \end{cases}$$

Step 3. Check which one of the following three cases holds:

Case a) If $\sum_{j=1}^{N} x_j = w_k$, then accept vector $(x_1, x_2, ..., x_N)$ as the equilibrium point, and stop.

Case b) If $\sum_{j=1}^{N} x_j > w_k$, then set k:=k+1, and go back to Step 2.

Case c) If $\sum_{j=1}^{N} x_j < w_k$, then go to Step 4.

Step 4. Define

$$I = \left\{ j \,\middle|\, \frac{w_{k-1} + w_k}{2} > u_j \right\}$$

and

$$J = \left\{ j \,\middle|\, \frac{w_{k-1} + w_k}{2} < v_j \right\}.$$

Then the equilibrium strategies can be obtained as

$$x_j = \begin{cases} 0, & \text{if } j \in I \\ L_j, & \text{if } j \in J \\ t_j, & \text{if } j \notin I \cup J, \end{cases}$$

where the values t_j are obtained as follows. First, solve equation

$$\sum_{j \in J} L_j + \sum_{j \notin I \cup J} (u_j - s) = s \tag{3.5.8}$$

for s, and then select

$$t_j = u_j - s^*,$$

where s^* is the solution of (3.5.8). Note that

$$s^* = \frac{\sum_{j \in J} L_j + \sum_{j \notin I \cup J} u_j}{N + 1 - |I \cup J|},$$

where $|I \cup J|$ is the number of elements in set $I \cup J$.

The above algorithm is very easy to implement and it is much more simple than the quadratic programming approach introduced by Mañas (1972).

3.6 Existence of Equilibrium in Rent Seeking Games

Rent seeking models were introduced earlier in Section 2.5, where we have shown that model (2.5.3) is equivalent to a single-product oligopoly game without product differentiation. In this section the existence of an equilibrium point will be verified under realistic assumptions on the agents' production functions $f_i(x_i)$. Assume that for all i and $x_i \geq 0$,

(A) f_i is twice differentiable;
(B) $f_i'(x_i)>0, f_i''(x_i)<0$;
(C) $f_i(0)=0$.

Recall that the strategy set of each agent is interval $[0,\infty)$, and the payoff function of agent *i* is defined as the net rent:

$$\varphi_i(x_1,\ldots,x_N)=\frac{f_i(x_i)}{\sum_{j=1}^{N} f_j(x_j)}-x_i. \tag{3.6.1}$$

If $x_1=x_2\ldots=x_N=0$, then φ_i is defined to be zero for all *i*.

Introduce the new variable $y_i=f_i(x_i)$, then $y_i\in[0,f_i(\infty))$, and payoff function φ_i can be rewritten as

$$\pi_i(y_1,\ldots,y_N)=y_i\cdot\frac{1}{\sum_{j=1}^{N} y_j}-g_i(y_i) \tag{3.6.2}$$

where g_i is the inverse of f_i, which exists since condition (B) implies that f_i is strictly increasing. Furthermore $g_i'(y_i)>0$ and $g_i''(y_i)>0$. We have shown earlier in Section 2.5 that this new formulation is a single-product oligopoly without product differentiation, where the strategy set of agent *i* is the interval $[0,f_i(\infty))$, its cost function is g_i, and the unit price function is $\frac{1}{s}$. Since interval $[0,f_i(\infty))$ may be unbounded and g_i is convex, the existence results presented in Section 3.3 for single-product oligopolies cannot be applied. However we can prove that the following theorem hold.

Theorem 3.6.1. Under condition (A), (B), and (C) the above rent-seeking game has exactly one equilibrium point.

Proof. First, we note that $y_1=y_2=\cdots y_n=0$ is not an equilibrium, since if any one of the agents changes his strategy selection from zero to a small positive y_i, then his payoff becomes positive:
$1-g_i(y_i)>0$.

Notice next that function (3.6.2) is concave in y_i. Therefore, with any fixed $y_j(j\neq i)$, the best response y_i^* of agent *i* is given as follows: If

$$g_i'(0) \geq \frac{1}{\sum_{j \neq i} y_j},$$

then

$$y_i^* = 0;$$

otherwise, y_i^* is the unique positive solution of equation

$$g_i'(y_i^*) = \frac{\sum_{j \neq i}^{N} y_j}{\left(\sum_{j \neq i} y_j + y_i^*\right)^2}.$$

It is well known that a vector $(y_1^*, ..., y_N^*)$ is an equilibrium point if and only if for all i, y_i^* is the best response with fixed values of $y_j^*(j \neq i)$.

Let $s = \sum_{i=1}^{N} y_i$ and for all s>0, define

$$y_i(s) = \begin{cases} 0 \text{ if } sg_i'(0) \geq 1 \\ \text{unique positive solution of equation} \\ s^2 g_i'(y_i) = s - y_i, \text{ otherwise.} \end{cases} \tag{3.6.3}$$

First, we show that $y_i(s)$ is well defined. If $sg_i'(0) < 1$, then at $y_i = 0$, $s^2 g_i'(y_i) < s - y_i$, and with $y_i = s, s^2 g_i'(y_i) > s - y_i$. Furthermore, $s^2 g_i'(y_i)$ is increasing in y_i, while s-y_i decreases. Hence, there is a unique positive solution in interval (0,s).

The above observation implies that $(y_1^*, ..., y_N^*)$ is a pure Nash equilibrium if and only if $s^* = \sum_{i=1}^{N} y_i^*$ satisfies equation

$$Y(s^*) = \sum_{i=1}^{N} y_i(s^*) - s^* = 0, \tag{3.6.4}$$

and then the equilibrium strategies are given as

$$y_i^* = y_i(s^*), \quad i = 1,2,...,N.$$

From equation (3.6.3), it is easy to see that $y_i(s)$ is continuous in s, and if $y_i(s)$=0 and s<s', then $y_i(s')$=0. Next we show that (3.6.4) has a unique solution by proving that there is a pair $S^* > S_* > 0$ such that no solution exists for

$s < S_*$ and $s > S^*$; furthermore, in the interval $[S_*, S^*]$, Y strictly decreases, $Y(S_*) \geq 0$, and $Y(S^*) \leq 0$. Assume therefore that $y_i(s)>0$. Differentiate equation $s^2 g_i'(y_i(s)) = s - y_i(s)$ with respect to s to see that

$$y_i'(s) = \frac{1 - 2sg_i'(y_i)}{1 + s^2 g_i''(y_i)} = \frac{1 - 2s((s - y_i)/s^2)}{1 + s^2 g_i''(y_i)}$$
$$= \frac{2y_i - s}{s(1 + s^2 g_i''(y_i))}.$$

If $y_i \leq s/2$, then y_i decreases. Notice that y_i decreases even if $y_i=0$. If $y_i > s/2$, then y_i strictly increases in s. From equation (3.6.3) we see that the second case occurs if and only if

$$s^2 g_i'\left(\frac{s}{2}\right) - s + \frac{s}{2} < 0,$$

which is equivalent to the inequality

$$2sg_i'\left(\frac{s}{2}\right) < 1. \tag{3.6.5}$$

The left-hand side is zero for $s=0$, strictly increases, and converges to ∞ as $s \to \infty$. Therefore, there is a unique positive value s_i such that $2s_i g_i'(s_i/2) = 1$, and inequality (3.6.5) holds if and only if $s<s_i$. Assume now that

$$s_1 \geq s_2 \geq \cdots \geq s_N.$$

If $s<s_2$, then $y_1(s) > s/2$ and $y_2(s) > s/2$. Hence, equation (3.6.4) has no solution. Select $S_* = s_2$. At $s = S_*$, $Y(s) \geq 0$. Assume next that $s > S_*$, then $y_2(s), \ldots, y_N(s)$ all decrease. If $y_1(s)$ is also decreasing, then $Y(s)$ obviously decreases. If $y_i'(s) \geq 0$, then assumption (B) implies that

$$Y'(s) = \sum_{i=1}^{N} y_i'(s) - 1 \leq y_1'(s) - 1 \leq \frac{2y_1(s) - s}{s} - 1$$
$$= \frac{2}{s}(y_1(s) - s) < 0,$$

since $y_1(s)<s$ from equation (3.6.3). That is $Y(s)$ decreases. Define finally $S^* = 1/\min_i g_i'(0)$. If $s \geq S^*$, then the first case of equation (3.6.3) implies that

for all i, $y_i(s)=0$; therefore, for $s \geq S^*$, $Y(s) < 0$, so no solution exists here. In order to complete the proof we have to show that $S_* < S^*$:

$$S_* = \frac{1}{2g_2'(S_*/2)} \leq \frac{1}{2g_2'(0)} \leq \frac{1}{2} \cdot \frac{1}{\min_i g_i(0)} = \frac{S^*}{2} < S^*.$$

Hence the theorem is completely proved. □

Corollary. Notice that for any agent i and any fixed values of $y_j (j \neq i)$, the solution $y_i=0$ always gives zero payoff value for this agent. Therefore, at the best response, his/her payoff must not be negative. Hence, we proved that under the conditions of the theorem each agent enjoys nonnegative expected net rent at the equilibrium.

Finally we mention that assumption (A) requiring that f_i is twice differentiable served only technical convenience. The existence of an equilibrium can be examined under only continuity assumption in the same way as the classical single-product oligopoly game without product differentiation was discussed earlier in Section 3.3.

3.7 Existence of Equilibrium in Labor-Managed Oligopolies

In this section the existence and uniqueness of the equilibrium points of labor-managed oligopolies will be examined.

Consider first the single-product case without product differentiation. Keeping the notation of Section 2.6, let $x_k \in [0, L_k]$ denote the output of firm k, where L_k is its capacity limit. If $p\left(\sum_{l=1}^{N} x_l\right)$ is the price function, w>0 the competitive wage rate, c_k>0 the fixed cost of firm k, and $h_k(x_k)$ the amount of labor necessary for producing output x_k, then the surplus of firm k per unit labor is given as

$$\varphi_k(x_1, \dots, x_N) = \left\{ x_k p\left(\sum_{l=1}^{N} x_l\right) - wh_k(x_k) - c_k \right\} \Big/ h_k(x_k). \tag{3.7.1}$$

Assume that

(A) Functions p and h_k (k=1,2,...,N) are continuous on $\left[0, \sum_{l=1}^{N} L_l\right]$ and $[0, L_k]$, respectively;

(B) $h_k(0) \geq 0$ and h_k is strictly increasing for all k;
(C) φ_k is concave in x_k with any fixed x_k $(l \neq k)$.

If $h_k(0)>0$ for all k, then the Nikaido-Isoda theorem (Nikaido and Isoda, 1955) guarantees the existence of at least one equilibrium point. If $h_k(0)=0$, then the equilibrium strategy for firm k is bounded away from 0, so its strategy set can be restricted to $x_k \geq \varepsilon$ with some small $\varepsilon > 0$.

Assume next that h_k $(k=1,2,\dots,N)$ and p are twice differentiable, then simple differentiation shows that

$$\frac{\partial \varphi_k}{\partial x_k} = \left\{ (p + x_k p' - w h'_k) h_k - (x_k p - w h_k - c_k) h'_k \right\} / h_k^2$$

$$= \left\{ (p + x_k p') h_k - (x_k p - c_k) h'_k \right\} / h_k^2$$

and

$$\frac{\partial^2 \varphi_k}{\partial x_k^2} = \left\{ \left[(2p' + x_k p'') h_k + (p + x_k p') h'_k - (p + x_k p') h'_k - (x_k p - c_k) h''_k \right] h_k^2 \right.$$

$$\left. - \left[(p + x_k p') h_k - (x_k p - c_k) h'_k \right] 2 h_k h'_k \right\} / h_k^4$$

$$= \left\{ \left[(2p' + x_k p'') h_k - (x_k p - c_k) h''_k \right] \right\} / h_k^2 - \frac{\partial \varphi_k}{\partial x_k} \cdot \frac{2h'_k}{h_k}.$$

Notice first that at $x_k=0$,

$$\frac{\partial \varphi_k}{\partial x_k} = (p h_k + c_k h'_k) / h_k^2 .$$

At $x_k=0$, $\partial \varphi_k / \partial x_k > 0$ showing that $x_k=0$ never maximizes φ_k. Similarly, at $x_k=L_k$,

$$\frac{\partial \varphi_k}{\partial x_k} = \left\{ (p + L_k p') h_k - (L_k p - c_k) h'_k \right\} / h_k^2 .$$

If we assume that

(D) For all k and $s_k \in \left[0, \sum_{l \neq k} L_l \right]$,

$$\left(p(L_k+s_k)+L_k p'(L_k+s_k)\right)h_k(L_k)-\left(L_k p(L_k+s_k)-c_k\right)h'_k(L_k)<0$$

then $x_k=L_k$ must not be the maximal choice of firm k, either. Therefore the maximum profit of each firm per labor occurs at a local optimum, where $\partial\varphi_k/\partial x_k=0$. If condition (D) does not hold, then there is no guarantee for interior equilibrium. In that case we have to consider both cases of interior and corner equilibria. In the case of corner equilibrium we may fix the value $x_k^*=L_k$ and find the corresponding equilibrium strategies of the other (N-1) players as the equilibrium of an (N-1)-person game. For the sake of simplicity assume that the equilibrium is interior. Let $\mathbf{x}^*=(x_1^*,\ldots,x_N^*)$ be an equilibrium point and let

$$s^*=\sum_{k=1}^{N}x_k^*.$$

Then for all k,

$$V_k(x_k^*,s^*)=\left(p(s^*)+x_k^* p'(s^*)\right)h_k(x_k^*)-\left(x_k^* p(s^*)-c_k\right)h'_k(x_k^*)=0 \tag{3.7.2}$$

Assume now that

(E) For all s^* and k, there is a unique x_k^* such that $V_k(x_k^*,s^*)=0$.

With fixed values of s^*,

$$\begin{aligned}\frac{\partial V_k}{\partial x_k^*}&=p'(s^*)h_k(x_k^*)+\left(p(s^*)+x_k^* p'(s^*)\right)h'_k(x_k^*)\\&\qquad -p(s^*)h'_k(x^*)-\left(x_k^* p(s^*)-c_k\right)h''_k(x_k^*)\\&=\left(h_k(x_k^*)+x_k^* h'_k(x_k^*)\right)p'(s^*)-\left(x_k^* p(s^*)-c_k\right)h''_k(x_k^*).\end{aligned}$$

Similarly, with fixed values of x_k^*,

$$\frac{\partial V_k}{\partial s^*}=\left(p'(s^*)+x_k^* p''(s^*)\right)h_k(x_k^*)-x_k^* p'(s^*)h'_k(x_k^*)$$

for all k. The chain-rule of differentiation of multi-variable functions implies that

$$\frac{dx_k^*}{ds^*}=\frac{-\dfrac{\partial V_k}{\partial s^*}}{\dfrac{\partial V_k}{\partial x_k^*}}. \tag{3.7:3}$$

Assume next that

(F) $\dfrac{dx_k^*}{ds^*} \le 0$ for all k and the inequality is strict for at least one k.

We can easily show that assumption (F) implies that there is no more than one equilibrium point. If $\mathbf{x}^* = (x_k^*)$ and $\mathbf{x}^{**} = (x_k^{**})$ are both equilibrium points, then let $s^* = \sum_{k=1}^{N} x_k^*$ and $s^{**} = \sum_{k=1}^{N} x_k^{**}$. If $s^* = s^{**}$, then assumption (E) implies that for all k, $x_k^* = x_k^{**}$. Otherwise we may assume that $s^* < s^{**}$. In this case (F) implies that

$$s^* = \sum_{k=1}^{N} x_k^* = \sum_{k=1}^{N} x_k^*(s^*) > \sum_{k=1}^{N} x_k^*(s^{**}) = \sum_{k=1}^{N} x_k^{**} = s^{**},$$

which is an obvious contradiction.

The equilibrium can be graphically obtained as follows. Figure 3.7.1 shows function $\sum_{k=1}^{N} x_k^*(s^*)$ as a strictly decreasing function of s^*.

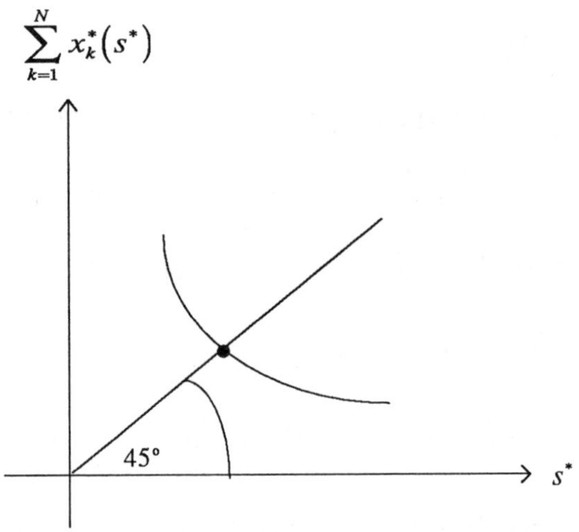

Figure 3.7.1 Graphical solution for s*

The intercept of the graph of the strictly decreasing function $\sum_{k=1}^{N} x_k^*(s^*)$ and the 45° line gives the equilibrium industry output, and the equilibrium outputs of the firms can be determined by solving equation (3.7.2) for all k.

The payoff functions of labor-managed firms were earlier introduced by equations (2.6.2) and (2.6.3), respectively. The application of the Nikaido-Isoda theorem first requires the sets of strategies being convex, closed, and bounded. These conditions are usually satisfied. The continuity of the payoff functions follows from the assumption that functions p and h_k are continuous and $h_k \neq 0$. In order to apply the Nikaido-Isoda theorem we also have to assume that φ_k is concave in x_k (or in $\mathbf{x}_k$ in the multi-product case). This additional condition holds if $\frac{\partial^2 \varphi_k}{\partial x_k^2} \leq 0$ and in the multi-product case, if the Hessian of φ_k with respect to $\mathbf{x}_k$ is negative semidefinite.

3.8 Existence of Equilibrium in Oligopsony

An oligopsony model was introduced earlier in Section 2.7. In this section the existence of the equilibrium point of that model will be first examined, and then - similarly to Cournot oligopolies - we will show that the equilibrium points can be obtained as solutions of nonlinear complementarity problems.

As in Section 2.7 an N-firm oligopsony is considered, where each firm produces M kinds of products with help of labor and capital. The strategy of each firm is its output vector $\mathbf{x}_k = \left(x_k^{(1)}, \ldots, x_k^{(M)}\right)$ and its labor and capital usage L_k and K_k, respectively. The set of feasible strategies of firm k is given by relations:

$$\mathbf{x}_k \in X_k(L_k, K_k), \;\; L_k \geq 0, \; K_k \geq 0 \tag{3.8.1}$$

where for all nonnegative pairs (L_k, K_k), set $X_k(L_k, K_k) \subseteq R_+^M$ such that $\mathbf{x}_k \in X_k(L_k, K_k)$ and $\mathbf{0} \leq \mathbf{z}_k \leq \mathbf{x}_k$ imply that $\mathbf{z}_k \in X_k(L_k, K_k)$. The strategies of the different firms are related by the additional requirement that

$$\left(\sum_{k=1}^{N} L_k, \sum_{k=1}^{N} K_k\right) \in X_s \tag{3.8.2}$$

where $X_s \subseteq R_+^2$ is the feasible resource-set such that $(L, K) \in X_s$ and $(0,0) \leq (L', K') \leq (L, K)$ imply that $(L', K') \in X_s$.

If $\mathbf{p}$ is the price function, w and r are the wage rate and rental of capital, then the profit of firm k can be expressed as follows:

$$\varphi_k(\mathbf{x}_1,L_1,K_1,\ldots,\mathbf{x}_N,L_N,K_N)=\mathbf{x}_k^T\mathbf{p}\left(\sum_{l=1}^{N}\mathbf{x}_l\right)-L_k w\left(\sum_{l=1}^{N}L_l\right)-K_k r\left(\sum_{l=1}^{N}K_l\right). \quad (3.8.3)$$

Assume that the following conditions hold:

(A) X_s is convex, closed, and bounded in R_+^2;
(B) For all k, set
$$S_k=\left\{(\mathbf{x}_k,L_k,K_k)\middle|\mathbf{x}_k\in X_k(L_k,K_k),\ (L_k,K_k)\in X_s\right\}$$
is convex, closed, and bounded in R^{M+2};
(C) $\mathbf{p}$ is continuous, each component of $\mathbf{p}$ is concave, and $-\mathbf{p}$ is monotonic (as given in Definition 3.1.1);
(D) Functions w and r are continuous, furthermore $L_k w(a+L_k)$ and $K_k r(b+K_k)$ are convex in L_k and K_k, respectively for all fixed a and b such that $(a+L_k,b+K_k)\in X_s$.

We will first prove the following result.

Theorem 3.8.1. Under the above conditions there is at least one equilibrium point.

Proof. The sets of S_k of strategies are convex, closed and bounded, the payoff functions are continuous as the consequence of conditions (C) and (D). In addition, condition (C) and Lemma 3.1.1 imply that φ_k is concave in $(\mathbf{x}_k,L_k,K_k)$. Therefore the Nikaido-Isoda theorem can be invoked to guarantee the existence of at least one equilibrium point. □

In the next part of this section the relation of the equilibrium problem of oligopsony to the solution of a nonlinear complementarity problem will be examined.

We assume that functions φ_k are differentiable with respect to $\mathbf{x}_k$ for all k. Introduce first the following notation

$$\mathbf{x}_k^{(-m)}=\left(x_k^{(1)},\ldots,x_k^{(m-1)},x_k^{(m+1)},\ldots,x_k^{(M)}\right),\quad \mathbf{L}=(L_1,\ldots,L_N),$$

$$\mathbf{K}=(K_1,\ldots,K_N),\quad \mathbf{L}_{-k}=(L_1,\ldots,L_{k-1},L_{k+1},\ldots,L_N),\ \text{and}$$

$$\mathbf{K}_{-k}=(K_1,\ldots,K_{k-1},K_{k+1},\ldots,K_N).$$

Define

$$X_k^{(m)}\left(\mathbf{x}_k^{(-m)},\mathbf{L},\mathbf{K}\right)=\left\{x_k^{(m)}\middle|\left(\mathbf{x}_k,L_k,K_k\right)\in S_k \text{ and } \left(\sum_{l=1}^{N}L_l,\sum_{l=1}^{N}K_l\right)\in X_s\right\},$$

$$L_k\left(\mathbf{x}_k,\mathbf{L}_{-k},\mathbf{K}\right)=\left\{L_k\middle|\left(\mathbf{x}_k,L_k,K_k\right)\in S_k \text{ and } \left(\sum_{l=1}^{N}L_l,\sum_{l=1}^{N}K_l\right)\in X_s\right\},$$

and

$$K_k\left(\mathbf{x}_k,\mathbf{L},\mathbf{K}_{-k}\right)=\left\{K_k\middle|\left(\mathbf{x}_k,L_k,K_k\right)\in S_k \text{ and} \left(\sum_{l=1}^{N}L_l,\sum_{l=1}^{N}K_l\right)\in X_s\right\}.$$

Conditions (A) and (B) imply that these sets are either empty or closed intervals in the real line. This observation implies that there exist ($2N$+M-1) - variable real, nonnegative functions $\alpha_k^{(m)},\beta_k^{\min},\beta_k^{\max},\gamma_k^{\min}$, and $\gamma_k^{\max}$ such that

$$X_k^{(m)}\left(\mathbf{x}_k^{(-m)},\mathbf{L},\mathbf{K}\right)=\left\{x_k^{(m)}\middle|0\le x_k^{(m)}\le\alpha_k^{(m)}\left(\mathbf{x}_k^{(-m)},\mathbf{L},\mathbf{K}\right)\right\}$$

$$L_k\left(\mathbf{x}_k,\mathbf{L}_{-k},\mathbf{K}\right)=\left\{L_k\middle|\beta_k^{\min}\left(\mathbf{x}_k,\mathbf{L}_{-k},\mathbf{K}\right)\le L_k\le\beta_k^{\max}\left(\mathbf{x}_k,\mathbf{L}_{-k},\mathbf{K}\right)\right.$$

and

$$K_k\left(\mathbf{x}_k,\mathbf{L},\mathbf{K}_{-k}\right)=\left\{K_k\middle|\gamma_k^{\min}\left(\mathbf{x}_k,\mathbf{L},\mathbf{K}_{-k}\right)\le K_k\le\gamma_k^{\max}\left(\mathbf{x}_k,\mathbf{L},\mathbf{K}_{-k}\right)\right\}.$$

The concavity of φ_k in $\left(\mathbf{x}_k,L_k,K_k\right)$ implies that a vector $\left(\mathbf{x}_1,\ldots,\mathbf{x}_N,\mathbf{L},\mathbf{K}\right)$ is a Nash-Cournot equilibrium if and only if for all k and m,

$$\frac{\partial\varphi_k}{\partial x_k^{(m)}}\begin{cases}\le 0 \text{ if } x_k^{(m)}=0\\ =0 \text{ if } 0<x_k^{(m)}<\alpha_k^{(m)}\left(\mathbf{x}_k^{(-m)},\mathbf{L},\mathbf{K}\right)\\ \ge 0 \text{ if } x_k^{(m)}=\alpha_k^{(m)}\left(\mathbf{x}_k^{(-m)},\mathbf{L},\mathbf{K}\right),\end{cases}\tag{3.8.4}$$

$$\frac{\partial\varphi_k}{\partial L_k}\begin{cases}\le 0 \text{ if } L_k=\beta_k^{\min}\left(\mathbf{x}_k,\mathbf{L}_{-k},\mathbf{K}\right)\\ =0 \text{ if } \beta_k^{\min}\left(\mathbf{x}_k,\mathbf{L}_{-k},\mathbf{K}\right)<L_k<\beta_k^{\max}\left(\mathbf{x}_k,\mathbf{L}_{-k},\mathbf{K}\right)\\ \ge 0 \text{ if } L_k=\beta_k^{\max}\left(\mathbf{x}_k,\mathbf{L}_{-k},\mathbf{K}\right),\end{cases}\tag{3.8.5}$$

and

$$\frac{\partial \varphi_k}{\partial K_k}\begin{cases}\leq 0 \text{ if } K_k = \gamma_k^{\min}(\mathbf{x}_k, \mathbf{L}, \mathbf{K}_{-k}) \\ = 0 \text{ if } \gamma_k^{\min}(\mathbf{x}_k, \mathbf{L}, \mathbf{K}_{-k}) < K_k < \gamma_k^{\max}(\mathbf{x}_k, \mathbf{L}, \mathbf{K}_{-k}) \\ \geq 0 \text{ if } K_k = \gamma_k^{\max}(\mathbf{x}_k, \mathbf{L}, \mathbf{K}_{-k}).\end{cases} \tag{3.8.6}$$

Introduce the slack variables

$$z_k^{(m)}\begin{cases} = 0 \text{ if } x_k^{(m)} > 0 \\ \geq 0 \text{ otherwise ,}\end{cases}$$

$$Z_k^{(m)}\begin{cases} = 0 \text{ if } x_k^{(m)} < \alpha_k^{(m)}(\mathbf{x}_k^{(-m)}, \mathbf{L}, \mathbf{K}) \\ \geq 0 \text{ otherwise ,}\end{cases}$$

$$u_k\begin{cases} = 0 \text{ if } L_k > \beta_k^{\min}(\mathbf{x}_k, \mathbf{L}_{-k}, \mathbf{K}) \\ \geq 0 \text{ otherwise ,}\end{cases}$$

$$U_k\begin{cases} = 0 \text{ if } L_k < \beta_k^{\max}(\mathbf{x}_k, \mathbf{L}_{-k}, \mathbf{K}) \\ \geq 0 \text{ otherwise ,}\end{cases}$$

$$v_k\begin{cases} = 0 \text{ if } K_k > \gamma_k^{\min}(\mathbf{x}_k, \mathbf{L}, \mathbf{K}_{-k}) \\ \geq 0 \text{ otherwise ,}\end{cases}$$

$$V_k\begin{cases} = 0 \text{ if } K_k < \gamma_k^{\max}(\mathbf{x}_k, \mathbf{L}, \mathbf{K}_{-k}) \\ \geq 0 \text{ otherwise .}\end{cases}$$

Then relations (3.8.4) - (3.8.6) can be rewritten as the following system of equations:

$$\frac{\partial \varphi_k}{\partial x_k^{(m)}} - Z_k^{(m)} + z_k^{(m)} = 0, \tag{3.8.7}$$

$$\frac{\partial \varphi_k}{\partial L_k} - U_k + u_k = 0, \tag{3.8.8}$$

$$\frac{\partial \varphi_k}{\partial K_k} - V_k + v_k = 0 \tag{3.8.9}$$

with the additional conditions:

$$\begin{aligned} z_k^{(m)}x_k^{(m)} &= Z_k^{(m)}\cdot\left(\alpha_k^{(m)}\left(\mathbf{x}_k^{(-m)},\mathbf{L},\mathbf{K}\right)-x_k^{(m)}\right)=u_k\cdot\left(L_k-\beta_k^{\min}\left(\mathbf{x}_k,\mathbf{L}_{-k},\mathbf{K}\right)\right)\\ &=U_k\cdot\left(\beta_k^{\max}\left(\mathbf{x}_k,\mathbf{L}_{-k},\mathbf{K}\right)-L_k\right)=v_k\cdot\left(K_k-\gamma_k^{\min}\left(\mathbf{x}_k,\mathbf{L},\mathbf{K}_{-k}\right)\right)\\ &=V_k\cdot\left(\gamma_k^{\max}\left(\mathbf{x}_k,\mathbf{L},\mathbf{K}_{-k}\right)-K_k\right)=0. \end{aligned} \tag{3.8.10}$$

These equations are equivalent to a nonlinear complementarity problem. In order to simplify further formulation introduce the additional notations:

$$\mathbf{z}_k=\left(z_k^{(m)}\right),\mathbf{Z}_k=\left(Z_k^{(m)}\right),\mathbf{z}=\left(\mathbf{z}_k\right),\mathbf{Z}=\left(\mathbf{Z}_k\right),\boldsymbol{\alpha}_k=\left(\alpha_k^{(m)}\right),\boldsymbol{\alpha}=(\boldsymbol{\alpha}_k)$$

$$\boldsymbol{\beta}^{\min}=\left(\beta_k^{\min}\right),\boldsymbol{\beta}^{\max}=\left(\beta_k^{\max}\right),\boldsymbol{\gamma}^{\min}=\left(\gamma_k^{\min}\right),$$

$$\boldsymbol{\gamma}^{\max}=\left(\gamma_k^{\max}\right),\nabla_x\varphi_k=\left(\frac{\partial\varphi_k}{\partial x_k^{(m)}}\right),\mathbf{u}=\left(u_k\right),\mathbf{U}=\left(U_k\right)$$

$$\mathbf{v}=\left(v_k\right),\mathbf{V}=\left(V_k\right),\nabla_L\varphi=\left(\frac{\partial\varphi_k}{\partial L_k}\right),\nabla_K\varphi=\left(\frac{\partial\varphi_k}{\partial K_k}\right),$$

furthermore

$$\mathbf{t}=\begin{pmatrix}\mathbf{x}_1\\ \vdots\\ \mathbf{x}_N\\ \mathbf{Z}_1\\ \vdots\\ \mathbf{Z}_N\\ \mathbf{u}\\ \mathbf{U}\\ \mathbf{v}\\ \mathbf{V}\end{pmatrix},\text{ and }\mathbf{h}(\mathbf{t})=\begin{pmatrix}\mathbf{Z}_1-\nabla_x\varphi_1\\ \vdots\\ \mathbf{Z}_N-\nabla_x\varphi_N\\ \boldsymbol{\alpha}_1\text{-}\mathbf{x}_1\\ \vdots\\ \boldsymbol{\alpha}_N\text{-}\mathbf{x}_N\\ \mathbf{L}\text{-}\boldsymbol{\beta}^{\min}\\ \boldsymbol{\beta}^{\max}\text{-}\mathbf{L}\\ \mathbf{K}\text{-}\boldsymbol{\gamma}^{\min}\\ \boldsymbol{\gamma}^{\max}\text{-}\mathbf{K}\end{pmatrix}.$$

Then relations (3.8.7) - (3.8.10) are equivalent to the nonlinear complementarity problem

$$\mathbf{t}\ge\mathbf{0},\mathbf{h}(\mathbf{t})\ge\mathbf{0},\mathbf{t}^T\mathbf{h}(\mathbf{t})=0. \tag{3.8.11}$$

Hence the equilibrium problem of an oligopsony is equivalent to problem (3.8.11), which can be solved by standard methodology. In addition, if function **h** is strictly monotone, then the equilibrium is unique. (For further details, see Section 3.2.)

3.9 Supplementary Notes and Discussions

3.1 The existence of the equilibrium point in concave multiproduct oligopoly game was first proven by Szidarovszky (1978). This result has been extended by Okuguchi and Szidarovszky (1985a) for continuously differentiable profit functions under the assumptions of the corollary of Theorem 3.1.2. In this paper numerical methods are also proposed for determining the equilibrium points by solving nonlinear complementarity problems. Theorems 3.1.1 and 3.1.2 can also be found in Szidarovszky and Okuguchi (1987a).

Further results on monotone and strictly monotone mappings are presented in Ortega and Rheinboldt (1970).

The original form of the Nikaido-Isoda theorem for the existence of equilibrium points for concave games is presented in Nikaido and Isoda (1955). The extension of this very important result for pseudogames is given in Debreu (1952). Analogous existence conditions are presented in Szép and Forgó (1985), and Friedman (1986).

An existence result is given in Friedman (1986) for models with product differentiation. His conditions are essentially the same as our assumptions in Theorem 3.1.4.

3.2 The best reply mapping is an old concept in game theory. Most existence proofs for equilibrium points are based on the applications of fixed point theorems to the best reply mapping. See for example, Rosen (1965) for a nice development of uniqueness results.

The fixed-point problem of Theorem 3.2.2 with lower dimension, was first formulated and analyzed by Szidarovszky (1978). Theorem 3.2.3 is a generalization of similar results presented by Friedman (1986). Note that part (a) of Theorem 3.2.3 is a slight generalization of the famous Gale-Nikaido univalence theorem (Gale and Nikaido, 1965). Similar univalence results are also presented in Ortega and Rheinboldt (1970). In Szidarovszky and Yakowitz (1978), a rigorous development of the contraction mapping theory is given with applications to the development of iterative methods. The uniqueness of the equilibrium for the classical Cournot model was first proven by Okuguchi (1976) by using univalent functions.

The relation of Cournot-Nash equilibrium problems to nonlinear complementarity problems has been widely analyzed. Details can be found in Karamardian (1969), Gabay and Moulin (1980), and Okuguchi (1983). Our results are partially taken form Okuguchi and Szidarovszky (1985b), where the linear version of Theorem 3.2.4 is discussed. The corollary of this theorem generalizes a similar result by Okuguchi (1983). The application of nonlinear complementarity problems to show the uniqueness of Nash-Cournot equilibria is given in Szidarovszky and Okuguchi (1988a).

3.3 In the case of the classical oligopoly game, the early existence results were based on twice differentiability of the price and cost functions. Under concavity conditions Burger (1959) proved existence and uniqueness by assuming that all cost functions are identical. He also presented a numerical method for finding the equilibrium point, which was based on the solution of a one variable monotone equation. This existence result has been extended by Frank and Quandt (1963) for the non-symmetric case. An analogous existence result and the extension of Burger's uniqueness theorem is given in Szidarovszky (1970), where the computation of the equilibrium point is also reduced to the solution of a single variable monotone equation. The same result is achieved in a more elegant framework by Szidarovszky and Yakowitz (1977). The existence of the classical oligopoly game is further discussed in Okuguchi (1976), Friedman (1977, 1981, 1986), Szidarovszky (1978), Szép and Forgó (1985), Szidarovszky and Molnár (1986), and Szidarovszky, Gershon and Duckstein (1986).

Theorems 3.3.1, 3.3.2, 3.3.3 are taken from Szidarovszky and Yakowitz (1982).

3.4 The results in this Section generalize the existence and uniqueness results of Mañas (1972) with the extension of his quadratic programming approach to multiproduct oligopolies. These results are taken from Okuguchi and Szidarovszky (1985b) and they are also discussed in Szidarovszky and Molnár (1986) and in Szidarovszky, Gershon and Duckstein (1986).

3.5 Fixed points of point-to-set and point-to-point mappings can be determined by the numerical solution of the governing system of nonlinear equations. Such methods are described in most texts on numerical analysis. A survey of iterative techniques is given in Ortega and Rheinboldt (1970). The diagonalization method for solving variational inequalities is presented in Dafermos (1983) and its application to Cournot oligopoly problems is described by Harker (1984). A similar algorithm to the solution of equation (3.5.5) is introduced in Murphy *et.al.* (1982), where the bisection (or secant) method is proposed to compute a dual variable with optimal value $\lambda = 0$. This method can be applied in a slightly more general case than the algorithm presented in Section 3.5.

3.6 Tullock's (1980) introductory paper initiated an extensive research on rent seeking games. Pérez-Castrillo and Verdier (1992) have analyzed the case of decreasing returns in rent seeking technology as well as that of increasing returns, and discussed the case when the agents' reaction functions are upward sloping. In Okuguchi (1995) a systematic approach is given to analyze the existence and uniqueness of the equilibrium under the same assumptions as given in this book, however identical production functions were assumed. The existence theorem and its proof has been first published in Szidarovszky and Okuguchi (1997a).

3.7 Labor-managed oligopolies have been first discussed by Ward (1958). Hill and Waterson (1983) have examined profit maximizing and labor-managed

Cournot oligopolies under the assumption that the firms have identical cost functions. Neary (1984) has generalized their results for the nonsymmetric case. The material of this section is based on Okuguchi (1996b).

3.8 Oligopsony has been introduced by Okuguchi (1996a), and Chiarella and Okuguchi (1996). Okuguchi (1996a) has analyzed the static game in which the problem of finding the equilibrium has been reduced to computing one-dimensional fixed points. Chiarella and Okuguchi (1996) examined a dynamic duopoly involving oligopsony. The material of this section is based on Szidarovszky and Okuguchi (1996). The nonlinear complementarity problem (3.8.11) can be solved by routine methods, which can be found for example, in Karamardian (1969).

4 Dynamic Oligopoly with Discrete Time Scale

In this chapter a special dynamic multiproduct oligopoly game and its modifications will be investigated. Throughout we assume the following conditions:

(A) Set X_k of feasible outputs of firm k ($1 \le k \le N$) is closed, convex, bounded in R_+^M such that $\mathbf{x}_k \in X_k$ and $\mathbf{0} \le \mathbf{t}_k \le \mathbf{x}_k$ imply that $\mathbf{t}_k \in X_k$.

Define set

$$S = \left\{ \mathbf{s} \middle| \mathbf{s} = \sum_{k=1}^{N} \mathbf{x}_k, \mathbf{x}_k \in X_k,\ k = 1,2,\ldots,N \right\}.$$

(B) The price function $\mathbf{p}$ is linear on S, that is,

$$\mathbf{p}(\mathbf{s}) = \mathbf{A}\mathbf{s} + \mathbf{b}, \tag{4.0.1}$$

where $\mathbf{A}$ and $\mathbf{b}$ are constant matrix and vector, respectively;

(C) Cost functions C_k are quadratic on X_k. That is,

$$C_k(\mathbf{x}_k) = \mathbf{x}_k^T \mathbf{B}_k \mathbf{x}_k + \mathbf{b}_k^T \mathbf{x}_k + c_k \quad (k = 1,2,\ldots,N), \tag{4.0.2}$$

where $\mathbf{B}_k$, $\mathbf{b}_k$ and c_k are constant matrix, constant vector, and a constant number, respectively;

(D) Matrix $(\mathbf{A} + \mathbf{A}^T) - (\mathbf{B}_k + \mathbf{B}_k^T)$ is negative definite for $k=1,2,\ldots,N$.

A rationale for assumption (B) was given earlier in Section 2.3. Condition (D) is satisfied if function $-\mathbf{p}$ is monotone and functions C_k ($k=1,2,\ldots,N$) are strictly convex, and either $-\mathbf{p}$ is strictly monotone or all C_k are convex. In the case of one product these conditions on $\mathbf{p}$ mean that it is (strictly) decreasing. Relations (4.0.1) and (4.0.2) imply that the profit or payoff functions

$$\varphi_k(\mathbf{x}_1,\ldots,\mathbf{x}_N) = \mathbf{x}_k^T(\mathbf{A}\mathbf{s}+\mathbf{b}) - (\mathbf{x}_k^T\mathbf{B}_k\mathbf{x}_k + \mathbf{b}_k^T\mathbf{x}_k + c_k) \tag{4.0.3}$$

are continuous on X, where $\mathbf{s} = \sum_{k=1}^{N} \mathbf{x}_k$. The Hessian of φ_k with respect to $\mathbf{x}_k$ equals $\mathbf{A}+\mathbf{A}^T - \mathbf{B}_k - \mathbf{B}_k^T$. Hence condition (D) implies that φ_k is concave in $\mathbf{x}_k$. Consequently, under conditions (A) - (D), the multiproduct oligopoly game has at least one equilibrium point, since all conditions of Theorem 3.3.1 are satisfied.

If at a certain time t, the firms are in an equilibrium, then - without assuming any kind of cooperation between the firms - the interest of each firm is to maintain the equilibrium position. In a disequilibrium situation at least one firm is able to select another strategy and improve its payoff. If the resulting new situation is an equilibrium, then the game will remain in this situation. Otherwise another firm changes its strategy, and so on. In analyzing such dynamic games, we require additional assumptions on the behavior of the firms. Their behavior can be modelled mathematically by certain adjustment processes. These additional assumptions can be divided into the following classes. The first type of models are based on discrete time scales. In this case four particular adjustment systems will be discussed. The first model uses the classical assumption of Cournot, the second model uses adaptive expectations, the third is based on a special sequential process, and in the fourth model extrapolative expectations are assumed. In the second type of model, continuous time scale is considered. The discussion of such models will be postponed until the next Chapter.

4.1 Cournot Expectations

Here assume that all firms form expectations on all *other firms' outputs à la Cournot*. It is assumed that at time t=0 each firm has an initial strategy selection, $x_k^{(0)}$ $(k=1,2,\ldots,N)$. At each t>0, it is assumed that the strategy selection of each firm is obtained by maximizing its payoff $\varphi_k(\mathbf{x}_1(t-1),\ldots,\mathbf{x}_{k-1}(t-1),\mathbf{x}_k,\mathbf{x}_{k+1}(t-1),\ldots,\mathbf{x}_N(t-1))$ by assuming all other firms will select again the same strategies which they have selected in the preceding time period. That is, the strategy selection $\mathbf{x}_k^{(t)}$ of firm k at time period t is the optimal solution of:

$$\text{maximize } \mathbf{x}_k^T\left(\mathbf{A}\left(\sum_{l\neq k}\mathbf{x}_l(t-1)+\mathbf{x}_k\right)+\mathbf{b}\right) - (\mathbf{x}_k^T\mathbf{B}_k\mathbf{x}_k + \mathbf{b}_k^T\mathbf{x}_k + c_k) \tag{4.1.1}$$

subject to $\mathbf{x}_k \in X_k$.

Assume that conditions (A) - (D) hold and

(E) The optimal solution $\mathbf{x}_k(t)$ of problem (4.1.1) is an interior point of X_k.

The first order optimality conditions imply that the gradient of the objective function with respect to $\mathbf{x}_k$ at the optimal solution equals zero. That is,

$$\left[\left(\mathbf{A}+\mathbf{A}^T\right)-\left(\mathbf{B}_k+\mathbf{B}_k^T\right)\right]\mathbf{x}_k(t)+\mathbf{A}\sum_{l\neq k}\mathbf{x}_l(t-1)+\mathbf{b}-\mathbf{b}_k=\mathbf{0}.$$

Since assumption (D) implies that the second order optimality condition holds and matrix $\left(\mathbf{A}+\mathbf{A}^T\right)-\left(\mathbf{B}_k+\mathbf{B}_k^T\right)$ is invertible,

$$\mathbf{x}_k(t)=-\left[\left(\mathbf{A}+\mathbf{A}^T\right)-\left(\mathbf{B}_k+\mathbf{B}_k^T\right)\right]^{-1}\mathbf{A}\sum_{l\neq k}\mathbf{x}_l(t-1)+\alpha,$$

where α is a constant vector. Using vector and matrix notation we can rewrite this recursion as

$$\mathbf{x}(t)=\mathbf{H}_c\mathbf{x}(t-1)+\beta_c, \tag{4.1.2}$$

where β_c is a constant vector,

$$\mathbf{x}(t)=\begin{bmatrix}\mathbf{x}_1(t)\\ \mathbf{x}_2(t)\\ \vdots\\ \mathbf{x}_N(t)\end{bmatrix},\quad \mathbf{x}(t-1)=\begin{bmatrix}\mathbf{x}_1(t-1)\\ \mathbf{x}_2(t-1)\\ \vdots\\ \mathbf{x}_N(t-1)\end{bmatrix},$$

and

$$\mathbf{H}_c=\begin{bmatrix}\mathbf{0} & -\mathbf{D}_1 & \cdots & -\mathbf{D}_1\\ -\mathbf{D}_2 & \mathbf{0} & \cdots & -\mathbf{D}_2\\ \vdots & \vdots & \ddots & \vdots\\ -\mathbf{D}_N & -\mathbf{D}_N & \cdots & \mathbf{0}\end{bmatrix}\quad \text{with } \mathbf{D}_k=\left(\mathbf{A}+\mathbf{A}^T-\mathbf{B}_k-\mathbf{B}_k^T\right)^{-1}\mathbf{A}.$$

The above derivation shows that the dynamic process based on Cournot expectations can be mathematically modelled by the linear difference equation (4.1.2) with constant coefficients.

Definition 4.1.1. An equilibrium point of the multiproduct oligopoly game is called globally asymptotically stable with respect to expectations à la Cournot, if process (4.1.2) converges to that equilibrium as $t \to \infty$ with arbitrary initial strategy selections.

It is known from the theory of linear systems (Szidarovszky and Bahill, 1992), that the equilibrium point is globally asymptotically stable if and only if all eigenvalues of matrix $\mathbf{H}_c$ are inside the unit circle of the complex plane. Thus, we have obtained:

Theorem 4.1.1. The equilibrium point of the multiproduct oligopoly game is globally asymptotically stable with respect to expectations à la Cournot if and only if all eigenvalues of matrix $\mathbf{H}_c$ are inside the unit circle of the complex plane.

Corollary. Under assumptions (A) - (E) the equilibrium point is unique, since as $t \to \infty$, vector $\mathbf{x}(t)$ has the same limit independently of the selection of the initial point $\mathbf{x}(0)$.

In most cases the application of Theorem 4.1.1 is difficult, since it requires the computation of the eigenvalues of matrix $\mathbf{H}_c$, which is usually nonsymmetric and may have a large size. In many practical cases however, simple sufficient stability conditions can be used, which are based on certain matrix norms. These conditions will be obtained next. First of all we introduce

Definition 4.1.2. The spectral norm of any real square matrix $\mathbf{M}$ is defined as

$$\|\mathbf{M}\|_2 = \sqrt{\max|\lambda_{\mathbf{M}^T\mathbf{M}}|},$$

where $\max|\lambda_{\mathbf{M}^T\mathbf{M}}|$ denotes the modulus of the eigenvalue of matrix $\mathbf{M}^T\mathbf{M}$ with largest absolute value.

It is well known from matrix theory (see e.g., Lancaster, 1969) that this matrix norm satisfies the following relations:

(i) $\|\mathbf{M}\|_2 \geq 0$ and $\|\mathbf{M}\|_2 = 0$ if and only if $\mathbf{M} = \mathbf{0}$;

(ii) $\|\alpha\mathbf{M}\|_2 = |\alpha| \cdot \|\mathbf{M}\|_2$, if α is any real or complex number;

(iii) $\|\mathbf{M}+\mathbf{N}\|_2 \leq \|\mathbf{M}\|_2 + \|\mathbf{N}\|_2$;

(iv) $\|\mathbf{M}\cdot\mathbf{N}\|_2 \leq \|\mathbf{M}\|_2 \cdot \|\mathbf{N}\|_2$,

where $\mathbf{M}$ and $\mathbf{N}$ are square matrices of the same size;

(v) $|\lambda| \leq \|\mathbf{M}\|_2$, if λ is any (real or complex) eigenvalue of matrix $\mathbf{M}$.

We mention here that if $\mathbf{M} = (m_{ij})$ is a square matrix then the following quantities can also serve as matrix norms:

$$\|\mathbf{M}\|_\infty = \max_i \sum_j |m_{ij}| \qquad \text{(row - norm);}$$

$$\|\mathbf{M}\|_1 = \max_j \sum_i |m_{ij}| \qquad \text{(column - norm);}$$

$$\|\mathbf{M}\|_F = \left\{ \sum_i \sum_j |m_{ij}|^2 \right\}^{\frac{1}{2}} \qquad \text{(Frobenius – norm).}$$

It is well known that each of these norms satisfies properties (i) - (v). Therefore, if $\|\mathbf{H}_c\| < 1$ with some matrix norm, then all eigenvalues of $\mathbf{H}_c$ are inside the unit circle, and hence the equilibrium is globally asymptotically stable with respect to expectations à la Cournot.

Note that the coefficient matrix $\mathbf{H}_c$ of difference equation (4.1.2) can be factored as $-\mathbf{H}_1 \cdot \mathbf{H}_2$, where

$$\mathbf{H}_1 = \begin{bmatrix} (\mathbf{A}+\mathbf{A}^T-\mathbf{B}_1-\mathbf{B}_1^T)^{-1} & & & \\ & (\mathbf{A}+\mathbf{A}^T-\mathbf{B}_2-\mathbf{B}_2^T)^{-1} & & 0 \\ & & \ddots & \\ & 0 & & (\mathbf{A}+\mathbf{A}^T-\mathbf{B}_N-\mathbf{B}_N^T)^{-1} \end{bmatrix} \tag{4.1.3}$$

and

$$\mathbf{H}_2 = \begin{bmatrix} \mathbf{0} & \mathbf{A} & \cdots & \mathbf{A} \\ \mathbf{A} & \mathbf{0} & \cdots & \mathbf{A} \\ \vdots & \vdots & \ddots & \vdots \\ \mathbf{A} & \mathbf{A} & \cdots & \mathbf{0} \end{bmatrix}. \tag{4.1.4}$$

Since $\mathbf{H}_1$ is symmetric, $\|\mathbf{H}_1\|_2$ equals the maximal absolute value of its eigenvalues. Let $\alpha_i^{(k)}$ denote the eigenvalues of matrix $\mathbf{A}+\mathbf{A}^T-\mathbf{B}_k-\mathbf{B}_k^T$, then the eigenvalues of $\mathbf{H}_1$ are the numbers $\left\{1/\alpha_i^{(k)}\right\}_{i,k}$.

Hence

$$\|\mathbf{H}_1\|_2 = \max_{i,k} \left\{ \frac{1}{|\alpha_i^{(k)}|} \right\} = \frac{1}{\min_{i,k} |\alpha_i^{(k)}|}. \tag{4.1.5}$$

Note next that matrix $\mathbf{H}_2$ has a very special structure, in which the same matrix **A** has shown up in the blocks. This structure is discussed next.

Definition 4.1.3. Let $\mathbf{M} = \left(m_{ij}\right)_{i,\ j=1}^{p,\ q}$ and **N** be real or complex matrices not necessarily having the same size. The Kronecker product of matrices **M** and **N** is defined by the block matrix

$$\mathbf{M} \otimes \mathbf{N} = \begin{bmatrix} m_{11}\mathbf{N} & \cdots & m_{1q}\mathbf{N} \\ \vdots & & \vdots \\ m_{p1}\mathbf{N} & \cdots & m_{pq}\mathbf{N} \end{bmatrix}.$$

The eigenvalues of matrix $\mathbf{M} \otimes \mathbf{N}$ can be directly obtained from the eigenvalues of matrices **M** and **N** as it is given in the following lemma.

Lemma 4.1.1. Let **M** and **N** be real or complex square matrices. Let λ_i and μ_j denote the eigenvalues of **M** and **N**, respectively. Then the eigenvalues of matrix $\mathbf{M} \otimes \mathbf{N}$ are the numbers $\lambda_i \cdot \mu_j$.

Proof. Consider the eigenvalue problem of matrix $\mathbf{M} \otimes \mathbf{N}$, where the eigenvectors are also rewritten in block form:

$$\begin{aligned} m_{11}\mathbf{N}\mathbf{u}_1 + m_{12}\mathbf{N}\mathbf{u}_2 + \cdots + m_{1q}\mathbf{N}\mathbf{u}_q &= \alpha\mathbf{u}_1 \\ m_{21}\mathbf{N}\mathbf{u}_1 + m_{22}\mathbf{N}\mathbf{u}_2 + \cdots + m_{2q}\mathbf{N}\mathbf{u}_q &= \alpha\mathbf{u}_2 \\ \vdots \qquad \vdots \qquad\qquad \vdots \qquad &\quad \vdots \\ m_{p1}\mathbf{N}\mathbf{u}_1 + m_{p2}\mathbf{N}\mathbf{u}_2 + \cdots + m_{pq}\mathbf{N}\mathbf{u}_q &= \alpha\mathbf{u}_p . \end{aligned} \tag{4.1.6}$$

Let us look for vectors $\mathbf{u}_k$ in the form $\beta_k\mathbf{v}$, where $\mathbf{v}$ is an eigenvector associated to an eigenvalue μ_j of matrix **N**, and the β_k's are constants. Then (4.1.6) implies that for l=1,2,...,p,

$$m_{l1}\beta_1\mu_j\mathbf{v} + \cdots + m_{lq}\beta_q u_j\mathbf{v} = \alpha\beta_k\mathbf{v}.$$

Since $\mathbf{v}\neq\mathbf{0}$, this equality implies relation

$$\mu_j\mathbf{M}\mathrm{ß} = \alpha\mathrm{ß}$$

with $\mathrm{ß}=\left(\beta_1,\ldots,\beta_q\right)^T$. Consequently $\alpha = \lambda_i\mu_j$, where λ_i is an eigenvalue of matrix **M**. Hence the theorem is proven for matrices $\mathbf{M} \otimes \mathbf{N}$ with distinct eigenvalues. The assertion of the theorem for matrices with multiple eigenvalues simply follows from the continuity of the eigenvalues on the matrix elements.□

We shall now find the norm of $\mathbf{H}_2$. Observe first that

$$\mathbf{H}_2^T\mathbf{H}_2 = \begin{bmatrix} (N-1)\mathbf{A}^T\mathbf{A} & (N-2)\mathbf{A}^T\mathbf{A} & \cdots & (N-2)\mathbf{A}^T\mathbf{A} \\ (N-2)\mathbf{A}^T\mathbf{A} & (N-1)\mathbf{A}^T\mathbf{A} & \cdots & (N-2)\mathbf{A}^T\mathbf{A} \\ \vdots & \vdots & \ddots & \vdots \\ (N-2)\mathbf{A}^T\mathbf{A} & (N-2)\mathbf{A}^T\mathbf{A} & \cdots & (N-1)\mathbf{A}^T\mathbf{A} \end{bmatrix} = \begin{bmatrix} N-1 & N-2 & \cdots & N-2 \\ N-2 & N-1 & \cdots & N-2 \\ \vdots & \vdots & \ddots & \vdots \\ N-2 & N-2 & \cdots & N-1 \end{bmatrix} \otimes \mathbf{A}^T\mathbf{A}. \tag{4.1.7}$$

The first factor can be rewritten as

$$\mathbf{I} + (N-2)\cdot\mathbf{1}, \tag{4.1.8}$$

where matrix $\mathbf{1}$ has all unit elements. First we prove that the eigenvalues of $\mathbf{1}$ are 0 and N. Consider therefore the eigenvalue equation of matrix $\mathbf{1}$:

$$u_1 + u_2 + \cdots u_N = \lambda u_k \quad (k = 1, 2, \ldots, N).$$

If $\lambda = 0$, then any arbitrary vector is an eigenvector such that $u_1 + u_2 + \cdots + u_N = 0$. If $\lambda \neq 0$, then $u_1 = u_2 = \cdots u_N$. If u denotes this common value, then simple substitution shows that

$$Nu = \lambda u.$$

That is,

$$\lambda = N.$$

Consequently, the eigenvalues of matrix (4.1.8) are 1 and $1+(N-2)N=(N-1)^2$. Let β_j denote the eigenvalues of $\mathbf{A}^T\mathbf{A}$, which are all nonnegative. Then

$$\|H_2\|_2 = \sqrt{(N-1)^2 \max_j\{\beta_j\}} = (N-1)\sqrt{\max_j\{\beta_j\}}.$$

And finally, if λ is any eigenvalue of matrix $\mathbf{H}_c$ then

$$|\lambda| \le \|\mathbf{H}_c\|_2 \le \|\mathbf{H}_1\|_2 \cdot \|\mathbf{H}_2\|_2 = \frac{1}{\min_{i,k}\left\{\left|\alpha_i^{(k)}\right|\right\}} \cdot (N-1)\sqrt{\max_j\{\beta_j\}}.$$

Hence λ is inside the unit circle of the complex plane if this upper bound for $|\lambda|$ is less than unity. Thus we have proven the following result.

Theorem 4.1.2. Let $\alpha_i^{(k)}$ denote the eigenvalues of matrix $\mathbf{A}+\mathbf{A}^T-\mathbf{B}_k-\mathbf{B}_k^T$ and let β_j denote the eigenvalues of matrix $\mathbf{A}^T\mathbf{A}$. Then the equilibrium point is globally asymptotically stable with respect to expectations à la Cournot if

$$\frac{\sqrt{\max_j\{\beta_j\}}}{\min_{i,k}\left|\alpha_i^{(k)}\right|} < \frac{1}{N-1}. \tag{4.1.9}$$

Corollary. Assume now that M=1. That is, the game is a classical single-product Cournot oligopoly without product differentiation. In this case matrices **A** and $\mathbf{B}_k$ are scalars, and therefore

$$\beta_j = A^2, \quad \alpha_i^{(k)} = 2A - 2B_k.$$

Hence the global asymptotical stability condition (4.1.9) now has the form:

$$(N-1)\,|A| < |2A - 2B_k| \quad (k = 1,2,\ldots,N).$$

Since assumption (D) implies that $2A - 2B_k < 0$, and $A < 0$ by the property of the price function, this inequality is equivalent to the following:

$$A < 0 \text{ and } B_k > \frac{(3-N)A}{2} \quad (k = 1,2,\ldots,N). \tag{4.1.10}$$

We can interpret (4.1.10) as follows:

If N=2 then global asymptotical stability is guaranteed for $B_k > \frac{A}{2}$, that is, if the cost functions are convex or slightly concave. If N=3 then the strict convexity of the cost functions implies the global asymptotical stability of the equilibrium, and if N>3 then only sufficiently large positive values of B_k satisfy (4.1.10). In the last case, the cost functions must be therefore strongly convex.

The above derivations are based on a spectral matrix norm and a special factorization of matrix $\mathbf{H}_c$. Analogous results can be obtained by different factorizations of $\mathbf{H}_c$ and by selecting another matrix norm. Such cases will be next discussed.

Note first that $\mathbf{H}_c = \mathbf{H}_3 \cdot \mathbf{H}_4$, where

$$\mathbf{H}_3 = \begin{bmatrix} -\mathbf{D}_1 & & & \\ & -\mathbf{D}_2 & & \\ & & \ddots & \\ & & & -\mathbf{D}_N \end{bmatrix} \text{ and } \mathbf{H}_4 = \begin{bmatrix} \mathbf{0} & \mathbf{I} & \cdots & \mathbf{I} \\ \mathbf{I} & \mathbf{0} & \cdots & \mathbf{I} \\ \vdots & \vdots & \ddots & \vdots \\ \mathbf{I} & \mathbf{I} & \cdots & \mathbf{0} \end{bmatrix}.$$

Simple calculation shows that

$$\|\mathbf{H}_3\|_2 = \max_k \|\mathbf{D}_k\|_2$$

and

$$\|\mathbf{H}_4\|_2 = N-1.$$

Therefore the global asymptotical stability of the equilibrium is implied by the condition

$$\|\mathbf{D}_k\|_2 < \frac{1}{N-1} \quad (k = 1,2,\dots,N). \tag{4.1.11}$$

Note that these relations hold if matrices $\mathbf{D}_k$ are sufficiently small.

If the block-row norm

$$\|\mathbf{H}\|_{\infty,B} = \max_i \sum_j \|\mathbf{H}_{ij}\|$$

of block matrices $\mathbf{H} = (\mathbf{H}_{ij})$ is selected, where $\|\bullet\|$ is any norm of the blocks, then $\|\mathbf{H}_c\|_{\infty,B} < 1$, if (4.1.11) holds with the selected norm of the blocks. Alternatively if one chooses the block-column norm then

$$\|\mathbf{H}\|_{1,B} = \max_j \sum_i \|\mathbf{H}_{ij}\|,$$

then $\|\mathbf{H}_c\|_{1,B} < 1$, if (4.1.12)

$$\sum_{l \neq k} \|\mathbf{D}_l\| < 1$$

for k=1,2,...,N. It is worthwhile to mention that these conditions are weaker than inequalities (4.1.11) with the same matrix norm.

In the special case where $\mathbf{B}_k = \mathbf{0}$ $(k = 1,2,\dots,N)$ a much stronger result can be derived.

Theorem 4.1.3. Assume that $\mathbf{B}_k = \mathbf{0}$ $(k = 1,2,...,N)$, and all eigenvalues of matrix $\mathbf{A}^{-1}\mathbf{A}^T$ are real. Then the equilibrium point is globally asymptotically stable with respect to expectations à la Cournot if and only if N=2.

Proof. If matrices $\mathbf{B}_k$ are all zeros, then (4.1.2) implies that

$$\mathbf{H}_c = \begin{bmatrix} 0 & 1 & \cdots & 1 \\ 1 & 0 & \cdots & 1 \\ \vdots & \vdots & \ddots & \vdots \\ 1 & 1 & \cdots & 0 \end{bmatrix} \otimes \left[\left(\mathbf{A} + \mathbf{A}^T \right)^{-1} \mathbf{A} \right]. \tag{4.1.13}$$

The second factor can be rewritten as

$$\left(\mathbf{A} + \mathbf{A}^T \right)^{-1} \left(\mathbf{A}^{-1} \right)^{-1} = \left(\mathbf{A}^{-1}\mathbf{A} + \mathbf{A}^{-1}\mathbf{A}^T \right)^{-1} = \left(\mathbf{I} + \mathbf{A}^{-1}\mathbf{A}^T \right)^{-1}.$$

We first verify that under the assumptions of the theorem all eigenvalues of matrix $\mathbf{A}^{-1}\mathbf{A}^T$ are equal to unity. Consider the eigenvalue equation of matrix $\mathbf{A}^{-1}\mathbf{A}^{\mathrm{T}}$:

$$\mathbf{A}^{-1}\mathbf{A}^T\mathbf{u} = \lambda \mathbf{u},$$

where λ and $\mathbf{u}$ are real. Premultiplying by $\mathbf{u}^T\mathbf{A}$ yields

$$\mathbf{u}^T\mathbf{A}^T\mathbf{u} = \lambda \mathbf{u}^T\mathbf{A}\mathbf{u}.$$

Since

$$\mathbf{u}^T\mathbf{A}^T\mathbf{u} = \mathbf{u}^T\mathbf{A}\mathbf{u}$$

and with $\mathbf{u} \neq \mathbf{0}$,

$$\mathbf{u}^T\mathbf{A}\mathbf{u} = \frac{1}{2}\mathbf{u}^T\left(\mathbf{A} + \mathbf{A}^T \right)\mathbf{u} < 0,$$

we may conclude that $\lambda = 1$. Hence the eigenvalues of the second factor in (4.1.13) are all equal to $(1+1)^{-1} = \frac{1}{2}$. The first factor equals **1-I** with eigenvalues N-1 and -1. By Lemma 4.1.1 we conclude that the eigenvalues of matrix $\mathbf{H}_c$ equal $\frac{1}{2} \cdot (-1)$ and $\frac{1}{2} \cdot (N-1)$. They are inside the unit circle if and only if their absolute values are less than unity; that is, if and only if

$$\frac{1}{2}(N-1) < 1.$$

This inequality holds if and only if N=2, which proves the assertion. □

Remark. The famous result of Theocharis (1959) is a special case of this theorem for M=1.

4.2 Adaptive Expectations

In this section expectations à la Cournot in multiproduct oligopoly markets are replaced by a different scheme of expectations. This more advanced model is a straightforward generalization of the classical Cournot model discussed in the previous section, since - as it will be shown - it can be obtained by a special selection of a model parameter. Consequently all results of this section also apply for the classical model.

Consider again the multiproduct oligopoly game discussed at the introduction of this chapter, and assume again that conditions (A) - (D) hold. The dynamic process is now defined as follows. At $t = 0$ the firms select the initial strategies $\mathbf{x}_k(0)$ independently of each other, and at each further time period $t > 0$ they form first expectations *adaptively on the output of the rest of the industry* according to the rule

$$\mathbf{s}_k^E(t) = \mathbf{s}_k^E(t-1) + \mathbf{M}_k \cdot \left(\mathbf{s}_k(t-1) - \mathbf{s}_k^E(t-1)\right), \quad (k = 1,2,...,N) \tag{4.2.1}$$

where $\mathbf{M}_k$ is a constant matrix, which is usually assumed to be diagonal, furthermore

$$\mathbf{s}_k(t-1) = \sum_{l \neq k} \mathbf{x}_l(t-1).$$

Then each firm maximizes its expected profit

$$\mathbf{x}_k^T\left(\mathbf{A}\mathbf{s}_k^E(t) + \mathbf{A}\mathbf{x}_k + \mathbf{b}\right) - \left(\mathbf{x}_k^T\mathbf{B}_k\mathbf{x}_k + \mathbf{b}_k^T\mathbf{x}_k + c_k\right) \tag{4.2.2}$$

subject to $\mathbf{x}_k \in X_k$.

It is also assumed that:

($E^{(1)}$) The optimal solution of (4.2.2) is an interior point in X_k, k=1,2,...,N.

The first order conditions in optimization problem (4.2.2) can be written as

$$\left(\mathbf{A} + \mathbf{A}^T - \mathbf{B}_k - \mathbf{B}_k^T\right)\mathbf{x}_k + \mathbf{A}\mathbf{s}_k^E(t) + \mathbf{b} - \mathbf{b}_k = 0. \tag{4.2.3}$$

Condition (D) implies that the second order optimality condition holds and matrix $\mathbf{A}+\mathbf{A}^T-\mathbf{B}_k-\mathbf{B}_k^T$ is invertible. By substituting relation (4.2.1) into (4.2.3) we have

$$\mathbf{x}_k(t)=-\left(\mathbf{A}+\mathbf{A}^T-\mathbf{B}_k-\mathbf{B}_k^T\right)^{-1}\mathbf{A}\left(\mathbf{s}_k^E(t-1)+\mathbf{M}_k\left(\mathbf{s}_k(t-1)-\mathbf{s}_k^E(t-1)\right)\right)+\boldsymbol{\alpha}, \quad (4.2.4)$$

where $\boldsymbol{\alpha}$ is a constant vector.

Thus, the above dynamic process can be described by the linear difference equation

$$\begin{bmatrix} \mathbf{x}_1(t) \\ \vdots \\ \mathbf{x}_N(t) \\ \mathbf{s}_1^E(t) \\ \vdots \\ \mathbf{s}_N^E(t) \end{bmatrix} = \mathbf{H}_A \cdot \begin{bmatrix} \mathbf{x}_1(t-1) \\ \vdots \\ \mathbf{x}_N(t-1) \\ \mathbf{s}_1^E(t-1) \\ \vdots \\ \mathbf{s}_N^E(t-1) \end{bmatrix} + \boldsymbol{\beta}_A, \quad (4.2.5)$$

where $\boldsymbol{\beta}_A$ is a constant vector,

$$\mathbf{H}_A = \begin{bmatrix} \mathbf{H}_{11} & \mathbf{H}_{12} \\ \mathbf{H}_{21} & \mathbf{H}_{22} \end{bmatrix}$$

with

$$\mathbf{H}_{11} = \begin{bmatrix} \mathbf{0} & -\mathbf{D}_1\mathbf{M}_1 & \cdots & -\mathbf{D}_1\mathbf{M}_1 \\ -\mathbf{D}_2\mathbf{M}_2 & \mathbf{0} & \cdots & -\mathbf{D}_2\mathbf{M}_2 \\ \vdots & \vdots & \ddots & \vdots \\ -\mathbf{D}_N\mathbf{M}_N & -\mathbf{D}_N\mathbf{M}_N & \cdots & \mathbf{0} \end{bmatrix}, \mathbf{D}_k = \left(\mathbf{A}+\mathbf{A}^T-\mathbf{B}_k-\mathbf{B}_k^T\right)^{-1}\mathbf{A};$$

$$\mathbf{H}_{12} = \begin{bmatrix} -\left(\mathbf{A}+\mathbf{A}^T-\mathbf{B}_1-\mathbf{B}_1^T\right)^{-1}\mathbf{A}\left(\mathbf{I}-\mathbf{M}_1\right) & & 0 \\ & \ddots & \\ 0 & & -\left(\mathbf{A}+\mathbf{A}^T-\mathbf{B}_N-\mathbf{B}_N^T\right)^{-1}\mathbf{A}\left(\mathbf{I}-\mathbf{M}_N\right) \end{bmatrix},$$

$$\mathbf{H}_{21} = \begin{bmatrix} \mathbf{0} & \mathbf{M}_1 & \cdots & \mathbf{M}_1 \\ \mathbf{M}_2 & \mathbf{0} & \cdots & \mathbf{M}_2 \\ \vdots & \vdots & & \vdots \\ \mathbf{M}_N & \mathbf{M}_N & \cdots & \mathbf{0} \end{bmatrix},$$

and

$$\mathbf{H}_{22} = \begin{bmatrix} \mathbf{I}-\mathbf{M}_1 & & 0 \\ & \ddots & \\ 0 & & \mathbf{I}-\mathbf{M}_N \end{bmatrix}.$$

In deriving (4.2.5) we used the fact that $\mathbf{s}_k(t-1) = \sum_{l \neq k} \mathbf{x}_l(t-1)$.

The above derivations imply:

Theorem 4.2.1. The equilibrium point of the multiproduct oligopoly game is globally asymptotically stable with respect to adaptive expectations (4.2.1) if and only if all eigenvalues of matrix $\mathbf{H}_A$ are inside the unit circle of the complex plane.

Remark 1. Consider the special case of $\mathbf{M}_k=\mathbf{I}$, $k=1,2,\ldots,N$. Then expectations (4.2.1) reduce to expectations à la Cournot. Furthermore $\mathbf{H}_{22}=\mathbf{0}$, and $\mathbf{H}_{11}$ equals matrix $\mathbf{H}_c$ of equation (4.1.2). Therefore all nonzero eigenvalues of $\mathbf{H}_A$ are the same as the eigenvalues of $\mathbf{H}_c$. That is, in this special case, the assertions of Theorem 4.1.1 and 4.2.1 are equivalent.

Remark 2. In practical cases it is usually a difficult task to check the validity of the conditions of the theorem since matrix $\mathbf{H}_A$ is usually large with dimension $2NM$. The following theorem makes a large reduction in the size of the matrix, the eigenvalues of which should be examined in order to check stability.

Theorem 4.2.2. The equilibrium point of the multiproduct oligopoly game is globally asymptotically stable with respect to adaptive expectations (4.2.1) if and only if all eigenvalues of matrix

$$\mathbf{H}_A^{(1)} = \begin{bmatrix} \mathbf{I}-\mathbf{M}_1 & -\mathbf{M}_1\mathbf{D}_2 & \cdots & -\mathbf{M}_1\mathbf{D}_N \\ -\mathbf{M}_2\mathbf{D}_1 & \mathbf{I}-\mathbf{M}_2 & \cdots & -\mathbf{M}_2\mathbf{D}_N \\ \vdots & \vdots & & \vdots \\ -\mathbf{M}_N\mathbf{D}_1 & -\mathbf{M}_N\mathbf{D}_2 & \cdots & \mathbf{I}-\mathbf{M}_N \end{bmatrix} \tag{4.2.6}$$

are inside the unit circle of the complex plane.

Proof. The eigenvalue problem of matrix $\mathbf{H}_A$ can be rewritten as

$$\begin{aligned} -\sum_{l \neq k} (\mathbf{D}_k\mathbf{M}_k)\mathbf{u}_l - \mathbf{D}_k(\mathbf{I}-\mathbf{M}_k)\mathbf{v}_k &= \lambda \mathbf{u}_k \\ \sum_{l \neq k} \mathbf{M}_k\mathbf{u}_l + (\mathbf{I}-\mathbf{M}_k)\mathbf{v}_k &= \lambda \mathbf{v}_k. \end{aligned} \tag{4.2.7}$$

Premultiplying the second equation by $\mathbf{D}_k$ and adding it to the first equation yields

$$\lambda(\mathbf{u}_k + \mathbf{D}_k\mathbf{v}_k) = \mathbf{0} \quad (k = 1,2,...,N).$$

If $\lambda = 0$, then it is inside the unit circle, and therefore does not destroy global asymptotical stability. If $\lambda \neq 0$, then

$$\mathbf{u}_k = -\mathbf{D}_k\mathbf{v}_k.$$

Substituting this relation into the second equation of (4.2.7), we obtain

$$-\sum_{l \neq k} \mathbf{M}_k\mathbf{D}_l\mathbf{v}_l + (\mathbf{I} - \mathbf{M}_k)\mathbf{v}_k = \lambda\mathbf{v}_k \quad (k = 1,2,...,N),$$

which is the eigenvalue problem of matrix (4.2.6). Thus the theorem is proven. □

Remark 1. The dimension of matrix (4.2.6) is NM, which is half of that of the original matrix $\mathbf{H}_A$.

Remark 2. Note that in the case of $\mathbf{M}_k = \mathbf{I}$ $(\forall k)$, relation (4.2.1) implies that $\mathbf{s}_k^E(t) = \mathbf{s}_k(t-1)$. That is, adaptive expectations coincide with expectations à la Cournot, which were discussed in the previous section. Observe also that in this special case matrix $\mathbf{H}_A^{(1)}$ has the form

$$\mathbf{H}_c^{(1)} = \begin{bmatrix} \mathbf{0} & -\mathbf{D}_2 & \cdots & -\mathbf{D}_N \\ -\mathbf{D}_1 & \mathbf{0} & \cdots & -\mathbf{D}_N \\ \vdots & \vdots & \ddots & \vdots \\ -\mathbf{D}_1 & -\mathbf{D}_2 & \cdots & \mathbf{0} \end{bmatrix}.$$

Since

$$\mathbf{H}_c^{(1)} = -\begin{bmatrix} \mathbf{0} & \mathbf{I} & \cdots & \mathbf{I} \\ \mathbf{I} & \mathbf{0} & \cdots & \mathbf{I} \\ \vdots & \vdots & \ddots & \vdots \\ \mathbf{I} & \mathbf{I} & \cdots & \mathbf{0} \end{bmatrix} \begin{bmatrix} \mathbf{D}_1 & & & \\ & \mathbf{D}_2 & & \\ & & \ddots & \\ & & & \mathbf{D}_N \end{bmatrix}$$

and

$$\mathbf{H}_c = -\begin{bmatrix} \mathbf{D}_1 & & & \\ & \mathbf{D}_2 & & \\ & & \ddots & \\ & & & \mathbf{D}_N \end{bmatrix} \begin{bmatrix} \mathbf{0} & \mathbf{I} & \cdots & \mathbf{I} \\ \mathbf{I} & \mathbf{0} & \cdots & \mathbf{I} \\ \vdots & \vdots & \ddots & \vdots \\ \mathbf{I} & \mathbf{I} & \cdots & \mathbf{0} \end{bmatrix},$$

they have the same eigenvalues. Here we use the well known fact that for square matrices $\mathbf{U}$ and $\mathbf{V}$ of the same size the eigenvalues of $\mathbf{UV}$ and $\mathbf{VU}$ are identical.

The application of the above results is usually difficult since it requires the knowledge of the eigenvalues of matrix $\mathbf{H}_A$ or $\mathbf{H}_c^{(1)}$. However in many cases simple sufficient conditions based on matrix norms can be applied, since if some norm of matrix (4.2.6) is less than one, then the equilibrium point is globally asymptotically stable with respect to adaptive expectations (4.2.1). By selecting the block-row norm we obtain the following sufficient conditions:

$$\|\mathbf{I}-\mathbf{M}_k\| + \sum_{l \neq k} \|\mathbf{M}_k \mathbf{D}_l\| < 1, \quad (k = 1,2,\ldots,N)$$

which holds if

$$\|\mathbf{I}-\mathbf{M}_k\| + \|\mathbf{M}_k\| \cdot \sum_{l \neq k} \|\mathbf{D}_l\| < 1 \quad (k = 1,2,\ldots,N).$$

The last condition can be explained as follows. If matrices $\mathbf{M}_k$ are given so that $\|\mathbf{I}-\mathbf{M}_k\| < 1$, then all matrices $\mathbf{D}_l$ must be small enough so that for all k,

$$\sum_{l \neq k} \|\mathbf{D}_l\| < \frac{1}{\|\mathbf{M}_k\|}\left(1 - \|\mathbf{I}-\mathbf{M}_k\|\right).$$

In the special case of expectations à la Cournot these relations reduce to (4.1.12). By selecting the block-column norm we get the following sufficient conditions:

$$\|\mathbf{I}-\mathbf{M}_k\| + \sum_{l \neq k} \|\mathbf{M}_l \mathbf{D}_k\| < 1 \quad (k = 1,2,\ldots,N)$$

which holds if

$$\|\mathbf{I}-\mathbf{M}_k\| + \|\mathbf{D}_k\| \cdot \sum_{l \neq k} \|\mathbf{M}_l\| < 1 \quad (k = 1,2,\ldots,N).$$

This last inequality can be rewritten as

$$\|\mathbf{D}_k\| < \frac{1 - \|\mathbf{I}-\mathbf{M}_k\|}{\sum_{l \neq k} \|\mathbf{M}_l\|} \quad (k = 1,2,\ldots,N).$$

Note that in the special case of expectations à la Cournot (that is, when $\mathbf{M}_k = \mathbf{I},\ k = 1,2,\dots,N$) these relations reduce to the requirement that for all k,

$$\|\mathbf{D}_k\| < \frac{1}{N-1}.$$

Next the eigenvalue problem of matrix (4.2.6) is further investigated. We shall reduce further the dimension of the matrix, but a nonlinear eigenvalue problem will be obtained. Assume now that $\mathbf{B}_k$ does not depend on k. Then $\mathbf{D}_k \equiv \mathbf{D}$. Note first that the eigenvalue equation of matrix (4.2.6) has the form

$$-\sum_{l \neq k} \mathbf{M}_k \mathbf{D} \mathbf{v}_l + (\mathbf{I} - \mathbf{M}_k)\mathbf{v}_k = \lambda \mathbf{v}_k \ (\forall k), \tag{4.2.8}$$

and by introducing the notation $\mathbf{v} = \sum_{k=1}^{N} \mathbf{v}_k$ and rearranging the terms we have

$$-\mathbf{M}_k \mathbf{D} \mathbf{v} + (\mathbf{I} - \mathbf{M}_k + \mathbf{M}_k \mathbf{D} - \lambda \mathbf{I})\mathbf{v}_k = \mathbf{0}.$$

Assume that matrix $(\mathbf{I} - \mathbf{M}_k + \mathbf{M}_k \mathbf{D})$ has eigenvalues only inside the unit circle. Then any other eigenvalue of matrix (4.2.6) satisfies the relation

$$\mathbf{v}_k = (\mathbf{I} + \mathbf{M}_k(\mathbf{D} - \mathbf{I}) - \lambda \mathbf{I})^{-1} \mathbf{M}_k \mathbf{D} \mathbf{v}.$$

By adding this equation for $k=1,2,\dots,N$ we have

$$\mathbf{v} = \sum_{k=1}^{N} (\mathbf{I} + \mathbf{M}_k(\mathbf{D} - \mathbf{I}) - \lambda \mathbf{I})^{-1} \mathbf{M}_k \mathbf{D} \mathbf{v}.$$

Consequently, we have proven the following result.

Theorem 4.2.3. Assume that $\mathbf{B}_k$ does not depend on k and all eigenvalues of matrices $(\mathbf{I} - \mathbf{M}_k + \mathbf{M}_k \mathbf{D})$ as well as those of the nonlinear eigenvalue problems

$$\det\left(\sum_{k=1}^{N} (\mathbf{I} + \mathbf{M}_k(\mathbf{D} - \mathbf{I}) - \lambda \mathbf{I})^{-1} \mathbf{M}_k \mathbf{D} - \mathbf{I} \right) = 0 \quad (k = 1,2,\dots,N) \tag{4.2.9}$$

are inside the unit circle. Then the equilibrium point of the multiproduct oligopoly game with respect to the adaptive expectations (4.2.1) is globally asymptotically stable.

Remark. In practical cases it is usually a difficult task to verify the conditions of the theorem. Note that the linear and nonlinear eigenvalue problems given in the conditions are all only M dimensional. Thus, we have again a drastic reduction in the dimension. However, nonlinear eigenvalue problems have to be solved.

Consider next the further special case when $\mathbf{M}_k \equiv \mathbf{M}$. That is, matrices $\mathbf{M}_k$ are identical for all values of k. Then (4.2.9) implies that there exists a $\mathbf{v} \neq \mathbf{0}$ such that

$$\left(\sum_{k=1}^{N} (\mathbf{I} + \mathbf{M}(\mathbf{D} - \mathbf{I}) - \lambda\mathbf{I})^{-1} \mathbf{MD} - \mathbf{I}\right)\mathbf{v} = \mathbf{0}.$$

Premultiplying this equation by $(\mathbf{I} + \mathbf{M}(\mathbf{D} - \mathbf{I}) - \lambda\mathbf{I})$ we have

$$[N\mathbf{MD} - (\mathbf{MD} - \mathbf{M} + \mathbf{I} - \lambda\mathbf{I})]\mathbf{v} = \mathbf{0}.$$

That is,

$$\det((N-1)\mathbf{MD} + \mathbf{M} - \mathbf{I} + \lambda\mathbf{I}) = 0.$$

From this identity and the assertion of the theorem we conclude that if all eigenvalues of matrices **I-M+MD** and -(N-1)**MD-M+I** are inside the unit circle, then the equilibrium is globally asymptotically stable. Note that both eigenvalue problems are liner and have common dimension M.

In the further special case when $\mathbf{B}_k = \mathbf{0}$, $\mathbf{M}_k = \alpha\mathbf{I}$ $(k = 1,2,\ldots N)$, and $\mathbf{A}=\mathbf{A}^T$, we have

$$\mathbf{D} = \left(\mathbf{A} + \mathbf{A}^T\right)^{-1}\mathbf{A} = \frac{1}{2}\mathbf{I},$$

$$\mathbf{I} - \mathbf{M} + \mathbf{MD} = \left(1 - \alpha + \frac{\alpha}{2}\right)\mathbf{I} = \left(1 - \frac{\alpha}{2}\right)\mathbf{I},$$

$$-(N-1)\mathbf{MD} - \mathbf{M} + \mathbf{I} = \left(-(N-1)\alpha \cdot \frac{1}{2} - \alpha + 1\right)\mathbf{I} = \left(1 - \frac{(N+1)\alpha}{2}\right)\mathbf{I}.$$

The eigenvalues of these matrices are $1 - \frac{\alpha}{2}$ and $1 - \frac{(N+1)\alpha}{2}$, respectively. We note that in this special case the nonzero eigenvalues of matrix $\mathbf{H}_A$ of (4.2.5) are the same values. Hence we have proven the following

Theorem 4.2.4. Assume that $\mathbf{A} = \mathbf{A}^T$, $\mathbf{B}_k = \mathbf{0}$, $\mathbf{M}_k = \alpha\mathbf{I}$ for all k. The equilibrium point of the multiproduct oligopoly game is globally asymptotically stable with respect to adaptive expectations (4.2.1) if and only if $0 < \alpha < \frac{4}{N+1}$.

Proof. The eigenvalues of matrix $\mathbf{H}_A$ are inside the unit circle if and only if

$$\left|1 - \frac{\alpha}{2}\right| < 1 \text{ and } \left|1 - \frac{(N+1)\alpha}{2}\right| < 1,$$

and these inequalities are equivalent to the assertion. □

Corollary. The fastest order of magnitude of the convergence speed of the dynamic process (4.2.5) occurs for the value α^* of α which minimizes the magnitude of the largest eigenvalue of $\mathbf{H}_A$. That is, the value of α^* is obtained by minimizing

$$g(\alpha) = \max\left\{\left|1 - \frac{\alpha}{2}\right|; \left|1 - \frac{(N+1)\alpha}{2}\right|\right\}.$$

This function is shown in Figure 4.2.1, and one may easily verify that $\alpha^* = \frac{4}{N+2}$.

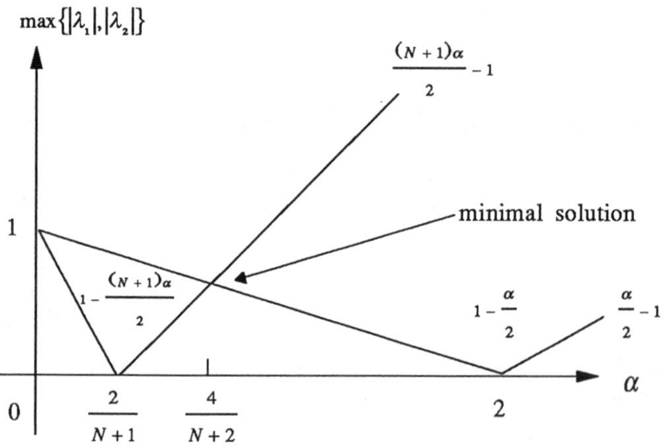

Figure 4.2.1. Selection of the fastest adjustment speed

Remark. Expectations à la Cournot, which were discussed in the previous section, are obtained by selecting $\alpha = 1$. This value of α satisfies the stability conditions of Theorem 4.2.4 if and only if N=2. Thus, a new kind of generalization of the classical result of Theocharis (1959) is obtained. Theorem 4.2.4 is also interesting from a different viewpoint. The theorem asserts that under certain conditions the equilibrium point is always globally asymptotically stable with arbitrary number of firms if the speed α of adjustment is sufficiently small.

Consider now the slightly more general case when $\mathbf{A}=\mathbf{A}^T$, $\mathbf{B}_k=\mathbf{0}$, and $\mathbf{M}_k$ is diagonal for all k. Introduce the notation $\mathbf{M}_k = \text{diag}\left(\alpha_{k1},...,\alpha_{kM}\right)$, and assume that $0<\alpha_{kj}\le 1$ for all k and j. Notice first that matrix (4.2.6) reduces to the following:

$$\mathbf{H}_A^{(1)} = \begin{pmatrix} \mathbf{I}-\mathbf{M}_1 & -\frac{1}{2}\mathbf{M}_1 & \cdots & -\frac{1}{2}\mathbf{M}_1 \\ -\frac{1}{2}\mathbf{M}_2 & \mathbf{I}-\mathbf{M}_2 & \cdots & -\frac{1}{2}\mathbf{M}_2 \\ \vdots & \vdots & & \vdots \\ -\frac{1}{2}\mathbf{M}_N & -\frac{1}{2}\mathbf{M}_N & \cdots & \mathbf{I}-\mathbf{M}_N \end{pmatrix}.$$

Since each block of this matrix is diagonal, simple permutation of the rows and corresponding columns of this matrix shows that it is similar to the block-diagonal matrix

$$\mathbf{H}_A^{(2)} = \begin{pmatrix} \mathbf{H}_1 & & & \\ & \mathbf{H}_2 & & \\ & & \ddots & \\ & & & \mathbf{H}_M \end{pmatrix}$$

with $N \times N$ diagonal blocks

$$\mathbf{H}_m = \begin{pmatrix} 1-\alpha_{1m} & -\frac{\alpha_{1m}}{2} & \cdots & -\frac{\alpha_{1m}}{2} \\ -\frac{\alpha_{2m}}{2} & 1-\alpha_{2m} & \cdots & -\frac{\alpha_{2m}}{2} \\ \cdots & \cdots & \cdots & \cdots \\ -\frac{\alpha_{Nm}}{2} & -\frac{\alpha_{Nm}}{2} & \cdots & 1-\alpha_{Nm} \end{pmatrix}.$$

The eigenvalues of $\mathbf{H}_A^{(1)}$ and $\mathbf{H}_A^{(2)}$ are the same, and the eigenvalues of matrix $\mathbf{H}_A^{(2)}$ are the eigenvalues of the blocks. Therefore under the above conditions the dynamic oligopoly model is globally asymptotically stable if and only if all eigenvalues of all matrices $\mathbf{H}_m$ are inside the unit circle. By using the special structure of $\mathbf{H}_m$, we can obtain its characteristic polynomial in a closed form. In the following discussion we will use the following:

Lemma 4.2.1. Let **a** and **b** be N-element real (or complex) vectors and **I** the $N \times N$ identity matrix. Then

$$\det\left(\mathbf{I} + \mathbf{a}\mathbf{b}^T\right) = 1 + \mathbf{a}^T\mathbf{b}.$$

Proof. We will use finite induction with respect to the size of the vectors **a** and **b**. If N=1, then **I**=1, **a**=a, **b**=b, and

$$\det\left(\mathbf{I} + \mathbf{a}\mathbf{b}^T\right) = \det(1 + ab) = 1 + ab = 1 + \mathbf{a}^T\mathbf{b}.$$

Assume next that the assertion holds for all $n<N$, and consider the $N \times N$ matrix

$$\mathbf{D}_N = \mathbf{I} + \mathbf{a}\mathbf{b}^T = \begin{bmatrix} 1 + a_1b_1 & a_1b_2 & \cdots & a_1b_{N-1} & a_1b_N \\ a_2b_1 & 1 + a_2b_2 & \cdots & a_2b_{N-1} & a_2b_N \\ \vdots & \vdots & & \vdots & \vdots \\ a_{N-1}b_1 & a_{N-1}b_2 & \cdots & 1 + a_{N-1}b_{N-1} & a_{N-1}b_N \\ a_Nb_1 & a_Nb_2 & \cdots & a_Nb_{N-1} & 1 + a_Nb_N \end{bmatrix}.$$

Subtract the a_N/a_{N-1} - multiple of the (N-1)st row from the Nth row, then subtract the a_{N-1}/a_{N-2} - multiple of the (N-2)th row from the (N-1)th row, and so on, and finally, subtract the a_2/a_1 - multiple of the first row from the second row. The resulting matrix has the same determinant as **I**+**ab**^{T} and has the form:

$$\begin{bmatrix} 1 + a_1b_1 & a_1b_2 & \cdots & a_1b_{N-1} & a_1b_N \\ -\frac{a_2}{a_1} & 1 & & & \\ & -\frac{a_3}{a_2} & \ddots & & \\ & & \ddots & 1 & \\ & & & -\frac{a_N}{a_{N-1}} & 1 \end{bmatrix},$$

where all other matrix elements are equal to zero. Expand the determinant of this matrix with respect to its last column to see that

$$\det(\mathbf{D}_N) = \det(\mathbf{D}_{N-1}) \cdot 1 + (-1)^{N-1} a_1b_N \cdot \frac{a_2}{a_1} \cdot \frac{a_3}{a_2} \cdot \ldots \cdot \frac{a_N}{a_{N-1}} (-1)^{N-1} = \det(\mathbf{D}_{N-1}) + a_Nb_N,$$

which completes the proof. □

The characteristic polynomial of $\mathbf{H}_m$ can be written as

$$\varphi_m(\lambda) = \det(\mathbf{H}_m - \lambda\mathbf{I}) = \det(\boldsymbol{\Delta}_m + \mathbf{a}_m \cdot \mathbf{1}^T - \lambda\mathbf{I}),$$

where

$$\boldsymbol{\Delta}_m = \begin{pmatrix} 1-\frac{\alpha_{1m}}{2} & & \\ & \ddots & \\ & & 1-\frac{\alpha_{Nm}}{2} \end{pmatrix}, \quad \mathbf{a}_m = \begin{pmatrix} -\frac{\alpha_{1m}}{2} \\ \vdots \\ -\frac{\alpha_{Nm}}{2} \end{pmatrix},$$

and all components of $\mathbf{1}$ are equal to one.

Using simple algebra and Lemma 4.2.1 we have

$$\varphi_m(\lambda) = \det(\boldsymbol{\Delta}_m - \lambda\mathbf{I}) \cdot \det(\mathbf{I} + (\boldsymbol{\Delta}_m - \lambda\mathbf{I})^{-1}\mathbf{a}_m\mathbf{1}^T) = \det(\boldsymbol{\Delta}_m - \lambda\mathbf{I}) \cdot \{1 + \mathbf{1}^T \cdot (\boldsymbol{\Delta}_m - \lambda\mathbf{I})^{-1}\mathbf{a}_m\},$$

since $(\boldsymbol{\Delta}_m - \lambda\mathbf{I})^{-1}\mathbf{a}_m$ is a column vector. Since $\boldsymbol{\Delta}_m - \lambda\mathbf{I}$ is a diagonal matrix,

$$\varphi_m(\lambda) = \mathop{\pi}_{k=1}^{N}\left(1 - \frac{\alpha_{km}}{2} - \lambda\right)\left\{1 + \sum_{k=1}^{N} \frac{\frac{-\alpha_{km}}{2}}{1 - \frac{\alpha_{km}}{2} - \lambda}\right\}.$$

Assume next that the different α_{km} numbers are ordered such that $\alpha_1^* > \alpha_2^* > \cdots > \alpha_l^*$ with multiplicities $r_1, r_2, \ldots, r_l$ such that $\sum_{i=1}^{l} r_i = N$. Using this notation

$$\varphi_m(\lambda) = \mathop{\pi}_{i=1}^{l}\left(1 - \frac{\alpha_i^*}{2} - \lambda\right)^{r_i}\left\{1 - \sum_{i=1}^{l} \frac{\alpha_i^* r_i}{2 - \alpha_i^* - 2\lambda}\right\}.$$

If r_i=1 with some i, then the factor $1 - \frac{\alpha_i^*}{2} - \lambda$ cancels, otherwise this factor remains in $\varphi_m(\lambda)$ with multiplicity r_i-1. Therefore, $\lambda = 1 - \frac{\alpha_i^*}{2}$ is a root of φ_m with multiplicity r_i-1. All other eigenvalues of $\mathbf{H}_A^{(1)}$ are the roots of the equation

$$\sum_{i=1}^{l} \frac{\alpha_i^* r_i}{2 - \alpha_i^* - 2\lambda} = 1.$$

Notice first that this is equivalent to a polynomial equation of degree l, therefore there are l real (or maybe complex) roots. If $g(\lambda)$ denotes the left hand side of the equation, then g locally strictly increases everywhere,

$$\lim_{\lambda \to 1-\frac{\alpha_i^*}{2}+0} g(\lambda) = -\infty,$$

$$\lim_{\lambda \to 1-\frac{\alpha_i^*}{2}-0} g(\lambda) = \infty,$$

and

$$\lim_{\lambda \to \pm\infty} g(\lambda) = 0.$$

The graph of function g is shown in Figure 4.2.2, which has exactly l intercepts with the horizontal line g=1, therefore all roots of the equation are real and they are located as follows. There is exactly one root inside each interval $(\alpha_i^*, \alpha_{i-1}^*)$ (i=2,3,...,l), and one root is before α_l^*. Since $0 < \alpha_i^* \le 1$ for all i, the first set of roots is inside the unit circle, and the last root is also inside the unit circle if and only if $g(-1)<1$. This condition can be rewritten as

$$\sum_{k=1}^{N} \frac{\alpha_{km}}{4-\alpha_{km}} < 1. \tag{4.2.10}$$

The above derivation implies the following result.

Theorem 4.2.5. Assume that $\mathbf{A} = \mathbf{A}^T$, $\mathbf{B}_k = \mathbf{0}$ and $\mathbf{M}_k = \text{diag}(\alpha_{k1}, \ldots, \alpha_{kM})$ with $0 < \alpha_{km} \le 1$ for all k and m. Then the dynamic oligopoly game with adaptive expectations is globally asymptotically stable if and only if relation (4.2.10) holds for all m.

Corollary 1. Assume that N=2, that is duopoly. Then

$$\sum_{k=1}^{2} \frac{\alpha_{km}}{4-\alpha_{km}} \le \sum_{k=1}^{2} \frac{1}{3} = \frac{2}{3} < 1,$$

therefore duopoly is always globally asymptotically stable.

Corollary 2. Assume next that $\alpha_{km} \equiv \alpha_m$ for all k. Then

$$\sum_{k=1}^{N} \frac{\alpha_m}{4-\alpha_m} = \frac{N\alpha_m}{4-\alpha_m} < 1$$

if and only if

$$\alpha_m < \frac{4}{N+1},$$

which coincides with the assertion of Theorem 4.2.4.

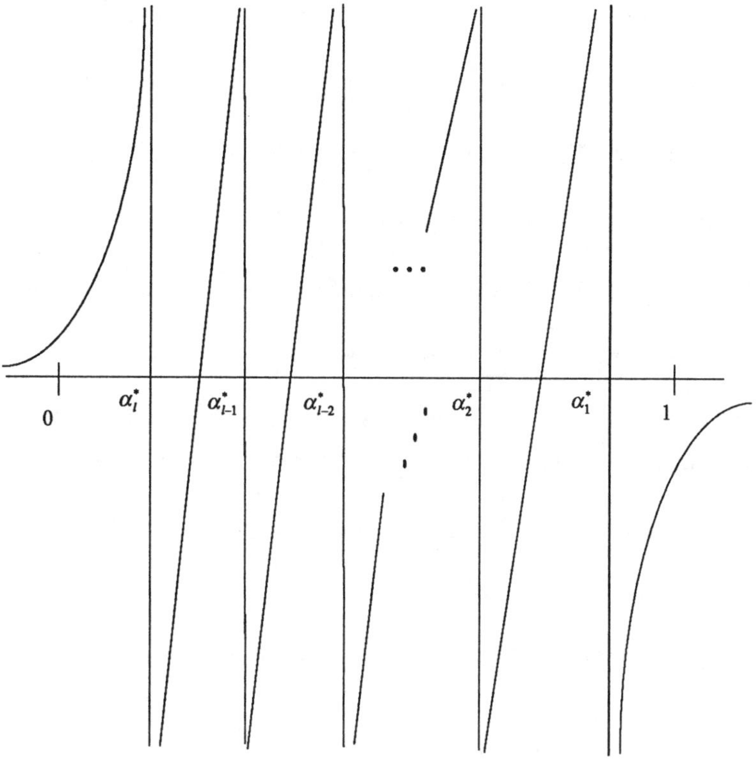

Figure 4.2.2 The graph of function g

In the next part of this section *adaptive expectations on the outputs of other firms* is investigated. The models with expectations on the output of the rest of the industry assume that each firm supposes the homogeneity in the sense that the behavior of all other firms can be described by a single adaptive equation. If such assumptions are not realistic then adaptive expectations are made on the individual strategies of all other firms. In these models we assume that at each time period $t > 0$ each firm k forms expectations $\mathbf{x}_{k1}^E(t), \ldots, \mathbf{x}_{k,k-1}^E(t), \mathbf{x}_{k,k+1}^E(t), \ldots, \mathbf{x}_{k,N}^E(t)$ adaptively on the strategies of all other firms and in the same period firm k maximizes its own expected profit. That is, in period t, firm k maximizes

$$\mathbf{x}_k^T\left(\mathbf{A}\sum_{l\neq k}\mathbf{x}_{kl}^E(t)+\mathbf{A}\mathbf{x}_k+\mathbf{b}\right)-\left(\mathbf{x}_k^T\mathbf{B}_k\mathbf{x}_k+\mathbf{b}_k^T\mathbf{x}_k+c_k\right) \tag{4.2.11}$$

subject to $\mathbf{x}_k \in X_k$.

Assume further that

($E^{(2)}$) The optimal solution of (4.2.11) is an interior point of X_k.

We also assume that the adaptive expectations on vectors $\mathbf{x}_l$ can be described by

$$\mathbf{x}_{kl}^E(t)=\mathbf{x}_{kl}^E(t-1)+\mathbf{M}_{kl}\left(\mathbf{x}_l(t-1)-\mathbf{x}_{kl}^E(t-1)\right),\quad (\forall k,\ l\neq k) \tag{4.2.12}$$

where $\mathbf{M}_{kl}$ is a constant matrix for all k and l.

Under assumption ($E^{(2)}$) the first order optimality conditions have the form

$$\left(\mathbf{A}+\mathbf{A}^T-\mathbf{B}_k-\mathbf{B}_k^T\right)\mathbf{x}_k+\mathbf{A}\sum_{l\neq k}\mathbf{x}_{kl}^E(t)+\mathbf{b}-\mathbf{b}_k=\mathbf{0}.$$

Condition (D) implies that matrix $\left(\mathbf{A}+\mathbf{A}^T-\mathbf{B}_k-\mathbf{B}_k^T\right)$ is invertible, and by substituting relation (4.2.11) into the first order condition we obtain

$$\mathbf{x}_k(t)=-\left(\mathbf{A}+\mathbf{A}^T-\mathbf{B}_k-\mathbf{B}_k^T\right)^{-1}\mathbf{A}\sum_{l\neq k}\left(\mathbf{x}_{kl}^E(t-1)+\mathbf{M}_{kl}\left(\mathbf{x}_l(t-1)-\mathbf{x}_{kl}^E(t-1)\right)\right)+\boldsymbol{\alpha}, \tag{4.2.13}$$

where $\boldsymbol{\alpha}$ is a constant vector. Combining equations (4.2.13) and (4.2.12) we get the recursive relation

$$\begin{bmatrix}\mathbf{x}_1(t)\\ \vdots\\ \mathbf{x}_N(t)\\ \mathbf{x}_{12}^E(t)\\ \vdots\\ \mathbf{x}_{1N}^E(t)\\ \vdots\\ \mathbf{x}_{N1}^E(t)\\ \vdots\\ \mathbf{x}_{N,N-1}^E(t)\end{bmatrix}=\mathbf{H}_A^*\cdot\begin{bmatrix}\mathbf{x}_1(t-1)\\ \vdots\\ \mathbf{x}_N(t-1)\\ \mathbf{x}_{12}^E(t-1)\\ \vdots\\ \mathbf{x}_{1N}^E(t-1)\\ \vdots\\ \mathbf{x}_{N1}^E(t-1)\\ \vdots\\ \mathbf{x}_{N,N-1}^E(t-1)\end{bmatrix}+\boldsymbol{\beta}_A^*, \tag{4.2.14}$$

where $\boldsymbol{\beta}_A^*$ is a constant vector, and

$$\mathbf{H}_A^* = \begin{bmatrix} \mathbf{H}_{00} & \mathbf{H}_{01} & \cdots & \mathbf{H}_{0N} \\ \mathbf{H}_{10} & \mathbf{H}_{11} & \cdots & \mathbf{H}_{1N} \\ \vdots & \vdots & & \vdots \\ \mathbf{H}_{N0} & \mathbf{H}_{N1} & \cdots & \mathbf{H}_{NN} \end{bmatrix}.$$

Here

$$\mathbf{H}_{00} = \begin{bmatrix} \mathbf{0} & -\mathbf{D}_1\mathbf{M}_{12} & \cdots & -\mathbf{D}_1\mathbf{M}_{1N} \\ -\mathbf{D}_1\mathbf{M}_{21} & \mathbf{0} & \cdots & -\mathbf{D}_2\mathbf{M}_{2N} \\ \vdots & \vdots & \ddots & \vdots \\ -\mathbf{D}_N\mathbf{M}_{N1} & -\mathbf{D}_N\mathbf{M}_{N2} & \cdots & \mathbf{0} \end{bmatrix}, \mathbf{D}_k = \left(\mathbf{A} + \mathbf{A}^T - \mathbf{B}_k - \mathbf{B}_k^T\right)^{-1}\mathbf{A};$$

$$\mathbf{H}_{0k} = \begin{bmatrix} \mathbf{0} & \mathbf{0} & \cdots & \mathbf{0} \\ \vdots & \vdots & & \vdots \\ \mathbf{0} & \mathbf{0} & & \mathbf{0} \\ -\mathbf{D}_k(\mathbf{I} - \mathbf{M}_{k1}) & -\mathbf{D}_k(\mathbf{I} - \mathbf{M}_{k2}) & \cdots & -\mathbf{D}_k(\mathbf{I} - \mathbf{M}_{kN}) \\ \mathbf{0} & \mathbf{0} & & \mathbf{0} \\ \vdots & \vdots & & \vdots \\ \mathbf{0} & \mathbf{0} & \cdots & \mathbf{0} \end{bmatrix},$$

where the "formal" diagonal block $-\mathbf{D}_k(\mathbf{I} - \mathbf{M}_{kk})$ is missing. Furthermore

$$\mathbf{H}_{k0} = \begin{bmatrix} \mathbf{M}_{k1} & & & & \mathbf{0} & & & \\ & \mathbf{M}_{k2} & & & \mathbf{0} & & & \\ & & \ddots & & \vdots & & & \\ & & & \mathbf{M}_{k,k-1} & \mathbf{0} & & & \\ & & & & \mathbf{0} & \mathbf{M}_{k,k+1} & & \\ & & & & \vdots & & \ddots & \\ & & & & \mathbf{0} & & & \mathbf{M}_{k,N} \end{bmatrix}; \; (k \geq 1)$$

and for $m \geq 1$,

$$\mathbf{H}_{km} = \begin{cases} \mathbf{0} \quad \text{if} \quad m \neq k, \\ \begin{bmatrix} \mathbf{I} - \mathbf{M}_{k1} & & \\ & \ddots & \\ & & \mathbf{I} - \mathbf{M}_{kN} \end{bmatrix} \quad \text{if} \;\; m = k, \end{cases}$$

where in the last matrix the "formal" diagonal block $\mathbf{I} - \mathbf{M}_{kk}$ is missing, so it has only (N-1) diagonal blocks.

Theorem 4.2.6. The equilibrium point of the multiproduct oligopoly game is globally asymptotically stable with respect to adaptive expectations (4.2.12) if and only if all eigenvalues of matrix $\mathbf{H}_A^*$ defined by (4.2.14) are inside the unit circle of the complex plane.

In practical cases it is very difficult to verify the conditions of the theorem, since matrix $\mathbf{H}_A^*$ has a large dimension, $MN + N \cdot (N-1)M = N^2 M$. However, Theorem 4.2.2 can be modified easily for this case and based on its assertion a significant dimension reduction will become possible.

Theorem 4.2.7. The equilibrium point of the multiproduct oligopoly game is globally asymptotically stable with respect to adaptive expectations (4.1.12) if and only if all eigenvalues of matrix

$$\mathbf{H}_A^{*(1)} = \left[\begin{array}{ccc|ccc|c|ccc}
\mathbf{I}-\mathbf{M}_{12} & & & -\mathbf{M}_{12}\mathbf{D}_2 & \cdots & -\mathbf{M}_{12}\mathbf{D}_2 & & & & \\
 & \ddots & & & & & \ddots & & & \\
 & & \mathbf{I}-\mathbf{M}_{1N} & & & & & -\mathbf{M}_{1N}\mathbf{D}_N & \cdots & -\mathbf{M}_{1N}\mathbf{D}_N \\
\hline
 & \vdots & & & \vdots & & \ddots & \vdots & & \\
\hline
-\mathbf{M}_{N1}\mathbf{D}_1 & \cdots & -\mathbf{M}_{N1}\mathbf{D}_1 & & & & & \mathbf{I}-\mathbf{M}_{N1} & & \\
 & & & -\mathbf{M}_{N2}\mathbf{D}_2 & \cdots & -\mathbf{M}_{N2}\mathbf{D}_2 & \cdots & & \ddots & \\
 & & & & & & & & & \mathbf{I}-\mathbf{M}_{N,N-1}
\end{array}\right] \tag{4.2.15}$$

are inside the unit circle.

Proof. Consider the eigenvalue problem of matrix $\mathbf{H}_A^*$:

$$\begin{aligned}
&-\sum_{l \neq k} \mathbf{D}_k \mathbf{M}_{kl} \mathbf{u}_l - \sum_{l \neq k} \mathbf{D}_k \left(\mathbf{I} - \mathbf{M}_{kl}\right) \mathbf{v}_{kl} = \lambda \mathbf{u}_k \quad (k = 1, \ldots, N). \\
&\mathbf{M}_{kl} \mathbf{u}_l + \left(\mathbf{I} - \mathbf{M}_{kl}\right) \mathbf{v}_{kl} = \lambda \mathbf{u}_{kl} \quad (k = 1, \ldots, N,\ l \neq k).
\end{aligned} \tag{4.2.16}$$

Multiplying the second equation of (4.2.16) by $\mathbf{D}_k$ and adding it to the first equation, for all $l \neq k$,

$$\lambda \left(\mathbf{u}_k + \sum_{l \neq k} \mathbf{D}_k \mathbf{v}_{kl} \right) = \mathbf{0} \quad (k = 1, 2, \ldots, N).$$

If $\lambda = 0$, then it is inside the unit circle of the complex plane so it does not affect global asymptotical stability. If $\lambda \neq 0$, then

$$\mathbf{u}_k = -\mathbf{D}_k \sum_{l \neq k} \mathbf{v}_{kl} .$$

Substituting this into the second equation of (4.2.16) we obtain

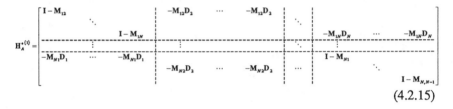

$$-\mathbf{M}_{kl}\mathbf{D}_l\sum_{p\neq l}\mathbf{v}_{lp}+(\mathbf{I}-\mathbf{M}_{kl})\mathbf{v}_{kl}=\lambda\mathbf{v}_{kl},\quad (k=1,2,\ldots,N;\ l\neq k)$$

which is the eigenvalue problem of matrix (4.2.15). Thus the theorem is proven. □

Remark. The dimension of matrix (4.2.15) is $N(N\text{-}1)M=N^2M\text{-}NM$, which is less by NM than the dimension of matrix $\mathbf{H}_A^*$ of the original difference equation (4.2.14).

Next the eigenvalue problem of matrix (4.2.15) will be further investigated. We will further reduce the dimension of the problem, however a nonlinear eigenvalue problem similar to (4.2.9) will be obtained. Note that the eigenvalue problem of matrix $\mathbf{H}_A^{*(1)}$ implies that

$$-\mathbf{M}_{kl}\mathbf{D}_l\mathbf{v}_l+(\mathbf{I}-\mathbf{M}_{kl})\mathbf{v}_{kl}=\lambda\mathbf{v}_{kl},\quad (k=1,\ldots,N;\ l\neq k)$$

where $\mathbf{v}_l=\sum_{p\neq l}\mathbf{v}_{lp}$. Assume that matrix ($\mathbf{I}$-$\mathbf{M}_{kl}$) has eigenvalues only inside the unit circle. Then any other eigenvalue of matrix (4.2.15) satisfies the relation

$$\mathbf{v}_{kl}=(\mathbf{I}-\mathbf{M}_{kl}-\lambda\mathbf{I})^{-1}\mathbf{M}_{kl}\mathbf{D}_l\mathbf{v}_l.$$

By adding this equation for $l\neq k$ we have

$$\mathbf{v}_k=\sum_{l\neq k}(\mathbf{I}-\mathbf{M}_{kl}-\lambda\mathbf{I})^{-1}\mathbf{M}_{kl}\mathbf{D}_l\mathbf{v}_l.$$

Consequently, we have

Theorem 4.2.8. Assume that all eigenvalues of matrices ($\mathbf{I}$-$\mathbf{M}_{kl}$) as well as all solutions of the nonlinear eigenvalue problem

$$\det\begin{bmatrix}\mathbf{I} & -(\mathbf{I}-\mathbf{M}_{12}-\lambda\mathbf{I})^{-1}\mathbf{M}_{12}\mathbf{D}_2 & \cdots & -(\mathbf{I}-\mathbf{M}_{1N}-\lambda\mathbf{I})^{-1}\mathbf{M}_{1N}\mathbf{D}_N\\ -(\mathbf{I}-\mathbf{M}_{21}-\lambda\mathbf{I})^{-1}\mathbf{M}_{21}\mathbf{D}_1 & \mathbf{I} & \cdots & -(\mathbf{I}-\mathbf{M}_{2N}-\lambda\mathbf{I})^{-1}\mathbf{M}_{2N}\mathbf{D}_N\\ \vdots & \vdots & & \vdots\\ -(\mathbf{I}-\mathbf{M}_{N1}-\lambda\mathbf{I})^{-1}\mathbf{M}_{N1}\mathbf{D}_1 & -(\mathbf{I}-\mathbf{M}_{N2}-\lambda\mathbf{I})^{-1}\mathbf{M}_{N2}\mathbf{D}_2 & \cdots & \mathbf{I}\end{bmatrix}=0 \tag{4.2.17}$$

are inside the unit circle. Then the equilibrium point of the multiproduct oligopoly game is globally asymptotically stable with respect to adaptive expectations (4.2.12).

Remark 1. As an analogy between Theorems 4.2.3 and 4.2.8, note that in the special case of $\mathbf{M}_{kl} \equiv \mathbf{M}_k$ $(\forall k)$, problem (4.2.17) formally reduces to the eigenvalue problem of matrix (4.2.6) when each block row is multiplied by $(\mathbf{I} - \mathbf{M}_k - \lambda \mathbf{I})$. If in addition $\mathbf{D}_k \equiv \mathbf{D}$ $(\forall k)$, then Theorem 4.2.3 remains valid, which results in a further reduction in the dimensions of the eigenvalue problems to be examined.

Remark 2. In practical cases it is usually difficult to verify the conditions of the theorem. Note that the linear eigenvalue problems are M dimensional and problem (4.2.17) is only MN dimensional. Thus a drastic reduction in the dimension is obtained, but the eigenvalue problem became more complicated, since it is usually nonlinear.

Consider finally the special case when $\mathbf{A} = \mathbf{A}^T$, $\mathbf{B}_k = \mathbf{0}$ $(\forall k)$ and $\mathbf{M}_{kl} = \alpha \mathbf{I}$ $(\forall k, l)$. Then $\mathbf{D}_k$ does not depend on k. Consequently, (as we have seen in Remark 1) equation (4.2.17) is identical to the eigenvalue problem of matrix (4.2.6). Hence all consequences of Theorem 4.2.2 such as Theorems 4.2.3 and 4.2.4, as well as the selection of the fastest speed of adjustment, remain valid.

The analogy of the two adjustment processes for this last special case is obvious, since if $\mathbf{M}_{kl} \equiv \mathbf{M}_k$, then adaptive expectations on the individual strategies of the firms are equivalent to those on the output of the rest of the industry.

4.3 Sequential Adjustment Processes

Consider again the multiproduct oligopoly game and assume that conditions (A) – (D) given in the introduction of this chapter hold. Assume furthermore that the firms can make actions over successive periods of time. From one play to the next, each firm updates its strategy based on the latest strategies of the other firms. In the case of the sequential adjustment process the firms update and announce their strategy selections one after another. At time $t = 0$, let $\mathbf{x}(0) = (\mathbf{x}_1(0), \ldots, \mathbf{x}_N(0))$ denote the strategies of the firms. Then for each $t > 0$, the following process is assumed. In the order k=1,2,...,N each firm updates his strategy $\mathbf{x}_k(t+1)$ for the next time period by maximizing his payoff value

$$\varphi_k\left(\mathbf{x}_1(t+1), \ldots, \mathbf{x}_{k-1}(t+1), \mathbf{x}_k, \mathbf{x}_{k+1}(t), \ldots, \mathbf{x}_N(t)\right).$$

This function is based on the latest information available.

Assume that

($E^{(3)}$) For all $t \geq 0$ and k, the optimal solutions $\mathbf{x}_k(t+1)$ are interior points in X_k.

In our case the first order optimality conditions imply that

$$\left(\mathbf{A}+\mathbf{A}^T-\mathbf{B}_k-\mathbf{B}_k^T\right)\mathbf{x}_k(t+1)+\mathbf{A}\sum_{l<k}\mathbf{x}_l(t+1)+\mathbf{A}\sum_{l>k}\mathbf{x}_l(t)+\left(\mathbf{b}-\mathbf{b}_k\right)=\mathbf{0} \quad (k=1,\dots,N).$$

That is,

$$(\mathbf{I}+\mathbf{L})\mathbf{x}(t+1)+\mathbf{U}\mathbf{x}(t)+\boldsymbol{\alpha}=\mathbf{0}, \tag{4.3.1}$$

where $\boldsymbol{\alpha}$ is a constant vector,

$$\mathbf{L}=\begin{bmatrix} \mathbf{0} & \mathbf{0} & \cdots & \mathbf{0} & \mathbf{0} \\ \mathbf{D}_2 & \mathbf{0} & \cdots & \mathbf{0} & \mathbf{0} \\ \vdots & \vdots & & \vdots & \vdots \\ \mathbf{D}_{N-1} & \mathbf{D}_{N-1} & \cdots & \mathbf{0} & \mathbf{0} \\ \mathbf{D}_N & \mathbf{D}_N & \cdots & \mathbf{D}_N & \mathbf{0} \end{bmatrix}, \mathbf{U}=\begin{bmatrix} \mathbf{0} & \mathbf{D}_1 & \cdots & \mathbf{D}_1 & \mathbf{D}_1 \\ \mathbf{0} & \mathbf{0} & \cdots & \mathbf{D}_2 & \mathbf{D}_2 \\ \vdots & \vdots & & \vdots & \vdots \\ \mathbf{0} & \mathbf{0} & \cdots & \mathbf{0} & \mathbf{D}_{N-1} \\ \mathbf{0} & \mathbf{0} & \cdots & \mathbf{0} & \mathbf{0} \end{bmatrix}$$

with

$$\mathbf{D}_k=\left(\mathbf{A}+\mathbf{A}^T-\mathbf{B}_k-\mathbf{B}_k^T\right)^{-1}\mathbf{A}, \quad k=1,2,\dots,N.$$

From (4.3.1) we obtain the recursion

$$\mathbf{x}(t+1)=-(\mathbf{I}+\mathbf{L})^{-1}\mathbf{U}\mathbf{x}(t)+\boldsymbol{\beta}_S, \tag{4.3.2}$$

where $\boldsymbol{\beta}_S$ is a constant vector. Hence the global asymptotical stability of the equilibrium with respect to the sequential adjustment process is equivalent to the global asymptotical stability of the system of linear difference equations with coefficient matrix

$$\mathbf{H}_S=-(\mathbf{I}+\mathbf{L})^{-1}\mathbf{U}. \tag{4.3.3}$$

Thus we have

Theorem 4.3.1. The equilibrium point of the multiproduct oligopoly game is globally asymptotically stable with respect to the sequential adjustment process if and only if all eigenvalues of matrix $\mathbf{H}_S$ are inside the unit circle of the complex plane.

Note that the dimension of matrix $\mathbf{H}_S$ is NM, which equals the dimension of the coefficient matrix $\mathbf{H}_c$ under Cournot assumptions. It is much less than the dimensions of coefficient matrices $\mathbf{H}_A$ and $\mathbf{H}_A^*$ when the adjustment processes were based on adaptive expectations.

Our main result is the following:

Theorem 4.3.2. Assume that $\mathbf{B}_k = \mathbf{0}$ $(\forall k)$ and $\mathbf{A} = \mathbf{A}^T$. Then the equilibrium point is globally asymptotically stable with respect to the sequential adjustment process for all $N \geq 2$.

The proof of the theorem is based on two lemmas.

Lemma 4.3.1. If $\mathbf{A} = \mathbf{A}^T$ and $\mathbf{B}_k = \mathbf{0}$ $(\forall k)$, then matrix

$$\mathbf{L}+\mathbf{U}+\mathbf{I} = \begin{bmatrix} \mathbf{I} & \mathbf{D} & \cdots & \mathbf{D} \\ \mathbf{D} & \mathbf{I} & \cdots & \mathbf{D} \\ \vdots & \vdots & \ddots & \vdots \\ \mathbf{D} & \mathbf{D} & \cdots & \mathbf{I} \end{bmatrix} \tag{4.3.4}$$

with $\mathbf{D} = \left(\mathbf{A}+\mathbf{A}^T\right)^{-1}\mathbf{A}$ being positive definite.

Proof. Using the notation $\otimes$ for Kronecker products we have

$$\mathbf{L}+\mathbf{U}+\mathbf{I} = \mathbf{I} + \begin{bmatrix} 0 & 1 & \cdots & 1 \\ 1 & 0 & \cdots & 1 \\ \vdots & \vdots & \ddots & \vdots \\ 1 & 1 & \cdots & 0 \end{bmatrix} \otimes \mathbf{D},$$

where now $\mathbf{D} = \left(\mathbf{A}+\mathbf{A}^T\right)^{-1}\mathbf{A} = \frac{1}{2}\mathbf{I}$.

Since the eigenvalues of the $N \times N$ matrix $\mathbf{1}$ are 0 and N (see Section 4.1), the eigenvalues of matrix

$$\begin{bmatrix} 0 & 1 & \cdots & 1 \\ 1 & 0 & \cdots & 1 \\ \vdots & \vdots & \ddots & \vdots \\ 1 & 1 & \cdots & 0 \end{bmatrix} = \mathbf{1} - \mathbf{I}$$

are -1 and N-1. Matrix $\mathbf{D}=\frac{1}{2}\mathbf{I}$ has eigenvalues $\frac{1}{2}$. Therefore Lemma 4.1.1 implies that the eigenvalues of matrix (4.3.4) are $1+(-1)\cdot\frac{1}{2}=\frac{1}{2}$ and $1+(N-1)\cdot\frac{1}{2}=\frac{N+1}{2}$, which are positive. Thus the proof is completed, since matrix (4.3.4) is symmetric. □

Lemma 4.3.2. Assume that $\mathbf{U}=\mathbf{L}^T$ and matrix $\mathbf{L}+\mathbf{U}+\mathbf{I}$ is positive definite. Then all eigenvalues of matrix $\mathbf{H}_S$ are inside the unit circle.

Proof. Consider the eigenvalue problem of matrix $\mathbf{H}_S$:

$$\mathbf{H}_s\mathbf{u}=\lambda\mathbf{u},$$

where λ and $\mathbf{u}$ may be complex. That is,

$$\mathbf{U}\mathbf{u}=-\lambda(\mathbf{I}+\mathbf{L})\mathbf{u}.$$

Premultiplying this relation by $\mathbf{u}^*$ (where $*$ denotes the conjugate transposed) we get

$$\mathbf{u}^*\mathbf{U}\mathbf{u}=-\lambda\left(\mathbf{u}^*\mathbf{u}+\mathbf{u}^*\mathbf{L}\mathbf{u}\right). \tag{4.3.5}$$

Denote $z=\mathbf{u}^*\mathbf{L}\mathbf{u}$, then

$$\mathbf{u}^*\mathbf{U}\mathbf{u}=\mathbf{u}^*\mathbf{L}^T\mathbf{u}=\left(\mathbf{u}^*\mathbf{L}\mathbf{u}\right)^*=\bar{z},$$

and from (4.3.5) we have

$$\bar{z}=-\lambda(v+z), \tag{4.3.6}$$

where $v=\mathbf{u}^*\mathbf{u}>0$. Since $\mathbf{L}+\mathbf{U}+\mathbf{I}$ is positive definite,

$$0<\mathbf{u}^*(\mathbf{L}+\mathbf{U}+\mathbf{I})\mathbf{u}=z+\bar{z}+v=v+2\operatorname{Re}z.$$

Then

$$|\bar{z}|^2=(\operatorname{Re}z)^2+(\operatorname{Im}z)^2<(v+\operatorname{Re}z)^2+(\operatorname{Im}z)^2=|v+z|^2,$$

and combining this relation with (4.3.6) leads to inequality

$$|\lambda| = \frac{|\bar{z}|}{|\nu + z|} < 1,$$

which completes the proof. □

On the basis of the above two lemmas, the theorem can be proven as follows:

Proof of the Theorem. Since $\mathbf{A}=\mathbf{A}^T$, Lemma 4.3.1 implies that matrix $\mathbf{L}+\mathbf{U}+\mathbf{I}$ is positive definite. Then Lemma 4.3.2 implies that all eigenvalues of matrix $\mathbf{H}_S$ are inside the unit circle from which the assertion follows. □

Remark 1. Gabay and Moulin (1980) investigated the sequential adjustment process in the case when M=1 and the Jacobian matrix

$$\mathbf{F}=\mathbf{L}+\mathbf{U}+\mathbf{I}$$

is strictly diagonally dominant. This property holds only for N=2. In this section the same process is examined under much more general conditions.

Remark 2. It is known (see Theorem 4.1.3) that the simultaneous adjustment process with expectations à la Cournot is stable only for N=2. If adaptative expectations are assumed, then stability can be assured for arbitrary number of firms with sufficiently small speed of adjustments, which implies that the corresponding dynamic process converges very slowly to the equilibrium. In Theorem 4.3.2 no such assumptions were made.

The sequential adjustment process is identical to a block variant of the Gauss-Seidel method for solving linear equations. This method can be further generalized as the successive overrelation (SOR) algorithm. This generalization of the sequential adjustment process will be examined next. It is well known from the theory of iteration processes (see Ortega and Rheinboldt, 1970) that the SOR method has the form

$$\mathbf{x}_k(t+1) = \mathbf{x}_k(t) + \mathbf{W}_k\left(-\sum_{l<k}\mathbf{D}_k\mathbf{x}_l(t+1) - \sum_{l>k}\mathbf{D}_k\mathbf{x}_l(t) - \mathbf{x}_k(t)\right) + \boldsymbol{\lambda}_k\,, \qquad (4.3.7)$$

where $\boldsymbol{\lambda}_k$ is a constant vector and $\mathbf{W}_k$ is the matrix of relaxation for firm k. As a special case take $\mathbf{W}_k = \mathbf{I}$ $(\forall k)$ to obtain the sequential adjustment method, and so this process is really a generalization. Define $\mathbf{W} = \mathrm{diag}(\mathbf{W}_1, \dots, \mathbf{W}_N)$, and introduce the notation

$$\tilde{\mathbf{L}} = \begin{bmatrix} \mathbf{0} & \mathbf{0} & \cdots & \mathbf{0} & \mathbf{0} \\ \mathbf{W}_2\mathbf{D}_2 & \mathbf{0} & \cdots & \mathbf{0} & \mathbf{0} \\ \vdots & \vdots & \ddots & \vdots & \vdots \\ \mathbf{W}_N\mathbf{D}_N & \mathbf{W}_N\mathbf{D}_N & \cdots & \mathbf{W}_N\mathbf{D}_N & \mathbf{0} \end{bmatrix}, \tilde{\mathbf{U}} = \begin{bmatrix} \mathbf{0} & \mathbf{W}_1\mathbf{D}_1 & \cdots & \mathbf{W}_1\mathbf{D}_1 & \mathbf{W}_1\mathbf{D}_1 \\ \mathbf{0} & \mathbf{0} & \cdots & \mathbf{W}_2\mathbf{D}_2 & \mathbf{W}_2\mathbf{D}_2 \\ \vdots & \vdots & \ddots & \vdots & \vdots \\ \mathbf{0} & \mathbf{0} & \cdots & \mathbf{0} & \mathbf{0} \end{bmatrix}.$$

Then (4.3.7) implies that

$$\mathbf{x}(t+1) = -\left(\mathbf{I}+\tilde{\mathbf{L}}\right)^{-1}\left(\mathbf{W}-\mathbf{I}+\tilde{\mathbf{U}}\right)\mathbf{x}(t) + \boldsymbol{\lambda}_S^{(1)}.$$

That is, the method ensures convergence to the equilibrium with arbitrary initial vector $\mathbf{x}(0)$ if and only if the eigenvalues of matrix

$$\mathbf{H}_S^{(1)} = -\left(\mathbf{I}+\tilde{\mathbf{L}}\right)^{-1}\left(\mathbf{W}-\mathbf{I}+\tilde{\mathbf{U}}\right) \tag{4.3.8}$$

are inside the unit circle. The main result on this process can be summarized in the following way.

Theorem 4.3.3. Assume that $\mathbf{B}_k = \mathbf{0}$ $(\forall k)$ and $\mathbf{A} = \mathbf{A}^T$, and furthermore for all k, $\mathbf{W}_k \equiv \mathbf{W}$, where $\mathbf{W}$ is a symmetric matrix with eigenvalues on (0,2). Then the equilibrium point is globally asymptotically stable with respect to the generalized sequential adjustment process (4.3.7).

Before proving the theorem, a generalized version of Lemma 4.3.2 is presented.

Lemma 4.3.3. Assume that $\mathbf{U} = \mathbf{L}^T$ and matrix **L+U+I** is positive definite, furthermore **W** is symmetric with eigenvalues from the interval (0,2). The all eigenvalues of matrix $\mathbf{H}_S^{(1)}$ are inside the unit circle.

Proof. We shall proceed analogously to the proof of Lemma 4.3.2. In this case the eigenvalue equation of matrix $\mathbf{H}_S^{(1)}$ implies that

$$\left(\mathbf{W}-\mathbf{I}+\tilde{\mathbf{U}}\right)\mathbf{u} = -\lambda\left(\mathbf{I}+\tilde{\mathbf{L}}\right)\mathbf{u}.$$

Since $\tilde{\mathbf{U}} = \mathbf{W}\mathbf{U}$ and $\tilde{\mathbf{L}} = \mathbf{W}\mathbf{L}$, we have

$$(\mathbf{W}-\mathbf{I}+\mathbf{W}\mathbf{U})\mathbf{u} = -\lambda(\mathbf{I}+\mathbf{W}\mathbf{L})\mathbf{u}.$$

Premultiplying by $\mathbf{u}^*\mathbf{W}^{-1}$ and defining $\boldsymbol{\Delta}=\mathbf{W}^{-1}$ yields relation

$$\mathbf{u}^*(\mathbf{I}-\boldsymbol{\Delta}+\mathbf{U})\mathbf{u} = -\lambda\mathbf{u}^*(\boldsymbol{\Delta}+\mathbf{L})\mathbf{u}.$$

Define

$$z = \mathbf{u}^*\mathbf{L}\mathbf{u},\ \bar{z} = \mathbf{u}^*\mathbf{U}\mathbf{u},\ v = \mathbf{u}^*\mathbf{u} > 0,\ w = \mathbf{u}^*\boldsymbol{\Delta}\mathbf{u} > 0,$$

then

$$v - w + \bar{z} = -\lambda(w + z). \tag{4.3.9}$$

We have again $v + 2\operatorname{Re} z > 0$, which follows from the assumption that matrix **L+U+I** is positive definite. Then we can easily verify that

$$|v - w + \bar{z}|^2 = (v - w + \operatorname{Re} z)^2 + (\operatorname{Im} z)^2 < |w + z|^2 = (w + \operatorname{Re} z)^2 + (\operatorname{Im} z)^2.$$

This inequality is equivalent to the relation

$$(v - 2w)(v + 2\operatorname{Re} z) < 0. \tag{4.3.10}$$

The first factor is negative, since **A** is symmetric with eigenvalues larger than $\frac{1}{2}$. The second factor is positive. Thus (4.3.10) is verified, and from (4.3.9) we may conclude that

$$|\lambda| = \frac{|v - w + \bar{z}|}{|w + z|} < 1.$$ □

The theorem is then the consequence of Lemma 4.3.3.

Remark 1. Theorem 4.3.3 has great importance in computing the equilibrium, since it provides the convergence of a large class of methods. As a special case the convergence of the sequential adjustment process can be obtained by selecting $\mathbf{W}_k$=**I** for all k.

Remark 2. The condition for matrix $\mathbf{W}_k$ is obviously satisfied if $\mathbf{W}_k = \operatorname{diag}(\omega_1, \ldots, \omega_M)$ with $0 < \omega_m < 2$ $(m = 1, 2, \ldots, M)$.

Remark 3. Theorem 4.3.3 is a linear block variant of the general convergence theorem of the SOR method (see Ortega and Rheinboldt, 1970, pp. 516-517). An interesting linear generalization of Theorem 4.3.3 can be given as follows.

Consider the linear equations

$$\sum_{l=1}^{N} \mathbf{A}_{kl}\mathbf{x}_l = \mathbf{b}_k \quad (k = 1, 2, \ldots, N),$$

where $\mathbf{A}_{kl}$ is a constant matrix, $\mathbf{b}_k$ is a constant vector, and vectors $\mathbf{x}_l$ are the unknowns. Starting from an initial approximation $\mathbf{x}(0) = (\mathbf{x}_1(0), \ldots, \mathbf{x}_N(0))$ the SOR method first determines

$$\bar{\mathbf{x}}_k(t+1) = \mathbf{A}_{kk}^{-1}\left[\mathbf{b}_k - \sum_{l<k} \mathbf{A}_{kl}\mathbf{x}_l(t+1) - \sum_{l>k} \mathbf{A}_{kl}\mathbf{x}_l(t)\right] \quad (k = 1,2,\ldots,N),$$

and then selects vectors

$$\mathbf{x}_k(t+1) = \mathbf{x}_k(t) + \mathbf{W}_k(\bar{\mathbf{x}}_k(t+1) - \mathbf{x}_k(t)) \quad (k = 1,2,\ldots,N)$$

as the new approximations. Assume that

(i) Matrix

$$\mathbf{A} = \begin{bmatrix} \mathbf{A}_{11} & \cdots & \mathbf{A}_{1N} \\ \vdots & & \vdots \\ \mathbf{A}_{N1} & \cdots & \mathbf{A}_{NN} \end{bmatrix}$$

is symmetric and positive definite;

(ii) For all k, matrix $\mathbf{W}_k$ is nonsingular and the symmetric matrix

$$\mathbf{W}_k^T \mathbf{A}_{kk} + \mathbf{A}_{kk}\mathbf{W}_k - \mathbf{W}_k^T \mathbf{A}_{kk}\mathbf{W}_k$$

is positive definite for all k.

Then the SOR method converges to the unique solution of the linear equations.

The dynamic process discussed in this section can be further generalized. Assume that the firms are divided into disjoint groups $G_1, G_2, \ldots, G_k$; that is, $G_k \cap G_l = \emptyset$ for $k \neq l$, and $G_1 \cup G_2 \cup \ldots \cup G_k = \{1,2,\ldots,N\}$. Let $\mathbf{x}_i(0)$ denote the output of firm i $(1 \le i \le N)$ at $t = 0$. Each further time period $t > 0$ is then divided into K subperiods $t(1),\ldots,t(K)$, and for each $t > 0$ and k $(1 \le k \le K)$, at subperiod $t(k)$ an equilibrium is formed by the firms from group G_k with fixed values of $\mathbf{x}_i = \mathbf{x}_i(t)$ $(i \in G_l, l < k)$ and $\mathbf{x}_i = \mathbf{x}_i(t+1)$ $(i \in G_l, l > k)$. In the special case, when each group consists of only one firm, this process coincides with the sequential adjustment process discussed. One may verify (see Szidarovszky and Okuguchi, 1987j), that Theorems 4.3.2 and 4.3.3 remain valid in the case of this more general dynamic process.

4.4 Extrapolative Expectations

Consider again the multiproduct oligopoly game and assume that conditions (A) - (D) hold. These conditions imply that the multiproduct oligopoly game has at least one equilibrium point. In this section a general dynamic model will be investigated, where the expectations may depend on several previous observations. That is, we assume that each firm forms expectation on vector $\mathbf{s}_k = \sum_{l \neq k} \mathbf{x}_l$ according to the formula

$$\mathbf{s}_k^E(t) = \sum_{i=1}^{L} \mathbf{E}_i^{(k)} \mathbf{s}_k(t-i), \tag{4.4.1}$$

where the $\mathbf{E}_i^{(k)}$'s are $M \times M$ constant matrices such that

$$\sum_{i=1}^{L} \mathbf{E}_i^{(k)} = \mathbf{I}.$$

It is usually assumed that matrices $\mathbf{E}_i^{(k)}$ are diagonal. Relation (4.4.1) means that expectation on $\mathbf{s}_k$ is extrapolated from its earlier values. Then, at time $t>0$, each firm k optimizes its expected profit

$$\mathbf{x}_k^T \left(\mathbf{A}\mathbf{s}_k^E(t) + \mathbf{A}\mathbf{x}_k + \mathbf{b} \right) - \left(\mathbf{x}_k^T \mathbf{B}_k \mathbf{x}_k + \mathbf{b}_k^T \mathbf{x}_k + c_k \right)$$

subject to $\mathbf{x}_k \in X_k$.

Assume that

($E^{(4)}$) The optimal solution is an interior point of X_k.

The first order optimality conditions imply that for all k and $t > 0$,

$$\begin{aligned} \mathbf{x}_k(t) &= -\left(\mathbf{A} + \mathbf{A}^T - \mathbf{B}_k - \mathbf{B}_k^T \right)^{-1} \left(\mathbf{A}\mathbf{s}_k^E(t) + \mathbf{b} - \mathbf{b}_k \right) \\ &= -\mathbf{D}_k \sum_{i=1}^{L} \mathbf{E}_i^{(k)} \sum_{l \neq k} \mathbf{x}_l(t-i) + \boldsymbol{\alpha}_k, \end{aligned} \tag{4.4.2}$$

where $\boldsymbol{\alpha}_k$ is a constant vector, and $\mathbf{D}_k = \left(\mathbf{A} + \mathbf{A}^T - \mathbf{B}_k - \mathbf{B}_k^T \right)^{-1} \mathbf{A}$ as before. We can summarize relations (4.4.2) with the difference equation

$$\mathbf{x}(t) = \sum_{i=1}^{L} \mathbf{H}_i \mathbf{x}(t-i) + \boldsymbol{\alpha}_E, \tag{4.4.3}$$

where

$$\mathbf{x}=\begin{bmatrix}\mathbf{x}_1\\ \vdots\\ \mathbf{x}_N\end{bmatrix},\boldsymbol{\alpha}_E=\begin{bmatrix}\alpha_1\\ \vdots\\ \alpha_N\end{bmatrix},\mathbf{H}_i=\begin{bmatrix}\mathbf{0} & -\mathbf{D}_1\mathbf{E}_i^{(1)} & \cdots & -\mathbf{D}_1\mathbf{E}_i^{(1)}\\ -\mathbf{D}_2\mathbf{E}_i^{(2)} & \mathbf{0} & \cdots & -\mathbf{D}_2\mathbf{E}_i^{(2)}\\ \vdots & \vdots & \ddots & \vdots\\ -\mathbf{D}_N\mathbf{E}_i^{(N)} & -\mathbf{D}_N\mathbf{E}_i^{(N)} & \cdots & \mathbf{0}\end{bmatrix}.$$

Observe that recursion (4.4.3) is an Lth order difference equation. Because of its linearity, sequence $\{\mathbf{x}(t)\}$ is convergent from arbitrary initial vectors $\mathbf{x}(0),\mathbf{x}(1),\ldots,\mathbf{x}(L-1)$ if and only if all solutions of the nonlinear eigenvalue problem

$$\det\left(\lambda^L\mathbf{I}-\sum_{i=1}^{L}\mathbf{H}_i\lambda^{L-i}\right)=0 \tag{4.4.4}$$

are inside the unit circle. It is well known from matrix theory, that (4.4.4) is equivalent to the usual eigenvalue problem of matrix

$$\mathbf{H}_E=\begin{bmatrix}\mathbf{H}_1 & \mathbf{H}_2 & \mathbf{H}_3 & \cdots & \mathbf{H}_{L-1} & \mathbf{H}_L\\ \mathbf{I} & & & & & \\ & \mathbf{I} & & & & \\ & & \mathbf{I} & & & \\ & & & \ddots & & \\ & & & & \mathbf{I} & \mathbf{0}\end{bmatrix}. \tag{4.4.5}$$

Thus we have the following-

Theorem 4.4.1. Starting from arbitrary initial vectors $\mathbf{x}(0),\ldots,\mathbf{x}(L-1)$ sequence (4.4.3) converges to the equilibrium point of the multiproduct oligopoly game if and only if all eigenvalues of matrix $\mathbf{H}_E$ are inside the unit circle.

An important stability condition is given in the next theorem, which is easy to apply in practical cases.

Theorem 4.4.2. Assume that $\sum_{i=1}^{L}\|\mathbf{H}_i\|<1$ with some matrix norm. Then the equilibrium is globally asymptotically stable with respect to process (4.4.3).

Proof. If λ is an eigenvalue of $\mathbf{H}_E$, then the eigenvalue equation implies that

$$\mathbf{H}_1\mathbf{u}_1+\mathbf{H}_2\mathbf{u}_2+\cdots+\mathbf{H}_L\mathbf{u}_L=\lambda\mathbf{u}_1,$$
$$\mathbf{u}_i=\lambda\mathbf{u}_{i+1}\quad(1\le i\le L-1).$$

Repeated application of the second equation shows that for i=1,...,L-1, $\mathbf{u}_i = \lambda^{L-i}\mathbf{u}_L$, and $\mathbf{u}_L \neq \mathbf{0}$. By substituting these relations into the first equation, a nonlinear eigenvalue problem

$$\left(\lambda^L \mathbf{I} - \lambda^{L-1}\mathbf{H}_1 - \cdots - \lambda \mathbf{H}_{L-1} - \mathbf{H}_L\right)\mathbf{u}_L = \mathbf{0}$$

is obtained which is therefore equivalent to the eigenvalue problem of matrix $\mathbf{H}_E$. From this equation we have

$$|\lambda|^L \|\mathbf{u}_L\| \leq \sum_{i=1}^{L} |\lambda|^{L-i} \|\mathbf{H}_i\| \cdot \|\mathbf{u}_L\|.$$

Assume that $|\lambda| \geq 1$, then the above inequality implies that

$$|\lambda|^L \leq \sum_{i=1}^{L} |\lambda|^{L-i} \|\mathbf{H}_i\| \leq |\lambda|^{L-1} \sum_{i=1}^{L} \|\mathbf{H}_i\| < |\lambda|^{L-1},$$

which implies that $|\lambda| < 1$. This is a contradiction. □

Corollary. Select the block-row norm for each matrix $\mathbf{H}_i$. Then we have the following sufficient conditions for the global asymptotic stability of process (4.4.3):

$$\sum_{i=1}^{L} \max_k \left\|\mathbf{D}_k \mathbf{E}_i^{(k)}\right\| < \frac{1}{N-1}. \tag{4.4.6}$$

By selecting the block-column norms for each matrix $\mathbf{H}_i$, the modified stability criterion

$$\sum_{i=1}^{L} \max_k \sum_{l \neq k} \left\|\mathbf{D}_l \mathbf{E}_i^{(l)}\right\| < 1 \tag{4.4.7}$$

is obtained.

Remark. Note that expectations à la Cournot are obtained if one selects L=1 and $\mathbf{E}_1^{(k)} = \mathbf{I}$ for all k. In this case relations (4.4.6) and (4.1.11) coincide, and (4.4.7) reduces to (4.1.12).

An interesting special case is discussed next, which is based on

Lemma 4.4.1. Consider the quadratic equation

$$\lambda^2 + a\lambda + b = 0$$

with real a and b. The roots of this equation are inside the unit circle if and only if the following inequalities hold:

$$\begin{aligned} &b < 1; \\ &a + b + 1 > 0; \\ &-a + b + 1 > 0. \end{aligned} \tag{4.4.8}$$

Proof. We consider two cases.

(i) If $a^2 - 4b \geq 0$, then the real roots are

$$\lambda_{12} = \frac{-a \pm \sqrt{a^2 - 4b}}{2}.$$

They are inside the unit circle if and only if

$$\frac{-a + \sqrt{a^2 - 4b}}{2} < 1 \text{ and } \frac{-a - \sqrt{a^2 - 4b}}{2} > -1.$$

Simple calculation shows that these relations hold if and only if the second and third inequalities of (4.4.8) are true.

(ii) If $a^2 - 4b < 0$, then there are two complex roots

$$\lambda_{12} = \frac{-a \pm i\sqrt{4b - a^2}}{2},$$

which are inside the unit circle if and only if

$$\left(-\frac{a}{2}\right)^2 + \frac{4b - a^2}{4} = b < 1.$$

Hence the lemma is proven. □

Theorem 4.4.3. Assume that for all k, $\mathbf{B}_k = \mathbf{0}$, and all eigenvalues of $\mathbf{A}^{-1}\mathbf{A}^T$ are real, furthermore $L = 2$ with $\mathbf{E}_1^{(k)} = \alpha\mathbf{I}$ and $\mathbf{E}_2^{(k)} = (1-\alpha)\mathbf{I}$ for all k. Then the equilibrium is globally asymptotically stable with respect to process (4.4.3) if and only if

$$-1/2 < \alpha < 3/2 \quad (\text{for } N = 2);$$

$$\frac{N-3}{N-1} < \alpha < \frac{1}{2} \cdot \frac{N+1}{N-1} \quad (\text{for } 2 < N < 7).$$

For $N \geq 7$ no such α exists.

Proof. Note first that in this case

$$\mathbf{H}_1 = \begin{bmatrix} \mathbf{0} & -\alpha\mathbf{D} & \cdots & -\alpha\mathbf{D} \\ -\alpha\mathbf{D} & \mathbf{0} & \cdots & -\alpha\mathbf{D} \\ \vdots & \vdots & \ddots & \vdots \\ -\alpha\mathbf{D} & -\alpha\mathbf{D} & \cdots & \mathbf{0} \end{bmatrix} = \alpha\mathbf{H}_E^*,$$

and

$$\mathbf{H}_2 = \begin{bmatrix} \mathbf{0} & -(1-\alpha)\mathbf{D} & \cdots & -(1-\alpha)\mathbf{D} \\ -(1-\alpha)\mathbf{D} & \mathbf{0} & \cdots & -(1-\alpha)\mathbf{D} \\ \vdots & \vdots & \ddots & \vdots \\ -(1-\alpha)\mathbf{D} & -(1-\alpha)\mathbf{D} & \cdots & \mathbf{0} \end{bmatrix} = (1-\alpha)\mathbf{H}_E^*$$

with $\mathbf{H}_E^* = -(\mathbf{1}-\mathbf{I}) \otimes \mathbf{D}$. Since the eigenvalues of $\mathbf{D}$ equal 1/2 (see the proof of Theorem 4.1.3) and the eigenvalues of **1-I** are -1 and N-1, the eigenvalues of $\mathbf{H}_E^*$ are equal to 1/2 and (1-N)/2. The triangular factorization of matrix $\mathbf{H}_E^*$ shows that in this case the nonlinear eigenvalue problem

$$\left(\lambda^2\mathbf{I} - \lambda\mathbf{H}_1 - \mathbf{H}_2\right)\mathbf{u} = \mathbf{0}$$

is equivalent to the pair of quadratic equations

$$\lambda^2 - \frac{\alpha}{2}\lambda - \frac{1-\alpha}{2} = 0 \tag{4.4.9}$$

and

$$\lambda^2 - \frac{\alpha(1-N)}{2}\lambda - \frac{(1-\alpha)(1-N)}{2} = 0. \tag{4.4.10}$$

The application of Lemma 4.4.1 and simple calculation imply the assertion. □

Remark. In the special case of α=1 extrapolative expectations coincide with expectations à la Cournot. Note that α=1 satisfies the conditions of the theorem if and only if N=2, which shows that this theorem is also a straightforward generalization of the famous result of Theocharis (1959).

4.5 Oligopoly with Market Saturation

A dynamic multiproduct oligopoly model will be examined with discrete time scale under the additional assumption that the inverse demand function depends not only on the present output of the industry but also on the saturation level of the market. Our basic model can be formulated as follows. Using the same notation as before, at each time period $t \geq 0$, the profit of firm k is given as

$$\mathbf{x}_k^T(t)\mathbf{p}(\mathbf{f}(t)) - C_k(\mathbf{x}_k(t)), \tag{4.5.1}$$

where it is assumed that the saturation level **f** follows the recursion

$$\mathbf{f}(t) = F(\mathbf{f}(t-1), \mathbf{s}(t)), \tag{4.5.2}$$

where $\mathbf{s}(t) = \sum_{k=1}^{N} \mathbf{x}_k(t)$. Since at time period t no complete information on the simultaneous outputs of the rivals is available to firm k, it is also assumed that at each time period t, each firm k forms expectation $\mathbf{s}_k^E(t)$ on the simultaneous output of the rest of the industry. Hence at time period t the expected profit of firm k is as follows:

$$\mathbf{x}_k^T\mathbf{p}\left(F\left(\mathbf{f}(t-1), \mathbf{s}_k^E(t) + \mathbf{x}_k\right)\right) - C_k(\mathbf{x}_k).$$

Assuming a unique optimizer, the output of firm k in time period t is determined by the relation

$$\mathbf{x}_k(t) = \arg\max_{\mathbf{x}_k}\left\{\mathbf{x}_k^T\mathbf{p}\left(F\left(\mathbf{f}(t-1), \mathbf{s}_k^E(t) + \mathbf{x}_k\right)\right) - C_k(\mathbf{x}_k)\right\}, \tag{4.5.3}$$

where the right hand side depends on $\mathbf{f}(t-1)$ and $\mathbf{s}_k^E(t)$. It is also assumed that the expectations $\mathbf{s}_k^E$ of the firms are formed by the dynamic rules:

$$\mathbf{s}_k^E(t) = \mathbf{S}_k\left(\mathbf{s}_k^E(t-1), \mathbf{s}_k^E(t-2), \ldots, \mathbf{s}_k(t-1), \mathbf{s}_k(t-2), \ldots\right), \tag{4.5.4}$$

where $\mathbf{s}_k = \sum_{l \neq k} \mathbf{x}_l$.

Equations (4.5.2), (4.5.3) and (4.5.4) form a discrete dynamic system. In addition to the assumptions given at the beginning of this chapter, assume that

(E) Function F is linear, that is, the recursion of the saturation level is given as

$$\mathbf{f}(t) = \mathbf{C}\mathbf{f}(t-1) + \mathbf{s}(t),$$

where $\mathbf{C}$ is a constant matrix.

Assuming interior optimum in (4.5.3), and expectations *à la Cournot*, the profit of firm k at time period t can be given as

$$\mathbf{x}_k^T\left[\mathbf{A}\left(\mathbf{C}\mathbf{f}(t-1) + \sum_{l\neq k}\mathbf{x}_l(t-1) + x_k\right) + \mathbf{b}\right] - \left(\mathbf{x}_k^T\mathbf{B}_k\mathbf{x}_k + \mathbf{b}_k^T\mathbf{x}_k + c_k\right).$$

Assuming interior optimum, equation (4.5.3) reduces to the following:

$$\mathbf{x}_k(t) = -\mathbf{D}_k\left(\mathbf{C}\mathbf{f}(t-1) + \sum_{l\neq k}\mathbf{x}_l(t-1)\right) + \boldsymbol{\alpha}_k \tag{4.5.5}$$

where $\boldsymbol{\alpha}_k$ is a constant vector and $\mathbf{D}_k = \left(\mathbf{A} + \mathbf{A}^T - \mathbf{B}_k - \mathbf{B}_k^T\right)^{-1}\mathbf{A}$, and from assumption (E) we have

$$\begin{aligned}\mathbf{f}(t) &= \mathbf{C}\mathbf{f}(t-1) + \sum_{k=1}^{N}\mathbf{x}_k(t)\\ &= \left(\mathbf{C} - \sum_{k=1}^{N}\mathbf{D}_k\mathbf{C}\right)\mathbf{f}(t-1) - \sum_{k=1}^{N}\mathbf{D}_k\sum_{l\neq k}\mathbf{x}_l(t-1) + \boldsymbol{\beta}_k\end{aligned} \tag{4.5.6}$$

where $\boldsymbol{\beta}_k$ is a constant vector.

By introducing the notation $\mathbf{x} = (\mathbf{x}_k)_{k=1}^{N}$ we have the dynamic system

$$\begin{pmatrix}\mathbf{x}(t)\\ \mathbf{f}(t)\end{pmatrix} = \mathbf{H}_S \cdot \begin{pmatrix}\mathbf{x}(t-1)\\ \mathbf{f}(t-1)\end{pmatrix} + \boldsymbol{\gamma}, \tag{4.5.7}$$

where $\boldsymbol{\gamma}$ is a constant vector and now

$$\mathbf{H}_S = \begin{pmatrix} \mathbf{0} & -\mathbf{D}_1 & \cdots & -\mathbf{D}_1 & -\mathbf{D}_1\mathbf{C}\\ -\mathbf{D}_2 & \mathbf{0} & \cdots & -\mathbf{D}_2 & -\mathbf{D}_2\mathbf{C}\\ \vdots & \vdots & \ddots & \vdots & \vdots\\ -\mathbf{D}_N & -\mathbf{D}_N & \cdots & \mathbf{0} & -\mathbf{D}_N\mathbf{C}\\ -\sum_{l\neq 1}\mathbf{D}_l & -\sum_{l\neq 2}\mathbf{D}_l & \cdots & -\sum_{l\neq N}\mathbf{D}_l & \mathbf{C} - \sum_k \mathbf{D}_k\mathbf{C} \end{pmatrix}.$$

Hence this system is globally asymptotically stable if and only if all eigenvalues of matrix $\mathbf{H}_S$ are inside the unit circle.

Before presenting particular stability conditions note that the model without market saturation corresponds to the special case of $\mathbf{C}=\mathbf{0}$, and in this case the last block-column of matrix $\mathbf{H}_S$ is zero. Therefore the nonzero eigenvalues of $\mathbf{H}_S$ coincide with the eigenvalues of the corresponding coefficient matrix $\mathbf{H}_c$ of the standard dynamic multiproduct oligopoly under Cournot expectations, which case was discussed earlier in Section 4.1.

The eigenvalue problem of $\mathbf{H}_S$ can be rewritten as

$$\mathbf{H}_c\mathbf{u} + \mathbf{R}\mathbf{v} = \lambda\mathbf{u} \qquad (4.5.8)$$

$$\mathbf{E}\mathbf{H}_c\mathbf{u} + (\mathbf{C} + \mathbf{E}\mathbf{R})\mathbf{v} = \lambda\mathbf{v} \qquad (4.5.9)$$

with

$$\mathbf{R} = \begin{pmatrix} -\mathbf{D}_1\mathbf{C} \\ -\mathbf{D}_2\mathbf{C} \\ \vdots \\ -\mathbf{D}_N\mathbf{C} \end{pmatrix} \text{ and } \mathbf{E} = (\mathbf{I}, \ldots, \mathbf{I}).$$

By premultiplying (4.5.8) by matrix $\mathbf{E}$ and subtracting it from (4.5.9) the following relation is obtained:

$$\mathbf{C}\mathbf{v} = \lambda(\mathbf{v} - \mathbf{E}\mathbf{u}),$$

that is,

$$(\mathbf{C} - \lambda\mathbf{I})\mathbf{v} = -\lambda\mathbf{E}\mathbf{u}.$$

Assume next that

(F) All eigenvalues of $\mathbf{C}$ are inside the unit circle.

Then we may assume that $\mathbf{C} - \lambda\mathbf{I}$ is nonsingular, and so

$$\mathbf{v} = -\lambda(\mathbf{C} - \lambda\mathbf{I})^{-1}\mathbf{E}\mathbf{u}.$$

By substituting this relation into (4.5.8) we have

$$\left(\mathbf{H}_c - \lambda\mathbf{R}(\mathbf{C} - \lambda\mathbf{I})^{-1}\mathbf{E} - \lambda\mathbf{I}\right)\mathbf{u} = \mathbf{0},$$

which has nontrivial solution if and only if

$$\det\left(\mathbf{H}_c - \lambda\mathbf{R}(\mathbf{C}-\lambda\mathbf{I})^{-1}\mathbf{E} - \lambda\mathbf{I}\right) = 0. \tag{4.5.10}$$

Thus, we proved the following result.

Theorem 4.5.1. Under conditions (A) - (F), system (4.5.7) is globally asymptotically stable if and only if all solutions of the nonlinear eigenvalue problem (4.5.10) are inside the unit circle.

Remark 1. The dimension of problem (4.5.10) is smaller by M than the size of matrix $\mathbf{H}_S$.

Remark 2. If $\mathbf{C}=\mathbf{0}$, then the usual multiproduct Cournot model is obtained. In that case (4.5.10) is the eigenvalue problem of matrix $\mathbf{H}_c$ as it should be.

Another approach to investigate the eigenvalues of the coefficient matrix $\mathbf{H}_S$ is based on writing its eigenvalue equation in the following form:

$$-\mathbf{D}_k\sum_{l\neq k}\mathbf{u}_l - \mathbf{D}_k\mathbf{C}\mathbf{v} = \lambda\mathbf{u}_k \quad (k=1,2,\ldots,N). \tag{4.5.11}$$

$$-\sum_{k=1}^{N}\left(\sum_{l\neq k}\mathbf{D}_l\right)\mathbf{u}_k + \left(\mathbf{C} - \sum_{k=1}^{N}\mathbf{D}_k\mathbf{C}\right)\mathbf{v} = \lambda\mathbf{v}. \tag{4.5.12}$$

Adding equation (4.5.11) for all values of k gives equality

$$-\sum_{k=1}^{N}\left(\sum_{l\neq k}\mathbf{D}_l\right)\mathbf{u}_k - \left(\sum_{k=1}^{N}\mathbf{D}_k\mathbf{C}\right)\mathbf{v} = \lambda\sum_{k=1}^{N}\mathbf{u}_k,$$

and a simple comparison of this equation and (4.5.12) shows that

$$\mathbf{C}\mathbf{v} = \lambda\mathbf{v} - \lambda\sum_{k=1}^{N}\mathbf{u}_k. \tag{4.5.13}$$

From (4.5.11) we have

$$\mathbf{D}_k\sum_{l=1}^{N}\mathbf{u}_l + \mathbf{D}_k\mathbf{C}\mathbf{v} = (\mathbf{D}_k - \lambda\mathbf{I})\mathbf{u}_k. \tag{4.5.14}$$

Assume now that

(G) All eigenvalues of $\mathbf{D}_k$ are inside the unit circle.

Then we may assume that $(\mathbf{D}_k - \lambda\mathbf{I})^{-1}$ exists, and

$$\mathbf{u}_k = (\mathbf{D}_k - \lambda\mathbf{I})^{-1}\mathbf{D}_k\sum_{l=1}^{N}\mathbf{u}_l + (\mathbf{D}_k - \lambda\mathbf{I})^{-1}\mathbf{D}_k\mathbf{C}\mathbf{v}.$$

By adding this equation for all values of k we have an equation for the sum of vectors $\mathbf{u}_k$:

$$\sum_{k=1}^{N}\mathbf{u}_k = \sum_{k=1}^{N}(\mathbf{D}_k - \lambda\mathbf{I})^{-1}\mathbf{D}_k\left(\sum_{l=1}^{N}\mathbf{u}_l + \mathbf{C}\mathbf{v}\right).$$

Combining this equation and (4.5.13) we see that

$$\left[\left(\mathbf{I} - \sum_{k=1}^{N}(\mathbf{D}_k - \lambda\mathbf{I})^{-1}\mathbf{D}_k\right)\frac{1}{\lambda}(\mathbf{C} - \lambda\mathbf{I}) + \sum_{k=1}^{N}(\mathbf{D}_k - \lambda\mathbf{I})^{-1}\mathbf{D}_k\mathbf{C}\right]\mathbf{v} = \mathbf{0}$$

which has nontrivial solution if and only if

$$\det\left\{\left(\mathbf{I} - \sum_{k=1}^{N}(\mathbf{D}_k - \lambda\mathbf{I})^{-1}\mathbf{D}_k\right)(\mathbf{C} - \lambda\mathbf{I}) + \lambda\sum_{k=1}^{N}(\mathbf{D}_k - \lambda\mathbf{I})^{-1}\mathbf{D}_k\mathbf{C}\right\} = 0. \qquad (4.5.15)$$

Thus, we have the following result.

Theorem 4.5.2. Under conditions (A) - (E) and (G), system (4.5.7) is globally asymptotically stable if and only if all solutions of the nonlinear eigenvalue problem (4.5.15) are inside the unit circle.

Remark. Notice that the dimension of problem (4.5.15) is only M, which is much smaller than the size of matrix $\mathbf{H}_S$ or problem (4.5.10).

Consider next the special case when $\mathbf{B}_k = \mathbf{0}$ $(k = 1, 2, \ldots, N)$ and $\mathbf{A}=\mathbf{A}^T$. Then for all k, $\mathbf{D}_k = \frac{1}{2}\mathbf{I}$. In this special case, problem (4.5.15) can be rewritten as

$$\det\left(\left(1 - N\cdot\frac{\frac{1}{2}}{\frac{1}{2} - \lambda}\right)(\mathbf{C}\text{-}\lambda\mathbf{I}) + \lambda\cdot N\frac{\frac{1}{2}}{\frac{1}{2} - \lambda}\mathbf{C}\right) = 0$$

which is equivalent to equation

$$\det\left(\left(\frac{1-N}{2}-\lambda\right)(\mathbf{C}-\lambda\mathbf{I})+\frac{\lambda N}{2}\mathbf{C}\right)=0. \tag{4.5.16}$$

Let $\gamma_1,\gamma_2,\ldots,\gamma_M$ denote the eigenvalues of matrix **C**. Then the triangular form of **C** implies that (4.5.16) holds if and only if for i=1,2,...,M,

$$\left(\frac{1-N}{2}-\lambda\right)(\gamma_i-\lambda)+\frac{\lambda N}{2}\gamma_i=0.$$

This equation can be rewritten as

$$\lambda^2+\lambda\frac{N-1-2\gamma_i+N\gamma_i}{2}+\gamma_i\frac{1-N}{2}=0.$$

By using Lemma 4.4.1 we see that the roots of this equation are inside the unit circle if and only if

$$\frac{\gamma_i-\gamma_i N}{2}<1$$

and

$$\pm\frac{N+N\gamma_i-2\gamma_i-1}{2}+\frac{\gamma_i-\gamma_i N}{2}+1>0. \tag{4.5.17}$$

That is, if

$$-\frac{2}{N-1}<\gamma_i<\min\left\{\frac{3-N}{2N-3};N+1\right\}. \tag{4.5.18}$$

The feasible set of this relation is shown in Figure 4.5.1.

The case of a nonnegative diagonal matrix **C** has some interest from an economic point of view. It is easy to verify that (4.5.18) is satisfied with nonnegative γ_i only for N=2, and in this case all $\gamma_i\in[0,1)$ satisfy (4.5.18). Since **C**=**0** (and therefore $\gamma_i=0$) corresponds to classical Cournot expectations, this result gives a new generalization of the classical result of Theocharis (1959).

Assume next that the firms form expectations *adaptively* on the output of the rest of the industry:

$$\mathbf{s}_k^E(t)=\mathbf{M}_k\sum_{l\neq k}\mathbf{x}_l(t-1)+(\mathbf{I}-\mathbf{M}_k)\mathbf{s}_k^E(t-1), \tag{4.5.19}$$

where $\mathbf{M}_k$ is a constant (usually diagonal) matrix. Then by assuming again that

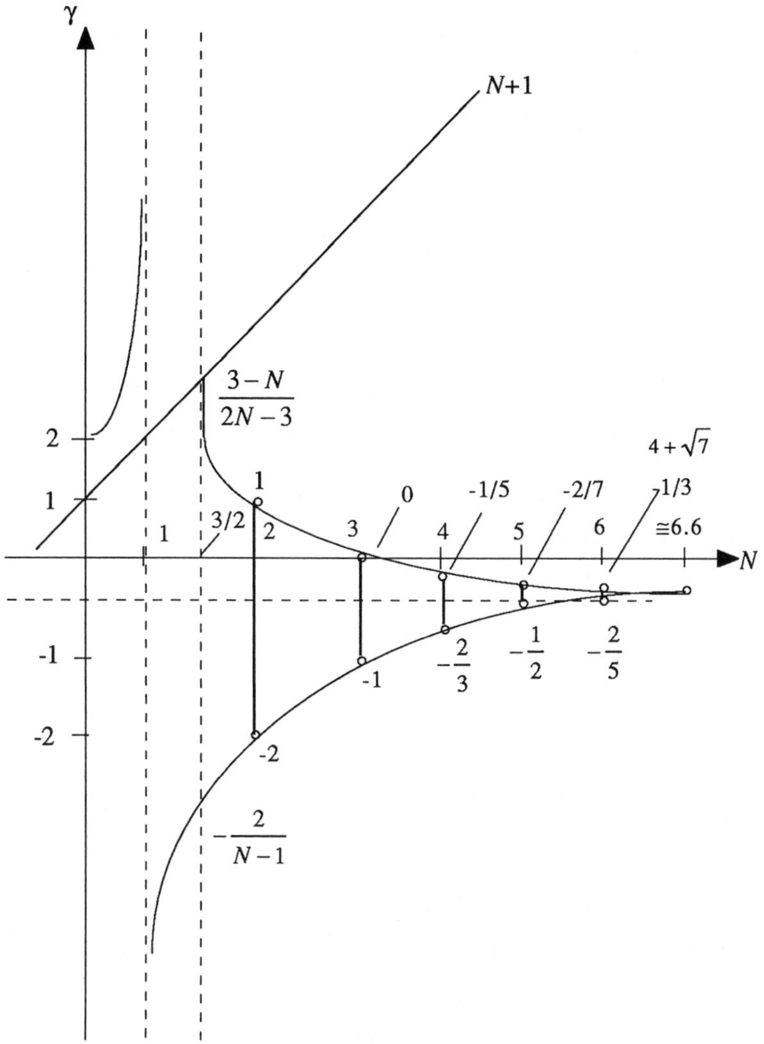

Fig. 4.5.1 Feasible set of relation (4.5.18)

the profit maximizing outputs are positive, equation (4.5.5) can be rewritten as

$$\mathbf{x}_k(t) = -\mathbf{D}_k\left(\mathbf{C}\mathbf{f}(t-1) + \mathbf{s}_k^E(t-1) + \mathbf{M}_k\left(\sum_{l\neq k}\mathbf{x}_l(t-1) - \mathbf{s}_k^E(t-1)\right)\right) + \boldsymbol{\alpha}_k. \quad (4.5.20)$$

Similarly, assumption (E) has the form

$$\mathbf{f}(t) = \mathbf{C}\mathbf{f}(t-1) + \sum_{k=1}^{N}\mathbf{x}_k(t) = \left(\mathbf{C} - \sum_{k=1}^{N}\mathbf{D}_k\mathbf{C}\right)\mathbf{f}(t-1)$$
$$-\sum_{k=1}^{N}\mathbf{D}_k(\mathbf{I}-\mathbf{M}_k)\mathbf{s}_k^E(t-1) - \sum_{k=1}^{N}\mathbf{D}_k\mathbf{M}_k\sum_{l\neq k}\mathbf{x}_l(t-1) + \boldsymbol{\beta}, \quad (4.5.21)$$

where $\boldsymbol{\beta}$ is a constant vector.

By combining the last three equations and introducing vectors $\mathbf{x} = (\mathbf{x}_k)_{k=1}^N$ and $\mathbf{s}^E = (\mathbf{s}_k^E)_{k=1}^N$, a linear difference equation is obtained:

$$\begin{pmatrix}\mathbf{x}(t)\\ \mathbf{s}^E(t)\\ \mathbf{f}(t)\end{pmatrix} = \mathbf{H}_{SA}\cdot\begin{pmatrix}\mathbf{x}(t-1)\\ \mathbf{s}^E(t-1)\\ \mathbf{f}(t-1)\end{pmatrix} + \boldsymbol{\gamma}, \quad (4.5.22)$$

where $\boldsymbol{\gamma}$ is a constant vector, and

$$\mathbf{H}_{SA} = \begin{pmatrix} -\mathbf{GM} & -\mathbf{GL} & -\mathbf{GK}\\ \mathbf{M} & \mathbf{L} & \mathbf{0}\\ -\mathbf{EGM} & -\mathbf{EGL} & \mathbf{C}-\mathbf{EGK}\end{pmatrix}$$

with

$$\mathbf{G} = \begin{pmatrix}\mathbf{D}_1 & & 0\\ & \ddots & \\ 0 & & \mathbf{D}_N\end{pmatrix},\ \mathbf{M} = \begin{pmatrix}\mathbf{0} & \mathbf{M}_1 & \cdots & \mathbf{M}_1\\ \mathbf{M}_2 & \mathbf{0} & \cdots & \mathbf{M}_2\\ \cdots & \cdots & \ddots & \cdots\\ \mathbf{M}_N & \mathbf{M}_N & \cdots & \mathbf{0}\end{pmatrix},$$

$$\mathbf{L} = \begin{pmatrix}\mathbf{I}-\mathbf{M}_1 & & \\ & \ddots & \\ & & \mathbf{I}-\mathbf{M}_N\end{pmatrix},\ \mathbf{K} = \begin{pmatrix}\mathbf{C}\\ \vdots\\ \mathbf{C}\end{pmatrix},\ \mathbf{E} = (\mathbf{I},\dots,\mathbf{I}).$$

Therefore system (4.5.22) is globally asymptotically stable if and only if all eigenvalues of $\mathbf{H}_{SA}$ are inside the unit circle. Similarly to the case discussed in the previous section, a large reduction in the size of the eigenvalue problem can be made, but the resulting eigenvalue problem becomes nonlinear. Consider therefore the eigenvalue problem of matrix $\mathbf{H}_{SA}$:

$$\begin{aligned} -\mathbf{GMu} - \mathbf{GLv} - \mathbf{GKw} &= \lambda\mathbf{u} \\ \mathbf{Mu} + \mathbf{Lv} &= \lambda\mathbf{v} \\ -\mathbf{EGMu} - \mathbf{EGLv} + (\mathbf{C} - \mathbf{EGK})\mathbf{w} &= \lambda\mathbf{w}. \end{aligned} \tag{4.5.23}$$

By adding the **G**-multiple of the second equation of (4.5.23) to the first equation we have

$$\mathbf{GKw} = \lambda(-\mathbf{Gv} - \mathbf{u}), \tag{4.5.24}$$

and by subtracting the **E**-multiple of the first equation from the third equation of (4.5.23) we obtain the relation

$$\mathbf{Cw} = \lambda(\mathbf{w} - \mathbf{Eu}). \tag{4.5.25}$$

If λ is an eigenvalue of $\mathbf{C}$, then it is inside the unit circle by assumption (F), otherwise we know that

$$\mathbf{w} = -\lambda(\mathbf{C} - \lambda\mathbf{I})^{-1}\mathbf{Eu}.$$

Substitute this equation into (4.5.24) to derive relation

$$\lambda\mathbf{Gv} = \left[\mathbf{GK}\lambda(\mathbf{C} - \lambda\mathbf{I})^{-1}\mathbf{E} - \lambda\mathbf{I}\right]\mathbf{u}.$$

If $\lambda=0$, then it is inside the unit circle. Assuming that $\lambda\neq 0$ and all matrices $\mathbf{D}_k$ are nonsingular, we have

$$\mathbf{v} = \left(\mathbf{K}(\mathbf{C} - \lambda\mathbf{I})^{-1}\mathbf{E} - \mathbf{G}^{-1}\right)\mathbf{u}.$$

By substituting this equality into the second equation of (4.5.23), the following nonlinear eigenvalue problem is obtained:

$$\left[\mathbf{MG} + (\mathbf{L} - \lambda\mathbf{I})\mathbf{K}(\mathbf{C} - \lambda\mathbf{I})^{-1}\mathbf{EG} - \mathbf{L} + \lambda\mathbf{I}\right]\tilde{\mathbf{u}} = \mathbf{0} \tag{4.5.26}$$

with $\tilde{\mathbf{u}} = \mathbf{G}^{-1}\mathbf{u}$. This equation has nontrivial solution if and only if

$$\det\left[\mathbf{MG} + (\mathbf{L} - \lambda\mathbf{I})\mathbf{K}(\mathbf{C} - \lambda\mathbf{I})^{-1}\mathbf{EG} - \mathbf{L} + \lambda\mathbf{I}\right] = 0. \tag{4.5.27}$$

Thus we have proven the following

Theorem 4.5.3. Assume that conditions (A) - (F) hold, and $\mathbf{D}_k$ is nonsingular for k=1,2,...,N. Then system (4.5.22) is globally asymptotically stable if and only if all solutions of the nonlinear eigenvalue problem (4.5.26) are inside the unit circle.

Remark 1. The size of problem (4.5.26) is less than half of the dimension of matrix $\mathbf{H}_{SA}$, which makes a large reduction in the size of the eigenvalue problem which has to be examined in order to verify stability.

Remark 2. If **C**=**0**, then **K**=**0**, and therefore problem (4.5.26) coincides with the usual eigenvalue problem of matrix –**MG**+**L**. This special case corresponds to the multiproduct Cournot market with adaptive expectations, and in this case the above result reduces to Theorem 4.2.2.

Consider next the special case when $\mathbf{A} = \mathbf{A}^T$, $\mathbf{B}_k = \mathbf{0}$ $(k = 1,2,\dots,N)$. For the sake of simplicity assume in addition that $\mathbf{C} = \gamma\mathbf{I}$ $(0 \le \gamma < 1)$ and for all k, $\mathbf{M}_k = \alpha\mathbf{I}$ $(0 < \alpha \le 1)$. Then $\mathbf{D}_k = \frac{1}{2}\mathbf{I}$ and therefore $\mathbf{G} = \frac{1}{2}\mathbf{I}$. Similarly, $\mathbf{L} = (1-\alpha)\mathbf{I}$, and equation (4.5.27) can be rewritten as follows

$$\begin{aligned}&\det\left(\frac{1}{2}\mathbf{M} + \frac{1-\alpha-\lambda}{2(\gamma-\lambda)}\mathbf{KE} + (\lambda - 1 + \alpha)\mathbf{I}\right)\\ &= \det\left(\left(\frac{\alpha}{2} + \frac{1-\alpha-\lambda}{2(\gamma-\lambda)}\gamma\right)\mathbf{1}\otimes\mathbf{I} + \left(\lambda - 1 + \frac{\alpha}{2}\right)\mathbf{I}\right) = 0\end{aligned} \tag{4.5.28}$$

since

$$\mathbf{M} = \begin{pmatrix} \mathbf{0} & \alpha\mathbf{I} & \cdots & \alpha\mathbf{I} \\ \alpha\mathbf{I} & \mathbf{0} & \cdots & \alpha\mathbf{I} \\ \vdots & \vdots & & \vdots \\ \alpha\mathbf{I} & \alpha\mathbf{I} & \cdots & \mathbf{0} \end{pmatrix} = (\alpha\mathbf{1})\otimes\mathbf{I} - \alpha\mathbf{I}$$

and

$$\mathbf{KE} = \begin{pmatrix} \gamma\mathbf{I} & \gamma\mathbf{I} & \cdots & \gamma\mathbf{I} \\ \gamma\mathbf{I} & \gamma\mathbf{I} & \cdots & \gamma\mathbf{I} \\ \vdots & \vdots & & \vdots \\ \gamma\mathbf{I} & \gamma\mathbf{I} & \cdots & \gamma\mathbf{I} \end{pmatrix} = (\gamma\mathbf{1})\otimes\mathbf{I}.$$

From this equation we see that $-\left(\lambda-1+\frac{\alpha}{2}\right)$ is the eigenvalue of matrix $\left(\frac{\alpha}{2}+\frac{1-\alpha-\lambda}{2(\gamma-\lambda)}\gamma\right)\mathbf{1}\otimes\mathbf{I}$. By recalling the fact that the eigenvalues of $\mathbf{1}$ are N and 0 (see Section 4.1) and using Lemma 4.1.1 this observation can be mathematically formulated as equations

$$\left(\frac{\alpha}{2}+\frac{1-\alpha-\lambda}{2(\gamma-\lambda)}\gamma\right)\cdot 0=-\left(\lambda-1+\frac{\alpha}{2}\right)$$

and

$$\left(\frac{\alpha}{2}+\frac{1-\alpha-\lambda}{2(\gamma-\lambda)}\gamma\right)\cdot N=-\left(\lambda-1+\frac{\alpha}{2}\right).$$

The first equation implies that $\lambda=1-\frac{\alpha}{2}$, which is inside the unit circle. The second equation can be rewritten as

$$\lambda^2+\lambda\frac{\alpha N+\alpha+\gamma N-2\gamma-2}{2}+\frac{2\gamma-\alpha\gamma-\gamma N}{2}=0.$$

Lemma 4.4.1 implies that the roots of this equation are inside the unit circle if and only if

$$\frac{2\gamma-\alpha\gamma-\gamma N}{2}<1,$$
$$\pm\frac{\alpha N+\alpha+\gamma N-2\gamma-2}{2}+\frac{2\gamma-\alpha\gamma-\gamma N}{2}+1>0.$$

These conditions are equivalent to the inequalities

$$\begin{aligned}&\gamma(2-\alpha-N)<2,\\&\alpha(-N-1+\gamma)<0,\end{aligned}\tag{4.5.29}$$

and

$$\alpha(N+1+\gamma)<4-2\gamma N+4\gamma.$$

The first two inequalities are always satisfied under our assumptions, and the third relation holds if and only if

$$\alpha < \frac{4 - 2\gamma N + 4\gamma}{N + 1 + \gamma}. \tag{4.5.30}$$

It is interesting to note that if $\alpha=1$ (that is, when expectations à la Cournot are assumed) inequalities (4.5.29) reduce to (4.5.17) as they should. It is also worthwhile to mention that the case of $\alpha=1$ and $\gamma=0$ is equivalent to multiproduct oligopolies without market saturation and with Cournot expectations, and in this case inequality (4.5.30) is satisfied if and only if $N=2$. Hence the above result is a further generalization of the classical stability theorem of Theocharis (1959). Figure 4.5.2 illustrates the feasible set of inequality (4.5.30).

Notice that $N=2$ is the only case, when for all $\alpha \in [0,1]$ and $0 \le \gamma < 1$ stability occurs, and with increasing value of N the stability region becomes smaller. In addition, with fixed N and increasing γ, the stability region for α also decreases, that is, α must be selected from an interval with less and less upper bound. This property coincides with the stability condition of multiproduct oligopolies without market saturation, when the upper bound for α decreases with increasing value of N. We can explain this analogy by considering the market saturation as buying from fictitious firms: larger value of the saturation coefficient γ corresponds to larger number of fictitious firms.

4.6 Quasioptimal Output Selections

Assume again that all conditions being presented at the beginning of this chapter hold, and assume first that each firm forms *expectations à la Cournot* on the output of the rest of the industry. From equation (4.1.2) we know that at time period t, the expected profit maximizing output is given as

$$\mathbf{x}_k^*(t) = -\left[\mathbf{A} + \mathbf{A}^T - \mathbf{B}_k - \mathbf{B}_k^T\right]^{-1} \mathbf{A} \sum_{l \neq k} \mathbf{x}_l(t-1) + \boldsymbol{\alpha}_k \tag{4.6.1}$$

where $\boldsymbol{\alpha}_k$ is a constant vector. If $\|\mathbf{x}_k^*(t) - \mathbf{x}_k(t-1)\|$ is large then firm k has to make a large adjustment in his output, which is sometimes hard to manage or even impossible. In such cases we assume that firm k selects his output $\mathbf{x}_k(t)$ as a point between $\mathbf{x}_k(t-1)$ and $\mathbf{x}_k^*(t)$:

$$\mathbf{x}_k(t) = \left(\mathbf{I} - \overline{\mathbf{M}}_k\right)\mathbf{x}_k(t-1) + \overline{\mathbf{M}}_k \mathbf{x}_k^*(t), \tag{4.6.2}$$

where $\overline{\mathbf{M}}_k$ is a constant (usually diagonal) matrix.

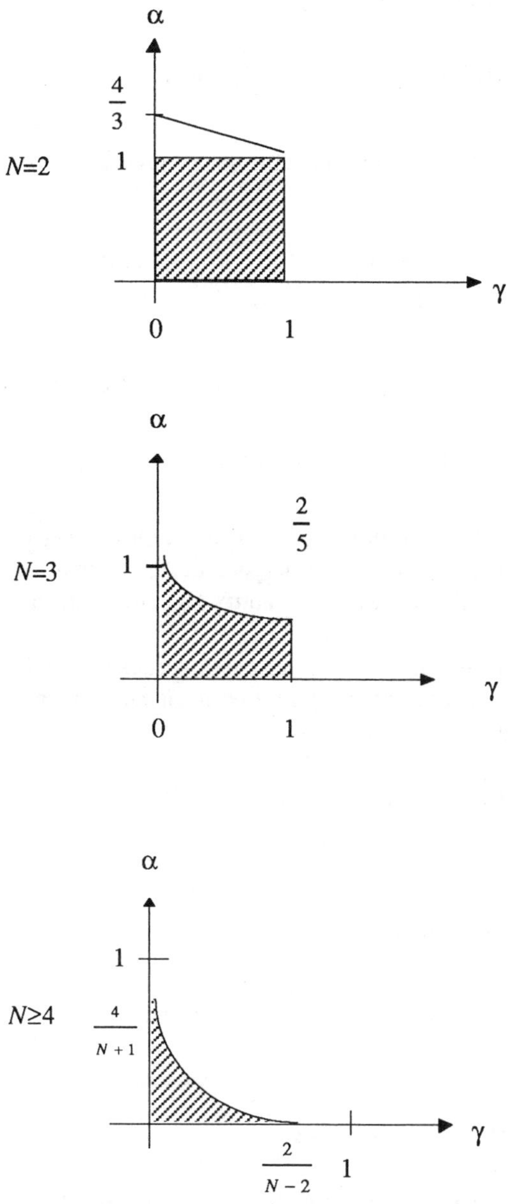

Fig. 4.6.1 Feasible set of relation (4.5.30)

Combining equations (4.6.1) and (4.6.2) we have

$$\mathbf{x}_k(t) = \left(\mathbf{I} - \overline{\mathbf{M}}_k\right)\mathbf{x}_k(t-1) - \overline{\mathbf{M}}_k\left(\mathbf{A} + \mathbf{A}^T - \mathbf{B}_k - \mathbf{B}_k^T\right)^{-1}\mathbf{A}\sum_{l\neq k}\mathbf{x}_l(t-1) + \boldsymbol{\alpha}_k \qquad (4.6.3)$$

which is a discrete dynamic system with state variables $\mathbf{x}_k$(t) (k=1,2,...,N) and coefficient matrix

$$\mathbf{H}_{QC} = \begin{pmatrix} \mathbf{I} - \overline{\mathbf{M}}_1 & -\overline{\mathbf{M}}_1\mathbf{D}_1 & \cdots & -\overline{\mathbf{M}}_1\mathbf{D}_1 \\ -\overline{\mathbf{M}}_2\mathbf{D}_2 & \mathbf{I} - \overline{\mathbf{M}}_2 & \cdots & -\overline{\mathbf{M}}_2\mathbf{D}_2 \\ \vdots & \vdots & & \vdots \\ -\overline{\mathbf{M}}_N\mathbf{D}_N & -\overline{\mathbf{M}}_N\mathbf{D}_N & \cdots & \mathbf{I} - \overline{\mathbf{M}}_N \end{pmatrix}$$

where $\mathbf{D}_k = \left(\mathbf{A} + \mathbf{A}^T - \mathbf{B}_k - \mathbf{B}_k^T\right)^{-1}\mathbf{A}$ as in Section 4.1.

Theorem 4.6.1. The equilibrium point of the multiproduct oligopoly game is globally asymptotically stable with respect to the output adjustment process (4.6.2) if and only if all eigenvalues of matrix $\mathbf{H}_{QA}$ are inside the unit circle.

By using special matrix norms, easy to check sufficient stability conditions can be obtained. By selecting the block-row norm of $\mathbf{H}_{QC}$ we obtain the following sufficient condition:

$$\left\|\mathbf{I} - \overline{\mathbf{M}}_k\right\| + (N-1)\left\|\overline{\mathbf{M}}_k\mathbf{D}_k\right\| < 1 \quad (k = 1,2,...,N)$$

which holds if

$$\left\|\mathbf{I} - \overline{\mathbf{M}}_k\right\| + (N-1)\left\|\overline{\mathbf{M}}_k\right\| \cdot \left\|\mathbf{D}_k\right\| < 1,$$

that is, when

$$\left\|\mathbf{D}_k\right\| < \frac{1 - \left\|\mathbf{I} - \overline{\mathbf{M}}_k\right\|}{(N-1)\left\|\overline{\mathbf{M}}_k\right\|}. \qquad (4.6.4)$$

By selecting the block-column norm of $\mathbf{H}_{QC}$ we obtain the sufficient stability condition:

$$\left\|\mathbf{I} - \overline{\mathbf{M}}_k\right\| + \sum_{l\neq k}\left\|\overline{\mathbf{M}}_l\mathbf{D}_l\right\| < 1$$

which holds if

$$\left\|\mathbf{I}-\overline{\mathbf{M}}_k\right\|+\sum_{l\neq k}\left\|\overline{\mathbf{M}}_l\right\|\cdot\left\|\mathbf{D}_l\right\|<1.$$

Notice that this inequality necessarily holds if

$$\left\|\mathbf{D}_l\right\|<\frac{1-\max_k\left\|\mathbf{I}-\overline{\mathbf{M}}_k\right\|}{(N-1)\left\|\overline{\mathbf{M}}_l\right\|}. \tag{4.6.5}$$

Consider next the eigenvalue problem of matrix $\mathbf{H}_{QC}$:

$$\left(\mathbf{I}-\overline{\mathbf{M}}_k\right)\mathbf{v}_k-\overline{\mathbf{M}}_k\mathbf{D}_k\sum_{l\neq k}\mathbf{v}_l=\lambda\mathbf{v}_k \quad (k=1,2,\ldots,N). \tag{4.6.6}$$

Let $\mathbf{v}=\sum_{k=1}^{N}\mathbf{v}_k$, then by rearranging the terms we have

$$-\overline{\mathbf{M}}_k\mathbf{D}_k\mathbf{v}+\left(\mathbf{I}-\overline{\mathbf{M}}_k+\overline{\mathbf{M}}_k\mathbf{D}_k-\lambda\mathbf{I}\right)\mathbf{v}_k=\mathbf{0}.$$

Assume that matrix $\left(\mathbf{I}-\overline{\mathbf{M}}_k+\overline{\mathbf{M}}_k\mathbf{D}_k\right)$ has eigenvalues only inside the unit circle, then any other eigenvalue of $\mathbf{H}_{QC}$ satisfies relation

$$\mathbf{v}_k=\left(\mathbf{I}+\overline{\mathbf{M}}_k\left(\mathbf{D}_k-\mathbf{I}\right)-\lambda\mathbf{I}\right)^{-1}\overline{\mathbf{M}}_k\mathbf{D}_k\mathbf{v}.$$

By adding this equation for k=1,2,...,N, we have

$$\mathbf{v}=\sum_{k=1}^{N}\left(\mathbf{I}+\overline{\mathbf{M}}_k\left(\mathbf{D}_k-\mathbf{I}\right)-\lambda\mathbf{I}\right)^{-1}\overline{\mathbf{M}}_k\mathbf{D}_k\mathbf{v}.$$

This equality implies the following result.

Theorem 4.6.2. Assume that all eigenvalues of matrix $\mathbf{I}-\overline{\mathbf{M}}_k+\overline{\mathbf{M}}_k\mathbf{D}_k$ are inside the unit circle. The process (4.6.3) is globally asymptotically stable if and only if all solutions of the nonlinear eigenvalue problem

$$\det\left(\sum_{k=1}^{N}\left(\mathbf{I}+\overline{\mathbf{M}}_k\left(\mathbf{D}_k-\mathbf{I}\right)-\lambda\mathbf{I}\right)^{-1}\overline{\mathbf{M}}_k\mathbf{D}_k-\mathbf{I}\right)=0 \tag{4.6.7}$$

are inside the unit circle.

Notice the analogy between matrix $\mathbf{H}_{QC}$ and $\mathbf{H}_A^{(1)}$ (given in equation (4.2.6)) in the case of adaptive expectations as well as between the nonlinear eigenvalue problems (4.2.9) and (4.6.7).

Consider next the special case when $\mathbf{A}=\mathbf{A}^T$, $\mathbf{B}_k=\mathbf{0}$, and $\overline{\mathbf{M}}_k$ is diagonal for all k. Since matrix $\mathbf{H}_{QC}$ formally coincides with $\mathbf{H}_A^{(1)}$, Theorem 2.4.5 also holds for this case.

Assume next that all firms form *adaptive expectations* on the output of the rest of the industry:

$$\mathbf{s}_k^E(t)=\mathbf{s}_k^E(t-1)+\mathbf{M}_k\cdot\left(\sum_{l\neq k}\mathbf{x}_l(t-1)-\mathbf{s}_k^E(t-1)\right) \tag{4.6.8}$$

where $\mathbf{M}_k$ is a constant matrix, which is usually assumed to be diagonal. The expected profit maximizing output of firm k at time period t is given by equation (4.2.4):

$$\mathbf{x}_k^*(t)=-\mathbf{D}_k\left(\mathbf{s}_k^E(t-1)+\mathbf{M}_k\left(\sum_{l\neq k}\mathbf{x}_l(t-1)-\mathbf{s}_k^E(t-1)\right)\right)+\boldsymbol{\alpha}_k$$

with some constant vector $\boldsymbol{\alpha}_k$. Assume again that firm k selects a point between $\mathbf{x}_k(t-1)$ and $\mathbf{x}_k^*(t)$:

$$\mathbf{x}_k(t)=\left(\mathbf{I}-\overline{\mathbf{M}}_k\right)\mathbf{x}_k(t-1)-\overline{\mathbf{M}}_k\mathbf{D}_k\left[\mathbf{s}_k^E(t-1)+\mathbf{M}_k\left(\sum_{l\neq k}\mathbf{x}_l(t-1)-\mathbf{s}_k^E(t-1)\right)\right]+\boldsymbol{\beta}_k \tag{4.6.9}$$

with some constant vector $\boldsymbol{\beta}_k$. Equations (4.6.8) and (4.6.9) form a discrete linear dynamic system with state variables $\mathbf{x}_k(t)$ and $\mathbf{s}_k^E(t)$ $(k=1,\dots,N)$. The coefficient matrix of this system has the form

$$\mathbf{H}_{QA}=\begin{pmatrix}\mathbf{H}_{11} & \mathbf{H}_{12}\\ \mathbf{H}_{21} & \mathbf{H}_{22}\end{pmatrix}$$

with

$$\mathbf{H}_{11}=\begin{pmatrix}\mathbf{I}-\overline{\mathbf{M}}_1 & -\overline{\mathbf{M}}_1\mathbf{D}_1\mathbf{M}_1 & \cdots & -\overline{\mathbf{M}}_1\mathbf{D}_1\mathbf{M}_1\\ -\overline{\mathbf{M}}_2\mathbf{D}_2\mathbf{M}_2 & \mathbf{I}-\overline{\mathbf{M}}_2 & \cdots & -\overline{\mathbf{M}}_2\mathbf{D}_2\mathbf{M}_2\\ \vdots & \vdots & & \vdots\\ -\overline{\mathbf{M}}_N\mathbf{D}_N\mathbf{M}_N & -\overline{\mathbf{M}}_N\mathbf{D}_N\mathbf{M}_N & \cdots & \mathbf{I}-\overline{\mathbf{M}}_N\end{pmatrix},$$

$$\mathbf{H}_{12} = \begin{pmatrix} -\overline{\mathbf{M}}_1\mathbf{D}_1(\mathbf{I}-\mathbf{M}_1) & & \\ & \ddots & \\ & & -\overline{\mathbf{M}}_N\mathbf{D}_N(\mathbf{I}-\mathbf{M}_N) \end{pmatrix},$$

$$\mathbf{H}_{21} = \begin{pmatrix} 0 & \mathbf{M}_1 & \cdots & \mathbf{M}_1 \\ \mathbf{M}_2 & 0 & \cdots & \mathbf{M}_2 \\ \vdots & \vdots & & \vdots \\ \mathbf{M}_N & \mathbf{M}_N & \cdots & \mathbf{0} \end{pmatrix},$$

and

$$\mathbf{H}_{22} = \begin{pmatrix} \mathbf{I}-\mathbf{M}_1 & & & \\ & \mathbf{I}-\mathbf{M}_2 & & \\ & & \ddots & \\ & & & \mathbf{I}-\mathbf{M}_N \end{pmatrix}.$$

Notice that the structure of matrix $\mathbf{H}_{QA}$ is analogous to that of matrix $\mathbf{H}_A$ given in equation (4.2.5) for adaptive expectations, and in the special case of $\mathbf{M}_k$=$\mathbf{I}$ (all k), matrix $\mathbf{H}_{QA}$ reduces to $\mathbf{H}_A$.

The above deviation implies the following result.

Theorem 4.6.3. The equilibrium point of system (4.6.8) - (4.6.9) is globally asymptotically stable if and only if all eigenvalues of $\mathbf{H}_{QA}$ are inside the unit circle.

Similarly to our earlier Theorem 4.2.2 we can reduce the dimension of the eigenvalue problem to be examined. The eigenvalue equation of matrix $\mathbf{H}_{QA}$ has the form:

$$\left(\mathbf{I}-\overline{\mathbf{M}}_k\right)\mathbf{u}_k - \overline{\mathbf{M}}_k\mathbf{D}_k\mathbf{M}_k \cdot \sum_{l\neq k}\mathbf{u}_l - \overline{\mathbf{M}}_k\mathbf{D}_k(\mathbf{I}-\mathbf{M}_k)\mathbf{v}_k = \lambda\mathbf{u}_k \tag{4.6.10}$$

$$\mathbf{M}_k\sum_{l\neq k}\mathbf{u}_l + (\mathbf{I}-\mathbf{M}_k)\mathbf{v}_k = \lambda\mathbf{v}_k. \tag{4.6.11}$$

Add the $\overline{\mathbf{M}}_k\mathbf{D}_k$-multiple of the second equation to the first equation to have

$$\left(\mathbf{I}-\overline{\mathbf{M}}_k\right)\mathbf{u}_k = \lambda\left(\mathbf{u}_k + \overline{\mathbf{M}}_k\mathbf{D}_k\mathbf{v}_k\right).$$

Assuming that all eigenvalues of matrix $\mathbf{I}-\overline{\mathbf{M}}_k$ are inside the unit circle we may assume that λ is not eigenvalue of $\mathbf{I}-\overline{\mathbf{M}}_k$, and therefore

$$\mathbf{u}_k = \lambda\left(\mathbf{I} - \overline{\mathbf{M}}_k - \lambda\mathbf{I}\right)^{-1}\overline{\mathbf{M}}_k\mathbf{D}_k\mathbf{v}_k.$$

Substituting this relation into (4.6.11) results in equation

$$\mathbf{M}_k \sum_{l \neq k} \lambda\left(\mathbf{I} - \overline{\mathbf{M}}_l - \lambda\mathbf{I}\right)^{-1}\overline{\mathbf{M}}_l\mathbf{D}_l\mathbf{v}_l + \left(\mathbf{I} - \mathbf{M}_k\right)\mathbf{v}_k = \lambda\mathbf{v}_k$$

which can be rewritten as a nonlinear eigenvalue problem

$$\det\begin{pmatrix} \mathbf{I} - \mathbf{M}_1 - \lambda\mathbf{I} & \lambda\mathbf{M}_1\left(\mathbf{I} - \overline{\mathbf{M}}_2 - \lambda\mathbf{I}\right)^{-1}\overline{\mathbf{M}}_2\mathbf{D}_2 & \cdots & \lambda\mathbf{M}_1\left(\mathbf{I} - \overline{\mathbf{M}}_N - \lambda\mathbf{I}\right)^{-1}\overline{\mathbf{M}}_N\mathbf{D}_N \\ \lambda\mathbf{M}_2\left(\mathbf{I} - \overline{\mathbf{M}}_1 - \lambda\mathbf{I}\right)^{-1}\overline{\mathbf{M}}_1\mathbf{D}_1 & \mathbf{I} - \mathbf{M}_2 - \lambda\mathbf{I} & \cdots & \lambda\mathbf{M}_2\left(\mathbf{I} - \overline{\mathbf{M}}_N - \lambda\mathbf{I}\right)^{-1}\overline{\mathbf{M}}_N\mathbf{D}_N \\ \vdots & \vdots & & \vdots \\ \lambda\mathbf{M}_N\left(\mathbf{I} - \overline{\mathbf{M}}_1 - \lambda\mathbf{I}\right)^{-1}\overline{\mathbf{M}}_1\mathbf{D}_1 & \lambda\mathbf{M}_N\left(\mathbf{I} - \overline{\mathbf{M}}_2 - \lambda\mathbf{I}\right)^{-1}\overline{\mathbf{M}}_2\mathbf{D}_2 & \cdots & \mathbf{I} - \mathbf{M}_N - \lambda\mathbf{I} \end{pmatrix} = 0. \tag{4.6.12}$$

Theorem 4.6.4. Assume that all eigenvalues of matrices $\mathbf{I} - \overline{\mathbf{M}}_k$ are inside the unit circle. The equilibrium of system (4.6.8) - (4.6.9) is globally asymptotically stable if and only if all solutions of the nonlinear eigenvalue problem (4.6.12) are inside the unit circle.

Remark. In the special case of $\overline{\mathbf{M}}_k = \mathbf{I}$, problem (4.6.12) reduces to the usual eigenvalue problem of matrix $\mathbf{H}_A^{(1)}$ (examined earlier in Theorem 4.2.2).

Consider finally the special case, when $\mathbf{A}=\mathbf{A}^T$, $\mathbf{B}_k=\mathbf{0}$, $\mathbf{M}_k = \mu\mathbf{I}$ and $\overline{\mathbf{M}}_k = \overline{\mu}\mathbf{I}$ for all k. Notice that $\mathbf{D}_k = \frac{1}{2}\mathbf{I}$, $\mathbf{I} - \mathbf{M}_k - \lambda\mathbf{I} = (1 - \mu - \lambda)\mathbf{I}$, and $\lambda\mathbf{M}_k\left(\mathbf{I} - \overline{\mathbf{M}}_l - \lambda\mathbf{I}\right)^{-1}\overline{\mathbf{M}}_l\mathbf{D}_l = \frac{\lambda\mu\overline{\mu}}{2(1-\overline{\mu}-\lambda)}\mathbf{I}$ for all k and l, and therefore problem (4.6.12) can be simplified as

$$\det\left(\frac{\lambda\mu\overline{\mu}}{2(1-\overline{\mu}-\lambda)}\mathbf{I} \otimes (\mathbf{1} - \mathbf{I}) + (1 - \mu - \lambda)\mathbf{I}\right) = 0.$$

That is, $\mu + \lambda - 1$ is an eigenvalue of matrix $\frac{\lambda\mu\overline{\mu}}{2(1-\overline{\mu}-\lambda)}\mathbf{I} \otimes (\mathbf{1} - \mathbf{I})$. Using Lemma 4.1.1 and the fact that the eigenvalues of $\mathbf{1}$ are 0 and N we have the following two equations:

$$\frac{\lambda\mu\overline{\mu}}{2(1-\overline{\mu}-\lambda)} \cdot (-1) = \mu + \lambda - 1$$

$$\frac{\lambda\mu\overline{\mu}}{2(1-\overline{\mu}-\lambda)} \cdot (N-1) = \mu + \lambda - 1.$$

These equations can be rewritten in the following form:

$$\lambda^2 - \lambda\frac{(\mu-2)(\bar{\mu}-2)}{2} + (\mu-1)(\bar{\mu}-1) = 0 \tag{4.6.13}$$

and

$$\lambda^2 + \lambda\frac{(N-1)\mu\bar{\mu}+2\mu+2\bar{\mu}-4}{2} + (\mu-1)(\bar{\mu}-1) = 0. \tag{4.6.14}$$

Using Lemma 4.4.1 we know that the roots of these quadratic polynomials are inside the unit circle if and only if

$$(\mu-1)(\bar{\mu}-1) < 1$$

$$\pm\frac{(\mu-2)(\bar{\mu}-2)}{2} + (\mu-1)(\bar{\mu}-1) + 1 > 0$$

$$\pm\frac{(N-1)\mu\bar{\mu}+2\mu+2\bar{\mu}-4}{2} + (\mu-1)(\bar{\mu}-1) + 1 > 0.$$

Simple calculation shows that these relations hold if and only if

$$0 < \mu\bar{\mu} < \mu + \bar{\mu} < \min\left\{\frac{3}{4}\mu\bar{\mu} + 2; \frac{3-N}{4}\mu\bar{\mu} + 2\right\}. \tag{4.6.15}$$

Notice that this inequality is symmetric in μ and $\bar{\mu}$, that is, it remains the same if μ and $\bar{\mu}$ are interchanged.

4.7 Production Adjustment Costs

For the sake of simplicity only the single-product case will be discussed, the multiproduct case can be examined in a similar manner. Assume that the price function is $p(s) = As + b$ with b>0 and A<0, and the cost function of each firm is linear: $C_k(x_k) = b_k x_k + c_k$ $(k = 1,2,\dots,N)$.

At $t = 0$, each firm selects an initial output $x_k(0)$, and at each later time period $t > 0$, they first predict the output of the rest of the industry adaptively by

$$s_k^E(t) = m_k \sum_{l \neq k} x_l(t-1) + (1-m_k)s_k^E(t-1) \tag{4.7.1}$$

with some constant $0 < m_k \le 1$, and then they select the profit maximizing output. In this model we assume that the expected profit of firm *k* is given as

$$x_k p\left(x_k + s_k^E(t)\right) - C_k(x_k) - K_k\left(x_k - x_k(t-1)\right)^2 \tag{4.7.2}$$

where the last term is the cost of changing output. Assume that $x_k(t) > 0$, then simple differentiation shows that $x_k(t)$ satisfies equation

$$b + A\left(x_k(t) + s_k^E(t)\right) + Ax_k(t) - b_k - 2K_k\left(x_k(t) - x_k(t-1)\right) = 0,$$

that is

$$x_k(t) = \frac{-K_k}{A+K_k} x_k(t-1) + \frac{A}{2(A+K_k)} s_k^E(t) - \frac{b-b_k}{2(A+K_k)}. \tag{4.7.3}$$

Since function (4.7.2) is strictly concave, $x_k(t)$ is the unique profit-maximizing output.

Combining this equation with (4.7.1) a discrete linear dynamic system is obtained with state variables $\left(x_k(t)\right)_{k=1}^N$ and $\left(s_k^E(t)\right)_{k=1}^N$ and coefficient matrix

$$\mathbf{H}_{AD} = \left(\begin{array}{cccc|cccc} \frac{K_1}{-A+K_1} & \frac{Am_1}{2(-A+K_1)} & \cdots & \frac{Am_1}{2(-A+K_1)} & \frac{A(1-m_1)}{2(-A+K_1)} & & & \\ \frac{Am_2}{2(-A+K_2)} & \frac{K_2}{-A+K_2} & \cdots & \frac{Am_2}{2(-A+K_2)} & & \frac{A(1-m_2)}{2(-A+K_2)} & & \\ \cdots & \cdots & \cdots & \cdots & & & \ddots & \\ \frac{Am_N}{2(-A+K_N)} & \frac{Am_N}{2(-A+K_N)} & \cdots & \frac{K_N}{-A+K_N} & & & & \frac{A(1-m_N)}{2(-A+K_N)} \\ \hline 0 & m_1 & \cdots & m_1 & 1-m_1 & & & \\ m_2 & 0 & \cdots & m_2 & & 1-m_2 & & \\ \cdots & \cdots & \cdots & \cdots & & & \ddots & \\ m_N & m_N & \cdots & 0 & & & & 1-m_N \end{array}\right).$$

Hence we have the following result.

Theorem 4.7.1. System (4.7.1) - (4.7.2) is globally asymptotically stable if and only if all eigenvalues of matrix $\mathbf{H}_{AD}$ are inside the unit circle.

The eigenvalue equation of matrix $\mathbf{H}_{AD}$ can be written as follows:

$$\begin{aligned} \frac{K_k}{-A+K_k} u_k + \frac{Am_k}{2(-A+K_k)} \sum_{l \ne k} u_l + \frac{A(1-m_k)}{2(-A+K_k)} v_k &= \lambda u_k \\ m_k \sum_{l \ne k} u_l + (1-m_k) v_k &= \lambda v_k \end{aligned} \tag{4.7.4}$$

for k=1,2,...,N, where u_k and v_k denote the components of the eigenvectors. Add the $-A/(2(-A+K_k))$ multiple of the second equation to the first equation to have

$$\frac{K_k}{-A+K_k}u_k = \lambda\left(u_k - \frac{A}{2(-A+K_k)}v_k\right).$$

Since zero eigenvalues do not influence asymptotical stability, we may assume that $\lambda \neq 0$. Then

$$v_k = \frac{-2K_k + 2\lambda(-A+K_k)}{\lambda A}u_k, \tag{4.7.5}$$

and substituting this relation into the second equation of (4.7.4) gives equality

$$m_k\sum_{l\neq k} u_l + (1-m_k-\lambda)\frac{-2K_k+2\lambda(-A+K_k)}{\lambda A}u_k = 0,$$

which can be further simplified as

$$-\lambda A m_k \sum_{l=1}^{N} u_l + \left[2(-A+K_k)\lambda^2 - \lambda(-Am_k + 2K_k + 2(1-m_k)(-A+K_k)) + 2K_k(1-m_k)\right]u_k = 0. \tag{4.7.6}$$

Introduce next the simplifying notation

$$\alpha_k = 2(-A+K_k)$$

$$\beta_k = -\left[-Am_k + 2K_k + 2(1-m_k)(-A+K_k)\right]$$

$$\gamma_k = 2K_k(1-m_k)$$

and

$$p_k(\lambda) = \alpha_k\lambda^2 + \beta_k\lambda + \gamma_k.$$

Then equation (4.7.6) can be summarized in matrix form as a homogeneous system of linear algebraic equations with coefficient matrix

$$\begin{pmatrix} -\lambda A m_1 & \cdots & -\lambda A m_1 \\ -\lambda A m_2 & \cdots & -\lambda A m_2 \\ \vdots & & \\ -\lambda A m_N & \cdots & -\lambda A m_N \end{pmatrix} + \begin{pmatrix} \alpha_1\lambda^2+\beta_1\lambda+\gamma_1 & & & \\ & \alpha_2\lambda^2+\beta_2\lambda+\gamma_2 & & \\ & & \ddots & \\ & & & \alpha_N\lambda^2+\beta_N\lambda+\gamma_N \end{pmatrix}$$

$$= \begin{pmatrix} -\lambda A m_1 \\ -\lambda A m_2 \\ \vdots \\ -\lambda A m_N \end{pmatrix}(1,1,\ldots,1) + \begin{pmatrix} \alpha_1\lambda^2+\beta_1\lambda+\gamma_1 & & & \\ & \alpha_2\lambda^2+\beta_2\lambda+\gamma_2 & & \\ & & \ddots & \\ & & & \alpha_N\lambda^2+\beta_N\lambda+\gamma_N \end{pmatrix}$$

$$= \begin{pmatrix} \alpha_1\lambda^2+\beta_1\lambda+\gamma_1 & & & \\ & \alpha_2\lambda^2+\beta_2\lambda+\gamma_2 & & \\ & & \ddots & \\ & & & \alpha_N\lambda^2+\beta_N\lambda+\gamma_N \end{pmatrix} \left(\mathbf{I} + \begin{pmatrix} \frac{-\lambda A m_1}{\alpha_1\lambda^2+\beta_1\lambda+\gamma_1} \\ \frac{-\lambda A m_2}{\alpha_2\lambda^2+\beta_2\lambda+\gamma_2} \\ \vdots \\ \frac{-\lambda A m_N}{\alpha_N\lambda^2+\beta_N\lambda+\gamma_N} \end{pmatrix}(1,1,\ldots,1) \right).$$

Therefore equations (4.7.6) have nontrivial solution if and only if the determinant of this matrix equals zero. Applying Lemma 4.2.1 we obtain the following equation:

$$\underset{k=1}{\overset{N}{\pi}}\left(\alpha_k\lambda^2+\beta_k\lambda+\gamma_k\right)\cdot\left\{1-\sum_{k=1}^{N}\frac{\lambda A m_k}{\alpha_k\lambda^2+\beta_k\lambda+\gamma_k}\right\}=0. \tag{4.7.7}$$

We will next prove that all quadratic polynomials $p_k(\lambda)$ have two real roots in the interval [0,1). Notice first that the discriminant of $p_k(\lambda)$ satisfies relation

$$\begin{aligned} D_k &= \beta_k^2 - 4\alpha_k\gamma_k = \left[-Am_k + 2K_k + 2(1-m_k)(-A+K_k)\right]^2 \\ &-4\left[2(-A+K_k)\right]\left[2K_k(1-m_k)\right] > \left[2K_k + 2(1-m_k)(-A+K_k)\right]^2 \\ &-4\left[2(-A+K_k)\right]\left[2K_k(1-m_k)\right] = \left[2K_k - 2(1-m_k)(-A+K_k)\right]^2 \ge 0, \end{aligned}$$

therefore there are two real roots. Since $\beta_k < 0$ and $\gamma_k \ge 0$, both roots are nonnegative, and if $m_k \ne 1$, then the roots are positive. Simple calculation shows that

$$\begin{aligned} \alpha_k - \beta_k + \gamma_k &> 0 \\ \alpha_k + \beta_k + \gamma_k &> 0 \\ -\alpha_k + \gamma_k &< 0, \end{aligned}$$

therefore Lemma 4.4.1 implies that the roots are inside the unit circle. If r_{1k} and r_{2k} $(r_{1k} < r_{2k})$ denote these roots, then equation (4.7.7) can be rewritten as

$$\mathop{\pi}_{k=1}^{N}\left[(\lambda - r_{1k})(\lambda - r_{2k})\right]\left\{1 - \sum_{k=1}^{N}\frac{\frac{\lambda A m_k}{\alpha_k}}{(\lambda - r_{1k})(\lambda - r_{2k})}\right\} = 0. \tag{4.7.8}$$

Therefore the system is globally asymptotically stable if and only if all roots of equation

$$1 - \sum_{k=1}^{N}\frac{\frac{\lambda A m_k}{\alpha_k}}{(\lambda - r_{1k})(\lambda - r_{2k})} = 0 \tag{4.7.9}$$

are inside the unit circle. Since this equation is equivalent to a polynomial equation, in particular cases, software packages (such as MATHLAB) can be used to find the roots.

Next, two special and important cases are examined. Consider first the case of Cournot expectations, when $m_k = 1$ for all k. Then $\lambda_k = 0$, $\alpha_k = 2(-A + K_k)$, and $\beta_k = -(-A + 2K_k)$. Consequently

$$p_k(\lambda) = \alpha_k \lambda^2 + \beta_k \lambda$$

and therefore $r_{1k} = 0$ and $r_{2k} = \dfrac{-A + 2K_k}{2(-A + K_k)}$.

Equation (4.7.9) now simplifies as follows:

$$1 - \sum_{k=1}^{N}\frac{\frac{A}{2(A + K_k)}}{\lambda - \frac{-A + 2K_k}{2(-A + K_k)}} = 0. \tag{4.7.10}$$

If we introduce the notation $E_k = \dfrac{-A}{-A + K_k}$, then this equation further simplifies as

$$1 + \sum_{k=1}^{N}\frac{\frac{E_k}{2}}{\lambda - \left(1 - \frac{E_k}{2}\right)} = 0.$$

A similar derivation to the one which was given earlier in Section 4.2 to obtain condition (4.2.10) shows that the system is globally asymptotically stable if and only if

$$\sum_{k=1}^{N} \frac{-A}{-3A+4K_k} < 1.$$

Assume next that the firms are identical, that is $K_k \equiv K^*$, $b_k \equiv b^*$, $c_k \equiv c^*$, and $m_k \equiv m^*$. Then

$$\alpha_k \equiv (\alpha =) 2\left(-A+K^*\right),$$
$$\beta_k \equiv (\beta =) -\left[-Am^* + 2K^* + 2\left(1-m^*\right)\left(-A+K^*\right)\right],$$
$$\gamma_k \equiv (\gamma =) 2K^*\left(1-m^*\right),$$

and so, equation (4.7.9) can be rewritten in the following way:

$$1 - \frac{N\lambda Am^*}{\alpha\lambda^2 + \beta\lambda + \gamma} = 0,$$

since the terms of the summation are identical. This equation is equivalent to the quadratic equation

$$\alpha\lambda^2 + \lambda\left(\beta - NAm^*\right) + \gamma = 0, \tag{4.7.11}$$

therefore the system is asymptotically stable if and only if

$$\alpha - \left(\beta - NAm^*\right) + \gamma > 0$$
$$\alpha + \left(\beta - NAm^*\right) + \gamma > 0$$
$$-\alpha + \gamma < 0.$$

The second and third inequalities are always satisfied, and the first inequality holds if and only if

$$N < \frac{\alpha - \beta + \gamma}{-Am^*} = \frac{-A\left(4-m^*\right) + 4K^*\left(2-m^*\right)}{-Am^*}. \tag{4.7.12}$$

Notice that for $m^* \in (0,1]$,

$$\frac{4-m^*}{m^*} \geq \frac{4-1}{1} = 3,$$

therefore the upper bound for N given in (4.7.12) is always greater than 3. Therefore for $N = 2$ and $N = 3$ we always have a globally asymptotically stable system. The upper bound increases if either K^* increases and/or A^* increases with given value of m^*. That is, larger production adjustment cost and/or smaller slope in the price function makes the system more stable. With fixed values of A^* and K^*, the upper bound decreases in m^*. As $m^* \to 0$ it converges to infinity, and at $m^* = 1$ it equals $3 - 4K^* / A$. Therefore we may obtain an asymptotically stable system with any number of firms, if m^* is sufficiently small. Notice, that a similar result was shown earlier for adaptive expectations without production adjustment costs.

4.8 Dynamic Rent Seeking Oligopolies

In this section we will examine the discrete dynamic extension of the rent seeking game earlier discussed in Sections 2.5 and 3.6. Keeping the earlier notation, assume that the production function of agent i is linear: $f_i(x_i) = a_i x_i$ with some positive constant a_i. Formula (3.6.1) implies that the payoff function of agent i is given as

$$\varphi_i(x_1, \ldots, x_N) = \frac{a_i x_i}{\sum_{j=1}^{N} a_j x_j} - x_i . \tag{4.8.1}$$

Before discussing the dynamic model, the static equilibrium of this game will be determined. Assuming interior optimum, simple differentiation shows that at the equilibrium

$$\frac{a_i \left(\sum_{j=1}^{N} a_j x_j \right) - a_i^2 x_i}{\left(\sum_{j=1}^{N} a_j x_j \right)^2} - 1 = 0.$$

By introducing the new variable $p = \sum_{j=1}^{N} a_j x_j$, this equation can be rewritten as

$$a_i p - a_i^2 x_i - p^2 = 0$$

which implies that

$$x_i = \frac{1}{a_i^2}\left(a_i p - p^2\right).$$

By multiplying this equation by a_i and adding the resulting equations for i=1,2,...,N a single equation is obtained for p:

$$p = Np - p^2 \sum_{i=1}^{N} \frac{1}{a_i}$$

which implies that at the equilibrium

$$p^* = \frac{N-1}{\sum_{i=1}^{N} \frac{1}{a_i}}, \tag{4.8.2}$$

therefore the equilibrium expenditures for agent i is

$$x_i^* = \frac{1}{a_i} \cdot \frac{N-1}{\sum_{i=1}^{N} \frac{1}{a_i}} - \frac{1}{a_i^2}\left(\frac{N-1}{\sum_{i=1}^{N} \frac{1}{a_i}}\right)^2. \tag{4.8.3}$$

Assume now that at $t = 0$, each agent selects an initial level $x_i(0)$ of expenditure, and at each later time period $t \geq 1$, first forms an adaptive expectation on the total production for lotteries of the competitors:

$$p_i^E(t) = p_i^E(t-1) + m_i\left(\sum_{j \neq i} a_j x_j(t-1) - p_i^E(t-1)\right) \tag{4.8.4}$$

where $0 < m_i \leq 1$ for all i. Then each firm maximizes his expected net rent

$$\frac{a_i x_i}{a_i x_i + p_i^E(t)} - x_i.$$

Assuming interior optimum, simple differentiation shows that

$$a_i p_i^E(t) - \left(a_i x_i + p_i^E(t)\right)^2 = 0,$$

that is, the best x_i selection of agent i at time period t is given as

$$x_i(t)=\frac{1}{a_i}\left(\sqrt{a_i p_i^E(t)}-p_i^E(t)\right).$$

Combining this equation with (4.8.4) we have the following recursion:

$$x_i(t)=\frac{1}{a_i}\left(\sqrt{a_i m_i \sum_{j\neq i} a_j x_j(t-1)+a_i(1-m_i)p_i^E(t-1)}-m_i\sum_{j\neq i} a_j x_j(t-1)-(1-m_i)p_i^E(t-1)\right).$$

(4.8.5)

Notice that equations (4.8.4) and (4.8.5) form a discrete nonlinear system with state variables $x_i(t)$ and $p_i^E(t)$ $(i=1,2,...,N)$.

It is known from the theory of difference equations (Li and Szidarovszky, 1997) that the above nonlinear system is locally asymptotically stable, if all eigenvalues of the Jacobian, computed at the equilibrium, are inside the unit circle. The Jacobian has the following special form:

$$J_{RS}^*=\left(\begin{array}{cccc|cccc} 0 & a_2\alpha_1 m_1 & \cdots & a_N\alpha_1 m_1 & \alpha_1(1-m_1) & & & \\ a_1\alpha_2 m_2 & 0 & \cdots & a_N\alpha_2 m_2 & & \alpha_2(1-m_2) & & \\ \vdots & \vdots & & \vdots & & & \ddots & \\ a_1\alpha_N m_N & a_2\alpha_N m_N & \cdots & 0 & & & & \alpha_N(1-m_N) \\ \hline 0 & a_2 m_1 & \cdots & a_N m_1 & 1-m_1 & & & \\ a_1 m_2 & 0 & \cdots & a_N m_2 & & 1-m_2 & & \\ \vdots & \vdots & & \vdots & & & \ddots & \\ a_1 m_N & a_2 m_N & \cdots & 0 & & & & 1-m_N \end{array}\right)$$

with $\alpha_i=\frac{1}{2\sqrt{p^*}}-\frac{1}{a_i}$ $(i=1,2,...,N)$. The above derivation implies the following result.

Theorem 4.8.1. Assume that for i=1,2,...,N, the equilibrium expenditures x_i^* are positive, and all eigenvalues of $\mathbf{J}_{RS}^*$ are inside the unit circle. Then system (4.8.4) - (4.8.5) is locally asymptotically stable.

Notice that the size of $\mathbf{J}_{RS}^*$ is $2N$. The structure of this matrix is very similar to that of matrix (4.2.5) introduced for adaptive expectations. In order to reduce the size of the problem, the same idea will be used as was shown there. The eigenvalue problem of $\mathbf{J}_{RS}^*$ has the form

$$\sum_{j\neq i} a_j\alpha_i m_i u_j+\alpha_i(1-m_i)v_i=\lambda u_i \tag{4.8.6}$$

$$\sum_{j\neq i} a_j m_i u_j+(1-m_i)v_i=\lambda v_i\,. \tag{4.8.7}$$

Multiply the second equation by α_i and subtract the resulting equation from the first one to get

$$\lambda(-\alpha_i v_i + u_i) = 0.$$

Since a zero eigenvalue does not destroy stability, we may assume that $\lambda \neq 0$. Then $u_i = \alpha_i v_i$, and by substituting this relation into (4.8.7) we have

$$\sum_{j \neq i} a_j m_i \alpha_j v_j + (1 - m_i) v_i = \lambda v_i$$

which is the eigenvalue problem of matrix

$$\mathbf{J}_{RS}^{(1)*} = \begin{pmatrix} 1-m_1 & m_1 a_2 \alpha_2 & \cdots & m_1 a_N \alpha_N \\ m_2 a_1 \alpha_1 & 1-m_2 & \cdots & m_2 a_N \alpha_N \\ \vdots & \vdots & & \vdots \\ m_N a_1 \alpha_1 & m_N a_2 \alpha_2 & \cdots & 1-m_N \end{pmatrix}.$$

Hence we have proved the following

Theorem 4.8.2. Assume that for i=1,2,...,N, the equilibrium expenditures x_i^* are positive and all eigenvalues of $\mathbf{J}_{RS}^{(1)*}$ are inside the unit circle. Then system (4.8.4)-(4.8.5) is locally asymptotically stable.

Notice first that the size of $\mathbf{J}_{RS}^{(1)*}$ is N, which is half of the size of the Jacobian $\mathbf{J}_{RS}^*$. The characteristic polynomial of $\mathbf{J}_{RS}^{(1)*}$ can be written as

$$\varphi(\lambda) = \det\left(\mathbf{D} - \lambda \mathbf{I} + \mathbf{a}\mathbf{b}^T\right)$$

with

$$\mathbf{D} = \begin{pmatrix} 1-m_1(1+a_1\alpha_1) & & & \\ & 1-m_2(1+a_2\alpha_2) & & \\ & & \ddots & \\ & & & 1-m_N(1+a_N\alpha_N) \end{pmatrix}, \mathbf{a} = \begin{pmatrix} m_1 \\ m_2 \\ \vdots \\ m_N \end{pmatrix}$$

and

$$\mathbf{b}^T = (a_1\alpha_1, a_2\alpha_2, \ldots, a_N\alpha_N).$$

Simple algebra and Lemma 4.2.1 imply that

$$\varphi(\lambda) = \det(\mathbf{D} - \lambda\mathbf{I}) \cdot \det\left[\mathbf{I} + (\mathbf{D} - \lambda\mathbf{I})^{-1}\mathbf{a}\mathbf{b}^T\right]$$

$$= \det(\mathbf{D} - \lambda\mathbf{I}) \cdot \left[1 + \mathbf{b}^T(\mathbf{D} - \lambda\mathbf{I})^{-1}\mathbf{a}\right]$$

$$= \mathop{\pi}_{i=1}^{N}\left(1 - m_i(1 + a_i\alpha_i) - \lambda\right) \cdot \left[1 + \sum_{i=1}^{N} \frac{m_i a_i \alpha_i}{1 - m_i(1 + a_i\alpha_i) - \lambda}\right].$$

Let $\gamma_1, \ldots, \gamma_l$ denote the distinct $1 - m_i(1 + a_i\alpha_i)$ numbers with multiplicities $r_1, \ldots, r_l$. Assume also that $\gamma_1 < \gamma_2 < \cdots < \gamma_l$. If r_i=1 with some i, then the factor $1 - m_i(1 + a_i\alpha_i) - \lambda$ cancels, otherwise this factor remains in $\varphi(\lambda)$ with the multiplicity r_i-1. Therefore, $\lambda = 1 - m_i(1 + a_i\alpha_i)$ is a root of φ with multiplicity r_i-1. All other eigenvalues of $\mathbf{J}_{RS}^{(1)*}$ are the roots of equation

$$\sum_{j=1}^{r} \frac{\delta_j}{\gamma_j - \lambda} = -1 \tag{4.8.8}$$

where

$$\delta_j = \sum_{i \in I_j} m_i a_i \alpha_i$$

with

$$I_j = \left\{i \middle| 1 - m_i(1 + a_i\alpha_i) = \gamma_j\right\}.$$

Hence we have the following result.

Theorem 4.8.3. Assume that for $r_i \geq 2, \left|1 - m_i(1 + a_i\alpha_i)\right| < 1$, furthermore all roots of equation (4.8.8) are inside the unit circle. Then system (4.8.4)-(4.8.5) is locally asymptotically stable.

Unfortunately we are unable to obtain such easy stability conditions as were given in Theorem 2.4.5, since in the case of nonsymmetric firms the sign of δ_j is indefinite. However, in the special case, when the α_i values have the same sign, all the values δ_j also have the same sign, therefore the method for proving Theorem 2.4.5 can be easily used. The details are left as an exercise for the reader. In the special case of symmetric firms we can proceed as follows. Assume that $a_i \equiv a$, $m_i \equiv m \in (0,1]$ for all i. In this special case, equation (4.8.2) implies that

$p^* = \frac{N-1}{N}a$ and $x_i^* \equiv \frac{N-1}{N} - \left(\frac{N-1}{N}\right)^2 = \frac{N-1}{N^2}$, furthermore $\alpha_i \equiv \frac{1}{2\sqrt{\frac{N-1}{N}a}} - \frac{1}{a}$.

Therefore

$$1 - m_i(1 + a_i\alpha_i) = 1 - m \cdot \left(1 + \frac{a}{2\sqrt{\frac{N-1}{N}a}} - 1\right)$$

$$= 1 - \frac{m\sqrt{Na}}{2\sqrt{N-1}},$$

and this number is between -1 and +1 if

$$m < \frac{4\sqrt{N-1}}{\sqrt{Na}}. \tag{4.8.9}$$

Equation (4.8.8) can be rewritten as

$$1 + \frac{Nma\alpha}{1 - m(1 + a\alpha) - \lambda} = 0,$$

and therefore the root is

$$\lambda = 1 - m(1 - (N-1)a\alpha),$$

which is between -1 and +1 if

$(N-1)a\alpha < 1$ and $m(1 - (N-1)a\alpha) < 2$.

Simple calculation shows that that these relations are equivalent to the following:

$$a < \frac{4N}{N-1} \text{ and } m < \frac{4}{2N - \sqrt{(N-1)Na}}. \tag{4.8.10}$$

Relations (4.8.9) and (4.8.10) can be interpreted as neither a nor m can have large values.

4.9 Dynamic Labor-Managed Oligopolies

In this section the dynamic extension of the labor managed oligopoly model (3.7.1) will be examined. Assume that the inverse demand (or price) function is linear:

$$p(s) = As + b \quad (A < 0, b > 0),$$

and for k=1,2,...,N, the inverse production function of firm k is also linear:

$$l_k = h_k(x_k) = a_k x_k + b_k$$

with constants a_k>0 and b_k≥0. Then the payoff of firm k, which is the surplus per unit of labor of this firm, can be given as

$$\varphi_k(x_1,\ldots,x_N) = \frac{x_k\left(A\sum_{l=1}^{N} x_l + b\right) - w(a_k x_k + b_k) - c_k}{a_k x_k + b_k}. \tag{4.9.1}$$

Recall that w is the competitive wage rate which is constant, and c_k is firms k's fixed cost.

Before the dynamic extension of this game is examined, the static equilibrium point will be determined. Assuming interior optimum, simple differentiation shows that at the equilibrium

$$(As + b + Ax_k - wa_k)(a_k x_k + b_k) - (Ax_k s + bx_k - a_k w x_k - b_k w - c_k)a_k = 0$$

where $s = \sum_{l=1}^{N} x_l$. That is,

$$Aa_k x_k^2 + Ab_k x_k + (Asb_k + bb_k + a_k c_k) = 0.$$

Since A<0, the positive root is

$$x_k = \frac{-Ab_k - \sqrt{A^2 b_k^2 - 4Aa_k(Asb_k + bb_k + a_k c_k)}}{2Aa_k}.$$

Introducing the notation

$$\alpha_k = A^2 b_k^2 - 4Aa_k(bb_k + a_k c_k)$$

the above equation has the form

$$x_k = \frac{-Ab_k - \sqrt{-4A^2 a_k b_k s + \alpha_k}}{2Aa_k}. \tag{4.9.2}$$

By adding this equation for k=1,2,...N, a single equation is obtained for s:

$$s + \sum_{k=1}^{N} \frac{b_k}{2a_k} = -\frac{1}{2A} \sum_{k=1}^{N} \frac{\sqrt{-4A^2 a_k b_k s + \alpha_k}}{a_k}. \tag{4.9.3}$$

Notice that the left hand side is increasing in s, and the right hand side decreases. Assume that

$$\sum_{k=1}^{N} \frac{b_k}{2a_k} < -\frac{1}{2A} \sum_{k=1}^{N} \frac{\sqrt{\alpha_k}}{a_k}, \tag{4.9.4}$$

then at $s = 0$, the left hand side is smaller than the right hand side. Assume furthermore that at $s_{\max} = \min_k \left\{ \alpha_k / \left(4A^2 a_k b_k \right) \right\}$,

$$s_{\max} + \sum_{k=1}^{N} \frac{b_k}{2a_k} > -\frac{1}{2A} \sum_{k=1}^{N} \frac{\sqrt{\alpha_k - 4A^2 a_k b_k s_{\max}}}{a_k}. \tag{4.9.5}$$

Under conditions (4.9.4) and (4.9.5), there is a unique positive s^* value satisfying equation (4.9.3). The corresponding individual firms equilibrium outputs are given by equation (4.9.2). In addition we have to assume that $x_k^* > 0$ for all k, which is true if

$$s^* < \min \left\{ \frac{-A^2 b_k^2 + \alpha_k}{4A^2 a_k b_k} \right\}. \tag{4.9.6}$$

Assume now that at the initial time period $t = 0$, each firm selects an initial output $x_k(0)$, and at each later time period $t \geq 1$, the firms maximize their expected payoff based on adaptive expectations. As before, let $s_k^E(t)$ denote the expectation of firm k on the output of the rest of the industry, then

$$s_k^E(t) = s_k^E(t-1) + m_k \left(\sum_{l \neq k} \mathbf{x}_l(t-1) - s_k^E(t-1) \right) \tag{4.9.7}$$

with some constant $m_k \in (0,1]$. The expected payoff of firm k at time period t is the following:

$$\frac{x_k\left(Ax_k + Am_k\sum_{l\neq k}\mathbf{x}_l(t-1) + A(1-m_k)s_k^E(t-1) + b\right) - w(a_kx_k + b_k) - c_k}{a_kx_k + b_k}.$$

Assuming interior optimum, simple differentiation shows that at the optimal x_k,

$$\left[2Ax_k + Am_k\sum_{l\neq k}\mathbf{x}_l(t-1) + A(1-m_k)s_k^E(t-1) + b - wa_k\right](a_kx_k + b_k)$$

$$-a_k\left[Ax_k^2 + Ax_km_k\sum_{l\neq k}\mathbf{x}_l(t-1) + A(1-m_k)x_ks_k^E(t-1) + x_kb - w(a_kx_k + b_k) - c_k\right] = 0$$

which is a quadratic equation for the unknown $x_k = x_k(t)$:

$$Aa_kx_k^2 + x_k(2Ab_k) + \left(b_kAm_k\sum_{l\neq k}\mathbf{x}_l(t-1) + A(1-m_k)b_ks_k^E(t-1) + bb_k + a_kc_k\right) = 0. \tag{4.9.8}$$

By differentiation, for $k\neq l$,

$$\frac{\partial x_k}{\partial x_l(t-1)} = \frac{-b_kAm_k}{2Aa_kx_k + 2Ab_k} = -\frac{b_km_k}{2(a_kx_k + b_k)} = -\frac{b_km_k}{2h_k}$$

with $h_k = ax_k + b_k$. Similarly,

$$\frac{\partial x_k}{\partial s_k^E(t-1)} = -\frac{b_k(1-m_k)}{2h_k}.$$

The Jacobian of the resulting nonlinear dynamic system has the special form:

$$J_L^* = \left(\begin{array}{cccc|cccc}
0 & -\frac{b_1m_1}{2h_1} & \cdots & -\frac{b_1m_1}{2h_1} & -\frac{b_1(1-m_1)}{2h_1} & & & \\
-\frac{b_2m_2}{2h_2} & 0 & \cdots & -\frac{b_2m_2}{2h_2} & & -\frac{b_2(1-m_2)}{2h_2} & & \\
\vdots & \vdots & & \vdots & & & \ddots & \\
-\frac{b_Nm_N}{2h_N} & -\frac{b_Nm_N}{2h_N} & \cdots & 0 & & & & -\frac{b_N(1-m_N)}{2h_N} \\
\hline
0 & m_1 & \cdots & m_1 & 1-m_1 & & & \\
m_2 & 0 & \cdots & m_2 & & 1-m_2 & & \\
\vdots & \vdots & & \vdots & & & \ddots & \\
m_N & m_N & \cdots & 0 & & & & 1-m_N
\end{array}\right).$$

Notice that this matrix is the same as the Jacobian $\mathbf{J}^*_{RS}$ appearing in Theorem 4.8.1 with the selection of a_k=1 and $\alpha_k = -\frac{b_k}{2h_k}$ $(k = 1,2,...,N)$.

Therefore Theorem 4.8.1 can be applied without any modification as well as the reduction given in Theorem 4.8.2. In addition, equation (4.8.8) implies that the nonzero eigenvalues of $\mathbf{J}^*_L$ are given as follows. Define $\gamma_1 < \gamma_2 < \cdots < \gamma_l$ as the distinct $1 - m_i\left(1 - \frac{b_i}{2h_i}\right)$ values with multiplicities $r_1, r_2, ..., r_l$, and let

$$\delta_j = -\sum_{i \in I_j} m_i \frac{b_i}{2h_i}$$

with

$$I_j = \left\{ i \,\middle|\, 1 - m_i\left(1 - \frac{b_i}{2h_i}\right) = \gamma_j \right\}.$$

Then for $r_i \geq 2$, $1 - m_i\left(1 - \frac{b_i}{2h_i}\right)$ is an eigenvalue with multiplicity r_i-1, and all other eigenvalues are the roots of equation (4.8.8) what we repeat here for convenience:

$$\sum_{j=1}^{r} \frac{\delta_j}{\gamma_j - \lambda} = -1.$$

Notice that $b_i \leq a_i x_i + b_i = h_i$, therefore $\gamma_i \in [0,1)$ and $\delta_j \leq 0$ for all j. Similarly to Theorem 2.4.5 one can prove the following result.

Theorem 4.9.1. Assume that at the equilibrium,

$$\sum_{i=1}^{N} \frac{\frac{m_i b_i}{2h_i}}{2 - m_i\left(1 - \frac{b_i}{2h_i}\right)} < 1. \tag{4.9.9}$$

Then the equilibrium is locally asymptotically stable.

Remark 1. Assume first that N=2. Then

$$\sum_{i=1}^{N} \frac{\frac{m_i b_i}{2h_i}}{2 - m_i\left(1 - \frac{b_i}{2h_i}\right)} < \sum_{i=1}^{N} \frac{\frac{m_i}{2}}{2 - m_i} = \sum_{i=1}^{2} \frac{m_i}{4 - 2m_i} \leq 1,$$

therefore the dynamic system is always locally asymptotically stable.

Remark 2. Relation (4.9.9) is always satisfied if the m_i speeds of adjustments are sufficiently small. As a special case assume that the firms are identical, that is, $a_i \equiv a$, $b_i \equiv b$, and $m_i \equiv m$. Since the uniqueness of the equilibrium implies that $h_i \equiv h$, condition (4.9.9) can be simplified as

$$\frac{\frac{Nmb}{2h}}{2 - m\left(1 - \frac{b}{2h}\right)} < 1,$$

which can be rewritten as

$$m < \frac{4h}{b(N-1) + 2h}. \tag{4.9.10}$$

Notice that this upper bound is always positive, and converges to zero as $N \to \infty$ with fixed values of b, since under our assumptions h is bounded.

4.10 Dynamic Oligopsonies

In this section dynamic oligopsonies will be examined. We will consider an N-firm oligopsony producing a single product and using M factors of production. Let $\mathbf{l}_i \in R_+^M$ be the production factor usage vector of firm i, and let $\mathbf{L} = \sum_{i=1}^{N} \mathbf{l}_i$ be the total production factor usage vector of the industry. Assume that the production factor prices depend on $\mathbf{L}$, that is, the factor price vector is $\mathbf{w}=\mathbf{w}(\mathbf{L})$. Let $f_i(\mathbf{l}_i)$ denote the production function of firm i, then its profit can be given as follows

$$\Pi_i = p\left(\sum_{j=1}^{N} f_j(\mathbf{l}_j)\right) \cdot f_i(\mathbf{l}_i) - \mathbf{l}_i^T \mathbf{w}\left(\sum_{j=1}^{N} \mathbf{l}_j\right) \tag{4.10.1}$$

where we assume that the product price function depends on the total output of the industry.

Assume that

(i) $p(s) = As + b$ with some constants $A < 0$ and $b > 0$;
(ii) $f_i(\mathbf{l}_i) = \mathbf{c}_i^T \mathbf{l}_i + d_i$ where $\mathbf{c}_i \in R^M$ and d_i is a constant;
(iii) $\mathbf{w}(\mathbf{L}) = \mathbf{BL} + \mathbf{b}$ with $\mathbf{B} \in R^{M \times M}$ and $\mathbf{b} \in R^M$.

Under these assumptions, the profit of firm i, can be written as

$$p(s)f_i(\mathbf{l}_i) - \mathbf{l}_i^T \mathbf{w}(\mathbf{L}) = (As + b)(\mathbf{c}_i^T \mathbf{l}_i + d_i) - \mathbf{l}_i^T (\mathbf{BL} + \mathbf{b}) \tag{4.10.2}$$

where

$$s = \sum_{j=1}^{N} f_j(\mathbf{l}_j) \text{ and } \mathbf{L} = \sum_{j=1}^{N} \mathbf{l}_j .$$

Assume that at the initial time period $t = 0$, each firm selects an initial production factor usage $\mathbf{l}_i(0)$. At each later time period $t \geq 1$, each firm first forms two expectations adaptively. The first expectation predicts the output of the rest of the industry, and the second expectation estimates the total production factor usage of the rivals. The need for two different expectations can be explained as follows. The total production factor usage and output of the rest of the industry are given as

$$\mathbf{L}_{-i} = \sum_{j \neq i} \mathbf{l}_j \text{ and } S_{-i} = \sum_{j \neq i} f_j(\mathbf{l}_j)$$

respectively, and in the case of different production functions, the value of $\mathbf{L}_{-i}$ does not determine S_{-i} uniquely. However, if the production functions of the firms are identical, then $\mathbf{c}_i = \mathbf{c}$ and $d_i = d$ for all i, and

$$S_{-i} = \sum_{j \neq i} (\mathbf{c}^T \mathbf{l}_j + d) = \mathbf{c}^T \mathbf{L}_{-i} + (N-1)d$$

which is a function relation between $\mathbf{L}_{-i}$ and S_{-i}. Therefore in the following discussion firms are assumed to have different production functions. If $S_i^E(t)$ and $\mathbf{L}_i^E(t)$ denote the two expectations of firm i, then for all $t \geq 1$,

$$S_i^E(t) = m_i \sum_{j \neq i} f_j(\mathbf{l}_j(t-1)) + (1 - m_i) S_i^E(t-1) \tag{4.10.3}$$

and

$$\mathbf{L}_i^E(t) = \mathbf{M}_i \sum_{j \neq i} \mathbf{l}_j(\mathbf{l}_j(t-1)) + (\mathbf{I} - \mathbf{M}_i)\mathbf{L}_i^E(t-1), \tag{4.10.4}$$

where $m_i \in (0,1]$ is a real number and $\mathbf{M}_i$ is an $M \times M$ real matrix. The expected profit of firm i (i=1,2,...,N) can be computed as

$$\begin{aligned}\Pi_i^E(t) &= p(f_i(\mathbf{l}_i) + S_i^E(t))f_i(\mathbf{l}_i) - \mathbf{l}_i^T \mathbf{w}(\mathbf{l}_i + \mathbf{L}_i^E(t)) \\ &= \left[A(\mathbf{c}_i^T \mathbf{l}_i + d_i + S_i^E(t)) + b\right](\mathbf{c}_i^T \mathbf{l}_i + d_i) - \mathbf{l}_i^T(\mathbf{B}\mathbf{l}_i + \mathbf{B}\mathbf{L}_i^E(t) + \mathbf{b}).\end{aligned}$$

Excluding corner optimum, simple differentiation shows that at the maximum

$$A\mathbf{c}_i(\mathbf{c}_i^T \mathbf{l}_i + d_i) + \left[A(\mathbf{c}_i^T \mathbf{l}_i + d_i + S_i^E(t)) + b\right]\mathbf{c}_i - (\mathbf{B} + \mathbf{B}^T)\mathbf{l}_i - \mathbf{B}\mathbf{L}_i^E(t) - \mathbf{b} = \mathbf{0},$$

which can be rewritten as

$$\mathbf{l}_i = (\mathbf{B} + \mathbf{B}^T - 2A\mathbf{c}_i\mathbf{c}_i^T)^{-1}\left[A\mathbf{c}_i S_i^E(t) - \mathbf{B}\mathbf{L}_i^E(t) + 2Ad_i\mathbf{c}_i + \beta\mathbf{c}_i - \mathbf{b}\right] \tag{4.10.5}$$

assuming that

(iv) matrix $\mathbf{B} + \mathbf{B}^T - 2A\mathbf{c}_i\mathbf{c}_i^T$ is positive definite.

Introducing the notation $\mathbf{B}_i = (\mathbf{B} + \mathbf{B}^T - 2A\mathbf{c}_i\mathbf{c}_i^T)^{-1}$ and combining equations (4.10.3), (4.10.4) and (4.10.5) we have

$$\begin{aligned}\mathbf{l}_i(t) &= \alpha\mathbf{B}_i\mathbf{c}_i\left[m_i \sum_{j \neq i}(\mathbf{c}_j^T \mathbf{l}_j(t-1) + d_j) + (1 - m_i)S_i^E(t-1)\right] \\ &-\mathbf{B}_i\mathbf{B}\left[\mathbf{M}_i \sum_{j \neq i} \mathbf{l}_j(t-1) + (\mathbf{I} - \mathbf{M}_i)\mathbf{L}_i^E(t-1)\right] + \mathbf{k}\end{aligned} \tag{4.10.6}$$

where $\mathbf{k}$ is a constant vector. Notice that relations (4.10.3), (4.10.4) and (4.10.6) define a linear, dynamic, discrete system with state variables $\mathbf{l}_i$, $\mathbf{L}_i^E$, and S_i^E. Notice that the coefficient matrix of the system has the form:

$$
\mathbf{H}_{OS}=\left(\begin{array}{cccc|cccc|cccc}
\mathbf{0} & \mathbf{D}_{12} & \cdots & \mathbf{D}_{1N} & \mathbf{E}_1 & & & & \mathbf{g}_1 & & & \\
\mathbf{D}_{21} & \mathbf{0} & \cdots & \mathbf{D}_{2N} & & \mathbf{E}_2 & & & & \mathbf{g}_2 & & \\
\vdots & \vdots & & \vdots & & & \ddots & & & & \ddots & \\
\mathbf{D}_{N1} & \mathbf{D}_{N2} & \cdots & \mathbf{0} & & & & \mathbf{E}_N & & & & \mathbf{g}_N \\
\hline
\mathbf{0} & \mathbf{M}_1 & \cdots & \mathbf{M}_1 & \mathbf{I}-\mathbf{M}_1 & & & & & & & \\
\mathbf{M}_2 & \mathbf{0} & \cdots & \mathbf{M}_2 & & \mathbf{I}-\mathbf{M}_2 & & & & & & \\
\vdots & \vdots & & \vdots & & & \ddots & & & & & \\
\mathbf{M}_N & \mathbf{M}_N & \cdots & \mathbf{0} & & & & \mathbf{I}-\mathbf{M}_N & & & & \\
\hline
\mathbf{0}^T & \mathbf{h}_{12}^T & \cdots & \mathbf{h}_{1N}^T & & & & & 1-m_1 & & & \\
\mathbf{h}_{21}^T & \mathbf{0}^T & \cdots & \mathbf{h}_{2N}^T & & & & & & 1-m_2 & & \\
\vdots & \vdots & & \vdots & & & & & & & \ddots & \\
\mathbf{h}_{N1}^T & \mathbf{h}_{N2}^T & \cdots & \mathbf{0}^T & & & & & & & & 1-m_N
\end{array}\right)
$$

with

$$
\left.\begin{array}{l}
\mathbf{D}_{ij}=\mathbf{B}_i\left(Am_i\mathbf{c}_i\mathbf{c}_j^T-\mathbf{B}\mathbf{M}_i\right) \\
\mathbf{h}_{ij}^T=m_i\mathbf{c}_j^T
\end{array}\right\} \qquad (i,j=1,2,\ldots,N;\ i\neq j)
$$

$$
\left.\begin{array}{l}
\mathbf{E}_i=-\mathbf{B}_i\mathbf{B}(\mathbf{I}-\mathbf{M}_i) \\
\mathbf{g}_i=A(1-m_i)\mathbf{B}_i\mathbf{c}_i
\end{array}\right\} \qquad (i=1,2,\ldots,N).
$$

Theorem 4.10.1. The dynamic oligopsony under conditions (i) - (iv) is globally asymptotically stable if and only if all eigenvalues of $\mathbf{H}_{0S}$ are inside the unit circle.

Notice that the eigenvalue equation of matrix $\mathbf{H}_{0S}$ can be summarized as follows:

$$
\begin{array}{lll}
\sum_{j\neq i}\mathbf{D}_{ij}\mathbf{u}_j-\mathbf{B}_i\mathbf{B}(\mathbf{I}-\mathbf{M}_i)\mathbf{v}_i+A(1-m_i)\mathbf{B}_i\mathbf{c}_i w_i & & =\lambda\mathbf{u}_i \\
\sum_{j\neq i}\mathbf{M}_i\mathbf{u}_j+(\mathbf{I}-\mathbf{M}_i)\mathbf{v}_i & & =\lambda\mathbf{v}_i \\
\sum_{j\neq i}m_i\mathbf{c}_j^T\mathbf{u}_j & +(1-m_i)w_i & =\lambda w_i .
\end{array}
\tag{4.10.7}
$$

From the third equation

$$
w_i=\frac{1}{\lambda-(1-m_i)}\sum_{j\neq i}\mathbf{m}_i\mathbf{c}_j^T\mathbf{u}_j, \tag{4.10.8}
$$

from the second equation

$$
\mathbf{v}_i=\left(\lambda\mathbf{I}-(\mathbf{I}-\mathbf{M}_i)\right)^{-1}\sum_{j\neq i}\mathbf{M}_i\mathbf{u}_j . \tag{4.10.9}
$$

We may assume here that $\lambda \neq 1-m_i$, since $1-m_i$ is inside the unit circle, and an eigenvalue $\lambda = 1-m_i$ will not destroy the asymptotical stability of the system. In equation (4.10.9) the inverse exists if λ is not an eigenvalue of matrix $\mathbf{I}-\mathbf{M}_i$. If we assume that

(v) all eigenvalues of $\mathbf{I}-\mathbf{M}_i$ are inside the unit circle,

then we need to consider only such eigenvalues of $\mathbf{H}_{0S}$ which are not eigenvalues of $\mathbf{I}-\mathbf{M}_i$. Substitute relations (4.10.8) and (4.10.9) into the first equation of (4.10.7) to obtain equality

$$\sum_{j\neq i}\left[\mathbf{D}_{ij}-\mathbf{B}_i\mathbf{B}(\mathbf{I}-\mathbf{M}_i)(\lambda\mathbf{I}-(\mathbf{I}-\mathbf{M}_i))^{-1}\mathbf{M}_i + A(1-m_i)\mathbf{B}_i\mathbf{c}_i m_i \mathbf{c}_j^T \frac{1}{\lambda-(1-m_i)}\right]\mathbf{u}_j = \lambda\mathbf{u}_i \,. \tag{4.10.10}$$

Notice that (4.10.10) is a nonlinear eigenvalue problem of dimension MN, while the size of matrix $\mathbf{H}_{0S}$ is $(2M+1)N$, which is much larger.

Theorem 4.10.2. The equilibrium of the above dynamic system is globally asymptotically stable if and only if all λ solutions of the MN - dimensional nonlinear eigenvalue problem (4.10.10) are inside the unit circle.

Consider next the important special case of Cournot expectations, where $m_i = 1$ and $\mathbf{M}_i = \mathbf{I}$ for all i. The eigenvalues of matrix $\mathbf{H}_{0S}$ are $\lambda = 0$ and the eigenvalues of matrix

$$\mathbf{H}_{0S}^{(1)} = \begin{pmatrix} \mathbf{0} & \mathbf{D}_{12} & \cdots & \mathbf{D}_{1N} \\ \mathbf{D}_{21} & \mathbf{0} & \cdots & \mathbf{D}_{2N} \\ \vdots & \vdots & & \vdots \\ \mathbf{D}_{N1} & \mathbf{D}_{N2} & \cdots & \mathbf{0} \end{pmatrix}.$$

Notice that problem (4.10.10) also reduces to the eigenvalue problem of $\mathbf{H}_{0S}^{(1)}$, where for all $i \neq j$,

$$\mathbf{D}_{ij} = \left(\mathbf{A}+\mathbf{A}^T - 2\alpha\mathbf{c}_i\mathbf{c}_i^T\right)^{-1}\left(\alpha\mathbf{c}_i\mathbf{c}_j^T - \mathbf{A}\right). \tag{4.10.11}$$

In the further special case of identical firms and symmetric $\mathbf{B}$, $\mathbf{D}_{ij} = -\frac{1}{2}\mathbf{I}$, and therefore

$$\mathbf{H}_{OS}^{(2)} = \begin{pmatrix} \mathbf{0} & -\frac{1}{2}\mathbf{I} & \cdots & -\frac{1}{2}\mathbf{I} \\ -\frac{1}{2}\mathbf{I} & \mathbf{0} & \cdots & -\frac{1}{2}\mathbf{I} \\ \vdots & \vdots & & \vdots \\ -\frac{1}{2}\mathbf{I} & -\frac{1}{2}\mathbf{I} & \cdots & \mathbf{0} \end{pmatrix}.$$

Notice that this matrix is the Kronecker product of the $N \times N$ matrix

$$\begin{pmatrix} 0 & -\frac{1}{2} & \cdots & -\frac{1}{2} \\ -\frac{1}{2} & 0 & \cdots & -\frac{1}{2} \\ \vdots & \vdots & & \vdots \\ -\frac{1}{2} & -\frac{1}{2} & \cdots & 0 \end{pmatrix} = -\frac{1}{2}(\mathbf{1} - \mathbf{I})$$

and the M- dimensional identity matrix, when all elements of matrix $\mathbf{1}$ are equal to one. From Section 4.1 we know that the eigenvalues of $\mathbf{1}$ are 0 and N, therefore the eigenvalues of $\mathbf{H}_{OS}^{(2)}$ are $-\frac{1}{2}(0-1) = \frac{1}{2}$ and $-\frac{1}{2}(N-1) = \frac{1-N}{2}$.

These eigenvalues are inside the unit circle if and only if $N \le 2$. That is, in this special case the equilibrium is asymptotically stable for only duopoly-oligopsony. This result is a new extension of the classical theorem of Theocharis (1959), which was discussed earlier in Section 4.1.

4.11 Supplementary Notes and Discussions

The theory of dynamic games is generally discussed by several authors. The reader can refer to Basar and Olsder (1982) or to Friedman (1986).

4.1 The classical theorem of Theocharis (1959) is generalized for multiproduct oligopolies in this section. Model (4.1.2) was formulated first by Szidarovszky and Okuguchi (1986). Theorem 4.1.1 is a simple consequence of the asymptotic stability theory of linear difference equations. Lemma 4.1.1 is known from Bellman (1970), but it is given in a more general framework in Rózsa (1974). Theorem 4.1.3 is taken from Szidarovszky and Okuguchi (1986). A similar development is given in Okuguchi and Szidarovszky (1987a).

4.2 Adaptive expectations for the classical oligopoly game with discrete time scale have been analyzed by Okuguchi (1970, 1976). Model (4.2.5) was originally formulated by Szidarovszky, Szép and Okuguchi (1987), and Okuguchi and Szidarovszky (1987b). In the second paper the continuous time scale counterpart is also analyzed. Theorems 4.2.1, 4.2.2, and 4.2.4 and the optimal selection of parameter α^* are taken from Szidarovszky, Szép and Okuguchi (1987). Theorem 4.2.5 was earlier published in Szidarovszky, Rassenti and Yen (1994). Adaptive expectations on the individual outputs of the rivals as well as Theorems 4.2.6, 4.2.7, and 4.2.8 were discussed in a more general framework in Szidarovszky and Okuguchi (1987b). The combination of the two kinds of adaptive expectations and relevant stability conditions were given in Section 4.3 of the earlier version of this book (Okuguchi and Szidarovszky, 1990).

4.3 Sequential adjustment processes have been introduced by Gabay and Moulin (1980) for the classical oligopoly game without product differentiation under the assumption that the Jacobian of the profit functions was strictly diagonally dominant. This property holds only for N=2. In this section not only the game but also the conditions are more general. The results of this section are taken from Okuguchi and Szidarovszky (1987c). Note that this model is a generalization of the two-persons leader-follower model of Stackelberg (1934), where for all k, firm k is the follower of firm k-1 (for $k \neq 1$), and firm 1 is the follower of firm N. For more details of Stackelberg duopoly see Henderson and Quandt (1958) or Okuguchi (1976).

4.4 The results of this section are taken from Szidarovszky and Okuguchi (1987h). A general description with convergence criteria and with conditions of monotone convergence for multi-step iterations is presented in Szidarovszky and Okuguchi (1987i), where several theorems for single-step iterations by Ortega and Rheinboldt (1970) are generalized.

4.5 The model and most stability conditions, except Theorem 4.5.2, given in this section have been earlier published in Szidarovszky (1990).

4.6 The single-product version of the model presented in this section has been introduced in Szidarovszky and Yen (1991), and relations (4.6.18) have been found as the necessary and sufficient conditions. The multiproduct extension of the model was first given in Szidarovszky, Rassenti and Yen (1992) under Cournot expectations. The multiproduct case with adaptive expectations is new material.

4.7 The model and stability conditions under Cournot expectations have been presented in Szidarovszky and Yen (1995). The case of adaptive expectations has not been published earlier.

4.8 The results of this section are all new, not being published before.

4.9 The model and stability conditions are new results.

4.10 Dynamic oligopsonies with perfectly competitive product prices under adaptive expectations have been analyzed in Szidarovszky and Okuguchi (1997b). The model and stability conditions presented in this section are new.

The methodology used in this chapter can be used to find necessary stability conditions, or equivalently, to find sufficient conditions for the instability of the equilibrium. Assume first that the system is linear and time-invariant, that is, it is described by a difference equation

$$\mathbf{x}(t+1) = \mathbf{H}\mathbf{x}(t) + \mathbf{b}$$

with a constant matrix **H** and a constant vector **b**. If at least one eigenvalue of **H** is outside the unit circle, then the equilibrium is unstable. Consider next a time-invariant nonlinear system

$$\mathbf{x}(t+1) = \mathbf{f}(\mathbf{x}(t)),$$

where $\mathbf{f}: D \mapsto D$ is a continuously differentiable function and D is a convex, open set in R^N. Let $\mathbf{x} \in D$ be an equilibrium, and let $\mathbf{J}(\mathbf{x}^*)$ denote the Jacobian of $\mathbf{f}$ at this equilibrium. If at least one eigenvalue of $\mathbf{J}(\mathbf{x}^*)$ is outside the unit circle, then $\mathbf{x}^*$ is unstable. A simple elementary proof of this important result can be found for example, in Li and Szidarovszky (1997).

Finally, we mention that dynamic oligopolies with discrete time-scale are discussed in Szidarovszky and Okuguchi (1989a), where a slightly different approach is used.

5 Dynamic Oligopoly with Continuous Time Scale

This chapter is devoted to analysis of different versions of dynamic multiproduct oligopolies with continuous time scale. The static game, which will be extended into a dynamic framework, is the same as that discussed in Chapter 3. Hence, the following assumptions are made:

(A) The set X_k of strategies of firm k ($1 \le k \le N$) is a closed, convex, bounded set in R_+^M, such that $\mathbf{x}_k \in X_k$ and $\mathbf{0} \le \mathbf{t}_k \le \mathbf{x}_k$ imply that $\mathbf{t}_k \in X_k$;

Define set

$$S = \left\{ \mathbf{s} \middle| \mathbf{s} = \sum_{k=1}^{N} \mathbf{x}_k,\ \mathbf{x}_k \in X_k,\ k = 1,2,\ldots,N \right\}.$$

(B) The price function $\mathbf{p}$ is linear on S:

$$\mathbf{p}(\mathbf{s}) = \mathbf{A}\mathbf{s} + \mathbf{b}, \tag{5.0.1}$$

where $\mathbf{A}$ and $\mathbf{b}$ are constant matrix and vector, respectively;

(C) Cost function C_k of firm k ($1 \le k \le N$) is quadratic on X_k, that is,

$$C_k(\mathbf{x}_k) = \mathbf{x}_k^T \mathbf{B}_k \mathbf{x}_k + \mathbf{b}_k^T \mathbf{x}_k + c_k, \tag{5.0.2}$$

where $\mathbf{B}_k$ is a constant matrix, $\mathbf{b}_k$ is a constant vector, and c_k is a constant number.

(D) Matrix $(\mathbf{A} + \mathbf{A}^T) - (\mathbf{B}_k + \mathbf{B}_k^T)$ is negative definite for all $(1 \le k \le N)$.

At the outset of Chapter 4 we introduced the payoff functions

$$\varphi_k(\mathbf{x}_1,\ldots,\mathbf{x}_N)=\mathbf{x}_k^T(\mathbf{A}\mathbf{s}+\mathbf{b})-(\mathbf{x}_k^T\mathbf{B}_k\mathbf{x}_k+\mathbf{b}_k^T\mathbf{x}_k+c_k). \tag{5.0.3}$$

These are continuous on X with $\mathbf{s}=\sum_{k=1}^{N}\mathbf{x}_k$, and furthermore the Hessian of φ_k with respect to $\mathbf{x}_k$ equals $\mathbf{A}+\mathbf{A}^T-(\mathbf{B}_k+\mathbf{B}_k^T)$. Thus, condition (D) implies that φ_k is concave in X_k, and therefore all conditions of Theorem 3.1.1 are satisfied. Consequently, under assumptions (A) - (D) the multiproduct oligopoly game has at lease one equilibrium. We note here that condition (D) has been examined earlier in Chapter 4.

Let t denote the time. If at a certain time $t\geq 0$ the firms are in an equilibrium point, then (without assuming cooperation among the firms) the interest of each firm is to remain in this equilibrium situation. If the strategies of the firms at a time $t\geq 0$ do not form an equilibrium point, then in this disequilibrium situation their behavior can be modelled on the basis of certain adjustment assumptions. This chapter will discuss three different kinds of such adjustment processes. In addition, some variants of the classical dynamic oligopoly model will be discussed under continuous time scale.

5.1 Classical Results

In this section we assume that conditions (A) - (D) hold and all firms form expectations on all *other firms' outputs à la Cournot*. On the basis of this last assumption two kinds of adjustment processes are discussed in the literature:

(a) Each firm adjusts its actual output proportionally to its expected marginal profit calculated under the Cournot assumption on rival firms' outputs;

(b) Each firm adjusts its actual output proportionally to the difference between its profit-maximizing and actual outputs, where the profit-maximizing output is calculated under the Cournot assumption on rival firms' outputs.

Let's first investigate case (a). If $\mathbf{x}_k(t)$ denotes the output of firm k at time $t\geq 0$, then the marginal expected profit equals the value at $(\mathbf{x}_1(t),\ldots,\mathbf{x}_N(t))$ of the gradient of function φ_k with respect to strategy vector $\mathbf{x}_k$. Consequently, the adjustment process can be mathematically described for k=1,2,...,N as

$$\frac{d\mathbf{x}_k(t)}{dt}=\mathbf{K}_k\left[(\mathbf{A}+\mathbf{A}^T-\mathbf{B}_k-\mathbf{B}_k^T)\mathbf{x}_k(t)+\mathbf{A}\sum_{l\neq k}\mathbf{x}_l(t)+\mathbf{b}-\mathbf{b}_k\right], \tag{5.1.1}$$

where $\mathbf{K}_k$ is a constant matrix for k=1,2,...,N. It is usually assumed that matrices $\mathbf{K}_k$ are diagonal with positive diagonal elements. These differential equations can be rewritten as

$$\frac{d\mathbf{x}(t)}{dt} = \begin{bmatrix} \mathbf{K}_1(\mathbf{A}+\mathbf{A}^T-\mathbf{B}_1+\mathbf{B}_1^T) & & \\ & \ddots & \\ & & \mathbf{K}_N(\mathbf{A}+\mathbf{A}^T-\mathbf{B}_N-\mathbf{B}_N^T) \end{bmatrix} \begin{bmatrix} \mathbf{I} & \mathbf{D}_1 & \cdots & \mathbf{D}_1 \\ \mathbf{D}_2 & \mathbf{I} & \cdots & \mathbf{D}_2 \\ \vdots & \vdots & \ddots & \vdots \\ \mathbf{D}_N & \mathbf{D}_N & \cdots & \mathbf{I} \end{bmatrix} \mathbf{x}(t) + \boldsymbol{\beta}_c \tag{5.1.2}$$

where $\mathbf{D}_k = \left(\mathbf{A}+\mathbf{A}^T-\mathbf{B}_k-\mathbf{B}_k^T\right)^{-1}\mathbf{A}$ $(k=1,2,...,N)$, $\boldsymbol{\beta}_c$ is a constant vector, and $\mathbf{x}(t)$ is the same as in (4.1.2). Thus, the dynamic adjustment process may be modelled by the linear differential equation (5.1.2) with the additional assumption:

(E) For all $t \geq 0$ and $k=1,2,...,N$, $\mathbf{x}_k(t) \in X_k$.

Consider next case (b). At time $t \geq 0$ the profit-maximizing output under the Cournot assumption is obtained by solving:

Maximize $\quad \mathbf{x}_k^T\left(A\left(\sum_{l \neq k}\mathbf{x}_l(t)+\mathbf{x}_k\right)+\mathbf{b}\right)-\left(\mathbf{x}_k^T\mathbf{B}_k\mathbf{x}_k+\mathbf{b}_k^T\mathbf{x}_k+c_k\right)$

subject to $\quad \mathbf{x}_k \in X_k$.

Assume that conditions (A) - (D) hold and the optimal solution $\mathbf{x}_k^*(t)$ is an interior point of X_k.

The first order conditions imply that

$$\left[\left(\mathbf{A}+\mathbf{A}^T\right)-\left(\mathbf{B}_k+\mathbf{B}_k^T\right)\right]\mathbf{x}_k+\mathbf{A}\sum_{l \neq k}\mathbf{x}_l(t)+\mathbf{b}-\mathbf{b}_k=\mathbf{0}.$$

That is,

$$\mathbf{x}_k^*(t)=-\left[\left(\mathbf{A}+\mathbf{A}^T\right)-\left(\mathbf{B}_k+\mathbf{B}_k^T\right)\right]^{-1}\mathbf{A}\sum_{l \neq k}\mathbf{x}_l(t)+\boldsymbol{\alpha},$$

where $\boldsymbol{\alpha}$ is a constant vector. Thus, the adjustment process under assumption (b) can be mathematically modelled as

$$\frac{d\mathbf{x}_k(t)}{dt}=\mathbf{K}_k^c\left[-\left(\mathbf{A}+\mathbf{A}^T-\mathbf{B}_k-\mathbf{B}_k^T\right)^{-1}\mathbf{A}\sum_{l \neq k}\mathbf{x}_l(t)+\boldsymbol{\alpha}-\mathbf{x}_k(t)\right]. \tag{5.1.3}$$

This equation may be rewritten as

$$\frac{d\mathbf{x}(t)}{dt} = -\begin{bmatrix} \mathbf{K}_1^c & & \\ & \ddots & \\ & & \mathbf{K}_N^c \end{bmatrix} \begin{bmatrix} \mathbf{I} & \mathbf{D}_1 & \cdots & \mathbf{D}_1 \\ \mathbf{D}_2 & \mathbf{I} & \cdots & \mathbf{D}_2 \\ \vdots & \vdots & \ddots & \vdots \\ \mathbf{D}_N & \mathbf{D}_N & \cdots & \mathbf{I} \end{bmatrix} \mathbf{x}(t) + \boldsymbol{\beta}_c, \tag{5.1.4}$$

where $\boldsymbol{\beta}_c$ is a constant vector. Note that by introducing the notation

$$\overline{\mathbf{K}}_k = -\mathbf{K}_k \left(\mathbf{A} + \mathbf{A}^T - \mathbf{B}_k - \mathbf{B}_k^T\right)^{-1},$$

model (5.1.2) formally reduces to model (5.1.4) with $\mathbf{K}_k^c$ replaced by $\overline{\mathbf{K}}_k$, $1 \le k \le N$. Consequently, in further discussions it is sufficient to consider only assumption (a) and differential equation (5.1.2).

Definition 5.1.1. The equilibrium point of the multiproduct oligopoly game is called globally asymptotically stable under adjustment assumption (a) if starting from arbitrary initial strategies $\mathbf{x}_1(0), \ldots, \mathbf{x}_N(0)$, the dynamic process (5.1.2) converges to the equilibrium point as time approaches infinity.

The following result is known from the theory of continuous linear system (see, for example, Szidarovszky and Bahill, 1992).

Theorem 5.1.1. The equilibrium point of the multiproduct oligopoly game is globally asymptotically stable with respect to the adjustment assumption (a) if and only if all eigenvalues of matrix

$$\begin{bmatrix} \mathbf{K}_1\left(\mathbf{A} + \mathbf{A}^T - \mathbf{B}_1 - \mathbf{B}_1^T\right) & & \\ & \ddots & \\ & & \mathbf{K}_N\left(\mathbf{A} + \mathbf{A}^T - \mathbf{B}_N - \mathbf{B}_N^T\right) \end{bmatrix} \begin{bmatrix} \mathbf{I} & \mathbf{D}_1 & \cdots & \mathbf{D}_1 \\ \mathbf{D}_2 & \mathbf{I} & \cdots & \mathbf{D}_2 \\ \vdots & \vdots & \ddots & \vdots \\ \mathbf{D}_N & \mathbf{D}_N & \cdots & \mathbf{I} \end{bmatrix} \tag{5.1.5}$$

have negative real parts.

Remark. In practical cases it is usually a difficult task to verify the condition of the theorem, since the eigenvalues of a large matrix must be determined. In the following part of this section sufficient conditions will be derived which guarantee - without computing the eigenvalues - that the conditions of the theorem hold, and therefore imply the global asymptotical stability of the equilibrium point.

In deriving sufficient stability conditions we use the following

Lemma 5.1.1. Assume that matrices $\mathbf{H}$ and $\mathbf{K}$ are quadratic and have the same size, furthermore $\mathbf{H}+\mathbf{H}^T$ is negative definite, and $\mathbf{K}$ is positive definite. Then all eigenvalues of matrix $\mathbf{K}\cdot\mathbf{H}$ have negative real parts.

Proof. Consider the eigenvalue problem of $\mathbf{K}\cdot\mathbf{H}$:

$$\mathbf{KHu}=\lambda\mathbf{u},\ \ (\mathbf{u}\neq\mathbf{0})$$

which is equivalent to equality

$$\mathbf{Hu}=\lambda\mathbf{K}^{-1}\mathbf{u}.$$

Premultiplying this equation by vector $\bar{\mathbf{u}}^T$, where overbar denotes complex conjugate, we get

$$\bar{\mathbf{u}}^T\mathbf{Hu}=\lambda\bar{\mathbf{u}}^T\mathbf{K}^{-1}\mathbf{u}. \tag{5.1.6}$$

Since $\mathbf{K}$ is positive definite, the same is true for $\mathbf{K}^{-1}$, and therefore

$$\bar{\mathbf{u}}^T\mathbf{K}^{-1}\mathbf{u}>0. \tag{5.1.7}$$

The left hand side of equation (5.1.6) satisfies the relation

$$2\,\mathrm{Re}\,\bar{\mathbf{u}}^T\mathbf{Hu}=\bar{\mathbf{u}}^T\left(\mathbf{H}+\mathbf{H}^T\right)\mathbf{u}<0. \tag{5.1.8}$$

Thus, relations (5.1.6), (5.1.7) and (5.1.8) imply that $\mathrm{Re}\,\lambda<0$, which proves the assertion. □

Corollary. Combining Theorem 5.1.1 and Lemma 5.1.1, we get the following assertion: The equilibrium point of the multiproduct oligopoly game is globally asymptotically stable with respect to the adjustment assumption (a) if all matrices $\mathbf{K}_k$ are positive definite and matrix $\mathbf{H}_c+\mathbf{H}_c^T$ is negative definite, where

$$\mathbf{H}_c=\begin{bmatrix}\mathbf{A}+\mathbf{A}^T-\mathbf{B}_1-\mathbf{B}_1^T & \mathbf{A} & \cdots & \mathbf{A}\\ \mathbf{A} & \mathbf{A}+\mathbf{A}^T-\mathbf{B}_2-\mathbf{B}_2^T & & \mathbf{A}\\ \vdots & \vdots & \ddots & \vdots\\ \mathbf{A} & \mathbf{A} & \cdots & \mathbf{A}+\mathbf{A}^T-\mathbf{B}_N-\mathbf{B}_N^T\end{bmatrix}. \tag{5.1.9}$$

The main result of this section is the following

Theorem 5.1.2. Assume that $\mathbf{A}+\mathbf{A}^T$ is negative definite, and $\mathbf{B}_k+\mathbf{B}_k^T$ is positive semidefinite for all k. Assume furthermore that matrices $\mathbf{K}_k$ are all positive definite. Then the equilibrium point of the multiproduct oligopoly game is globally asymptotically stable with respect to adjustment system (a).

Proof. According to the corollary of Lemma 5.1.1 it is sufficient to prove that matrix $\mathbf{H}_c + \mathbf{H}_c^T$ is negative definite, where $\mathbf{H}_c$ is defined by (5.1.9). Observe first that

$$\mathbf{H}_c + \mathbf{H}_c^T = \begin{bmatrix} 2(\mathbf{A}+\mathbf{A}^T) & \mathbf{A}+\mathbf{A}^T & \cdots & \mathbf{A}+\mathbf{A}^T \\ \mathbf{A}+\mathbf{A}^T & 2(\mathbf{A}+\mathbf{A}^T) & \cdots & \mathbf{A}+\mathbf{A}^T \\ \vdots & \vdots & \ddots & \vdots \\ \mathbf{A}+\mathbf{A}^T & \mathbf{A}+\mathbf{A}^T & \cdots & 2(\mathbf{A}+\mathbf{A}^T) \end{bmatrix} + \begin{bmatrix} -2(\mathbf{B}_1+\mathbf{B}_1^T) & & 0 \\ & \ddots & \\ 0 & & -2(\mathbf{B}_N+\mathbf{B}_N^T) \end{bmatrix}. \tag{5.1.10}$$

The first term equals

$$\begin{bmatrix} 2 & 1 & \cdots & 1 \\ 1 & 2 & \cdots & 1 \\ \vdots & \vdots & \ddots & \vdots \\ 1 & 1 & \cdots & 2 \end{bmatrix} \otimes \left(\mathbf{A}+\mathbf{A}^T\right).$$

The eigenvalues of $\mathbf{A}+\mathbf{A}^T$ are negative, and we can easily show that the eigenvalues of the first factor are all positive. Then Lemma 4.1.1 implies that the eigenvalues of the first term in (5.1.10) are all negative, therefore the first term is negative definite. To prove this fact note that

$$\begin{bmatrix} 2 & 1 & \cdots & 1 \\ 1 & 2 & \cdots & 1 \\ \vdots & \vdots & \ddots & \vdots \\ 1 & 1 & \cdots & 2 \end{bmatrix} = \mathbf{I} + \mathbf{1},$$

where $\mathbf{1}$ is the matrix with all unit elements. In proving Theorem 4.1.2 we have seen that the eigenvalues of $\mathbf{1}$ are 0 and N, and therefore the eigenvalues of $\mathbf{I}+\mathbf{1}$ are 1 and N+1, which are positive. Since the second term of (5.1.10) is negative semidefinite, the proof is completed. □

Remark. If $\mathbf{A}+\mathbf{A}^T$ is negative definite and $\mathbf{B}_k + \mathbf{B}_k^T$ is positive semidefinite for all k, then global asymptotical stability holds for arbitrary positive definite matrices $\mathbf{K}_k$.

Corollary. In the case of adjustment assumptions (b) and the conditions of the theorem, we have to assume that matrices $\mathbf{K}_k$ and $\mathbf{A}+\mathbf{A}^T - \mathbf{B}_k - \mathbf{B}_k^T$ commute in order to guarantee that matrix $\overline{\mathbf{K}}_k$ is positive definite. In this case we might apply the following result.

Lemma 5.1.2. If matrices **K** and **H** are positive definite and commute, then matrix **KH** is also positive definite.

Proof. First we verify that matrix **KH** is symmetric: $(\mathbf{KH})^T = \mathbf{H}^T\mathbf{K}^T = \mathbf{HK} = \mathbf{KH}$. Next we prove that all eigenvalues of **KH** are positive. Since -**H** is negative definite so is matrix $-\mathbf{H}-\mathbf{H}^T$. Therefore Lemma 5.1.1 implies that the real parts of the eigenvalues of $\mathbf{K}(-\mathbf{H}-\mathbf{H}^T) = -2\mathbf{KH}$ are negative. Since the eigenvalue of **KH** are real, the proof is complete. □

5.2 Adaptive Expectations

In this section two models with adaptive expectations will be introduced. In the first model it will be assumed that each firm forms adaptive expectations on the rest of the industry output. In the second model we assume that each firm forms expectations on rivals' outputs adaptively. Both models assume that conditions (A) - (D) presented at the introduction of this chapter hold.

Let $\mathbf{s}_k^E(t)$ denote the expectation of firm k on the *output of the rest of the industry* at time t. Assume that each firm adjusts its actual output proportionally to its expected marginal profit, where $\mathbf{s}_k^E(t)$ is assumed to be the total output of the rivals. Thus, the adjustment process can be described as

$$\frac{d\mathbf{x}_k(t)}{dt} = \mathbf{K}_k\left[\left(\mathbf{A}+\mathbf{A}^T-\mathbf{B}_k-\mathbf{B}_k^T\right)\mathbf{x}_k(t)+\mathbf{A}\mathbf{s}_k^E(t)+\mathbf{b}-\mathbf{b}_k\right], \tag{5.2.1}$$

which can be derived similarly to (5.1.1). It is also assumed that each firm's expectation is made adaptively according to equation

$$\frac{d\mathbf{s}_k^E(t)}{dt} = \mathbf{M}_k\left(\mathbf{s}_k(t)-\mathbf{s}_k^E(t)\right), \tag{5.2.2}$$

where $\mathbf{M}_k$ is a constant matrix, usually diagonal with positive diagonal elements, and $\mathbf{s}_k(t) = \sum_{l\neq k}\mathbf{x}_l(t)$. Equations (5.2.1) and (5.2.2) can be summarized as the differential equation

$$
\frac{d}{dt}\begin{bmatrix} \mathbf{x}_1 \\ \mathbf{x}_2 \\ \vdots \\ \mathbf{x}_N \\ \mathbf{s}_1 \\ \mathbf{s}_2 \\ \vdots \\ \mathbf{s}_N \end{bmatrix} = \begin{bmatrix} \mathbf{K}_1 & & & & & & & \\ & \mathbf{K}_2 & & & & & & \\ & & \ddots & & & & & \\ & & & \mathbf{K}_N & & & & \\ & & & & \mathbf{M}_1 & & & \\ & & & & & \mathbf{M}_2 & & \\ & & & & & & \ddots & \\ & & & & & & & \mathbf{M}_N \end{bmatrix} \cdot \mathbf{H}_A \cdot \begin{bmatrix} \mathbf{x}_1 \\ \mathbf{x}_2 \\ \vdots \\ \mathbf{x}_N \\ \mathbf{s}_1 \\ \mathbf{s}_2 \\ \vdots \\ \mathbf{s}_N \end{bmatrix} + \boldsymbol{\alpha}_A \tag{5.2.3}
$$

where $\boldsymbol{\alpha}_A$ is a constant vector, and

$$
\mathbf{H}_A = \left[\begin{array}{cccc|cccc} \mathbf{E}_1 & & & 0 & \mathbf{A} & & & 0 \\ & \mathbf{E}_2 & & & & \mathbf{A} & & \\ & & \ddots & & & & \ddots & \\ 0 & & & \mathbf{E}_N & 0 & & & \mathbf{A} \\ \hline 0 & \mathbf{I} & \cdots & \mathbf{I} & -\mathbf{I} & & & 0 \\ \mathbf{I} & 0 & \cdots & \mathbf{I} & & -\mathbf{I} & & \\ \vdots & \vdots & \ddots & \vdots & & & \ddots & \\ \mathbf{I} & \mathbf{I} & \cdots & 0 & 0 & & & -\mathbf{I} \end{array}\right] \text{with } \mathbf{E}_k = \mathbf{A} + \mathbf{A}^T - \mathbf{B}_k - \mathbf{B}_k^T,\ k = 1,2,\ldots N.
$$

Assume that

(E') For all $t \geq 0, \mathbf{x}_k(t) \in X_k$ and $\mathbf{x}_k(t) + \mathbf{s}_k^E(t) \in S$ $(\forall k)$.

The above derivation implies the following result.

Theorem 5.2.1. Under the above adjustment assumptions the equilibrium point of the multiproduct oligopoly game is globally asymptotically stable if and only if the real parts of all eigenvalues of matrix $\text{diag}\left(\mathbf{K}_1,\ldots,\mathbf{K}_N,\mathbf{M}_1,\ldots,\mathbf{M}_N\right)\cdot\mathbf{H}_A$ are negative.

Remark. In practical cases it is usually difficult to verify the conditions of the theorem since the eigenvalues of a large nonsymmetric matrix have to be determined. Therefore practical sufficient conditions will be derived next which can simplify the stability check.

The following result is a straightforward consequence of Lemma 5.1.1:

Theorem 5.2.2. Assume that matrices $\mathbf{K}_k$ and $\mathbf{M}_k$ are positive definite for all k, and matrix $\mathbf{H}_A + \mathbf{H}_A^T$ is negative definite. Then the equilibrium point is globally asymptotically stable with respect to adaptive expectations (5.2.2).

Remark. The dimension of $\mathbf{H}_A + \mathbf{H}_A^T$ is $2NM$. For practical purposes it is very important to reduce this dimension. Such reductions will be discussed next.

Introduce first the notation

$$\mathbf{F} = \begin{bmatrix} \mathbf{E}_1 & & & \\ & \mathbf{E}_2 & & \\ & & \ddots & \\ & & & \mathbf{E}_N \end{bmatrix}, \mathbf{A}_0 = \begin{bmatrix} \mathbf{A}^T & \mathbf{I} & \cdots & \mathbf{I} \\ \mathbf{I} & \mathbf{A}^T & \cdots & \mathbf{I} \\ \vdots & \vdots & \ddots & \vdots \\ \mathbf{I} & \mathbf{I} & \cdots & \mathbf{A}^T \end{bmatrix}.$$

Using this notation we first prove

Theorem 5.2.3. Assume that matrix $4\mathbf{F}+\mathbf{A}_0^T\mathbf{A}_0$ is negative definite, and matrices $\mathbf{K}_k$ and $\mathbf{M}_k$ are positive definite for all k. Then the equilibrium point is globally asymptotically stable with respect to adaptive expectations (5.2.2).

Proof. Consider the eigenvalue problem of matrix $\mathbf{H}_A+\mathbf{H}_A^T$:

$$2\mathbf{F}\mathbf{u}+\mathbf{A}_0^T\mathbf{v}=\lambda\mathbf{u}$$
$$\mathbf{A}_0\mathbf{u}-2\mathbf{v}=\lambda\mathbf{v},$$

where $\mathbf{u}$, $\mathbf{v}$ and λ are real. From the second equation

$$\mathbf{v}=\frac{1}{\lambda+2}\mathbf{A}_0\mathbf{u},$$

and by substituting it into the first equation we get

$$\left(2\mathbf{F}+\frac{1}{\lambda+2}\mathbf{A}_0^T\mathbf{A}_0-\lambda\mathbf{I}\right)\mathbf{u}=\mathbf{0}.$$

We may assume here that $\lambda \neq -2$, since a negative eigenvalue does not destroy stability. Multiply this equation by $\mathbf{u}^T$ and introduce the notation

$$\alpha^*=\frac{\mathbf{u}^T\mathbf{F}\mathbf{u}}{\mathbf{u}^T\mathbf{u}}, \quad \beta^*=\frac{\mathbf{u}^T\mathbf{A}_0^T\mathbf{A}_0\mathbf{u}}{\mathbf{u}^T\mathbf{u}}$$

to obtain

$$\lambda^2-(2\alpha^*-2)\lambda-(4\alpha^*+\beta^*)=0.$$

The assumptions of the theorem imply that $4\alpha^*+\beta^*<0$, and assumption (D) implies that $2\alpha^*-2<0$. Consequently both roots of this quadratic equation are negative.

□

Remark. The dimension of $4\mathbf{F}+\mathbf{A}_0^T\mathbf{A}_0$ is MN, which is the half of the dimension of $\mathbf{H}_A+\mathbf{H}_A^T$.

In certain special cases further reductions in the dimension is possible, as the following results show.

Theorem 5.2.4. Assume that

(i) Matrices $\mathbf{K}_k$ and $\mathbf{M}_k$ are positive definite for all k;
(ii) $\mathbf{B}_k \equiv \mathbf{B}$ for all k;
(iii) Matrices
$(\mathbf{A}-\mathbf{I})(\mathbf{A}^T-\mathbf{I})+4\mathbf{E}$ and $(\mathbf{A}+(N-1)\mathbf{I})(\mathbf{A}^T+(N-1)\mathbf{I})+4\mathbf{E}$
are negative definite, where $\mathbf{E}=\mathbf{A}+\mathbf{A}^T-\mathbf{B}-\mathbf{B}^T$.

Then the equilibrium point is globally asymptotically stable with respect to adaptive expectations (5.2.2).

Proof. On the basis of Theorem 5.2.2 it is sufficient to prove that all eigenvalues of matrix $\mathbf{H}_A+\mathbf{H}_A^T$ have negative real parts. In order to verify this statement consider the eigenvalue equation of matrix $\mathbf{H}_A+\mathbf{H}_A^T$:

$$\begin{aligned} &2\mathbf{E}\mathbf{u}_k+\mathbf{A}\mathbf{v}_k+\sum_{i\neq k}\mathbf{v}_i=\lambda\mathbf{u}_k \\ &\mathbf{A}^T\mathbf{u}_k+\sum_{i\neq k}\mathbf{u}_i-2\mathbf{v}_k=\lambda\mathbf{v}_k, \end{aligned} \tag{5.2.4}$$

where $\mathbf{u}_k$, $\mathbf{v}_k$, $\mathbf{u}_i$, $\mathbf{v}_i$ are all M dimensional real vectors, and λ is a real number. By adding equations (5.2.4) for k=1,2,...,N we have

$$\begin{aligned} &2\mathbf{E}\mathbf{u}+\mathbf{A}\mathbf{v}+(N-1)\mathbf{v}=\lambda\mathbf{u} \\ &\mathbf{A}^T\mathbf{u}+(N-1)\mathbf{u}-2\mathbf{v}=\lambda\mathbf{v} \end{aligned} \tag{5.2.5}$$

with

$$\mathbf{u}=\sum_{k=1}^N\mathbf{u}_k \text{ and } \mathbf{v}=\sum_{k=1}^N\mathbf{v}_k .$$

If λ=-2, then we have nothing to prove, since this eigenvalue is negative. If $\lambda\neq$-2, then the second equation of (5.2.5) implies that

$$\mathbf{v}=\frac{1}{\lambda+2}\left(\mathbf{A}^T+(N-1)\mathbf{I}\right)\mathbf{u}. \tag{5.2.6}$$

Substituting this relation into the first equation of (5.2.5) we see that

$$\left[2\mathbf{E}-\lambda\mathbf{I}+\frac{1}{\lambda+2}(\mathbf{A}+(N-1)\mathbf{I})\left(\mathbf{A}^T+(N-1)\mathbf{I}\right)\right]\mathbf{u}=\mathbf{0};$$

that is,

$$\left[-\lambda^2\mathbf{I}+2\lambda(\mathbf{E}-\mathbf{I})+(\mathbf{A}+(N-1)\mathbf{I})\left(\mathbf{A}^T+(N-1)\mathbf{I}\right)+4\mathbf{E}\right]\mathbf{u}=\mathbf{0}. \tag{5.2.7}$$

Assume first that **u=0**. Then from (5.2.6) we obtain **v=0**, and from (5.2.4) we conclude that

$$\begin{aligned}2\mathbf{E}\mathbf{u}_k+(\mathbf{A}-\mathbf{I})\mathbf{v}_k&=\lambda\mathbf{u}_k\\ \left(\mathbf{A}^T-\mathbf{I}\right)\mathbf{u}_k-2\mathbf{v}_k&=\lambda\mathbf{v}_k.\end{aligned} \tag{5.2.8}$$

The second equation of (5.2.8) implies

$$\mathbf{v}_k=\frac{1}{\lambda+2}\left(\mathbf{A}^T-\mathbf{I}\right)\mathbf{u}_k. \tag{5.2.9}$$

By substituting this relation into the first equation of (5.2.8) the following equality is obtained:

$$\left[2\mathbf{E}-\lambda\mathbf{I}+\frac{1}{\lambda+2}(\mathbf{A}-\mathbf{I})\left(\mathbf{A}^T-\mathbf{I}\right)\right]\mathbf{u}_k=\mathbf{0}.$$

That is,

$$\left[-\lambda^2\mathbf{I}+2\lambda(\mathbf{E}-\mathbf{I})+(\mathbf{A}-\mathbf{I})\left(\mathbf{A}^T-\mathbf{I}\right)+4\mathbf{E}\right]\mathbf{u}_k=\mathbf{0}. \tag{5.2.10}$$

If $\mathbf{u}_k=\mathbf{0}$ for all k, then (5.2.9) implies that $\mathbf{v}_k=\mathbf{0}$ for all k. This situation cannot occur, since eigenvectors must differ from zero. Thus, for at least one k, $\mathbf{u}_k\neq\mathbf{0}$.

In summary, we conclude that if **u=0**, then (5.2.10) holds for at least one nonzero vector $\mathbf{u}_k$, and if $\mathbf{u}\neq\mathbf{0}$, then (5.2.7) holds. That is, for some nonzero vector **w** (which is either $\mathbf{u}_k$ or **u**),

$$\left(-\lambda^2\mathbf{I}+2\lambda(\mathbf{E}-\mathbf{I})+(\mathbf{A}+Q\cdot\mathbf{I})\left(\mathbf{A}^T+Q\cdot\mathbf{I}\right)+4\mathbf{E}\right)\mathbf{w}=\mathbf{0},$$

where Q equals either -1 or $(N-1)$.

Multiplying this equation by $\mathbf{w}^T$ leads to the quadratic equation

$$\lambda^2 - 2\alpha^*\lambda - \beta^* = 0, \tag{5.2.11}$$

where

$$\alpha^* = \frac{\mathbf{w}^T(\mathbf{E}-\mathbf{I})\mathbf{w}}{\mathbf{w}^T\mathbf{w}} < 0$$

and

$$\beta^* = \frac{\mathbf{w}^T\left[(\mathbf{A}+Q\mathbf{I})(\mathbf{A}^T+Q\mathbf{I})+4\mathbf{E}\right]\mathbf{w}}{\mathbf{w}^T\mathbf{w}} < 0.$$

Since the eigenvalue is real, λ must be negative. □

Remark 1. Note that the dimension of matrices

$$(\mathbf{A}+Q\mathbf{I})(\mathbf{A}^T+Q\mathbf{I})+4\mathbf{E} \quad \left(Q \in \{-1;\, N-1\}\right)$$

equals M, which is really a large reduction in the size of matrices compared to the dimension $2MN$ of matrix $\mathbf{H}_A$.

Remark 2. The economic interpretations of the conditions of the Theorem are as follows. Usually we take $\mathbf{K}_k = \text{diag}\left(K_k^{(1)},\ldots,K_k^{(M)}\right)$ and $\mathbf{M}_k = \text{diag}\left(M_k^{(1)},\ldots,M_k^{(M)}\right)$, where the speeds of adjustment $K_k^{(m)}$ and $M_k^{(m)}$ are assumed positive. These conditions imply that matrices $\mathbf{K}_k$ and $\mathbf{M}_k$ are positive definite for all k. Condition (ii) means that in its cost function each firm has the same quadratic term. Condition (iii) can be explained directly in the special case of M=1, that is, in the case of the classical oligopoly game without product differentiation. By introducing appropriate unit in price, we may assume that $A=-1$ and $B=d/2$. Then $E=-2-d$, and assumptions (iii) are equivalent to the inequalities

$$(-2)(-2)+4(-2-d)<0 \text{ and } (-1+N-1)(-1+N-1)+4(-2-d)<0.$$

These relations hold if and only if

$$d > \max\left\{-1;\, \frac{(N-2)^2-8}{4}\right\};$$

that is,

$$d > \begin{cases} -1, & \text{if } N \le 4 \\ \dfrac{(N-2)^2 - 8}{4} & \text{if } N \ge 5. \end{cases} \tag{5.2.12}$$

Remark 3. Finally consider the special case when $\mathbf{A} = \mathbf{A}^T$ and $\mathbf{B}_k = \mathbf{0}$ for all k. In this case $\mathbf{E}$=2$\mathbf{A}$. If α_i denotes the eigenvalues of matrix $\mathbf{A}$, then $\alpha_i < 0$, furthermore the eigenvalues of the matrices in condition (iii) are

$$(\alpha_i - 1)^2 + 8\alpha_i \text{ and } (\alpha_i + N - 1)^2 + 8\alpha_i.$$

They are negative if and only if

$$\alpha_i \in \left(-3 - \sqrt{8},\ -3 + \sqrt{8}\right)$$

and (5.2.13)

$$\alpha_i \in \left(-(N+3) - \sqrt{8(N+1)},\ -(N+3) + \sqrt{8(N+1)}\right).$$

In this case we have the following

Theorem 5.2.5. Assume that $\mathbf{A} = \mathbf{A}^T$ and $\mathbf{B}_k = \mathbf{0}$ for all k. Assume furthermore that all eigenvalues α_i of matrix $\mathbf{A}$ satisfy the following conditions:

$$\begin{aligned} &\alpha_i \in \left(-3 - \sqrt{8}, -3 + \sqrt{8}\right) && \text{if } N = 2; \\ &\alpha_i \in \left(-3 - \sqrt{8}, -(N+3) + \sqrt{8(N+1)}\right) && \text{if } 3 \le N \le 13. \end{aligned} \tag{5.2.14}$$

Then the equilibrium point is globally asymptotically stable with respect to adaptive expectations (5.2.2).

Proof. We have to verify that (5.2.14) is equivalent to (5.2.13). In order to prove this equivalence note that for N=2,

$$-3 - \sqrt{8} > -(N+3) - \sqrt{8(N+1)} \text{ and } -3 + \sqrt{8} < -(N+3) + \sqrt{8(N+1)}.$$

For $N \ge 3$,

$$-3 - \sqrt{8} > -(N+3) - \sqrt{8(N+1)} \text{ and } -(N+3) + \sqrt{8(N+1)} < -3 + \sqrt{8}.$$

Furthermore, no real α_i satisfies the second condition of (5.2.14) for $N \ge 14$.

□

In the next part of this section adaptive expectations on the *rivals' outputs* will be examined. Let $\mathbf{x}_{kl}^{E}(t)$ denote the expectation of firm k at time t on the output $\mathbf{x}_l(t)$ of firm $l(l \neq k)$. The adjustment process can now be described as

$$\frac{d\mathbf{x}_k(t)}{dt} = \mathbf{K}_k \left[\left(\mathbf{A} + \mathbf{A}^T - \mathbf{B}_k - \mathbf{B}_k^T\right)\mathbf{x}_k(t) + \mathbf{A}\sum_{l \neq k} \mathbf{x}_{kl}^{E}(t) + \mathbf{b} - \mathbf{b}_k \right], \tag{5.2.15}$$

since the right hand side is the $\mathbf{K}_k$-multiple of the expected marginal profit of firm k. It is also assumed that the expectations of firm k are given adaptively as

$$\frac{d\mathbf{x}_{kl}^{E}(t)}{dt} = \mathbf{M}_{kl}\left(\mathbf{x}_l(t) - \mathbf{x}_{kl}^{E}(t)\right), \tag{5.2.16}$$

where $\mathbf{M}_{kl}$ is a constant matrix for all k and $l \neq k$, which is usually assumed to be diagonal with positive diagonal elements. Equations (5.2.15) and (5.2.16) are analogous to the corresponding equations (5.2.1) and (5.2.2), where adaptive expectations on the output of the rest of the industry are assumed. Relation (5.2.15) and (5.2.16) can be summarized as

$$\frac{d}{dt}\begin{bmatrix} \mathbf{x}_1 \\ \mathbf{x}_2 \\ \vdots \\ \mathbf{x}_N \\ \mathbf{x}_{12} \\ \vdots \\ \mathbf{x}_{1N} \\ \vdots \\ \mathbf{x}_{N1} \\ \vdots \\ \mathbf{x}_{N,N-1} \end{bmatrix} = \begin{bmatrix} \mathbf{K}_1 & & & & & & & & & \\ & \mathbf{K}_2 & & & & & & & \mathbf{0} & \\ & & \ddots & & & & & & & \\ & & & \mathbf{K}_N & & & & & & \\ & & & & \mathbf{M}_{12} & & & & & \\ & & & & & \ddots & & & & \\ & & & & & & \mathbf{M}_{1N} & & & \\ & & \mathbf{0} & & & & & \ddots & & \\ & & & & & & & & \mathbf{M}_{N1} & \\ & & & & & & & & & \ddots \\ & & & & & & & & & & \mathbf{M}_{N,N-1} \end{bmatrix} \cdot \mathbf{H}_A^{*} \cdot \begin{bmatrix} \mathbf{x}_1 \\ \mathbf{x}_2 \\ \vdots \\ \mathbf{x}_N \\ \mathbf{x}_{12} \\ \vdots \\ \mathbf{x}_{1N} \\ \vdots \\ \mathbf{x}_{N1} \\ \vdots \\ \mathbf{x}_{N,N-1} \end{bmatrix} + \boldsymbol{\alpha}_A^{*}, \tag{5.2.17}$$

where $\boldsymbol{\alpha}_A^{*}$ is a constant vector, and

$$\mathbf{H}_A^{*} = \left[\begin{array}{ccc|ccc|c|ccc} \mathbf{E}_1 & & & \mathbf{A} & \cdots & \mathbf{A} & & \mathbf{0} & \cdots & \mathbf{0} \\ & & & \mathbf{0} & \cdots & \mathbf{0} & & \vdots & & \vdots \\ & \ddots & & \vdots & & \vdots & & \mathbf{0} & & \mathbf{0} \\ & & \mathbf{E}_N & \mathbf{0} & \cdots & \mathbf{0} & & \mathbf{A} & \cdots & \mathbf{A} \\ \hline \mathbf{0} & \mathbf{I} & & -\mathbf{I} & & & & & & \\ & \ddots & & & \ddots & & & & & \\ & & \mathbf{I} & & & -\mathbf{I} & & & & \\ \hline & \vdots & & & & & \ddots & & & \\ \hline \mathbf{I} & & & & & & & -\mathbf{I} & & \\ & \ddots & & & & & \cdots & & \ddots & \\ & \mathbf{I} & \mathbf{0} & & & & & & & -\mathbf{I} \end{array}\right] \begin{array}{l} \left.\vphantom{\begin{array}{c}1\\1\\1\\1\end{array}}\right\} N \\ \left.\vphantom{\begin{array}{c}1\\1\\1\end{array}}\right\} N-1 \\ \\ \left.\vphantom{\begin{array}{c}1\\1\\1\end{array}}\right\} N-1 \end{array}$$

with column blocks of widths $\underbrace{}_{N}$, $\underbrace{}_{N-1}$, …, $\underbrace{}_{N-1}$.

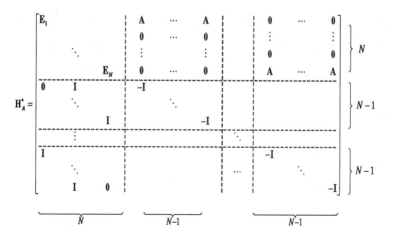

with $\mathbf{E}_k = \mathbf{A} + \mathbf{A}^T - \mathbf{B}_k - \mathbf{B}_k^T$ as before.

Assume that

(E") For all t, $\mathbf{x}_k(t) \in X_k$ and $\mathbf{x}_k(t) + \sum_{l \neq k} \mathbf{x}_{kl}^E(t) \in S$ $(\forall k)$.

The above derivation implies the following result.

Theorem 5.2.6. Under the above adjustment assumptions the equilibrium point of the multiproduct oligopoly game is globally asymptotically stable if and only if the real parts of all eigenvalues of matrix $\text{diag}\left(\mathbf{K}_1, ..., \mathbf{K}_N, \mathbf{M}_{12}, ..., \mathbf{M}_{1N}, ..., \mathbf{M}_{N,1}, ..., \mathbf{M}_{N,N-1}\right) \cdot \mathbf{H}_A^*$ have negative real parts.

In a manner similar to the proof of Theorem 5.2.2, we can obtain the following

Theorem 5.2.7. Assume that matrices $\mathbf{K}_k$ and $\mathbf{M}_{kl}$ $(k = 1, ..., N, l \neq k)$ are all positive definite and matrix $\mathbf{H}_A^* + \mathbf{H}_A^{*T}$ is negative definite. Then the equilibrium point is globally asymptotically stable with respect to adaptive expectations (5.2.16).

Remark. The dimension of matrix $\mathbf{H}_A^* + \mathbf{H}_A^{*T}$ is $NM + N(N-1)M = N^2M$, which can be very large if many firms and a large number of products are present. Therefore reduction in the dimension of matrices (the eigenvalues of which should be examined) may have significant practical importance. Such reductions will be discussed next.

Introduce the notation

$$\mathbf{A}_1 = \begin{bmatrix} \mathbf{A}^T & \mathbf{I} & & \\ \vdots & & \ddots & \\ \mathbf{A}^T & & & \mathbf{I} \end{bmatrix}, ..., \mathbf{A}_N = \begin{bmatrix} \mathbf{I} & & & \mathbf{A}^T \\ & \ddots & & \vdots \\ & & \mathbf{I} & \mathbf{A}^T \end{bmatrix}, \mathbf{F} = \begin{bmatrix} \mathbf{E}_1 & & \\ & \ddots & \\ & & \mathbf{E}_N \end{bmatrix},$$

then

$$\mathbf{H}_A^* + \mathbf{H}_A^{*T} = \begin{bmatrix} 2\mathbf{F} & \mathbf{A}_1^T & \cdots & \mathbf{A}_N^T \\ \mathbf{A}_1 & -2\mathbf{I} & & \\ \vdots & & \ddots & \\ \mathbf{A}_N & & & -2\mathbf{I} \end{bmatrix}.$$

Our first reduction theorem can be formulated as a straightforward extension of Theorem 5.2.3.

Theorem 5.2.8. Assume that matrices $\mathbf{K}_k$ and $\mathbf{M}_{kl}$ $(k=1,...,N, l \neq k)$ are all positive definite and furthermore matrix

$$4\mathbf{F} + \sum_{k=1}^{N} \mathbf{A}_k^T \mathbf{A}_k \tag{5.2.18}$$

is negative definite. Then the equilibrium point is globally asymptotically stable with respect to adaptive expectations (5.2.16).

Proof. On the basis of Theorem 5.2.7 it is sufficient to prove that matrix $\mathbf{H}_A^* + \mathbf{H}_A^{*T}$ is negative definite. To verify this assertion consider the eigenvalue problem of matrix $\mathbf{H}_A^* + \mathbf{H}_A^{*T}$:

$$\begin{aligned} &2\mathbf{F}\mathbf{u} + \sum_{k=1}^{N} \mathbf{A}_k^T \mathbf{v}_k = \lambda \mathbf{u} \\ &\mathbf{A}_k \mathbf{u} - 2\mathbf{v}_k = \lambda \mathbf{v}_k \quad (k = 1,2,...,N). \end{aligned} \tag{5.2.19}$$

We have to prove that $\lambda < 0$, since matrix $\mathbf{H}_A^* + \mathbf{H}_A^{*T}$ is symmetric. If $\lambda = -2$, then we have nothing to prove. If $\lambda \neq -2$, then the second equation of (5.2.19) implies that

$$\mathbf{v}_k = \frac{1}{\lambda+2} \mathbf{A}_k \mathbf{u}, \tag{5.2.20}$$

and by substituting this relation into the first equation of (5.2.19) we obtain

$$\left(2\mathbf{F} + \frac{1}{\lambda+2} \sum_{k=1}^{N} \mathbf{A}_k^T \mathbf{A}_k - \lambda \mathbf{I}\right) \mathbf{u} = \mathbf{0}. \tag{5.2.21}$$

If **u=0**, then (5.2.20) implies that for all k, $\mathbf{v}_k = \mathbf{0}$. This case cannot occur, since eigenvectors must differ from zero. If **u≠0**, then by multiplying relation (5.2.21) by vector $\mathbf{u}^T(\lambda+2)$ and introducing the notation

$$\alpha^* = \frac{\mathbf{u}^T \mathbf{F} \mathbf{u}}{\mathbf{u}^T \mathbf{u}} < 0 \text{ and } \beta^* = \frac{\mathbf{u}^T \left(\sum_{k=1}^{N} \mathbf{A}_k^T \mathbf{A}_k \right) \mathbf{u}}{\mathbf{u}^T \mathbf{u}}$$

equation (5.2.21) can be reduced to the quadratic equation

$$\lambda^2 - (2\alpha^* - 2)\lambda - (4\alpha^* + \beta^*) = 0.$$

Since both roots λ_1 and λ_2 are real and inequalities

$$\lambda_1 + \lambda_2 = 2(\alpha^* - 1) < 0,$$
$$\lambda_1 \lambda_2 = -(4\alpha^* + \beta^*) > 0$$

hold, we conclude that both roots λ_1 and λ_2 are negative. Thus the proof is completed. □

Remark. The dimension of matrix (5.2.18) is MN, which is usually much smaller than that of matrix $\mathbf{H}_A^* + \mathbf{H}_A^{*T}$. If M and N are large, MN may still be large. This situation makes further reductions in the dimension of matrices very important.

Consider finally the special case when $\mathbf{A}^T = \mathbf{A}$, and $\mathbf{B}_k = \mathbf{0}$ for all k. Then simple calculations show that matrix (5.2.18) can be rewritten as

$$\begin{bmatrix} 8\mathbf{A} & & & \\ & 8\mathbf{A} & & \\ & & \ddots & \\ & & & 8\mathbf{A} \end{bmatrix} + \begin{bmatrix} (N-1)(\mathbf{A}^2+\mathbf{I}) & 2\mathbf{A} & \cdots & 2\mathbf{A} \\ 2\mathbf{A} & (N-1)(\mathbf{A}^2+\mathbf{I}) & & 2\mathbf{A} \\ \vdots & \vdots & \ddots & \vdots \\ 2\mathbf{A} & 2\mathbf{A} & \cdots & (N-1)(\mathbf{A}^2+\mathbf{I}) \end{bmatrix}$$
$$= ((N-1)\mathbf{I} \otimes \mathbf{A}^2) + ((2\mathbf{1} + 6\mathbf{I}) \otimes \mathbf{A}) + ((N-1)\mathbf{I} \otimes \mathbf{A}^0), \tag{5.2.22}$$

where all elements of matrix $\mathbf{1}$ are unity. This matrix structure is slightly more general than the Kronecker product of two matrices. A general formulation of such constructs can be defined as follows.

Definition 5.2.1. Let $\mathbf{M}$ and $\mathbf{N}$ be real square matrices and $p_0(x), \ldots, p_r(x)$ be real polynomials. Then the construct

$$p_r(\mathbf{N}) \otimes \mathbf{M}^r + \cdots + p_1(\mathbf{N}) \otimes \mathbf{M}^1 + p_0(\mathbf{N}) \otimes \mathbf{M}^0 \tag{5.2.23}$$

is called the *Kronecker polynomial* of $\mathbf{M}$ and $\mathbf{N}$.

It is possible to generalize Lemma 4.1.1 for Kronecker polynomials. This generalization can be verified analogously to Lemma 4.1.1, and can be stated as follows:

Lemma 5.2.1. Let $\mathbf{M}$ and $\mathbf{N}$ be real quadratic matrices. Let λ_i and μ_j denote the eigenvalues of $\mathbf{M}$ and $\mathbf{N}$, respectively. Then the eigenvalues of matrix (5.2.23) are the numbers

$$\lambda_i^r \cdot p_r(\mu_j) + \cdots + \lambda_i^1 \cdot p_1(\mu_j) + \lambda_i^0 \cdot p_0(\mu_j).$$

By using the lemma, the eigenvalues of matrix (5.2.22) can be determined easily. We know from the proof of Theorem 4.1.2 that the eigenvalues of **1** are 0 and N. Let α_i denote the eigenvalues of matrix **A**. If we take r=2,

$$p_2(x) = N-1,\ p_1(x) = 2x+6,\ p_0(x) = N-1,$$
$$\mathbf{M} = \mathbf{A} \text{ and } \mathbf{N} = \mathbf{1},$$

then Lemma 5.2.1 implies that the eigenvalues of matrix (5.2.22) are the numbers

$$(N-1)\alpha_i^2 + 6\alpha_i + (N-1) \text{ and } (N-1)\alpha_i^2 + (2N+6)\alpha_i + (N-1).$$

These eigenvalues are all negative if and only if

$$\frac{-3-\sqrt{8+2N-N^2}}{N-1} < \alpha_i < \frac{-3+\sqrt{8+2N-N^2}}{N-1}$$

and (5.2.24)

$$\frac{-(N+3)-\sqrt{8(N+1)}}{N-1} < \alpha_i < \frac{-(N+3)+\sqrt{8(N+1)}}{N-1}.$$

Thus we have the following

Theorem 5.2.9. Assume that $\mathbf{A} = \mathbf{A}^T$ and $\mathbf{B}_k = \mathbf{0}$ for all k. Assume furthermore that all eigenvalues α_i of matrix **A** satisfy the conditions:

$$\alpha_i \in \left(-3-\sqrt{8},\ -3+\sqrt{8}\right) \quad \text{if} \quad N=2;$$

$$\alpha_i \in \left(\frac{-3-\sqrt{5}}{2},\ \frac{-3+\sqrt{5}}{2}\right) \quad \text{if} \quad N=3.$$

Then the equilibrium point is globally asymptotically stable with respect to adaptive expectations (5.2.16).

Proof. If N=2, then

$$\max\left\{\frac{-3-\sqrt{8+2N-N^2}}{N-1};\ \frac{-(N+3)-\sqrt{8(N+1)}}{N-1}\right\} = -3-\sqrt{8}$$

and

$$\min\left\{\frac{-3+\sqrt{8+2N-N^2}}{N-1};\ \frac{-(N+3)+\sqrt{8(N+1)}}{N-1}\right\}=-3+\sqrt{8}.$$

If N=3, then

$$\max\left\{\frac{-3-\sqrt{8+2N-N^2}}{N-1};\ \frac{-(N+3)-\sqrt{8(N+1)}}{N-1}\right\}=\frac{-3-\sqrt{5}}{2}$$

and

$$\min\left\{\frac{-3+\sqrt{8+2N-N^2}}{N-1};\ \frac{-(N+3)+\sqrt{8(N+1)}}{N-1}\right\}=\frac{-3+\sqrt{5}}{2}.$$

If $N \geq 4$, then no α_i satisfies inequalities of (5.2.24). □

Remark 1. Let us compare the stability conditions of Theorems 5.2.5 and 5.2.9. In the case of Theorem 5.2.5 stability may be guaranteed for up to 13 firms, however, in the case of Theorem 5.2.9 stability can be guaranteed only up to 3 firms. In addition, for duopolies, the stability intervals of α_i are the same in the two cases. This is as they should, since for duopolies $\mathbf{x}_{kl} = \mathbf{s}_k$ and therefore the two models are necessarily the same. If N=3, then the range for α_i which guarantees stability is larger in Theorem 5.2.5 than that in case of Theorem 5.2.9. Hence we may conclude that adaptive expectations on the output of the rest of the industry give a more stable process than adaptive expectations on the rivals' outputs.

Remark 2. It is very interesting to note that the assertions of Theorems 5.2.5 and 5.2.9 do not depend on the number M of products.

5.3 Extrapolative Expectations

In this section it is also assumed that conditions (A) - (D) hold. In the case of extrapolative expectations at all $t \geq 0$, each firm k adjusts its expectation on the output of the rest of the industry according to the rule

$$\mathbf{s}_k^E(t) = \mathbf{s}_k(t) + \mathbf{M}_k \frac{d}{dt}\mathbf{s}_k(t), \tag{5.3.1}$$

where $\mathbf{M}_k$ is a constant (usually diagonal) matrix. If expectations are formed on the rivals' outputs, then a similar method to the one presented in this section, can be used. As in the previous section, it is also assumed that each firm adjusts its output by

$$\frac{d}{dt}\mathbf{x}_k(t) = \mathbf{K}_k\left[\left(\mathbf{A} + \mathbf{A} - \mathbf{B}_k - \mathbf{B}_k^T\right)\mathbf{x}_k(t) + \mathbf{A}\mathbf{s}_k^E(t) + \mathbf{b} - \mathbf{b}_k\right].$$

Combining this equation with (5.3.1) we get the differential equation:

$$\frac{d}{dt}\mathbf{x}(t) = \mathbf{H}_E\mathbf{x}(t) + \boldsymbol{\beta}_E, \tag{5.3.2}$$

where $\boldsymbol{\beta}_E$ is a constant vector,

$$\mathbf{H}_E = \mathbf{E}^{-1}\mathbf{K}\mathbf{F}$$

with

$$\mathbf{E} = \begin{bmatrix} \mathbf{I} & -\mathbf{K}_1\mathbf{A}\mathbf{M}_1 & \cdots & -\mathbf{K}_1\mathbf{A}\mathbf{M}_1 \\ -\mathbf{K}_2\mathbf{A}\mathbf{M}_2 & \mathbf{I} & \cdots & -\mathbf{K}_2\mathbf{A}\mathbf{M}_2 \\ \vdots & \vdots & \ddots & \vdots \\ -\mathbf{K}_N\mathbf{A}\mathbf{M}_N & -\mathbf{K}_N\mathbf{A}\mathbf{M}_N & \cdots & \mathbf{I} \end{bmatrix},$$

$$\mathbf{K} = \begin{bmatrix} \mathbf{K}_1\left(\mathbf{A} + \mathbf{A}^T - \mathbf{B}_1 - \mathbf{B}_1^T\right) & & \\ & \ddots & \\ & & \mathbf{K}_N\left(\mathbf{A} + \mathbf{A}^T - \mathbf{B}_N - \mathbf{B}_N^T\right) \end{bmatrix},$$

and

$$\mathbf{F} = \begin{bmatrix} \mathbf{I} & \mathbf{D}_1 & \cdots & \mathbf{D}_1 \\ \mathbf{D}_2 & \mathbf{I} & \cdots & \mathbf{D}_2 \\ \vdots & \vdots & \ddots & \vdots \\ \mathbf{D}_N & \mathbf{D}_N & \cdots & \mathbf{I} \end{bmatrix},$$

where $\mathbf{D}_k = \left(\mathbf{A} + \mathbf{A}^T - \mathbf{B}_k - \mathbf{B}_k^T\right)^{-1}\mathbf{A}$ as before.

Here we assume that $\mathbf{E}$ is nonsingular, furthermore

($E^{(3)}$) For all $t \geq 0$ and $k = 1,2,\ldots,N$, $\mathbf{x}_k(t) \in X_k$.

From the theory of ordinary differential equations the following result is well known:

Theorem 5.3.1. The equilibrium point of the multiproduct oligopoly game is globally asymptotically stable with respect to the dynamic process (5.3.2) if and only if all eigenvalues of $\mathbf{H}_E$ have negative real parts.

From Lemma 5.1.1 we know that the conditions of the theorem hold if $\mathbf{H}_E + \mathbf{H}_E^T$ is negative definite by selecting **K=I** and **H=H**$_E$ in the assertion of the lemma. Since the size of matrix $\mathbf{H}_E$ is usually large, it is generally difficult to verify the conditions of the theorem, or even to prove that matrix $\mathbf{H}_E + \mathbf{H}_E^T$ is negative definite. A further difficulty arises from the fact that the structure of $\mathbf{H}_E$ is rather complicated. However, in certain special cases these conditions can be simplified and therefore easily verified. Such a case will be discussed next.

Observe first that $\mathbf{H}_E$ can be rewritten as

$$\mathbf{H}_E = \mathbf{U}^{-1}\mathbf{V},$$

where

$$\mathbf{U} = \begin{bmatrix} \mathbf{K}_1^{-1} & -\mathbf{AM}_1 & \cdots & -\mathbf{AM}_1 \\ -\mathbf{AM}_2 & \mathbf{K}_2^{-1} & \cdots & -\mathbf{AM}_2 \\ \vdots & \vdots & \ddots & \vdots \\ -\mathbf{AM}_N & -\mathbf{AM}_N & \cdots & \mathbf{K}_N^{-1} \end{bmatrix}$$

and

$$\mathbf{V} = \begin{bmatrix} \mathbf{A}+\mathbf{A}^T-\mathbf{B}_1-\mathbf{B}_1^T & \mathbf{A} & \cdots & \mathbf{A} \\ \mathbf{A} & \mathbf{A}+\mathbf{A}^T-\mathbf{B}_2-\mathbf{B}_2^T & \cdots & \mathbf{A} \\ \vdots & \vdots & \ddots & \vdots \\ \mathbf{A} & \mathbf{A} & \cdots & \mathbf{A}+\mathbf{A}^T-\mathbf{B}_N-\mathbf{B}_N^T \end{bmatrix}.$$

Note that

$$\mathbf{V}+\mathbf{V}^T = (\mathbf{1}+\mathbf{I})\otimes(\mathbf{A}+\mathbf{A}^T) - \mathrm{diag}(\mathbf{B}_1+\mathbf{B}_1^T,\dots,\mathbf{B}_N+\mathbf{B}_N^T),$$

and assume that $\mathbf{A}+\mathbf{A}^T$ is negative definite and for all k, $\mathbf{B}_k+\mathbf{B}_k^T$ is positive semidefinite. The eigenvalues of $\mathbf{A}+\mathbf{A}^T$ are negative and the eigenvalues of $\mathbf{1}+\mathbf{I}$ are 1 and N+1. Therefore Lemma 4.1.1 implies that the first term has only negative eigenvalues. Since it is symmetric, it is necessarily negative definite. Therefore $\mathbf{V}+\mathbf{V}^T$ is negative definite. Lemma 5.1.1 implies that in this case it is sufficient to guarantee that **U** is symmetric and positive definite (since then the same is true for $\mathbf{U}^{-1}$). Such conditions are presented in the following

Theorem 5.3.2. Assume that $\mathbf{A}+\mathbf{A}^T$ is negative definite and for all k, $\mathbf{B}_k+\mathbf{B}_k^T$ is positive semidefinite. Assume furthermore that $\mathbf{M}_k \equiv \mathbf{M}$ $(\forall k)$, and matrices $\mathbf{K}_k$ and $\mathbf{AM}$ are symmetric. Let γ_{ki} and υ_j denote the eigenvalues of $\mathbf{K}_k$ and $\mathbf{AM}$, respectively. If $\gamma_{ki} > 0$ for all k and i, and

$$\frac{-1}{\max_{k,i}\{\gamma_{ki}\}} < \upsilon_j < \frac{1}{(N-1)\max_{k,i}\{\gamma_{ki}\}} \tag{5.3.3}$$

for all j, then the equilibrium point is globally asymptotically stable with respect to dynamic process (5.3.2).

Proof. Under the assumptions of the theorem, matrix $\mathbf{U}$ is symmetric and

$$\mathbf{U} = \mathrm{diag}\left(\mathbf{K}_1^{-1},\ldots,\mathbf{K}_N^{-1}\right) + (\mathbf{I}-\mathbf{1}) \otimes (\mathbf{AM}). \tag{5.3.4}$$

The eigenvalues of the first term are γ_{ki}^{-1}, and the eigenvalues of the second term are υ_j and $(1-N)\upsilon_j$. Here we use the fact that the eigenvalues of **I-1** are 1-0=1 and 1-N. Let $\mathbf{U}_1$ and $\mathbf{U}_2$ denote the two terms of the right hand side of (5.3.4), then for all real vectors $\mathbf{u}$,

$$\frac{\mathbf{u}^T\mathbf{U}\mathbf{u}}{\mathbf{u}^T\mathbf{u}} = \frac{\mathbf{u}^T\mathbf{U}_1\mathbf{u}}{\mathbf{u}^T\mathbf{u}} + \frac{\mathbf{u}^T\mathbf{U}_2\mathbf{u}}{\mathbf{u}^T\mathbf{u}} \geq \min_{k,i}\{\gamma_{ki}^{-1}\} + \min_j \min\{\upsilon_j;\ (1-N)\upsilon_j\} > 0.$$

Thus, the proof is complete. □

Corollary. Assume, in addition, that $\mathbf{M} = \alpha\mathbf{I}$ and $\mathbf{A} = \mathbf{A}^T$. Let μ_l denote the eigenvalues of $\mathbf{A}$. Then (5.3.3) is equivalent to relations

$$\frac{-1}{\max_{k,i}\{\gamma_{ki}\}} < \mu_l\alpha < \frac{1}{(N-1)\max_{k,i}\{\gamma_{ki}\}} \quad \text{for all } l.$$

5.4 Oligopoly with Market Saturation

In this section the continuous counterpart of the discrete model introduced in Section 4.5 will be discussed. Using the earlier notation, at each time period the profit of each firm is given as

$$\mathbf{x}_k^T \cdot (\mathbf{Af}(t) + \mathbf{b}) - \left(\mathbf{x}_k^T\mathbf{B}_k\mathbf{x}_k + \mathbf{b}_k^T\mathbf{x}_k + c_k\right) \tag{5.4.1}$$

where we assume that functions $\mathbf{p}$ and C_k satisfy conditions (B) and (C) given at the beginning of this chapter. It is now assumed that market saturation changes accordingly to the rule

$$\dot{\mathbf{f}}(t) = \mathbf{s}(t) - \mathbf{C}\mathbf{f}(t), \tag{5.4.2}$$

when the first term represents the total production level of the industry, and the second term shows that in time the products already consumed by the market lose value and usage. Notice that this equation is a continuous counterpart of assumption (E) of Section 4.5 with the difference that in (5.4.2) the change in the market saturation level is given by the right hand side of the equation. The marginal profit of firm k $(k = 1,2,\dots,N)$ has the special form

$$\mathbf{A}\mathbf{f}(t) + \mathbf{b} - \left(\mathbf{B}_k + \mathbf{B}_k^T\right)\mathbf{x}_k - \mathbf{b}_k,$$

where we assume that firm k does not care about the fact that the rate of change of the market saturation in time depends on its current output. If we assume again that each firm adjusts its actual output proportionally to its marginal profit, then

$$\frac{d\mathbf{x}_k(t)}{dt} = \mathbf{K}_k\left(\mathbf{A}\mathbf{f}(t) + \mathbf{b} - \left(\mathbf{B}_k + \mathbf{B}_k^T\right)\mathbf{x}_k(t) - \mathbf{b}_k\right). \tag{5.4.3}$$

Combining equations (5.4.2) and (5.4.3) a continuous, linear dynamic system is obtained with coefficient matrix

$$\mathbf{H}_s = \begin{pmatrix} -\mathbf{K}_1\left(\mathbf{B}_1 + \mathbf{B}_1^T\right) & & & & \mathbf{K}_1\mathbf{A} \\ & -\mathbf{K}_2\left(\mathbf{B}_2 + \mathbf{B}_2^T\right) & & & \mathbf{K}_2\mathbf{A} \\ & & \ddots & & \vdots \\ & & & -\mathbf{K}_N\left(\mathbf{B}_N + \mathbf{B}_N^T\right) & \mathbf{K}_N\mathbf{A} \\ \mathbf{I} & \mathbf{I} & \cdots & \mathbf{I} & -\mathbf{C} \end{pmatrix}$$

$$= \mathbf{K}_s\mathbf{H}_s^*$$

with

$$\mathbf{K}_s = \operatorname{diag}\left(\mathbf{K}_1\left(\mathbf{B}_1 + \mathbf{B}_1^T\right), \dots, \mathbf{K}_N\left(\mathbf{B}_N + \mathbf{B}_N^T\right), \mathbf{I}\right)$$

and

$$\mathbf{H}_s^* = \begin{pmatrix} -\mathbf{I} & & & & \mathbf{F}_1 \\ & -\mathbf{I} & & & \mathbf{F}_2 \\ & & \ddots & & \vdots \\ & & & -\mathbf{I} & \mathbf{F}_N \\ \mathbf{I} & \mathbf{I} & \cdots & \mathbf{I} & -\mathbf{C} \end{pmatrix}$$

where $\mathbf{F}_k = \left(\mathbf{B}_k + \mathbf{B}_k^T\right)^{-1}\mathbf{A}$.

Theorem 5.4.1. System (5.4.2) - (5.4.3) is globally asymptotically stable if and only if all eigenvalues of matrix $\mathbf{K}_s\mathbf{H}_s^*$ have negative real parts.

In addition to the previous conditions assume that $\mathbf{K}_k\left(\mathbf{B}_k + \mathbf{B}_k^T\right)$ is symmetric and positive definite for all k. Then $\mathbf{K}_s$ is positive definite. Notice that

$$\mathbf{H}_s^* + \mathbf{H}_s^{*T} = \begin{pmatrix} -2\mathbf{I} & & & & \mathbf{F}_1 + \mathbf{I} \\ & -2\mathbf{I} & & & \mathbf{F}_2 + \mathbf{I} \\ & & \ddots & & \vdots \\ & & & -2\mathbf{I} & \mathbf{F}_N + \mathbf{I} \\ \mathbf{I} + \mathbf{F}_1^T & \mathbf{I} + \mathbf{F}_2^T & \cdots & \mathbf{I} + \mathbf{F}_N^T & -\left(\mathbf{C} + \mathbf{C}^T\right) \end{pmatrix}$$

with eigenvalue equations

$$\begin{aligned} &-2\mathbf{u}_k + \left(\mathbf{F}_k + \mathbf{I}\right)\mathbf{v} = \lambda \mathbf{u}_k \quad (k = 1,2,...,N) \\ &\sum_{k=1}^{N}\left(\mathbf{I} + \mathbf{F}_k^T\right)\mathbf{u}_k - \left(\mathbf{C} + \mathbf{C}^T\right)\mathbf{v} = \lambda \mathbf{v}. \end{aligned} \tag{5.4.4}$$

From the first equation we have

$$\mathbf{u}_k = \frac{1}{\lambda + 2}\left(\mathbf{F}_k + \mathbf{I}\right)\mathbf{v}$$

and by substituting this relation into the second equation of (5.4.4) we see that

$$\left[\frac{1}{\lambda + 2} \cdot \sum_{k=1}^{N}\left(\mathbf{I} + \mathbf{F}_k^T\right)\left(\mathbf{I} + \mathbf{F}_k\right) - \left(\mathbf{C} + \mathbf{C}^T\right) - \lambda\mathbf{I}\right]\mathbf{v} = \mathbf{0}.$$

Multiplying this equation from the left hand side by $\mathbf{v}^T$ and simplifying the resulting relation we get a quadratic equation for λ:

$$\lambda^2 + \lambda(2 + \gamma) + (2\gamma - \alpha) = 0$$

where

$$\gamma = \frac{\mathbf{v}^T\left(\mathbf{C} + \mathbf{C}^T\right)\mathbf{v}}{\mathbf{v}^T\mathbf{v}} \text{ and } \alpha = \frac{\mathbf{v}^{\mathrm{T}}\left(\sum_{k=1}^{N}\left(\mathbf{I} + \mathbf{F}_k^T\right)\left(\mathbf{I} + \mathbf{F}_k\right)\right)\mathbf{v}}{\mathbf{v}^T\mathbf{v}}.$$

If $2+\gamma>0$ and $2\gamma-\alpha>0$, then $\lambda<0$. Hence we have proven the following result.

Theorem 5.4.2. Assume that for all k, $\mathbf{K}_k(\mathbf{B}_k+\mathbf{B}_k^T)$ is symmetric, furthermore matrices $\mathbf{K}_k(\mathbf{B}_k+\mathbf{B}_k^T)$, $2\mathbf{I}+\mathbf{C}+\mathbf{C}^T$, and $2(\mathbf{C}+\mathbf{C}^T)-\sum_{k=1}^{N}(\mathbf{I}+\mathbf{F}_k^T)(\mathbf{I}+\mathbf{F}_k)$ are positive definite. Then system (5.4.2) - (5.4.3) is globally asymptotically stable.

Consider the special case of single-product oligopolies without product differentiation. In this case, matrices $\mathbf{A}$, $\mathbf{B}_k$, $\mathbf{K}_k$ and $\mathbf{C}$ are scalars, therefore $\mathbf{F}_k=A/(2B_k)$,

$$\mathbf{K}_k(\mathbf{B}_k+\mathbf{B}_k^T)=2K_kB_k,$$

$$2\mathbf{I}+\mathbf{C}+\mathbf{C}^T=2+2C,$$

and

$$2(\mathbf{C}+\mathbf{C}^T)-\sum_{k=1}^{N}(\mathbf{I}+\mathbf{F}_k^T)(\mathbf{I}+\mathbf{F}_k)=4C-\sum_{k=1}^{N}\left(1+\frac{A}{2B_k}\right)^2.$$

From the adjustment process, $K_k>0$, therefore the above quantities are positive if for all k,

$$B_k>0,\text{ and } C>\frac{1}{4}\sum_{k=1}^{N}\left(1+\frac{A}{2B_k}\right)^2.$$

5.5 Production Adjustment Costs

In addition to the conditions presented at the beginning of this chapter assume that at each time period, each firm faces an additional cost resulting by changing output. For the sake of simplicity we will assume that model (5.1.1) is modified in the following way:

$$\frac{d\mathbf{x}_k(t)}{dt}=\mathbf{K}_k\left[(\mathbf{A}+\mathbf{A}^T-\mathbf{B}_k-\mathbf{B}_k^T)\mathbf{x}_k(t)+\mathbf{A}\sum_{l\neq k}\mathbf{x}_l(t)+\mathbf{b}-\mathbf{b}_k-\mathbf{C}_k\frac{d\mathbf{x}_k(t)}{dt}\right],\qquad(5.5.1)$$

where $\mathbf{C}_k$ is a diagonal matrix with positive diagonal elements. The appearance of the additional term $-\mathbf{C}_k\dot{\mathbf{x}}_k$ in the marginal cost can be explained as a slowing effect in changing output in the cases of both positive and negative values of the components of $\dot{\mathbf{x}}_k(t)$.

Notice that equation (5.5.1) can be rewritten as

$$\frac{d\mathbf{x}_k(t)}{dt} = (\mathbf{I} + \mathbf{C}_k)^{-1}\mathbf{K}_k\left[(\mathbf{A} + \mathbf{A}^T - \mathbf{B}_k - \mathbf{B}_k^T)\mathbf{x}_k(t) + \mathbf{A}\sum_{l \neq k}\mathbf{x}_l(t) + \mathbf{b} - \mathbf{b}_k\right]$$

which is equivalent to model (5.1.1) with $\mathbf{K}_k$ being replaced by matrix $(\mathbf{I} + \mathbf{C}_k)^{-1}\mathbf{K}_k$. Therefore all results of Section 5.1 can be applied. The cases of adaptive and extrapolative expectations can be examined in a similar manner as it has been demonstrated in Sections 5.2 and 5.3.

5.6 Dynamic Rent Seeking Oligopolies

Using the notation of the discrete rent seeking games (studied earlier in Section 4.8) we see that the marginal payoff of agent i $(i = 1, 2, ..., N)$ is given as the derivative of the payoff function (4.8.1) with respect to x_k:

$$\frac{\partial \varphi_k(x_1, ..., x_N)}{\partial x_k} = \frac{a_k \sum_{j=1}^{N} a_j x_j - a_k^2 x_k}{\left(\sum_{j=1}^{N} a_j x_j\right)^2} - 1,$$

therefore model (5.1.1) is modified as the system of nonlinear differential equations

$$\frac{dx_k(t)}{dt} = K_k \cdot \left[\frac{a_k \sum_{j \neq k} a_j x_j}{\left(\sum_{j=1}^{N} a_j x_j\right)^2} - 1\right]. \tag{5.6.1}$$

It is well known from the theory of differential equations (see, for example, Bellman, 1969) that the equilibrium of this system is locally asymptotically stable, if all eigenvalues of the Jacobian, computed at the equilibrium, have negative real parts. The Jacobian has the following special form:

$$\mathbf{J}_{RS}^{*} = \frac{1}{p^3} \cdot \begin{pmatrix} 2K_1 a_1^2 (a_1 x_1 - p) & 2K_1 a_2 a_1 \left(a_1 x_1 - \frac{p}{2}\right) & \cdots & 2K_1 a_N a_1 \left(a_1 x_1 - \frac{p}{2}\right) \\ 2K_2 a_1 a_2 \left(a_2 x_2 - \frac{p}{2}\right) & 2K_2 a_2^2 (a_2 x_2 - p) & \cdots & 2K_2 a_N a_2 \left(a_2 x_2 - \frac{p}{2}\right) \\ \vdots & \vdots & \ddots & \vdots \\ 2K_N a_1 a_N \left(a_N x_N - \frac{p}{2}\right) & 2K_N a_2 a_N \left(a_N x_N - \frac{p}{2}\right) & \cdots & 2K_N a_N^2 (a_N x_N - p) \end{pmatrix}$$

with $p = \sum_{j=1}^{N} a_j x_j$. Since $\frac{1}{p^3} > 0$, all eigenvalues of $\mathbf{J}_{RS}^{*}$ have negative real parts if and only if the same holds for matrix

$$p^3 \mathbf{J}_{RS}^{*} = \mathbf{D} + \mathbf{a}\mathbf{b}^T \tag{5.6.2}$$

where

$$\mathbf{D} = \operatorname{diag}\left(-K_1 a_1^2 p, -K_2 a_2^2 p, \ldots, -K_N a_N^2 p\right),$$

$$\mathbf{a} = \begin{pmatrix} 2K_1 a_1 \left(a_1 x_1 - \frac{p}{2}\right) \\ 2K_2 a_2 \left(a_2 x_2 - \frac{p}{2}\right) \\ \vdots \\ 2K_N a_N \left(a_N x_N - \frac{p}{2}\right) \end{pmatrix}, \text{ and } \mathbf{b}^T = (a_1, a_2, \ldots, a_N).$$

The characteristic polynomial of this matrix can be obtained similarly to the way of obtaining condition (4.2.10) or proving Theorem 4.8.3 earlier:

$$\varphi(\lambda) = \prod_{k=1}^{N} \left(-K_k a_k^2 p - \lambda\right) \left[1 + \sum_{k=1}^{N} \frac{2K_k a_k^2 \left(a_k x_k - \frac{p}{2}\right)}{-K_k a_k^2 p - \lambda}\right].$$

Assume that at the equilibrium, $a_k x_k \le \frac{p}{2}$ for all agents, which is certainly true in the case of symmetric agents. Let $\pi_1 \le \pi_2 \le \cdots \le \pi_l \le 0$ denote the distinct $-K_k a_k^2 p$ values with multiplicities $r_1, r_2, \ldots, r_l$, then

$$\varphi(\lambda) = \prod_{i=1}^{l} (\pi_i - \lambda)^{r_i} \left[1 + \sum_{i=1}^{l} \frac{\alpha_i}{\pi_i - \lambda}\right]$$

with

$$\alpha_i = \sum_{k \in I_i} 2K_k a_k^2 \left(a_k x_k - \frac{p}{2} \right) \leq 0$$

where

$$I_i = \left\{ k \middle| -K_k a_k^2 p = \pi_i \right\}.$$

All eigenvalues $\lambda \neq \pi_i$ $(i = 1,2,...,l)$ are roots of equation

$$g(\lambda) = \sum_{i=1}^{l} \frac{\alpha_i}{\pi_i - \lambda} + 1 = 0. \tag{5.6.3}$$

Notice that for all i, $\alpha_i \leq 0$ and $\pi_i \leq 0$, and function g has the following properties:

$$\lim_{\lambda \to \pm\infty} g(\lambda) = 1,$$
$$\lim_{\lambda \to \pi_i + 0} g(\lambda) = +\infty, \quad \lim_{\lambda \to \pi_i - 0} g(\lambda) = -\infty,$$

and g is strictly decreasing. Therefore there are l-1 real roots inside intervals (π_i, π_{i+1}) $(i = 1,2,...,l-1)$, and one real root below π_1, furthermore all roots are real. Therefore all eigenvalues are real and negative implying the asymptotical stability of the system.

Theorem 5.6.1. Assume that at the equilibrium, $a_k x_k \leq \frac{p}{2}$ for all k. Then the equilibrium of system (5.6.1) is locally asymptotically stable.

If we drop the assumption that $a_k x_k \leq \frac{p}{2}$ for all k, then there is no guarantee that for all i, $\alpha_i \geq 0$, and even the equilibrium may be unstable. For example, consider the case of $N = 3$, $K_1 = K_2 = K_3 = 1$, $a_1 = a_2 = 1$, and $a_3 = 10^{25}$, when two eigenvalues of $\mathbf{J}_{RS}^*$ are positive and only one eigenvalue is negative.

5.7 Dynamic Labor-Managed Oligopolies

In this section the continuous counterpart of the model given earlier in Section 4.9 will be introduced and examined. Using the same notation as earlier, the payoff function of firm k $(k = 1,2,...,N)$ is the surplus per unit of labor, which can be expressed as

$$\varphi_k(x_1,\ldots,x_N)=\frac{x_k\left(A\sum_{l=1}^{N}x_l+b\right)-w(a_kx_k+b_k)-c_k}{a_kx_k+b_k}, \tag{5.7.1}$$

where $p(s)=As+b\ (A<0,b>0)$ is the price function, $h_k(x_k)=a_kx_k+b_k$ $(a_k>0,b_k\geq 0)$ and c_k is the inverse production function and fixed cost of firm k, respectively and w is the competitive wage rate. The marginal payoff to labor in firm k can be obtained by differentiation:

$$\frac{\partial\varphi_k}{\partial x_k}=\left[(As+b+Ax_k-a_kw)(a_kx_k+b_k)-x_ka_k(As+b)+a_kw(a_kx_k+b_k)+a_kc_k\right]/(a_kx_k+b_k)^2$$

where we used the notation $s=\sum_{k=1}^{N}x_k$. Simple calculation shows that

$$\frac{\partial\varphi_k}{\partial x_k}=\frac{Aa_kx_k^2+Ab_kx_k+(Asb_k+bb_k+a_kc_k)}{(a_kx_k+b_k)^2}.$$

Therefore the dynamic adjustment process can be written as the following system of nonlinear differential equations:

$$\frac{dx_k}{dt}=K_k\cdot\frac{Aa_kx_k^2+Ab_kx_k+(Asb_k+bb_k+a_kc_k)}{(a_kx_k+b_k)^2} \tag{5.7.2}$$

for $k=1,2,\ldots,N$. In order to find stability conditions, the Jacobian of the right hand sides of the differential equations will be first determined. The diagonal elements are the following:

$$K_k\frac{(2Aa_kx_k+Ab_k)(a_kx_k+b_k)^2-(Aa_kx_k^2+Ab_kx_k+(Asb_k+bb_k+a_kc_k))2(a_kx_k+b_k)a_k}{(a_kx_k+b_k)^4}$$

$$=K_k\frac{Aa_kb_kx_k+(Ab_k^2-2Asa_kb_k-2ba_kb_k-2a_k^2c_k)}{(a_kx_k+b_k)^3},$$

and the off-diagonal (k,l) $(k\neq l)$ elements are given as follows:

$$K_k\frac{Ab_k}{(a_kx_k+b_k)^2}.$$

Hence, the Jacobian has the special form:

$$\mathbf{J}_L^* = \mathbf{D} + \mathbf{a}\mathbf{b}^T \tag{5.7.3}$$

with

$$\mathbf{D} = \mathrm{diag}\left(-2Asa_1b_1 - 2a_1b_1b - 2a_1^2c_1, \ldots, -2Asa_Nb_N - 2a_Nb_Nb - 2a_N^2c_N\right),$$

$$\mathbf{a} = \begin{pmatrix} \dfrac{Ab_1}{(a_1x_1+b_1)^2} \\ \cdots \\ \dfrac{Ab_N}{(a_Nx_N+b_N)^2} \end{pmatrix}, \quad \mathbf{b}^T = (1, \ldots, 1).$$

In Section 4.9 we have shown that in order to have meaningful equilibrium we have to assume that at the equilibrium,

$$s < \min\left\{\frac{-A^2b_k^2 + \alpha_k}{4A^2a_kb_k}\right\}. \tag{5.7.4}$$

Under this condition, all diagonal elements of matrix $\mathbf{D}$ are negative. Let $\delta_1, \ldots, \delta_N$ denote these diagonal elements. The characteristic polynomial of matrix $\mathbf{J}_L^*$ can be obtained similarly to the proof of Theorem 4.8.3, and is the following:

$$\varphi(\lambda) = \pi_{k=1}^{N}(\delta_k - \lambda)\left[1 + \sum_{k=1}^{N}\frac{\dfrac{Ab_k}{(a_kx_k+b_k)^2}}{\delta_k - \lambda}\right].$$

Similarly to the proof of Theorem 5.6.1 we can easily verify that all roots of φ are negative. Hence we have the following result.

Theorem 5.7.1. Under condition (5.7.4), the equilibrium of system (5.7.2) is locally asymptotically stable.

5.8 Dynamic Oligopsonies

In the model to be discussed in this section we will use the notation of Section 4.10. Let $p(s) = As + b$ denote the price function of a single product, where $A < 0$ and $b > 0$. Assume that $f_k(\mathbf{l}_k) = \mathbf{c}_k^T\mathbf{l}_k + d_k$ is the production function of firm k $(k = 1, 2, \ldots, N)$, where $\mathbf{c}_k \in R^M$ and d_k is a constant, furthermore $\mathbf{w}(\mathbf{L}) = \mathbf{B}\mathbf{L} + \mathbf{b}$, with some $M \times M$ matrix $\mathbf{B}$ and M-element vector $\mathbf{b}$, is the production factor price vector.

The profit of firm k is given as

$$p(s)f_k(\mathbf{l}_k)-\mathbf{l}_k^T\mathbf{w}(\mathbf{L})=\left(A\sum_{i=1}^N(\mathbf{c}_i^T\mathbf{l}_i+d_i)+b\right)(\mathbf{c}_k^T\mathbf{l}_k+d_k)-\mathbf{l}_k^T\left(\mathbf{B}\sum_{i=1}^N\mathbf{l}_i+\mathbf{b}\right), \quad (5.8.1)$$

since $s=\sum_{i=1}^N f_i(\mathbf{l}_i)$. Notice that the marginal profit of firm k can be obtained as the gradient of this profit function with respect to $\mathbf{l}_k$:

$$A\mathbf{c}_k(\mathbf{c}_k^T\mathbf{l}_k+d_l)+\left(A\sum_{i=1}^N(\mathbf{c}_i^T\mathbf{l}_i+d_i)+b\right)\mathbf{c}_k-\left(\mathbf{B}\sum_{i=1}^N\mathbf{l}_i+\mathbf{b}\right)-\mathbf{B}^T\mathbf{l}_k.$$

Therefore the dynamic process can be formulated as follows:

$$\frac{d}{dt}\mathbf{l}_k=\mathbf{K}_k\cdot\left[A\mathbf{c}_k(\mathbf{c}_k^T\mathbf{l}_k+d_k)+\left(A\sum_{i=1}^N(\mathbf{c}_i^T\mathbf{l}_i+d_i)+b\right)\mathbf{c}_k-\left(\mathbf{B}\sum_{i=1}^N\mathbf{l}_i+\mathbf{b}\right)-\mathbf{B}^T\mathbf{l}_k\right]. \quad (5.8.2)$$

Notice that this is a linear system with a constant coefficient matrix

$$\mathbf{H}_{0S}=\begin{pmatrix}\mathbf{K}_1 & & & \\ & \mathbf{K}_2 & & \\ & & \ddots & \\ & & & \mathbf{K}_N\end{pmatrix}\cdot\mathbf{H}_{0S}^* \quad (5.8.3)$$

with

$$\mathbf{H}_{0S}^*=\begin{pmatrix}2A\mathbf{c}_1\mathbf{c}_1^T-(\mathbf{B}+\mathbf{B}^T) & A\mathbf{c}_1\mathbf{c}_2^T-\mathbf{B} & \cdots & A\mathbf{c}_1\mathbf{c}_N^T-\mathbf{B}\\ A\mathbf{c}_2\mathbf{c}_1^T-\mathbf{B} & 2A\mathbf{c}_2\mathbf{c}_2^T-(\mathbf{B}+\mathbf{B}^T) & \cdots & A\mathbf{c}_2\mathbf{c}_N^T-\mathbf{B}\\ \vdots & \vdots & & \vdots\\ A\mathbf{c}_N\mathbf{c}_1^T-\mathbf{B} & A\mathbf{c}_N\mathbf{c}_2^T-\mathbf{B} & \cdots & 2A\mathbf{c}_N\mathbf{c}_N^T-(\mathbf{B}+\mathbf{B}^T)\end{pmatrix}.$$

Hence we have the following

Theorem 5.8.1. The equilibrium of system (5.8.2) is globally asymptotically stable if and only if all eigenvalues of matrix $\mathbf{H}_{0S}$ have negative real parts.

The analysis of the characteristic equation of this matrix can be performed similarly to the previously discussed models, therefore the details are omitted.

5.9 Supplementary Notes and Discussions

On dynamic games in general the reader may refer to Basar and Olsder (1982), or to Friedman (1986),

5.1 Assumption (a) was analyzed earlier by Al-Nowaihi and Levine (1985), Dixit (1986), and Furth (1986). Assumption (b) is more commonly applied. A general model for quadratic games under assumption (a) is used, for example, in Szidarovszky and Okuguchi (1987d), and in Okuguchi and Szidarovszky (1987b). Our model (5.1.2) is taken from Okuguchi and Szidarovszky (1987a). Theorem 5.1.1 is a simple consequence of well known results from the theory of the stability of differential equations. Lemma 5.1.1 is known from Arrow and McManus (1958). The statement of the Lemma is further generalized in the theory of H- and D-stability of matrices (see Carlson, 1968; Johnson, 1974). Theorem 5.1.2 is taken from Okuguchi and Szidarovszky (1987a) in a slightly more general form, since in that paper only linear cost functions were considered.

Okuguchi (1976) provides a comprehensive survey of the main contributions. We note that Hadar (1966) was the first to analyze the stability of Cournot oligopoly equilibrium for a model with product differentiation and with single product firms.

5.2 The origin of continuous adaptive adjustment processes can be traced back to Nerlove (1958) in a different context. Adaptive expectations for the classical oligopoly game were analyzed by Okuguchi (1968, 1970, 1976 and 1986). All results of this section are generalizations of those special results. A different development can be found in Szidarovszky and Okuguchi (1987e). Model (5.2.17) was first formulated in Szidarovszky and Okuguchi (1987f). Theorems 5.2.6 and 5.2.7 are analogous statements to Theorems 5.2.1 and 5.2.2 for the adaptive expectations case of the rivals' outputs. Theorems 5.2.8 and 5.2.9 are taken also from Szidarovszky and Okuguchi (1987f). A general formulation and proof of Lemma 5.2.1 can be found in Rozsa (1974). The combination of adaptive and Cournot expectation and relevant stability conditions were given in Section 5.3 of the earlier version of this book (Okuguchi and Szidarovszky, 1990).

5.3 This section generalizes some results of Okuguchi (1976, Sections 6.2, 6.3). The combination of extrapolative expectations with Cournot and adaptive expectations can be discussed similarly to Section 5.3 of Okuguchi and Szidarovszky (1990).

5.4 The model and stability conditions discussed in this section are new. Combining this model with adaptive or extrapolative expectation can be made in an analogous manner.

5.5 The reduction of oligopolies with production adjustment costs to the classical multi-product model is a very simple idea. The cases of adaptive and extrapolative expectations can be discussed similarly.

5.6 The results given in this section are new. Notice that condition $a_k x_k \leq \frac{p}{2}$ (for all k) means that there is no dominating agent with probability higher than 50% to get the rent.

5.7-5.8 The models and stability conditions given in these sections are all new. The cases of adaptive and extrapolative expectations can be discussed in a similar way, the details are left as exercises to the reader.

The methodology used in this chapter can be applied to find necessary stability conditions, or equivalently to find sufficient conditions for the instability of the equilibrium. Assume first that the system is linear and time-invariant, that is, it is governed by a differential equation

$$\dot{\mathbf{x}}(t) = \mathbf{H}\mathbf{x}(t) + \mathbf{b}$$

with constant matrix $\mathbf{H}$ and a constant vector $\mathbf{b}$. If at least one eigenvalue of $\mathbf{H}$ has positive real part, then the equilibrium is unstable. Consider next a time-invariant nonlinear system

$$\dot{\mathbf{x}}(t) = \mathbf{f}(\mathbf{x}(t)),$$

where $\mathbf{f}$ is continuously differentiable in the neighborhood of an equilibrium $\mathbf{x}^*$. Let $\mathbf{J}(\mathbf{x}^*)$ denote the Jacobian of $\mathbf{f}$ at $\mathbf{x}^*$. If at least one eigenvalue of $\mathbf{J}(\mathbf{x}^*)$ has positive real part, then the equilibrium is unstable. This important result with an elegant proof can be found, for example, in Bellman (1969).

Finally we note that dynamic oligopolies with continuous time scale were discussed with a different approach in Szidarovszky and Okuguchi (1989b).

6 Extensions and Generalizations

This chapter will generalize and extend the results on dynamic oligopolies presented in Chapters 4 and 5. The first two subsections discuss a natural extension of oligopoly problems, namely quadratic games. Sections 6.3 and 6.4 introduce nonlinear models and conditions for the stability of equilibria in nonlinear oligopolies.

6.1 Quadratic Games Under Discrete Time Scale

In this section some models discussed in Chapter 4 will be generalized under a more general expectation scheme that contains assumptions á la Cournot and adaptive expectations as special cases.

In this section an N-person game

$$\Gamma = \{N;\ X_1,\dots,X_N;\ \varphi_1,\dots,\varphi_N\}$$

will be examined, where

(A) For all k, the strategy set X_k of player k is a closed, convex, bounded subset of finite dimensional Euclidean space;

(B) For all k, the payoff function of player k is given as

$$\varphi_k(\mathbf{x}_1,\dots,\mathbf{x}_N) = \mathbf{x}^{(k)T}\begin{bmatrix} \mathbf{A}_{00}^{(k)} & \cdots & \mathbf{A}_{0i_k}^{(k)} \\ \vdots & & \vdots \\ \mathbf{A}_{i_k0}^{(k)} & \cdots & \mathbf{A}_{i_ki_k}^{(k)} \end{bmatrix}\mathbf{x}^{(k)} + \mathbf{b}^{(k)T}\mathbf{x}^{(k)} + c^{(k)}, \tag{6.1.1}$$

where $\mathbf{x}_k \in X_k \ (\forall k)$,

$$\mathbf{x}^{(k)} = \begin{bmatrix} \mathbf{x}_k \\ \mathbf{s}_{k1} \\ \vdots \\ \mathbf{s}_{k,i_k} \end{bmatrix}, \mathbf{s}_{kl} = \sum_{m \neq k} \mathbf{B}_{lm}^{(k)} \mathbf{x}_m \quad (1 \le k \le N, 1 \le l \le i_k). \tag{6.1.2}$$

Notice that the selection $i_k = 1$, $\mathbf{B}_{1m}^{(k)} = \mathbf{I}$ corresponds to $s_{k1} = \sum_{m \neq k} \mathbf{x}_m$ which is the case of expectations on the output of the rest of the industry. Another special case is obtained when each firm forms expectations on the individual outputs of all other firms: $i_k = N-1$,

$$\mathbf{s}_{k1} = \mathbf{x}_1, \ldots, \mathbf{s}_{k,k-1} = \mathbf{x}_{k-1}, \mathbf{s}_{k,k} = \mathbf{x}_{k+1}, \ldots, \mathbf{s}_{k,N-1} = \mathbf{x}_N.$$

It is also assumed that

(C) Matrix $\mathbf{A}_{00}^{(k)} + \mathbf{A}_{00}^{(k)T}$ is negative definite for all k.

Note that payoff function (6.1.1) is a quadratic function of the strategy of player k and a linear function of the other players' strategies.

If $\mathbf{x}^{(k)}$ depends directly on the strategies, then the components of $\mathbf{x}^{(k)}$ are $\mathbf{x}_k, \mathbf{x}_1, \ldots, \mathbf{x}_{k-1}, \mathbf{x}_{k+1}, \ldots, \mathbf{x}_N$, and therefore

$$\mathbf{B}_{lm}^{(k)} = \begin{cases} \mathbf{I}, & \text{if } l < k \text{ and } l = m, \text{ or } l \ge k \text{ and } l+1 = m; \\ \mathbf{0} & \text{otherwise.} \end{cases}$$

Under assumptions (A) and (B) the quadratic game satisfies the conditions for the Nikaido-Isoda theorem (Nikaido and Isoda, 1955), therefore the game must have at least one equilibrium point.

The dynamic process discussed in this section can be described as follows. At t=0, let $\mathbf{x}_k(0)$ denote the initial strategy of player k $(1 \le k \le N)$, and let

$$\mathbf{s}_{kl}(0) = \sum_{m \neq k} \mathbf{B}_{lm}^{(k)} \mathbf{x}_m(0) \quad (1 \le k \le N,\ 1 \le l \le i_k).$$

For each $t > 0$, let $\mathbf{s}_{kl}^E(t)$ denote the expectation of player k on $\mathbf{s}_{kl}(t)$. It is assumed that at each t>0 each player maximizes his own payoff value under these expectations. That is, each player selects his strategy $\mathbf{x}_k(t)$ by solving the optimization problem

$$\text{maximize } \mathbf{x}^{(k)T} \begin{bmatrix} \mathbf{A}_{00}^{(k)} & \cdots & \mathbf{A}_{0i_k}^{(k)} \\ \vdots & & \vdots \\ \mathbf{A}_{i_k0}^{(k)} & \cdots & \mathbf{A}_{i_ki_k}^{(k)} \end{bmatrix} \mathbf{x}^{(k)} + \mathbf{b}^{(k)T} \mathbf{x}^{(k)} + c^{(k)} \tag{6.1.3}$$

subject to $\mathbf{x}_k \in X_k$,

$\mathbf{s}_{kl} = \mathbf{s}_{kl}^E(t) \quad (l = 1,2,\ldots,i_k)$.

Assume that

(D) The optimal solution of (6.1.3) is an interior point of X_k.

Under the above assumptions the first order optimality conditions imply that

$$\mathbf{x}_k(t) = -\left(\mathbf{A}_{00}^{(k)} + \mathbf{A}_{00}^{(k)T}\right)^{-1} \sum_{l=1}^{i_k} \left(\mathbf{A}_{0l}^{(k)} + \mathbf{A}_{l0}^{(k)T}\right) \mathbf{s}_{kl}^E(t) + \boldsymbol{\alpha} \tag{6.1.4}$$

where $\boldsymbol{\alpha}$ is a constant vector.

It is also assumed that each player's adaptive expectations on $\mathbf{s}_{kl}(t)$ can be written as

$$\mathbf{s}_{kl}^E(t) = \mathbf{s}_{kl}^E(t-1) + \mathbf{M}_{kl}\left(\mathbf{s}_{kl}(t-1) - \mathbf{s}_{kl}^E(t-1)\right), \tag{6.1.5}$$

where $\mathbf{M}_{kl}$ is a constant matrix. It is usually assumed that matrices $\mathbf{M}_{kl}$ are diagonal with positive diagonal elements. Note that expectation á la Cournot on any vector $\mathbf{s}_{kl}^E(t)$ can be modelled as a special case of (6.1.5) by selecting $\mathbf{M}_{kl} = \mathbf{I}$.

Combining equations (6.1.4) and (6.1.5) we obtain the following difference equation:

$$\mathbf{x}_k(t) = -\left(\mathbf{A}_{00}^{(k)} + \mathbf{A}_{00}^{(k)T}\right)^{-1} \sum_{l=1}^{i_k} \left(\mathbf{A}_{0l}^{(k)} + \mathbf{A}_{l0}^{(k)T}\right) \left[\sum_{m \neq k} \mathbf{M}_{kl}\mathbf{B}_{lm}^{(k)}\mathbf{x}_m(t-1) + \left(\mathbf{I} - \mathbf{M}_{kl}\right)\mathbf{s}_{kl}^E(t-1)\right] + \boldsymbol{\alpha}, \tag{6.1.6}$$

and by summarizing equations (6.1.5) and (6.1.6) we get the following form:

$$\begin{bmatrix} \mathbf{x}_1(t) \\ \vdots \\ \mathbf{x}_N(t) \\ \mathbf{s}_{11}^E(t) \\ \vdots \\ \mathbf{s}_{1,i_1}^E(t) \\ \vdots \\ \mathbf{s}_{N1}^E(t) \\ \vdots \\ \mathbf{s}_{N,i_N}^E(t) \end{bmatrix} = \begin{bmatrix} \mathbf{H}_{00} & \mathbf{H}_{01} & \cdots & \mathbf{H}_{0N} \\ \mathbf{H}_{10} & \mathbf{H}_{11} & \cdots & \mathbf{H}_{1N} \\ \vdots & \vdots & & \vdots \\ \mathbf{H}_{N0} & \mathbf{H}_{N1} & \cdots & \mathbf{H}_{NN} \end{bmatrix} \begin{bmatrix} \mathbf{x}_1(t-1) \\ \vdots \\ \mathbf{x}_N(t-1) \\ \mathbf{s}_{11}^E(t-1) \\ \vdots \\ \mathbf{s}_{1,i_1}^E(t-1) \\ \vdots \\ \mathbf{s}_{N1}^E(t-1) \\ \vdots \\ \mathbf{s}_{N,i_N}^E(t-1) \end{bmatrix} + \boldsymbol{\alpha}_K, \qquad (6.1.7)$$

where

$$\mathbf{H}_{00} = \begin{bmatrix} \mathbf{K}_{11} & \cdots & \mathbf{K}_{1N} \\ \vdots & & \vdots \\ \mathbf{K}_{N1} & \cdots & \mathbf{K}_{NN} \end{bmatrix}$$

with

$$\mathbf{K}_{km} = \begin{cases} \mathbf{0}, \text{ if } m = k \\ -\left(\mathbf{A}_{00}^{(k)} + \mathbf{A}_{00}^{(k)T}\right)^{-1} \sum_{l=1}^{i_k} \left(\mathbf{A}_{0l}^{(k)} + \mathbf{A}_{l0}^{(k)T}\right) \mathbf{M}_{kl} \mathbf{B}_{lm}^{(k)}, \text{ if } m \neq k; \end{cases}$$

$$\mathbf{H}_{0k} = \begin{bmatrix} \mathbf{L}_{11} & \cdots & \mathbf{L}_{1N} \\ \vdots & & \vdots \\ \mathbf{L}_{N1} & \cdots & \mathbf{L}_{NN} \end{bmatrix}$$

with

$$\mathbf{L}_{ml} = \begin{cases} \mathbf{0}, \text{ if } m \neq k \\ -\left(\mathbf{A}_{00}^{(k)} + \mathbf{A}_{00}^{(k)T}\right)^{-1} \left(\mathbf{A}_{0l}^{(k)} + \mathbf{A}_{l0}^{(k)T}\right)\left(\mathbf{I} - \mathbf{M}_{kl}\right) \text{ if } m = k; \end{cases}$$

$$\mathbf{H}_{k0} = \begin{bmatrix} \mathbf{M}_{k1}\mathbf{B}_{11}^{(k)} & \cdots & \mathbf{M}_{k1}\mathbf{B}_{1,k-1}^{(k)} & \mathbf{0} & \mathbf{M}_{k1}\mathbf{B}_{1,k+1}^{(k)} & \cdots & \mathbf{M}_{k1}\mathbf{B}_{1,N}^{(k)} \\ \vdots & & \vdots & \vdots & \vdots & & \vdots \\ \mathbf{M}_{ki_k}\mathbf{B}_{i_k 1}^{(k)} & \cdots & \mathbf{M}_{ki_k}\mathbf{B}_{i_k,k-1}^{(k)} & \mathbf{0} & \mathbf{M}_{ki_k}\mathbf{B}_{i_k,k+1}^{(k)} & \cdots & \mathbf{M}_{ki_k}\mathbf{B}_{i_k N}^{(k)} \end{bmatrix};$$

and

$$\mathbf{H}_{km} = \begin{cases} \mathbf{0} \text{ if } m \neq k \\ \begin{bmatrix} \mathbf{I} - \mathbf{M}_{k1} & & \\ & \ddots & \\ & & \mathbf{I} - \mathbf{M}_{ki_k} \end{bmatrix}, \text{ if } m = k. \end{cases}$$

If $\mathbf{H}_K$ denotes the matrix of coefficients of the linear difference equation (6.1.7) then it can be rewritten as:

$$\mathbf{H}_K = \begin{bmatrix} \mathbf{H}_{00} & \mathbf{H}_{01} & \cdots & \mathbf{H}_{0N} \\ \mathbf{H}_{10} & \mathbf{H}_{11} & & 0 \\ \vdots & & \ddots & \\ \mathbf{H}_{N0} & 0 & & \mathbf{H}_{NN} \end{bmatrix}.$$

Before presenting general stability conditions the special case of oligopolies will be derived from our general formulation. Since the payoff function of the linear oligopoly game is

$$\mathbf{x}_k^T\left(\mathbf{A}\sum_{l\neq k}\mathbf{x}_l + \mathbf{A}\mathbf{x}_k + b\right) - \left(\mathbf{x}_k^T\mathbf{B}_k\mathbf{x}_k + \mathbf{b}_k^T\mathbf{x}_k + c_k\right),$$

all vectors $\mathbf{s}_{kl}$ are assumed to be the sum of certain strategies $\mathbf{x}_i$ $(i \neq k)$. By defining the sets $I_{k1},\ldots,I_{ki_k}$ such that

$$I_{ki} \cap I_{kj} = \varnothing \ (i \neq j)$$

and

$$I_{k1} \cup I_{k2} \cup \cdots \cup I_{ki_k} = \{1,2,\ldots,k-1,k+1,\ldots,N\},$$

we may assume that for all k and l,

$$\mathbf{s}_{kl} = \sum_{i\in I_{kl}} \mathbf{x}_i.$$

That is, firm k forms expectations on the total output of firms belonging to groups $I_{k1}, I_{k2},\ldots,I_{ki_k}$.

That is, in this case we may select

$$\mathbf{A}_{ij}^{(k)} = \begin{cases} \mathbf{A} - \mathbf{B}_k, & \text{if } i = 0,\ j = 0; \\ \mathbf{A}, & \text{if } i = 0,\ j > 0; \\ \mathbf{0} & \text{otherwise} \end{cases}$$

and

$$\mathbf{B}_{lm}^{(k)} = \begin{cases} \mathbf{I}, & \text{if } m \in I_{kl} \\ \mathbf{0} & \text{otherwise.} \end{cases}$$

Our first stability theorem is the consequence of well known facts from the theory of difference equations.

Theorem 6.1.1. The equilibrium point of the quadratic game under combined expectations is globally asymptotically stable if and only if all eigenvalues of matrix $\mathbf{H}_K$ are inside the unit circle.

Theorem 6.1.2. The equilibrium point of the quadratic game is globally asymptotically stable with respect to expectations (6.1.5) if and only if all eigenvalues of matrix

$$
\mathbf{H}_K^{(1)} = \left[\begin{array}{ccc|ccc|c|ccc}
\mathbf{I}-\mathbf{M}_{11} & & & -\mathbf{M}_{11}\mathbf{B}_{12}^{(1)}\mathbf{D}_1^{(2)} & \cdots & -\mathbf{M}_{11}\mathbf{B}_{12}^{(1)}\mathbf{D}_{i_2}^{(2)} & & -\mathbf{M}_{11}\mathbf{B}_{1N}^{(1)}\mathbf{D}_1^{(N)} & \cdots & -\mathbf{M}_{11}\mathbf{B}_{1N}^{(1)}\mathbf{D}_{i_N}^{(N)} \\
 & \ddots & & \vdots & & \vdots & \cdots & \vdots & & \vdots \\
 & & \mathbf{I}-\mathbf{M}_{1i_1} & -\mathbf{M}_{1i_1}\mathbf{B}_{i_1 2}^{(1)}\mathbf{D}_1^{(2)} & \cdots & -\mathbf{M}_{1i_1}\mathbf{B}_{i_1 2}^{(1)}\mathbf{D}_{i_2}^{(2)} & & -\mathbf{M}_{1i_1}\mathbf{B}_{i_1,N}^{(1)}\mathbf{D}_1^{(N)} & \cdots & -\mathbf{M}_{1i_1}\mathbf{B}_{i_1,N}^{(1)}\mathbf{D}_{i_N}^{(N)} \\
\hline
-\mathbf{M}_{21}\mathbf{B}_{11}^{(2)}\mathbf{D}_1^{(1)} & \cdots & -\mathbf{M}_{21}\mathbf{B}_{11}^{(2)}\mathbf{D}_{i_1}^{(1)} & \mathbf{I}-\mathbf{M}_{21} & & & & -\mathbf{M}_{21}\mathbf{B}_{1N}^{(2)}\mathbf{D}_1^{(N)} & \cdots & -\mathbf{M}_{21}\mathbf{B}_{1N}^{(2)}\mathbf{D}_{i_N}^{(N)} \\
\vdots & & \vdots & & \ddots & & \cdots & \vdots & & \vdots \\
-\mathbf{M}_{2i_2}\mathbf{B}_{i_2 1}^{(2)}\mathbf{D}_1^{(1)} & \cdots & -\mathbf{M}_{2i_2}\mathbf{B}_{i_2 1}^{(2)}\mathbf{D}_{i_1}^{(1)} & & & \mathbf{I}-\mathbf{M}_{2i_2} & & -\mathbf{M}_{2i_2}\mathbf{B}_{i_2,N}^{(2)}\mathbf{D}_1^{(N)} & \cdots & -\mathbf{M}_{2i_2}\mathbf{B}_{i_2,N}^{(2)}\mathbf{D}_{i_N}^{(N)} \\
\hline
 & \vdots & & & \vdots & & \ddots & & \vdots & \\
\hline
-\mathbf{M}_{N1}\mathbf{B}_{11}^{(N)}\mathbf{D}_1^{(1)} & \cdots & -\mathbf{M}_{N1}\mathbf{B}_{11}^{(N)}\mathbf{D}_{i_1}^{(1)} & -\mathbf{M}_{N1}\mathbf{B}_{12}^{(N)}\mathbf{D}_1^{(2)} & \cdots & -\mathbf{M}_{N1}\mathbf{B}_{12}^{(N)}\mathbf{D}_{i_2}^{(2)} & \cdots & \mathbf{I}-\mathbf{M}_{N1} & & \\
 & & & \vdots & & \vdots & & & \ddots & \\
-\mathbf{M}_{Ni_N}\mathbf{B}_{i_N 1}^{(N)}\mathbf{D}_1^{(1)} & \cdots & -\mathbf{M}_{Ni_N}\mathbf{B}_{i_N 1}^{(N)}\mathbf{D}_{i_1}^{(1)} & -\mathbf{M}_{Ni_N}\mathbf{B}_{i_N,2}^{(N)}\mathbf{D}_1^{(N)} & \cdots & -\mathbf{M}_{Ni_N}\mathbf{B}_{i_N,2}^{(N)}\mathbf{D}_{i_2}^{(2)} & & & & \mathbf{I}-\mathbf{M}_{Ni_N}
\end{array}\right] \tag{6.1.8}
$$

are inside the unit circle, where $\mathbf{D}_i^{(m)} = \left(\mathbf{A}_{00}^{(m)} + \mathbf{A}_{00}^{(m)T}\right)^{-1}\left(\mathbf{A}_{0i}^{(m)} + \mathbf{A}_{i0}^{(m)T}\right)$.

Proof. Consider first the eigenvalue problem of matrix $\mathbf{H}_K$,

$$-\sum_{m \neq k}\left(\mathbf{A}_{00}^{(k)} + \mathbf{A}_{00}^{(k)T}\right)^{-1}\sum_{l=1}^{i_k}\left(\mathbf{A}_{0l}^{(k)} + \mathbf{A}_{l0}^{(k)T}\right)\mathbf{M}_{kl}\mathbf{B}_{lm}^{(k)}\mathbf{u}_m$$

$$-\sum_{l=1}^{i_k}\left(\mathbf{A}_{00}^{(k)} + \mathbf{A}_{00}^{(k)T}\right)^{-1}\left(\mathbf{A}_{0l}^{(k)} + \mathbf{A}_{l0}^{(k)T}\right)\left(\mathbf{I} - \mathbf{M}_{kl}\right)\mathbf{v}_{kl} = \lambda \mathbf{u}_k \quad (\forall k) \tag{6.1.9}$$

$$\sum_{m \neq k}\mathbf{M}_{kl}\mathbf{B}_{lm}^{(k)}\mathbf{u}_m + \left(\mathbf{I} - \mathbf{M}_{kl}\right)\mathbf{v}_{kl} = \lambda \mathbf{v}_{kl} \quad (\forall k, l).$$

By adding $\left(\mathbf{A}_{0l}^{(k)} + \mathbf{A}_{l0}^{(k)T}\right)$-multiple of the second equation of (6.1.9) for $l = 1, 2, \ldots, i_k$ and then by adding $\left(\mathbf{A}_{00}^{(k)} + \mathbf{A}_{00}^{(k)T}\right)^{-1}$-multiple of the resulting equation to the first equation of (6.1.9) the following relation is obtained:

$$\lambda\left[\mathbf{u}_k + \left(\mathbf{A}_{00}^{(k)} + \mathbf{A}_{00}^{(k)T}\right)^{-1}\sum_{l=1}^{i_k}\left(\mathbf{A}_{0l}^{(k)} + \mathbf{A}_{l0}^{(k)T}\right)\mathbf{v}_{kl}\right] = \mathbf{0} \; (\forall k, l).$$

If $\lambda = 0$, then is is inside the unit circle. If $\lambda \neq 0$, then

$$\mathbf{u}_k = -\left(\mathbf{A}_{00}^{(k)} + \mathbf{A}_{00}^{(k)T}\right)^{-1}\sum_{l=1}^{i_k}\left(\mathbf{A}_{0l}^{(k)} + \mathbf{A}_{l0}^{(k)T}\right)\mathbf{v}_{kl}.$$

By substituting this relation into the second equation of (6.1.9) we obtain

$$-\sum_{m \neq k}\mathbf{M}_{kl}\mathbf{B}_{lm}^{(k)}\left(\mathbf{A}_{00}^{(m)} + \mathbf{A}_{00}^{(m)T}\right)^{-1}\sum_{i=1}^{i_m}\left(\mathbf{A}_{0i}^{(m)} + \mathbf{A}_{i0}^{(m)T}\right)\mathbf{v}_{mi} + \left(\mathbf{I} - \mathbf{M}_{kl}\right)\mathbf{v}_{kl} = \lambda \mathbf{v}_{kl}.$$

With the notation

$$\mathbf{D}_i^{(m)} = \left(\mathbf{A}_{00}^{(m)} + \mathbf{A}_{00}^{(m)T}\right)^{-1}\left(\mathbf{A}_{0i}^{(m)} + \mathbf{A}_{i0}^{(m)T}\right),$$

the last equation can be simplified to

$$-\sum_{m \neq k}\mathbf{M}_{kl}\mathbf{B}_{lm}^{(k)}\sum_{i=1}^{i_m}\mathbf{D}_i^{(m)}\mathbf{v}_{mi} + \left(\mathbf{I} - \mathbf{M}_{kl}\right)\mathbf{v}_{kl} = \lambda \mathbf{v}_{kl},$$

which is identical to the eigenvalue problem of $\mathbf{H}_K^{(1)}$.

□

Remark. The dimension of matrix $\mathbf{H}_K^{(1)}$ is less by $n_1 + ... + n_N$ than the dimension of $\mathbf{H}_K$, where n_k is the dimension of vector $\mathbf{x}_k$, $k = 1,2,...,N$.

We can make further reductions in the dimension of the eigenvalue problems. The solutions of these eigenvalue problems must be examined to verify the global asymptotical stablity of the equilibrium point. This result can be formulated as follows.

Theorem 6.1.3. Assume that $\mathbf{D}_i^{(k)} \equiv \mathbf{D}^{(k)}$ $(\forall i)$, and all eigenvalues of matrices $\mathbf{I} - \mathbf{M}_{ki}$ are inside the unit circle as well as are all solutions of the nonlinear eigenvalue problem

$$\det\begin{bmatrix} \mathbf{I} & -\sum_{l=1}^{i_1}(\mathbf{I}-\mathbf{M}_{1l}-\lambda\mathbf{I})^{-1}\mathbf{M}_{1l}\mathbf{B}_{l2}^{(1)}\mathbf{D}^{(2)} & \cdots & -\sum_{l=1}^{i_1}(\mathbf{I}-\mathbf{M}_{1l}-\lambda\mathbf{I})^{-1}\mathbf{M}_{1l}\mathbf{B}_{lN}^{(1)}\mathbf{D}^{(N)} \\ -\sum_{l=1}^{i_2}(\mathbf{I}-\mathbf{M}_{2l}-\lambda\mathbf{I})^{-1}\mathbf{M}_{2l}\mathbf{B}_{l1}^{(2)}\mathbf{D}^{(1)} & \mathbf{I} & \cdots & -\sum_{l=1}^{i_2}(\mathbf{I}-\mathbf{M}_{2l}-\lambda\mathbf{I})^{-1}\mathbf{M}_{2l}\mathbf{B}_{lN}^{(2)}\mathbf{D}^{(N)} \\ \vdots & \vdots & \ddots & \vdots \\ -\sum_{l=1}^{i_N}(\mathbf{I}-\mathbf{M}_{Nl}-\lambda\mathbf{I})^{-1}\mathbf{M}_{Nl}\mathbf{B}_{l1}^{(N)}\mathbf{D}^{(1)} & -\sum_{l=1}^{i_N}(\mathbf{I}-\mathbf{M}_{Nl}-\lambda\mathbf{I})^{-1}\mathbf{M}_{Nl}\mathbf{B}_{l2}^{(N)}\mathbf{D}^{(2)} & \cdots & \mathbf{I} \end{bmatrix} = 0. \tag{6.1.10}$$

Then the equilibrium point of the quadratic game is globally asymptotically stable with respect to expectations (6.1.5).

Proof. Consider now the eigenvalue problem of matrix (6.1.8). For $k = 1,2,...,N$ and $l = 1,2,...,i_k$,

$$(\mathbf{I} - \mathbf{M}_{kl})\mathbf{v}_{kl} - \sum_{m \neq k} \mathbf{M}_{kl}\mathbf{B}_{lm}^{(k)}\mathbf{D}^{(m)}\mathbf{v}_m = \lambda \mathbf{v}_{kl},$$

where $\mathbf{v}_m = \sum_l \mathbf{v}_{ml}$, which implies that

$$\mathbf{v}_{kl} = (\mathbf{I} - \mathbf{M}_{kl} - \lambda \mathbf{I})^{-1} \sum_{m \neq k} \mathbf{M}_{kl}\mathbf{B}_{lm}^{(k)}\mathbf{D}^{(m)}\mathbf{v}_m.$$

By adding this equation for $l = 1,2,...,i_k$, we have

$$\mathbf{v}_k = \sum_{l=1}^{i_k} (\mathbf{I} - \mathbf{M}_{kl} - \lambda \mathbf{I})^{-1} \sum_{m \neq k} \mathbf{M}_{kl}\mathbf{B}_{lm}^{(k)}\mathbf{D}^{(m)}\mathbf{v}_m,$$

which is equivalent to the nonlinear eigenvalue problem (6.1.10). □

Remark. The dimension of this problem is $n_1 + ... + n_N$, which makes an additional drastic reduction, but as its consequence the eigenvalue problem becomes nonlinear.

Corollary. Assume that $\mathbf{M}_{kl} \equiv \mathbf{M}_k$, that is, $\mathbf{M}_{kl}$ is independent of l. If one multiplies the kth block row of the nonlinear eigenvalue problem (6.1.10) by $(\mathbf{I} - \mathbf{M}_{kl} - \lambda \mathbf{I})$, then the usual eigenvalue problem of matrix

$$\mathbf{H}_K^{(2)} = \begin{bmatrix} \mathbf{I} - \mathbf{M}_1 & -\mathbf{M}_1\left(\sum_{l=1}^{i_1} \mathbf{B}_{l2}^{(1)}\right)\mathbf{D}^{(2)} & \cdots & -\mathbf{M}_1\left(\sum_{l=1}^{i_1} \mathbf{B}_{lN}^{(1)}\right)\mathbf{D}^{(N)} \\ -\mathbf{M}_2\left(\sum_{l=1}^{i_2} \mathbf{B}_{l1}^{(2)}\right)\mathbf{D}^{(1)} & \mathbf{I} - \mathbf{M}_2 & \cdots & -\mathbf{M}_2\left(\sum_{l=1}^{i_2} \mathbf{B}_{lN}^{(2)}\right)\mathbf{D}^{(N)} \\ \vdots & \vdots & \ddots & \vdots \\ -\mathbf{M}_N\left(\sum_{l=1}^{i_N} \mathbf{B}_{l1}^{(N)}\right)\mathbf{D}^{(1)} & -\mathbf{M}_N\left(\sum_{l=1}^{i_N} \mathbf{B}_{l2}^{(N)}\right)\mathbf{D}^{(2)} & \cdots & \mathbf{I} - \mathbf{M}_N \end{bmatrix} \tag{6.1.11}$$

can be obtained.

The next part of this section introduces an alternative form of nonlinear eigenvalue problems, which can be useful in analyzing the global asymptotical stability of equilibrium points in quadratic games. This form can be derived as follows.

Consider the eigenvalue problem of $\mathbf{H}_K$:

$$\mathbf{H}_{00}\mathbf{u} + \sum_{k=1}^{N} \mathbf{H}_{0k}\mathbf{v}_k = \lambda\mathbf{u}$$
$$\mathbf{H}_{k0}\mathbf{u} + \mathbf{H}_{kk}\mathbf{v}_k = \lambda\mathbf{v}_k \quad (k = 1,2,...,N). \tag{6.1.12}$$

The second equation implies that

$$(\mathbf{H}_{kk} - \lambda\mathbf{I})\mathbf{v}_k = -\mathbf{H}_{k0}\mathbf{u}. \tag{6.1.13}$$

Assume that the eigenvalues of matrix $\mathbf{H}_{kk}$ are inside the unit circle for $k = 1,2,...,N$. Note that this is equivalent to the condition that the eigenvalues of matrices $\mathbf{M}_{kl}$ are inside the circle where the center and radius are unity. If, in addition, matrices $\mathbf{M}_{kl}$ are positive definite, which is the usual assumption in adaptive expectations, then this condition is equivalent to the condition that all eigenvalues of $\mathbf{M}_{kl}$ are less than two. If $\mathbf{M}_{kl}$ is diagonal, with positive diagonal elements, then all diagonal elements must be less than two.

If in (6.1.13) λ is an eigenvalue of $\mathbf{H}_{kk}$, then we have nothing to prove. Otherwise

$$\mathbf{v}_k = -(\mathbf{H}_{kk} - \lambda\mathbf{I})^{-1}\mathbf{H}_{k0}\mathbf{u}. \tag{6.1.14}$$

By substituting this relation into the first equation of (6.1.12) we have that

$$\left(\mathbf{H}_{00} - \sum_{k=1}^{N} \mathbf{H}_{0k}(\mathbf{H}_{kk} - \lambda\mathbf{I})^{-1}\mathbf{H}_{k0} - \lambda\mathbf{I}\right)\mathbf{u} = \mathbf{0}. \tag{6.1.15}$$

If $\mathbf{u}=\mathbf{0}$, then for all k, $\mathbf{v}_k = \mathbf{0}$. This case never occurs, since the eigenvectors are nonzero. Hence $\mathbf{u}\neq\mathbf{0}$, which proves the following

Theorem 6.1.4. Assume that the eigenvalues of $\mathbf{H}_{kk}$ are inside the unit circle for $k = 1,2,...,N$. Then the equilibrium point is globally asymptotically stable with respect to expectations (6.1.5) if and only if all roots of equation

$$\det\left[\mathbf{H}_{00} - \sum_{k=1}^{N} \mathbf{H}_{0k}(\mathbf{H}_{kk} - \lambda\mathbf{I})^{-1}\mathbf{H}_{k0} - \lambda\mathbf{I}\right] = 0 \tag{6.1.16}$$

are inside the unit circle.

Remark. Note that the dimension of problems (6.1.16) and (6.1.10) are the same. Problem (6.1.10) has the advantage that in the special case of $\mathbf{M}_{kl} \equiv \mathbf{M}_k$ it reduces to the usual eigenvalue problem of matrix (6.1.11). Note that problem (6.1.16) becomes linear only in very special cases.

Before concluding this section we consider the special case of expectations á la Cournot. We may now select $i_k = 1$ and $\mathbf{M}_{k1} = \mathbf{I}$ $(k = 1,2,...,N)$. Consequently, $\mathbf{H}_{0k} = \mathbf{0}$ and $\mathbf{H}_{kk} = \mathbf{0}$ for all k, and therefore all nonzero eigenvalues of $\mathbf{H}_k$ are the eigenvalues of $\mathbf{H}_{00}$, which now has the form:

$$\mathbf{H}_{00} = -\mathbf{H}_1 \cdot \mathbf{H}_2,$$

where

$$\mathbf{H}_1 = \begin{bmatrix} \left(\mathbf{A}_{00}^{(1)} + \mathbf{A}_{00}^{(1)T}\right)^{-1} & & 0 \\ 0 & \ddots & \\ & & \left(\mathbf{A}_{00}^{(N)} + \mathbf{A}_{00}^{(N)T}\right)^{-1} \end{bmatrix},$$

and

$$\mathbf{H}_2 = \begin{bmatrix} \mathbf{0} & \left(\mathbf{A}_{01}^{(1)} + \mathbf{A}_{10}^{(1)T}\right)\mathbf{B}_{12}^{(1)} & \cdots & \left(\mathbf{A}_{01}^{(1)} + \mathbf{A}_{10}^{(1)T}\right)\mathbf{B}_{1N}^{(1)} \\ \left(\mathbf{A}_{01}^{(2)} + \mathbf{A}_{10}^{(2)T}\right)\mathbf{B}_{11}^{(2)} & \mathbf{0} & \cdots & \left(\mathbf{A}_{01}^{(2)} + \mathbf{A}_{10}^{(2)T}\right)\mathbf{B}_{1N}^{(2)} \\ \vdots & \vdots & \ddots & \vdots \\ \left(\mathbf{A}_{01}^{(N)} + \mathbf{A}_{10}^{(N)T}\right)\mathbf{B}_{11}^{(N)} & \left(\mathbf{A}_{01}^{(N)} + \mathbf{A}_{10}^{(N)T}\right)\mathbf{B}_{12}^{(N)} & \cdots & \mathbf{0} \end{bmatrix}.$$

Let $\alpha_i^{(k)}$ denote the eigenvalues of $\mathbf{A}_{00}^{(k)} + \mathbf{A}_{00}^{(k)T}$, then the spectral norm (see Definition 4.1.2) of $\mathbf{H}_1$ can be obtained as

$$\|\mathbf{H}_1\|_2 = \frac{1}{\min_{i,k}\left|\alpha_i^{(k)}\right|}$$

in a manner similar to (4.1.5). Then a sufficient stability condition can be obtained as follows:

Theorem 6.1.5. Assume that $\|\mathbf{H}_2\|_2 < \min_{i,k}\left|\alpha_i^{(k)}\right|$, then the equilibrium point is globally asymptotically stable with respect to expectations á la Cournot.

Proof. Note that under the assumptions of the theorem

$$|\lambda| \le \|\mathbf{H}_K\|_2 \le \|\mathbf{H}_1\|_2 \cdot \|\mathbf{H}_2\|_2 < \frac{1}{\min_{i,k}\left|\alpha_i^{(k)}\right|} \cdot \min_{i,k}\left|\alpha_i^{(k)}\right| = 1,$$

where λ is an arbitrary eigenvalue of $\mathbf{H}_K$. □

Remark. This result is analogous to the earlier Theorem 4.1.2.

Corollary. Note that

$$\mathbf{H}_2 = \begin{bmatrix} \mathbf{A}_{01}^{(1)} + A_{10}^{(1)T} & & & \\ & \mathbf{A}_{01}^{(2)} + A_{10}^{(2)T} & & \\ & & \ddots & \\ & & & \mathbf{A}_{01}^{(N)} + A_{10}^{(N)T} \end{bmatrix} \begin{bmatrix} \mathbf{0} & \mathbf{B}_{12}^{(1)} & \cdots & \mathbf{B}_{1N}^{(1)} \\ \mathbf{B}_{11}^{(2)} & \mathbf{0} & & \mathbf{B}_{1N}^{(2)} \\ \vdots & & \ddots & \vdots \\ \mathbf{B}_{11}^{(N)} & \mathbf{B}_{12}^{(N)} & \cdots & \mathbf{0} \end{bmatrix}. \tag{6.1.17}$$

Let $\mathbf{H}_{21}$ and $\mathbf{H}_{22}$ denote the first and second factor, respectively. Then

$$\|\mathbf{H}_{21}\|_2 = \max_k \left\|\mathbf{A}_{01}^{(k)} + \mathbf{A}_{10}^{(k)T}\right\|_2 = \max_k A^{(k)},$$

where $A^{(k)}$ denotes the spectral norm of matrix $\mathbf{A}_{01}^{(k)} + \mathbf{A}_{10}^{(k)T}$.

(a) Assume first that matrices $\mathbf{B}_{1l}^{(k)}$ have the same size and are diagonal for all k and l, and furthermore all diagonal elements of these matrices are from the interval $[-\gamma, \gamma]$. Then

$$\left|\mathbf{H}_{22}^T \mathbf{H}_{22}\right| \le \begin{bmatrix} (N-1)\gamma^2\mathbf{I} & (N-2)\gamma^2\mathbf{I} & \cdots & (N-2)\gamma^2\mathbf{I} \\ (N-2)\gamma^2\mathbf{I} & (N-1)\gamma^2\mathbf{I} & \cdots & (N-2)\gamma^2\mathbf{I} \\ \vdots & \vdots & \ddots & \vdots \\ (N-2)\gamma^2\mathbf{I} & (N-2)\gamma^2\mathbf{I} & \cdots & (N-1)\gamma^2\mathbf{I} \end{bmatrix}, \tag{6.1.18}$$

and the right hand side matrix is the Kronecker product of $(N-2)\mathbf{1}+\mathbf{I}$ and $\gamma^2\mathbf{I}$. Thus the eigenvalues of this matrix are $\gamma^2 \cdot 1 = \gamma^2$ and $\gamma^2 \cdot ((N-2)N+1) = \gamma^2(N-1)^2$.

Consequently (see Ortega and Rheinboldt, 1970, p. 54),

$$\|\mathbf{H}_{22}\|_2 \le \gamma(N-1),$$

and hence, the following result: If

$$\max_k A^{(k)} \cdot \gamma(N-1) < \min_{i,k} \left|\alpha_i^{(k)}\right|, \tag{6.1.19}$$

then under the above conditions, the equilibrium point is globally asymptotically stable. Note, that in the case of oligopolies a similar result was proven in Theorem 4.1.2, in which $\gamma = 1$, $\mathbf{A}_{01}^{(k)} = \mathbf{A}$ and $\mathbf{A}_{10}^{(k)} = \mathbf{0}$. So (6.1.19) is identical to (4.1.9).

(b) Drop now the assumption that matrices $B_{1l}^{(k)}$ are diagonal but assume that all elements of these matrices are from the interval $[-\gamma, \gamma]$. Then, similarly to (6.1.18) we have that

$$\left|\mathbf{H}_{22}^T \mathbf{H}_{22}\right| \leq ((N-2)M\mathbf{1} + M\mathbf{I}) \otimes \gamma^2 \mathbf{1},$$

where the eigenvalues of the right hand side are 0,

$$\gamma^2 M \cdot ((N-2)M \cdot 0 + M \cdot 1) \text{ and } \gamma^2 M \cdot ((N-2)M \cdot N + M).$$

That is, they are $0, \gamma^2 M^2$ and $\gamma^2 M^2 (N-1)^2$. Hence

$$\left\|\mathbf{H}_{22}\right\|_2 \leq \gamma M(N-1),$$

and we have obtained the following result: If

$$\max_k A^{(k)} \cdot \gamma M(N-1) < \min_{i,k} \left|\alpha_i^{(k)}\right|, \tag{6.1.20}$$

then the equilibrium point is globally asymptotically stable under the above assumptions.

Note finally that other sufficient global asymptotical stability conditions can be derived by selecting other matrix norms, such as block-row and block-column norms. These results are analogous to those obtained earlier in Section 4.1. and 4.2 and the details are omitted.

6.2 Quadratic Games Under Continuous Time Scale

In this section the quadratic games discussed in the previous section will be investigated for the case of continuous time scale. Hence, the results of this section can be considered not only as the generalizations of the corresponding models and results presented in Chapter 5, but also as the continuous time scale counterparts of the results of the previous section.

Consider again the quadratic game discussed in the previous section and assume that conditions (A) - (C) hold. We now give the continuous time scale dynamic model under assumption (a) introduced in Section 5.1. Now we have

$$\frac{d\mathbf{x}_k(t)}{dt} = \mathbf{K}_k\left(\left(\mathbf{A}_{00}^{(k)} + \mathbf{A}_{00}^{(k)T}\right)\mathbf{x}_k(t) + \sum_{l=1}^{i_k}\left(\mathbf{A}_{0l}^{(k)} + \mathbf{A}_{l0}^{(k)T}\right)\mathbf{s}_{kl}^E(t) + \mathbf{b}_0^{(k)}\right), \tag{6.2.1}$$

where $\mathbf{s}_{kl}^E(t)$ denotes the expectation of firm k on vector $\mathbf{s}_{kl}(t)$, and $\mathbf{b}_0^{(k)}$ is a constant vector.

It is assumed that the expectations on vectors $\mathbf{s}_{kl}(t)$ $(1 \le l \le i_k - 1)$ are adaptive and expectation on $\mathbf{s}_{ki_k}(t)$ is á la Cournot. Thus, we assume that

$$\begin{aligned}
&\frac{d\mathbf{s}_{kl}^E(t)}{dt} = \mathbf{M}_{kl}\left(\mathbf{s}_{kl}(t) - \mathbf{s}_{kl}^E(t)\right) \qquad (l = 1,2,\ldots,i_k - 1),\\
&\mathbf{s}_{ki_k}^E(t) = \mathbf{S}_{ki_k}(t),\\
&\mathbf{s}_{kl}(t) = \sum_{m \ne k}\mathbf{B}_{lm}^{(k)}\mathbf{x}_m^{(t)} \qquad (l = 1,2,\ldots,i_k).
\end{aligned} \tag{6.2.2}$$

In summarizing equations (6.2.1) and (6.2.2) we obtain the following differential equation

$$\frac{d}{dt}\begin{bmatrix}\mathbf{x}_1\\ \vdots\\ \mathbf{x}_N\\ \mathbf{s}_{11}\\ \vdots\\ \mathbf{s}_{1i_1-1}\\ \vdots\\ \mathbf{s}_{N1}\\ \vdots\\ \mathbf{s}_{Ni_N-1}\end{bmatrix} = \begin{bmatrix}\mathbf{K}_1 & & & & & & & \\ & \ddots & & & & & 0 & \\ & & \mathbf{K}_N & & & & & \\ & & & \mathbf{M}_{11} & & & & \\ & & & & \ddots & & & \\ & & & & & \mathbf{M}_{1i_1-1} & & \\ & 0 & & & & & \ddots & \\ & & & & & & \mathbf{M}_{N1} & \\ & & & & & & & \ddots \\ & & & & & & & & \mathbf{M}_{Ni_N-1}\end{bmatrix}\mathbf{H}_K\begin{bmatrix}\mathbf{x}_1\\ \vdots\\ \mathbf{x}_N\\ \mathbf{s}_{11}\\ \vdots\\ \mathbf{s}_{1i_1-1}\\ \vdots\\ \mathbf{s}_{N1}\\ \vdots\\ \mathbf{s}_{Ni_N-1}\end{bmatrix} + \boldsymbol{\alpha}_K, \tag{6.2.3}$$

where $\boldsymbol{\alpha}_K$ is a constant vector,

$$\mathbf{H}_K = \begin{bmatrix}\mathbf{H}_{00} & \mathbf{H}_{01} & \cdots & \mathbf{H}_{0N}\\ \mathbf{H}_{10} & \mathbf{H}_{11} & \cdots & \mathbf{H}_{1N}\\ \vdots & \vdots & \ddots & \vdots\\ \mathbf{H}_{N0} & \mathbf{H}_{N1} & \cdots & \mathbf{H}_{NN}\end{bmatrix}$$

with blocks $\mathbf{H}_{ij}$ $(i, j \ge 0)$ having the following structures:

$$\mathbf{H}_{00} = \begin{bmatrix}\mathbf{E}_{11} & \cdots & \mathbf{E}_{1N}\\ \vdots & & \vdots\\ \mathbf{E}_{N1} & \cdots & \mathbf{E}_{NN}\end{bmatrix}$$

with

$$\mathbf{E}_{kl} = \begin{cases} \mathbf{A}_{00}^{(k)} + \mathbf{A}_{00}^{(k)T} & \text{if } k = l \\ \mathbf{A}_{0i_k}^{(k)} + \mathbf{A}_{i_k 0}^{(k)T} & \text{if } l \in I_{ki_k} \\ \mathbf{0} & \text{otherwise;} \end{cases}$$

$$\mathbf{H}_{0k} = \begin{bmatrix} \mathbf{0} & \cdots & \mathbf{0} \\ \vdots & & \vdots \\ \mathbf{0} & \cdots & \mathbf{0} \\ \mathbf{A}_{01}^{(k)} + \mathbf{A}_{10}^{(k)T} & \cdots & \mathbf{A}_{0,i_k-1}^{(k)} + \mathbf{A}_{i_k-1,0}^{(k)T} \\ \mathbf{0} & \cdots & \mathbf{0} \\ \vdots & & \vdots \\ \mathbf{0} & \cdots & \mathbf{0} \end{bmatrix} \quad (k \geq 1);$$

$$\mathbf{H}_{k0} = \begin{bmatrix} \mathbf{B}_{11}^{(k)} & \cdots & \mathbf{B}_{1,k-1}^{(k)} & \mathbf{0} & \mathbf{B}_{1,k+1}^{(k)} & \cdots & \mathbf{B}_{1,N}^{(k)} \\ \vdots & & \vdots & \vdots & \vdots & & \vdots \\ \mathbf{B}_{i_k-1,1}^{(k)} & \cdots & \mathbf{B}_{i_k-1,k-1}^{(k)} & \mathbf{0} & \mathbf{B}_{i_k-1,k+1}^{(k)} & \cdots & \mathbf{B}_{i_k-1,N}^{(k)} \end{bmatrix} \quad (k \geq 1);$$

$$\mathbf{H}_{km} = \begin{cases} \mathbf{0}, & \text{if } k \neq m \\ -\mathbf{I}, & \text{if } k = m. \end{cases}$$

Assume that

(D') For $t \geq 0$, $\mathbf{x}_k(t) \in X_k$.

Our first result is the consequence of the stability theory of ordinary differential equations:

Theorem 6.2.1. The equilibrium point of a quadratic game is globally asymptotically stable with respect to the above combined expectations if and only if the real parts of all eigenvalues of matrix

$$\text{diag}\left(\mathbf{K}_1, \ldots, \mathbf{K}_N, \mathbf{M}_{11}, \ldots, \mathbf{M}_{1,i_1-1}, \ldots, \mathbf{M}_{N,1}, \ldots, \mathbf{M}_{N,i_N-1}\right)\mathbf{H}_K$$

have negative real parts.

From Lemma 5.1.1 we have the following result.

Theorem 6.2.2. Assume that matrices $\mathbf{K}_k$ and $\mathbf{M}_{ki}$ are positive definite for all k and i, and matrix $\mathbf{H}_K + \mathbf{H}_K^T$ is negative definite. Then the equilibrium point is globally asymptotically stable with respect to expectations (6.2.2).

Remark. As we have discussed earlier in Section 5.3, the main advantage in applying this theorem is the fact that the eigenvalues of $\mathbf{H}_K + \mathbf{H}_K^T$ are always real.

The main reduction theorem of this section will be formulated next. This result will generalize Theorems 5.2.3 and 5.2.8. Define

$$\mathbf{F} = \frac{1}{2}\left(\mathbf{H}_{00} + \mathbf{H}_{00}^T\right),\ \mathbf{A}_k = \mathbf{H}_{k0} + \mathbf{H}_{0k}^T \quad (k = 1, 2, ..., N),$$

then

$$\mathbf{H}_K + \mathbf{H}_K^T = \begin{bmatrix} 2\mathbf{F} & \mathbf{A}_1^T & \cdots & \mathbf{A}_N^T \\ \mathbf{A}_1 & -2\mathbf{I} & & \\ \vdots & & \ddots & \\ \mathbf{A}_N & & & -2\mathbf{I} \end{bmatrix}.$$

Consequently, analogously to Theorems 5.2.3 and 5.2.8, we can prove the following statement:

Theorem 6.2.3. Assume that matrices $\mathbf{K}_k$ and $\mathbf{M}_{ki}$ $(\forall k, \forall i)$ are positive definite, and furthermore matrix **F-I** is negative semidefinite and

$$4\mathbf{F} + \sum_{k=1}^{N} \mathbf{A}_k^T \mathbf{A}_k$$

is negative definite. Then the equilibrium point is globally asymptotically stable with respect to the above combined expectations.

6.3 Nonlinear Oligopolies Under Discrete Time Scale

In this section the nonlinear counterpart of the dynamic processes given in Chapter 4 will be introduced and analyzed. A nonlinear N-firm multiproduct oligopoly will be considered. It is assumed that the conditions of Theorem 3.1.1 are satisfied, that is,

(A) The feasible output set X_k of firm k is a closed, convex, bounded set in R_+^M, where M is the number of products. Furthermore, $\mathbf{x}_k \in X_k$ and $\mathbf{0} \le \mathbf{t}_k \le \mathbf{x}_k$ imply that $\mathbf{t}_k \in X_k$;

(B) There exists a convex, closed set S in R_+^M such that $S \neq \{\mathbf{0}\}$. The unit price function satisfies the relation $\mathbf{p}(\mathbf{s}) = \mathbf{0}$ if $\mathbf{s} \notin S$, and $\mathbf{s} \in S$ and $\mathbf{0} \leq \mathbf{t} \leq \mathbf{s}$ imply that $\mathbf{t} \in S$;

(C) For all k cost function $C_k(\mathbf{x}_k)$ is strictly increasing in each component $x_k^{(m)}$, and continuous on X_k;

(D) For all k, the profit function of firm k is

$$\varphi_k(\mathbf{x}_1,\ldots,\mathbf{x}_N) = \mathbf{x}_k^T \mathbf{p}\left(\sum_{l=1}^{N} \mathbf{x}_l\right) - C_k(\mathbf{x}_k), \tag{6.3.1}$$

which is continuous on $X_1 \times X_2 \times \ldots \times X_N$ and concave in $\mathbf{x}_k$ for any fixed $\mathbf{x}_l \in X_l$ $(l \neq k)$ in the set

$$X^* = \left\{(\mathbf{x}_1,\ldots,\mathbf{x}_N) \middle| \mathbf{x}_k \in X_k \ (\forall k),\ \sum_{k=1}^{N} \mathbf{x}_k \in S\right\}. \tag{6.3.2}$$

If these conditions are met then there exists at least one equilibrium point. The stability of the equilibrium will be analyzed in this section under discrete time scale.

Most of the discrete and continuous time scale models of earlier chapters were based on the assumption that at each time $t \geq 0$, each firm forms expectation on the output of the rest of the industry. These expectations are denoted by $\mathbf{s}_k^E(t)$ $(k = 1,2,\ldots,N)$, and they can be obtained under several different assumptions. In the case of discrete time scales and under expectations á la Cournot, $\mathbf{s}_k^E(t) = \mathbf{s}_k(t-1)$; in the case of adaptive expectations $\mathbf{s}_k^E(t)$ satisfies difference equation (4.2.1); if expectations are assumed on the individual outputs of the rivals, then $\mathbf{s}_k^E(t) = \sum_{l \neq k} \mathbf{x}_{kl}^E(t)$, where $\mathbf{x}_{kl}^E(t)$ is the expectation of firm k on the output of firm l. In the case of sequential adjustment processes $\mathbf{s}_k^E(t) = \sum_{l<k} \mathbf{x}_l(t) + \sum_{l>k} \mathbf{x}_l(t-1)$. In the case of extrapolative expectations, $\mathbf{s}_k^E(t)$ satisfies relation (4.4.1).

In this section nonlinear discrete time models will be analyzed. If the expectation $\mathbf{s}_k^E$ is based on the output of the rest of the industry, then the profit of firm k can be written as

$$\mathbf{x}_k^T \mathbf{p}\left(\mathbf{x}_k + \mathbf{s}_k^E(t)\right) - C_k(\mathbf{x}_k).$$

Now assume:

(E) The profit maximizing output is an interior point of X_k, and functions $\mathbf{p}$ and C_k are differentiable to the order required in our derivations.

Simple differentiation shows that the profit maximizing output satisfies the equation

$$\frac{\partial}{\partial x_k^{(m)}}\left\{\mathbf{x}_k^T\mathbf{p}\left(\mathbf{x}_k+\mathbf{s}_k^E(t)\right)-C_k(\mathbf{x}_k)\right\}$$

$$=\sum_{v=1}^{M} x_k^{(v)}\frac{\partial p_v}{\partial s_m}\left(\mathbf{x}_k+\mathbf{s}_k^E(t)\right)+p_m\left(\mathbf{x}_k+\mathbf{s}_k^E(t)\right)-\frac{\partial C_k}{\partial x_k^{(m)}}(\mathbf{x}_k)=0 \qquad (6.3.3)$$

$$(k=1,\ldots,N;\ m=1,\ldots,M).$$

Assume that with fixed k and for all m, these relations determine the functions

$$\mathbf{x}_k=\mathbf{h}_k\left(\mathbf{s}_k^E(t)\right). \qquad (6.3.4)$$

Here it is assumed that these functions are single valued and differentiable.

Next we determine the Jacobian of $\mathbf{h}_k$. Differentiating (6.3.3) with respect to $s_k^{(\mu)E}(t)$, where $s_k^{(\mu)E}(t)$ is the μth element of vector $\mathbf{s}_k^E(t)$, the following relations are obtained:

$$\sum_{v=1}^{M}\left\{\frac{\partial x_k^{(v)}}{\partial s_k^{(\mu)}}\cdot\frac{\partial p_v}{\partial s_m}+x_k^{(v)}\left(\sum_{l=1}^{M}\frac{\partial^2 p_v}{\partial s_m\partial s_l}\cdot\frac{\partial x_k^{(l)}}{\partial s_k^{(\mu)}}+\frac{\partial^2 p_v}{\partial s_m\partial s_\mu}\right)\right\}$$

$$+\sum_{l=1}^{M}\frac{\partial p_m}{\partial s_l}\cdot\frac{\partial x_k^{(l)}}{\partial s_k^{(\mu)}}+\frac{\partial p_m}{\partial s_\mu}-\sum_{l=1}^{M}\frac{\partial^2 C_k}{\partial x_k^{(m)}\partial x_k^{(l)}}\cdot\frac{\partial x_k^{(l)}}{\partial s_k^{(\mu)}}=0.$$

After rearranging the terms, we have the identity

$$\sum_{l=1}^{M}\frac{\partial x_k^{(l)}}{\partial s_k^{(\mu)}}\cdot\left[\frac{\partial p_l}{\partial s_m}+\frac{\partial p_m}{\partial s_l}+\sum_{v=1}^{M}x_k^{(v)}\frac{\partial^2 p_v}{\partial s_m\partial s_l}-\frac{\partial^2 C_k}{\partial x_k^{(m)}\partial x_k^{(l)}}\right]$$

$$+\left[\sum_{v=1}^{M}x_k^{(v)}\frac{\partial^2 p_v}{\partial s_m\partial s_\mu}+\frac{\partial p_m}{\partial s_\mu}\right]=0 \quad (1\le m\le M,\ 1\le\mu\le M).$$

In order to simplify these relations let $\mathbf{J}_\mathbf{p}$ denote the Jacobian of $\mathbf{p}$, and let $\mathbf{H}_{p_v}$ and $\mathbf{H}_{C_k}$ denote the Hessian of functions p_v and C_k, respectively. Then the above relations are equivalent to the compact form

$$\left(\mathbf{J}_{\mathbf{p}}+\mathbf{J}_{\mathbf{p}}^{T}+\sum_{\nu=1}^{M}x_{k}^{(\nu)}\mathbf{H}_{\mathbf{p}_{\nu}}-\mathbf{H}_{C_{k}}\right)\mathbf{J}_{k}=-\sum_{\nu=1}^{M}x_{k}^{(\nu)}\mathbf{H}_{p_{\nu}}-\mathbf{J}_{\mathbf{p}},$$

where $\mathbf{J}_k$ denotes the Jacobian of $\mathbf{x}_k$ with respect to $\mathbf{s}_k^E(t)$. Assuming that the first factor of the left hand side is invertible, we conclude that

$$\mathbf{J}_{k}=-\left(\mathbf{J}_{p}+\mathbf{J}_{p}^{T}+\sum_{\nu=1}^{M}x_{k}^{(\nu)}\mathbf{H}_{p_{\nu}}-\mathbf{H}_{C_{k}}\right)^{-1}\left(\mathbf{J}_{p}+\sum_{\nu=1}^{M}x_{k}^{(\nu)}\mathbf{H}_{p_{\nu}}\right). \tag{6.3.5}$$

Thus the Jacobian of function (6.3.4) can be rewritten as (6.3.5).

Consider first the case of *expectations á la Cournot*, where

$$\mathbf{s}_k^E(t)=\sum_{l\neq k}\mathbf{x}_l(t-1).$$

Therefore the profit maximizing output is given as

$$\mathbf{x}_k^*(t)=\mathbf{h}_k\left(\sum_{l\neq k}\mathbf{x}_l(t-1)\right).$$

With this behind us, we can generalize the output adjustment system discussed in Chapter 4. It is now assumed that the output changes according to the equation

$$\mathbf{x}(t)=\mathbf{x}_k(t-1)+\mathbf{g}_k\left(\mathbf{x}_k^*(t)-\mathbf{x}_k(t-1)\right),\ (\forall k) \tag{6.3.6}$$

where $\mathbf{g}_k$ is an increasing function in each component.

Easy calculation shows that the Jacobian of this recursion can be given as

$$\mathbf{Q}_c=\begin{bmatrix}\mathbf{Q}_{11} & \cdots & \mathbf{Q}_{1N}\\ \vdots & & \vdots\\ \mathbf{Q}_{N1} & \cdots & \mathbf{Q}_{NN}\end{bmatrix},$$

where

$$\begin{aligned}\mathbf{Q}_{kl}&=\delta_{kl}\mathbf{I}+\mathbf{J}_{\mathbf{g}_k}\cdot\left(\mathbf{J}_k\cdot\mathbf{I}\cdot(1-\delta_{kl})-\delta_{kl}\mathbf{I}\right)\\&=\mathbf{J}_{\mathbf{g}_k}\cdot\mathbf{J}_k+\delta_{kl}\left(\mathbf{I}-\mathbf{J}_{\mathbf{g}_k}-\mathbf{J}_{\mathbf{g}_k}\cdot\mathbf{J}_k\right)\end{aligned} \tag{6.3.7}$$

with δ_{kl} being the Kronecker symbol

$$\delta_{kl} = \begin{cases} 1 & \text{if } k = l \\ 0 & \text{if } k \neq l, \end{cases}$$

and $\mathbf{J}_{\mathbf{g}_k}$ is the Jacobian of $\mathbf{g}_k$.

Consider now the special case of

$$\mathbf{p}(\mathbf{s}) = \mathbf{A}\mathbf{s} + \mathbf{b},\ C_k(\mathbf{x}_k) = \mathbf{x}_k^T \mathbf{B}_k \mathbf{x}_k + \mathbf{b}_k^T \mathbf{x}_k + c_k\ (\forall k)$$

and

$$\mathbf{g}_k(\mathbf{t}) = \mathbf{t}\ \left(\forall \mathbf{t} \in R^M\right). \tag{6.3.8}$$

Then

$$\mathbf{J}_{\mathbf{g}_k} \equiv \mathbf{I},\ \mathbf{J}_k = -\left(\mathbf{A} + \mathbf{A}^T - \mathbf{B}_k - \mathbf{B}_k^T\right)^{-1} \mathbf{A},$$

and (6.3.7) implies that

$$\mathbf{Q}_{kl} = \begin{cases} \mathbf{0} & \text{if } k = l \\ \mathbf{J}_k & \text{if } k \neq l. \end{cases}$$

Thus, matrix $\mathbf{Q}_c$ coincides with the matrix $\mathbf{H}_c$ of coefficients of difference equations (4.1.2), since in this case $\mathbf{J}_k \equiv -\mathbf{D}_k$. Note that $\mathbf{D}_k$ was defined in (4.1.2).

The following result is well known from the theory of difference equations (see Ortega and Rheinboldt, 1970).

Theorem 6.3.1. Assume that for all $\mathbf{x} \in X^*$, $\|\mathbf{Q}_c(\mathbf{x})\| \leq q < 1$, where q is a constant. Then the equilibrium is globally asymptotically stable with respect to dynamic process (6.3.6).

Special stability conditions can be derived by the particular selections of matrix norms.

Corollary 1. Consider the block-row norm, which was earlier discussed in Section 4.1:

$$\|\mathbf{Q}_c\|_{\infty,B} = \max_k \sum_l \|Q_{kl}\|,$$

where $\|\cdot\|$ denotes a norm of the blocks Q_{ij}. Relations (6.3.7) imply that $\|\mathbf{Q}_c\|_{\infty,B} \leq q < 1$, if

$$\left\|\mathbf{I}-\mathbf{J}_{\mathbf{g}_k}\right\|+(N-1)\left\|\mathbf{J}_{g_k}\mathbf{J}_k\right\|\le q<1. \tag{6.3.9}$$

That is, if (6.3.9) holds for all k, then the equilibrium is globally asymptotically stable with respect to the dynamic process (6.3.6).

Corollary 2. Consider next the block-columns norm

$$\left\|\mathbf{Q}_c\right\|_{1,B}=\max_{l}\sum_{k}\left\|\mathbf{Q}_{kl}\right\|,$$

then

$\left\|\mathbf{Q}_c\right\|_{1,B}\le q<1$, if for all k,

$$\left\|\mathbf{I}-\mathbf{J}_{\mathbf{g}_k}\right\|+\sum_{l\ne k}\left\|\mathbf{J}_{\mathbf{g}_l}\mathbf{J}_l\right\|\le q<1. \tag{6.3.10}$$

Consider now the special case of $\mathbf{g}_k(t)=\alpha_k\cdot\mathbf{t}$, where $1\ge\alpha_k>0$ is a constant. Then $\mathbf{J}_{\mathbf{g}_k}=\alpha_k\mathbf{I}$, therefore (6.3.10) has the special form

$$\sum_{\substack{l=1\\ l\ne k}}^{N}\alpha_l\left\|\mathbf{J}_l\right\|+\left(1-\alpha_k\right)\le q<1.$$

That is, for all k,

$$\sum_{\substack{l=1\\ l\ne k}}^{N}\alpha_l\left\|\mathbf{J}_l\right\|-\alpha_k\le q-1 \tag{6.3.11}$$

$$\left(\forall\mathbf{x}_k\in X_k,\ k=1,2,\ldots,N\right).$$

Consider next the special case, where M=1. Then (6.3.5) implies that

$$J_k=-\left(p'+x_kp''\right)/\left(2p'+x_kp''-c_k''\right),$$

and thus condition (6.3.11) generalizes the stability conditions derived by Okuguchi (1976) for the classical oligopoly game.

Remark. In the special case of (6.3.8), conditions (6.3.9) and (6.3.10) reduce to relations (4.1.11) and (4.1.12), respectively.

Consider next the case of *adaptive expectations on the output of the rest of the industry*. In this case it is assumed that the expectations $\mathbf{s}_k^E(t)$ of the firms are adjusted adaptively according to difference equation

$$\mathbf{s}_k^E(t) = \mathbf{s}_k^E(t-1) + \mathbf{e}_k\left(\mathbf{s}_k(t-1) - \mathbf{s}_k^E(t-1)\right), \tag{6.3.12}$$

where $\mathbf{e}_k$ is a function which increases in each component. It is also assumed that the actual output $\mathbf{x}_k(t)$ is adjusted again according to (6.3.6). Thus, vectors $\mathbf{x}_k(t)$ and $\mathbf{s}_k^E(t)$ satisfy the nonlinear difference equation

$$\begin{aligned}
\mathbf{x}_k(t) &= \mathbf{x}_k(t-1) + \mathbf{g}_k\left(\mathbf{h}_k\left(\mathbf{s}_k^E(t-1) + \mathbf{e}_k\left(\sum_{l\neq k}\mathbf{x}_l(t-1) - \mathbf{s}_k^E(t-1)\right)\right) - \mathbf{x}_k(t-1)\right) \\
\mathbf{s}_k^E(t) &= \mathbf{s}_k^E(t-1) + \mathbf{e}_k\left(\sum_{l\neq k}\mathbf{x}_k(t-1) - \mathbf{s}_k^E(t-1)\right).
\end{aligned} \tag{6.3.13}$$

The Jacobian of this recursion has the form

$$\mathbf{Q}_A = \begin{bmatrix}
\mathbf{Q}_{11} & \cdots & \mathbf{Q}_{1N} & \mathbf{S}_{11} & \cdots & \mathbf{S}_{1N} \\
\vdots & & \vdots & \vdots & & \vdots \\
\mathbf{Q}_{N1} & \cdots & \mathbf{Q}_{NN} & \mathbf{S}_{N1} & \cdots & \mathbf{S}_{NN} \\
\mathbf{R}_{11} & \cdots & \mathbf{R}_{1N} & \mathbf{T}_{11} & \cdots & \mathbf{T}_{1N} \\
\vdots & & \vdots & \vdots & & \vdots \\
\mathbf{R}_{N1} & \cdots & \mathbf{R}_{NN} & \mathbf{T}_{N1} & \cdots & \mathbf{T}_{NN}
\end{bmatrix}, \tag{6.3.14}$$

where

$$\begin{aligned}
\mathbf{Q}_{kl} &= \delta_{kl}\mathbf{I} + \mathbf{J}_{\mathbf{g}_k}\cdot\left(\mathbf{J}_k\cdot\mathbf{J}_{\mathbf{e}_k}\cdot\mathbf{I}(1-\delta_{kl}) - \delta_{kl}\mathbf{I}\right) \\
&= \begin{cases}\mathbf{I}-\mathbf{J}_{\mathbf{g}_k} & \text{if } k=l \\ \mathbf{J}_{\mathbf{g}_k}\mathbf{J}_k\mathbf{J}_{\mathbf{e}_k} & \text{if } k\neq l;\end{cases} \\
\mathbf{S}_{kl} &= \mathbf{J}_{\mathbf{g}_k}\cdot\mathbf{J}_k\left(\delta_{kl}\mathbf{I} + \mathbf{J}_{\mathbf{e}_k}\cdot(-\mathbf{I})\cdot\delta_{kl}\right) \\
&= \begin{cases}\mathbf{J}_{\mathbf{g}_k}\cdot\mathbf{J}_k\cdot\left(\mathbf{I}-\mathbf{J}_{\mathbf{e}_k}\right) & \text{if } k=l \\ \mathbf{0} & \text{otherwise;}\end{cases} \\
\mathbf{R}_{kl} &= \mathbf{J}_{\mathbf{e}_k}\cdot\mathbf{I}\cdot(1-\delta_{kl}) = \begin{cases}\mathbf{0} & \text{if } k=l \\ \mathbf{J}_{\mathbf{e}_k} & \text{otherwise;}\end{cases}
\end{aligned}$$

and finally,

$$\mathbf{T}_{kl} = \mathbf{I} \cdot \delta_{kl} + \mathbf{J}_{\mathbf{e}_k} \cdot (-\mathbf{I})\delta_{kl}$$
$$= \begin{cases} \mathbf{I} - \mathbf{J}_{\mathbf{e}_k} & \text{if } k = l \\ \mathbf{0} & \text{otherwise.} \end{cases}$$

Consider again the special case of (6.3.8) and assume that $\mathbf{e}_k(\mathbf{t}) = \mathbf{M}_k \cdot \mathbf{t}$.

Note that this case was discussed in Section 4.2, and the general formulation (6.3.14) reduces to the following:

$$\mathbf{Q}_{kl} = \mathbf{I} \cdot \mathbf{J}_k \cdot \mathbf{M}_k + \delta_{kl} \cdot (\mathbf{I} - \mathbf{I} - \mathbf{I} \cdot \mathbf{J}_k \cdot \mathbf{M}_k)$$
$$= \begin{cases} \mathbf{J}_k \mathbf{M}_k & \text{if } k \neq l \\ \mathbf{0} & \text{if } k = l;. \end{cases}$$

$$\mathbf{S}_{kl} = \begin{cases} \mathbf{J}_k (\mathbf{I} - \mathbf{M}_k) & \text{if } k = l \\ \mathbf{0} & \text{otherwise} \end{cases}$$

with

$$\mathbf{J}_k = -(\mathbf{A} + \mathbf{A}^T - \mathbf{B}_k - \mathbf{B}_k^T)^{-1} \mathbf{A} = -\mathbf{D}_k;$$

$$\mathbf{R}_{kl} = \begin{cases} \mathbf{0} & \text{if } k = l \\ \mathbf{M}_k & \text{otherwise;} \end{cases}$$

and

$$\mathbf{T}_{kl} = \begin{cases} \mathbf{I} - \mathbf{M}_k & \text{if } k = l \\ \mathbf{0} & \text{otherwise.} \end{cases}$$

Observe that in this case $\mathbf{Q}_A$ coincides with matrix $\mathbf{H}_A$ of difference equations (4.2.5).

Theorem 6.3.2. Assume that for all $\mathbf{x} \in X^*, \|\mathbf{Q}_A\| \le q < 1$, where q is a constant. Then the equilibrium is globally asymptotically stable with respect to dynamic process (6.3.13).

Corollary 1. By selecting a block-row norm the following sufficient conditions for the global asymptotical stability are obtained:

$$\left\|\mathbf{I} - \mathbf{J}_{\mathbf{g}_k}\right\| + (N-1)\left\|\mathbf{J}_{\mathbf{g}_k} \mathbf{J}_k \mathbf{J}_{\mathbf{e}_k}\right\| + \left\|\mathbf{J}_{\mathbf{g}_k} \mathbf{J}_k (\mathbf{I} - \mathbf{J}_{\mathbf{e}_k})\right\| \le q < 1 \tag{6.3.15}$$

and

$$(N-1)\left\|\mathbf{J}_{\mathbf{e}_k}\right\|+\left\|\mathbf{I}-\mathbf{J}_{\mathbf{e}_k}\right\| \le q<1,$$

for all k.

Corollary 2. If the block-column norm is selected, then these conditions are modified as follows:

$$\sum_{l\neq k}\left(\left\|\mathbf{J}_{\mathbf{g}_l}\mathbf{J}_l\mathbf{J}_{\mathbf{e}_l}\right\|+\left\|\mathbf{J}_{\mathbf{e}_l}\right\|\right)+\left\|\mathbf{I}-\mathbf{J}_{\mathbf{g}_k}\right\| \le q<1$$

and (6.3.16)

$$\left\|\mathbf{J}_{\mathbf{g}_k}\mathbf{J}_k\left(\mathbf{I}-\mathbf{J}_{\mathbf{e}_k}\right)\right\|+\left\|\mathbf{I}-\mathbf{J}_{\mathbf{e}_k}\right\| \le q<1.$$

Consider again the special case when $\mathbf{g}_k(\mathbf{t})=\alpha_k\mathbf{t}$, where $1\ge\alpha_k>0$ is a constant. Then $\mathbf{J}_{\mathbf{g}_k}=\alpha_k\mathbf{I}$, therefore conditions (6.3.16) can be simplified as

$$\begin{aligned}&\sum_{l\neq k}\left(\alpha_l\cdot\left\|\mathbf{J}_l\mathbf{J}_{\mathbf{e}_l}\right\|+\left\|\mathbf{J}_{\mathbf{e}_l}\right\|\right)-\alpha_k\le q-1,\\&\alpha_k\cdot\left\|\mathbf{J}_k\left(\mathbf{I}-\mathbf{J}_{\mathbf{e}_k}\right)\right\|+\left\|\mathbf{I}-\mathbf{J}_{\mathbf{e}_k}\right\|\le q,\end{aligned} \tag{6.3.17}$$

for $k=1,2,\ldots,N$.

The cases of *adaptive expectations on the rivals' outputs* can be similarly discussed.

Next we will study *sequential adjustment* processes in nonlinear oligopolies. The dynamic process is now as follows. For all t>0 and all k, $\mathbf{x}_k(t)$ is the solution of the equation

$$\begin{aligned}&\sum_{v=1}^{M}\mathbf{x}_k^{(v)}\frac{\partial p_v}{\partial s_m}\left(\mathbf{x}_k+\sum_{l<k}\mathbf{x}_l(t)+\sum_{l>k}\mathbf{x}_l(t-1)\right)\\&+p_m\left(\mathbf{x}_k+\sum_{l<k}\mathbf{x}_l(t)+\sum_{l>k}\mathbf{x}_l(t-1)\right)-\frac{\partial C_k}{\partial x_k^{(m)}}(\mathbf{x}_k)=\mathbf{0}\end{aligned} \tag{6.3.18}$$

$(m=1,2,\ldots,M)$. Assume that

(E') All vectors $\mathbf{x}_k(t)$ are uniquely determined and are interior points of X_k.

Note that equation (6.3.18) is obtained from relation (6.3.3) by substituting $\mathbf{s}_k^E(t)=\sum_{l\neq k}\mathbf{x}_l$ with fixed $\mathbf{x}_l=\mathbf{x}_l(t)$ $(l<k)$ and $\mathbf{x}_l=\mathbf{x}_l(t-1)$ $(l>k)$. The

Jacobian of function (6.3.18) will be determined first. Simple calculations show that its derivative with respect to $x_l^{(\mu)}$ equals

$$\sum_{\nu=1}^{M} x_k^{(\nu)} \frac{\partial^2 p_\nu}{\partial s_m \partial s_\mu} + \frac{\partial p_\mu}{\partial s_m} + \frac{\partial p_m}{\partial s_\mu} - \frac{\partial^2 C_k}{\partial x_k^{(m)} \partial x_k^{(\mu)}} \quad (l = k)$$

and

$$\sum_{\nu=1}^{M} x_k^{(\nu)} \frac{\partial^2 p_\nu}{\partial s_m \partial s_\mu} + \frac{\partial p_m}{\partial s_\mu} \quad (l \neq k).$$

Hence the Jacobian can be written in the form

$$\mathbf{Q}_S = \begin{bmatrix} \mathbf{Q}_{11} & \cdots & \mathbf{Q}_{1N} \\ \vdots & & \vdots \\ \mathbf{Q}_{N1} & \cdots & \mathbf{Q}_{NN} \end{bmatrix} \tag{6.3.19}$$

with

$$\mathbf{Q}_{kl} = \begin{cases} \mathbf{J}_p + \mathbf{J}_p^T + \sum_{\nu=1}^{M} x_k^{(\nu)} \mathbf{H}_{p_\nu} - \mathbf{H}_{C_k}, & \text{if } k = l \\ \mathbf{J}_p + \sum_{\nu=1}^{M} x_k^{(\nu)} \mathbf{H}_{p_\nu}, & \text{if } k \neq l. \end{cases}$$

The global SOR (successive overrelaxation) theorem (see Ortega and Rheinboldt, 1970) implies the following result:

Theorem 6.3.3. Assume that $\mathbf{Q}_{kl}$ is continuous for all k and l, $\mathbf{Q}_S$ is symmetric, and furthermore there exists a constant $c < 0$, such that

$$\mathbf{u}^T \mathbf{Q}_S(\mathbf{x}) \mathbf{u} \le c \mathbf{u}^T \mathbf{u} \quad \left(\forall \mathbf{u}, \mathbf{x} \in R^{MN}\right). \tag{6.3.20}$$

Then the equilibrium is globally asymptotically stable with respect to the sequential adjustment process.

Corollary. Assume that

$$\mathbf{p}(\mathbf{s}) = \mathbf{A}\mathbf{s} + \mathbf{b},$$

$\mathbf{A} = \mathbf{A}^T$ and $\mathbf{A}$ is negative definite, furthermore C_k is convex for all k. Then the equilibrium is globally asymptotically stable with respect to the sequential adjustment process.

Proof. Under our assumptions

$$\mathbf{Q}_S = \begin{bmatrix} 2\mathbf{A} & \mathbf{A} & \cdots & \mathbf{A} \\ \mathbf{A} & 2\mathbf{A} & \cdots & \mathbf{A} \\ \vdots & \vdots & \ddots & \vdots \\ \mathbf{A} & \mathbf{A} & \cdots & 2\mathbf{A} \end{bmatrix} - \begin{bmatrix} \mathbf{H}_{C_1} & & & 0 \\ & \mathbf{H}_{C_2} & & \\ 0 & & \ddots & \\ & & & \mathbf{H}_{C_N} \end{bmatrix}.$$

We have seen in Section 5.1 that the first term is negative definite. Let λ_0 denote the largest eigenvalue of the first term. Note also that the convexity of C_k for all k implies that matrices $\mathbf{H}_{C_k}$ are nonnegative definite. Consequently

$$\frac{\mathbf{u}^T \mathbf{Q}_S \mathbf{u}}{\mathbf{u}^T \mathbf{u}} \le \lambda_0 < 0.$$

That is, (6.3.20) is satisfied with $c = \lambda_0$. □

We will next consider an alternative way to analyze the global asymptotical stability of the sequential adjustment process. Observe first that this dynamic process can also be described as

$$\mathbf{x}_k(t) = \mathbf{h}_k\left(\sum_{l<k} \mathbf{x}(t) + \sum_{l>k} \mathbf{x}_l(t-1)\right) \quad (k = 1, 2, \ldots, N). \tag{6.3.21}$$

Assume there exists a constant a_k such that

$$\|\mathbf{J}_k(\mathbf{x})\| \le a_k < \frac{1}{N-1} \left(\text{all } \mathbf{x} \in X^* \text{ and } k\right). \tag{6.3.22}$$

Then (6.3.21) and the mean value theorem of the derivatives of vector-vector functions imply that

$$\|\mathbf{x}_k(t) - \mathbf{x}_k^*\| = \left\|\mathbf{h}_k\left(\sum_{l<k} \mathbf{x}_l(t) + \sum_{l>k} \mathbf{x}_l(t-1)\right) - \mathbf{h}_k\left(\sum_{l<k} \mathbf{x}_l^* + \sum_{l>k} \mathbf{x}_l^*\right)\right\|$$
$$\le a_k \cdot \left(\sum_{l<k} \|\mathbf{x}_l(t) - \mathbf{x}_l^*\| + \sum_{l>k} \|\mathbf{x}_l(t-1) - \mathbf{x}_l^*\|\right),$$

where $\left(\mathbf{x}_1^*, \ldots, \mathbf{x}_N^*\right)$ is the equilibrium, which is assumed to be an interior point of X^*. Introduce the notation

$$\varepsilon(t) = \max_k \left\| \mathbf{x}_k(t) - \mathbf{x}_k^* \right\|,$$

and notice that the last inequality implies that

$$\left\| \mathbf{x}_k(t) - \mathbf{x}_k^* \right\| \le a_k \big((k-1)\varepsilon(t) + (N-k)\varepsilon(t-1) \big).$$

Assume that the left hand side becomes maximal for $k = k_0$, then we conclude that

$$\varepsilon(t) \le a_{k_0} \big((k_0 - 1)\varepsilon(t) + (N - k_0)\varepsilon(t-1) \big).$$

That is,

$$\varepsilon(t) \le \frac{(N-k_0)a_{k_0}}{1-(k_0-1)a_{k_0}} \varepsilon(t-1). \tag{6.3.23}$$

We prove next that the right hand side is always less than or equal to $(N-1)a_{k_0}\varepsilon(t-1)$. Toward proving this fact consider inequality

$$\frac{(N-k_0)a_{k_0}}{1-(k_0-1)a_{k_0}} \le (N-1)a_{k_0}.$$

If $a_{k_0} = 0$, then the inequality holds. If $a_{k_0} \ne 0$, then it is equivalent to relation

$$a_{k_0} \le \frac{1}{k_0 - 1} \cdot \left(1 - \frac{N-k_0}{N-1} \right) = \frac{1}{N-1}.$$

Hence from (6.3.23) we conclude that there exists a $0 \le q < 1$ such that for all $t > 0$,

$$\varepsilon(t) \le q < 1,$$

which implies that for all k, $\mathbf{x}_k(t) \to \mathbf{x}_k^*$ for $t \to \infty$. This result can be summarized as follows:

Theorem 6.3.4. Under assumptions (6.3.22) the equilibrium is globally asymptotically stable with respect to the sequential adjustment process.

Remark. In the case of M=1 (that is, in the case of the classical Cournot oligopoly),

$$J_k = -\frac{p' + x_k p''}{2p' + x_k p'' - C_k''}.$$

Assume that $p' < 0$, p'' and $-C_k''$ are nonpositive. Then condition (6.3.22) is the following:

$$\frac{-p' - x_k p''}{-2p' - x_k p'' + C_k''} \leq \varepsilon, \quad \left(\varepsilon < \frac{1}{N-1}\right)$$

that is, for all k,

$$C_k'' \geq \frac{1}{\varepsilon}\left[(2\varepsilon - 1)p' + x_k(\varepsilon - 1)p''\right].$$

This condition can be interpreted as the requirement that C_k'' must be sufficiently large.

Before discussing models with continuous time scale some additional remarks are in order.

1. In the above derivations special matrix norms were used. Similar results can be obtained by using other matrix norms, but the derivation of the stability conditions remains the same.

2. The conditions of Theorems 6.3.1 and 6.3.2 can be weakened in the following way. Rewrite the dynamic adjustment process as

$$\mathbf{x}(t) = \mathbf{h}(\mathbf{x}(t-1)), \tag{6.3.24}$$

where $\mathbf{h}$ is a continuously differentiable function of R^{MN}. Assume also that

(i) For all $\mathbf{x} \in R^{MN}, \left\|\mathbf{Q}(\mathbf{x}^*)\mathbf{x}\right\|_2 < \|\mathbf{x}\|_2$;

(ii) If $\|\mathbf{x}\|_2 = \left\|\mathbf{h}(\mathbf{x} + \mathbf{x}^*) - \mathbf{x}^*\right\|_2$, then $\|\mathbf{Q}(\mathbf{x})\mathbf{x}\|_2 < \|\mathbf{x}\|_2$.

Then the equilibrium $\mathbf{x}^*$ is globally asymptotically stable with respect to the dynamic process (6.3.24). Here $\|\mathbf{x}\|_2 = \sqrt{\mathbf{x}^T\mathbf{x}}$ for all $\mathbf{x} \in R^{MN}$. This statement follows from the main result of Brock and Scheinkman (1975) if we rewrite relation (6.3.24) as

$$\mathbf{y}(t) = \mathbf{h}(\mathbf{y}(t-1) + \mathbf{x}^*) - \mathbf{x}^*$$

with $\mathbf{y}(t) = \mathbf{x}(t) - \mathbf{x}^*$. Observe that $\mathbf{y}^* = \mathbf{0}$ is the solution to this equation.

3. We can verify that the conditions of the previous remark can be further weakened in the following ways (see Szidarovszky and Okuguchi, 1987k).
   (a) Let $\mathbf{G}$ be any nonsingular matrix. Then the Euclidean norm $\|\mathbf{x}\|_2$ can be replaced by the norm $\|\mathbf{x}\| = \|\mathbf{Gx}\|_2$.
   (b) Introduce the notation
   $\mathbf{h}_1(\mathbf{y}) = \mathbf{h}(\mathbf{y}+\mathbf{x}^*) - \mathbf{x}^*$, $\mathbf{h}_2(\mathbf{y}) = (\mathbf{h}_1 \circ \mathbf{h}_1)(\mathbf{y}), \ldots,$
   $\mathbf{h}_k(\mathbf{y}) = (\mathbf{h}_1 \circ \mathbf{h}_{k-1})(\mathbf{y}) \quad (k \geq 2).$

   If there exists a $k \geq 1$ such that function $\mathbf{h}_k$ satisfies the conditions of the assertion with the generalized Euclidean norm $\|\mathbf{x}\| = \|\mathbf{Gx}\|_2$ (G is nonsingular), then the equilibrium is globally asymptotically stable.

   These generalizations have significant interest. If $\mathbf{h}_1(\mathbf{y}) = \mathbf{Q} \cdot \mathbf{y}$ with constant $\mathbf{Q}$, then it is known that the equilibrium is globally asymptotically stable if and only if all eigenvalues of $\mathbf{Q}$ are inside the unit circle. It is worthwhile to mention that even in this special case the conditions of Brock and Scheinkman are weaker than this sufficient and necessary condition. However the more general condition 3.(b) are already equivalent to this sufficient and necessary condition.

   This equivalence can be verified in the following way. Assume that $\mathbf{h}_k$ satisfies conditions (i) and (ii) of 2. Then $\mathbf{Q}(\mathbf{x}^*) = \mathbf{Q}$ and $\|\mathbf{Q}\| < 1$, which implies that all eigenvalues of $\mathbf{Q}$ are inside the unit circle. Assume next that all eigenvalues of $\mathbf{Q}$ are inside the unit circle. Then for $k \to \infty$, $\mathbf{Q}^k \to \mathbf{0}$. Consequently, for sufficiently large values of k, $\|\mathbf{Q}^k\|_2 < 1$. Since $\mathbf{h}_k(\mathbf{y}) = \mathbf{Q}^k\mathbf{y}$, function $\mathbf{h}_k$ satisfies conditions (i) and (ii) of 2.

4. In the previous discussions, the global asymptotical stability of the equilibrium was examined. The asymptotical stability of the equilibrium can be discussed in a similar way as it has been illustrated earlier in Sections 4.8 and 4.9. In order to prove (local) asymptotical stability we have to assume that $\mathbf{Q}(\mathbf{x})$ is continuous in the neighborhood of the equilibrium $\mathbf{x}^*$ and all eigenvalues of $\mathbf{Q}(\mathbf{x}^*)$ are inside the unit circle. This condition is certainly satisfied if with some matrix norm, $\|\mathbf{Q}(\mathbf{x}^*)\| < 1$. The particular stability conditions are the same as presented in this section with the difference that the inequalities should hold only at the equilibrium.

5. An alternative way of proving the global or local asymptotical stability of the equilibrium is based on Lyapunov functions. For discrete systems we followed the method based on the norm of the Jacobian. In the next section the Lyapunov method will be illustrated to find stability conditions for continuous models.

6.4 Nonlinear Oligopolies Under Continuous Time Scale

In this section dynamic oligopolies will be examined under *continuous time scale*. Consider the nonlinear multiproduct oligopoly game and assume the conditions (A) - (D) introduced at the beginning of the previous section. Assume also that functions $\mathbf{p}$ and C_k are differentiable to the order required. Let $\mathbf{s}_k^E(t)$ again denote the expectation of firm k $(1 \le k \le N)$ on the total output of the rest of the industry. The two major dynamic models are as follows:

(a) By assuming that the output of each firm is adjusted proportionally to its expected marginal profit computed under its expectations, the dynamic process can be described by the differential equation

$$\frac{d\mathbf{x}_k}{dt} = \mathbf{g}_k\left(\mathbf{J}_\mathbf{p}^T\left(\mathbf{x}_k + \mathbf{s}_k^E(t)\right)\mathbf{x}_k + \mathbf{p}_k\left(\mathbf{x}_k + \mathbf{s}_k^E(t)\right) - \nabla C_k(\mathbf{x}_k)\right) \quad (k = 1, 2, ..., N) \tag{6.4.1}$$

where ∇C_k denotes the gradient (as a column vector) of C_k. In deriving this relation equation (6.3.3) was used. Note that function $\mathbf{g}_k$ is sign preserving.

(b) By assuming that the outputs of the firms are adjusted proportionally to the difference of the profit maximizing and actual outputs, we obtain the following dynamic process

$$\frac{d\mathbf{x}_k}{dt} = \mathbf{g}_k\left(\mathbf{h}_k\left(\mathbf{s}_k^E(t)\right) - \mathbf{x}_k\right), \tag{6.4.2}$$

where notation (6.3.4) is used.

Consider first the case of *expectations á la Cournot*. In this case $\mathbf{s}_k^E(t) = \sum_{l \ne k} \mathbf{x}_l(t)$, which implies that under assumption (a) the Jacobian of the right hand side of (6.4.1) is the block matrix

$$\mathbf{Q}_C = \begin{bmatrix} \mathbf{Q}_{11} & \cdots & \mathbf{Q}_{1N} \\ \vdots & & \vdots \\ \mathbf{Q}_{N1} & \cdots & \mathbf{Q}_{NN} \end{bmatrix},$$

where

$$\mathbf{Q}_{kl} = \mathbf{J}_{\mathbf{g}_k} \cdot \left[\mathbf{J}_{\mathbf{p}} + \sum_{\nu=1}^{M} x_k^{(\nu)} \mathbf{H}_{p_\nu} + \delta_{kl} \left(\mathbf{J}_p^T - \mathbf{H}_{C_k} \right) \right]$$

$$= \begin{cases} \mathbf{J}_{\mathbf{g}_k} \cdot \left[\mathbf{J}_{\mathbf{p}} + \mathbf{J}_p^T + \sum_{\nu=1}^{M} x_k^{(\nu)} \mathbf{H}_{p_\nu} - \mathbf{H}_{C_k} \right] & \text{if } k = l \\ \mathbf{J}_{\mathbf{g}_k} \cdot \left[\mathbf{J}_{\mathbf{p}} + \sum_{\nu=1}^{M} x_k^{(\nu)} \mathbf{H}_{p_\nu} \right] & \text{if } k \neq l. \end{cases}$$

Hence

$$\mathbf{Q}_C = \begin{bmatrix} \mathbf{J}_{\mathbf{g}_1} & & 0 \\ & \mathbf{J}_{\mathbf{g}_2} & \\ 0 & & \ddots \\ & & & \mathbf{J}_{\mathbf{g}_N} \end{bmatrix} \cdot \left\{ \begin{bmatrix} \mathbf{J}_{\mathbf{p}} + \mathbf{J}_{\mathbf{p}}^T & \mathbf{J}_p & \cdots & \mathbf{J}_{\mathbf{p}} \\ \mathbf{J}_p & \mathbf{J}_{\mathbf{p}} + \mathbf{J}_{\mathbf{p}}^T & \cdots & \mathbf{J}_{\mathbf{p}} \\ \vdots & \vdots & \ddots & \vdots \\ \mathbf{J}_{\mathbf{p}} & \mathbf{J}_{\mathbf{p}} & \cdots & \mathbf{J}_{\mathbf{p}} + \mathbf{J}_{\mathbf{p}}^T \end{bmatrix} + \right.$$

$$\left. \sum_{\nu=1}^{M} \begin{bmatrix} x_1^{(\nu)} \mathbf{H}_{p_\nu} & \cdots & x_1^{(\nu)} \mathbf{H}_{p_\nu} \\ x_2^{(\nu)} \mathbf{H}_{p_\nu} & \cdots & x_2^{(\nu)} \mathbf{H}_{p_\nu} \\ \vdots & & \vdots \\ x_N^{(\nu)} \mathbf{H}_{p_\nu} & \cdots & x_N^{(\nu)} \mathbf{H}_{p_\nu} \end{bmatrix} - \begin{bmatrix} \mathbf{H}_{C_1} & & 0 \\ & \mathbf{H}_{C_2} & \\ 0 & & \ddots \\ & & & \mathbf{H}_{C_N} \end{bmatrix} \right\}. \tag{6.4.3}$$

We may similarly verify that the Jacobian of the right hand side of (6.4.2) can be written as

$$\tilde{\mathbf{Q}}_C = \begin{bmatrix} \tilde{\mathbf{Q}}_{11} & \cdots & \tilde{\mathbf{Q}}_{1N} \\ \vdots & & \vdots \\ \tilde{\mathbf{Q}}_{N1} & \cdots & \tilde{\mathbf{Q}}_{NN} \end{bmatrix},$$

where

$$\tilde{\mathbf{Q}}_{kl} = \mathbf{J}_{\mathbf{g}_k} \cdot \left[\mathbf{J}_k \cdot (1 - \delta_{kl}) - \mathbf{I} \cdot \delta_{kl} \right].$$

By using relation (6.3.5) we may conclude that

$$\tilde{\mathbf{Q}}_{kl} = -\mathbf{J}_{\mathbf{g}_k} \cdot \left(\mathbf{J}_{\mathbf{p}} + \mathbf{J}_p^T + \sum_{\nu=1}^{M} x_k^{(\nu)} \mathbf{H}_{p_\nu} - \mathbf{H}_{C_k} \right)^{-1} \cdot \left[(1 - \delta_{kl}) \cdot \left(\mathbf{J}_{\mathbf{p}} + \sum_{\nu=1}^{M} x_k^{(\nu)} \mathbf{H}_{p_\nu} \right) + \right.$$

$$\left. \delta_{kl} \left(\mathbf{J}_{\mathbf{p}} + \mathbf{J}_p^T + \sum_{\nu=1}^{M} x_k^{(\nu)} \mathbf{H}_{p_\nu} - \mathbf{H}_{C_k} \right) \right]$$

$$
= \begin{cases} \tilde{\mathbf{J}}_{\mathbf{g}_k} \cdot \left(\mathbf{J}_p + \mathbf{J}_p^T + \sum_{\nu=1}^{M} x_k^{(\nu)} \mathbf{H}_{p_\nu} - \mathbf{H}_{C_k} \right) & \text{if } k = l \\ \tilde{\mathbf{J}}_{\mathbf{g}_k} \cdot \left(\mathbf{J}_p + \sum_{\nu=1}^{M} x_k^{(\nu)} \mathbf{H}_{p_\nu} \right) & \text{if } k \neq l, \end{cases}
$$

where

$$
\tilde{\mathbf{J}}_{\mathbf{g}_k} = -\mathbf{J}_{\mathbf{g}_k} \cdot \left(\mathbf{J}_p + \mathbf{J}_p^T + \sum_{\nu=1}^{M} x_k^{(\nu)} \mathbf{H}_{p_\nu} - \mathbf{H}_{C_k} \right)^{-1} \quad (\forall k).
$$

Consider now the special case of (6.3.8) with $\mathbf{g}_k(t) = \mathbf{K}_k \mathbf{t}$, when $\mathbf{J}_p = \mathbf{A}$, $\mathbf{H}_{p_\nu} = \mathbf{0}$, $\mathbf{H}_{C_k} = \mathbf{B}_k + \mathbf{B}_k^T$, and $\mathbf{J}_{\mathbf{g}_k} = \mathbf{K}_k$. Matrices $\mathbf{Q}_C$ and $\tilde{\mathbf{Q}}_C$ coincide with the coefficient matrices of differential equations (5.1.2) and (5.1.4), respectively.

Since $\tilde{\mathbf{Q}}_C$ has the same form as $\mathbf{Q}_C$ where $\mathbf{J}_{\mathbf{g}_k}$ is replaced by $\tilde{\mathbf{J}}_{\mathbf{g}_k}$ for all k, only assumption (a) will be discussed. It is assumed that $\mathbf{Q}_C$ is continuous on X^*.

Our investigation on the global asymptotic stability of the autonomous differential equation (6.4.1) is based on a classical result of Uzawa (1961). This theory will be first discussed.

Definition 6.4.1. Consider the autonomous system

$$
\frac{d}{dt}\mathbf{x} = \mathbf{f}(\mathbf{x}), \tag{6.4.4}
$$

where function $\mathbf{f}(\mathbf{x})$ is defined on a subset T of a finite dimensional Euclidean space. Assume that for all $\mathbf{x}_0 \in T$, there is unique solution $\mathbf{x}(t, \mathbf{x}_0)$ of (6.4.4) such that $\mathbf{x}(0, \mathbf{x}_0) = \mathbf{x}_0$ and this solution is defined and remains in T for all $t \geq 0$. System (6.4.4) is said to be quasi-stable, if there exists a $K>0$ such that for any $\mathbf{x}_0 \in T$,

(i) $\|\mathbf{x}(t, \mathbf{x}_0)\| \leq K \quad (\forall t \geq 0)$;

(ii) If for any sequence $t_\nu \to \infty$, the limit $\lim_{\nu \to \infty} \mathbf{x}(t_\nu, \mathbf{x}_0)$ exists, then the limit $\mathbf{x}^*$ is an equilibrium (that is, $\mathbf{f}(\mathbf{x}^*) = \mathbf{0}$).

Remark. In the definition it is not required that $\lim_{t \to \infty} \mathbf{x}(t, \mathbf{x}_0)$ exists for all $\mathbf{x}_0 \in T$.

Lemma 6.4.1. Assume that function $\mathbf{f}(\mathbf{x})$ is continuous on T, and for all $\mathbf{x}_0 \in T$, the solution $\mathbf{x}(t, \mathbf{x}_0)$ exists and is unique. It is also assumed that the solution is in T for all $t \geq 0$ and is continuous in $\mathbf{x}_0$. Assume furthermore that set T is compact and there exists a real valued function $\phi(\mathbf{x}(t, \mathbf{x}_0))$ which is continuous in $\mathbf{x}$ and strictly decreasing in t unless $\mathbf{x}$ is an equilibrium. Then process (6.4.4) is quasi-stable.

The proof of the lemma is given in Uzawa (1961). Notice that ϕ is a Lyapunov function of system (6.4.4).

Remark. If function $\phi(\mathbf{x})$ is differentiable with respect to $\mathbf{x}$, then $\phi(\mathbf{x}(t, \mathbf{x}_0))$ is strictly decreasing in t if

$$\sum_i \frac{\partial \phi}{\partial x_i}(\mathbf{x}) \cdot f_i(\mathbf{x}) < 0,$$

where f_i denotes the ith component of $\mathbf{f}$.

Our stability analysis for continuous time scale models will be based on the following consequence of Lemma 6.4.1.

Theorem 6.4.1. Assume that the equilibrium is unique. Then under the condition of Lemma 6.4.1 system (6.4.4) is globally asymptotically stable in T. That is, for arbitrary $\mathbf{x}_0 \in T$, $\lim_{t\to\infty} \mathbf{x}(t, \mathbf{x}_0)$ exists and equals the equilibrium.

Proof. In contrary to the assumptions suppose that for an $\mathbf{x}_0 \in T$, $\lim_{t\to\infty} \mathbf{x}(t, \mathbf{x}_0)$ does not exist. Therefore there is a sequence $t_\nu \to \infty$ and a positive $\varepsilon > 0$ such that for all $\nu \geq 1$, $\|\mathbf{x}(t_\nu, \mathbf{x}_0) - \mathbf{x}^*\| \geq \varepsilon$, where $\mathbf{x}^*$ is the equilibrium. Since for all ν, $\mathbf{x}(t_\nu, \mathbf{x}_0) \in T$ and T is compact, there is a subsequence $\{t_{\nu_k}\} \subset \{t_\nu\}$ such that $\lim_{k\to\infty} \mathbf{x}(t_{\nu_k}, \mathbf{x}_0)$ exists. Then Lemma 6.4.1 implies that this limit equals $\mathbf{x}^*$. This fact contradicts the selection of ε. Thus the proof is complete. □

Remark. Practical stability conditions can be obtained by the particular selections of function $\phi(\mathbf{x})$. In the next part of this section some important forms of $\phi(\mathbf{x})$ will be analyzed.

1. Assume first that

$$\phi(\mathbf{x}) = (\mathbf{x} - \mathbf{x}^*)^T \mathbf{G}(\mathbf{x} - \mathbf{x}^*),$$

where $\mathbf{G}$ is a constant symmetric matrix. Assume that the right hand side of (6.4.1) is continuously differentiable on X^* for all k, and the equilibrium is unique. Then Theorem 6.4.1 implies that if $\mathbf{x}(t,\mathbf{x}_0) \in T$ for $t \geq 0$, and $\phi(\mathbf{x}(t,\mathbf{x}_0))$ is strictly decreasing in t for $\mathbf{x} \neq \mathbf{x}^*$, then the equilibrium is globally asymptotically stable. Simple calculation shows that

$$\frac{d}{dt}\phi(\mathbf{x}(t,\mathbf{x}_0)) = 2(\mathbf{x}-\mathbf{x}^*)^T \mathbf{G}\mathbf{f}(\mathbf{x}), \tag{6.4.5}$$

where $\mathbf{f} = (\mathbf{f}_1,\ldots,\mathbf{f}_N)$, $\mathbf{f}_k(\mathbf{x})$ is the right hand side of (6.4.1) with $\mathbf{s}_k^E(t) = \sum_{l \neq k} \mathbf{x}_l$. Our first particular result is the following

Theorem 6.4.2. Assume that the above conditions hold and matrix $\mathbf{GQ}+\mathbf{Q}^T\mathbf{G}$ is negative definite for all $\mathbf{x} \in X^*$. Then the equilibrium is globally asymptotically stable with respect to the dynamic process (6.4.1).

Proof. Observe that $\mathbf{GQ}_C$ is the Jacobian of function $\mathbf{Gf}(\mathbf{x})$, and therefore (see Ortega and Rheinboldt, 1970) function $-\mathbf{Gf}(\mathbf{x})$ is strictly monotone. Thus

$$0 > (\mathbf{x}-\mathbf{x}^*)^T(\mathbf{Gf}(\mathbf{x}) - \mathbf{Gf}(\mathbf{x}^*)) = (\mathbf{x}-\mathbf{x}^*)^T \mathbf{Gf}(\mathbf{x}).$$

So (6.4.5) is negative for $\mathbf{x} \neq \mathbf{x}^*$, and therefore $\phi(\mathbf{x}(t,\mathbf{x}_0))$ is strictly decreasing if $\mathbf{x} \neq \mathbf{x}^*$. □

Consider the special case when for all k, $\mathbf{g}_k(\mathbf{t}) = \mathbf{K}_k\mathbf{t}$, where $\mathbf{K}_k$ is a constant symmetric matrix. Then it is convenient to select $\mathbf{G} = \text{diag}(\mathbf{K}_1,\ldots,\mathbf{K}_N)^{-1}$, and for this selection

$$\mathbf{GQ}_C + \mathbf{Q}_C^T\mathbf{G} = \begin{bmatrix} 2(\mathbf{J_p}+\mathbf{J_p}^T) & \mathbf{J_p}+\mathbf{J_p}^T & \cdots & \mathbf{J_p}+\mathbf{J_p}^T \\ \mathbf{J_p}+\mathbf{J_p}^T & 2(\mathbf{J_p}+\mathbf{J_p}^T) & \cdots & \mathbf{J_p}+\mathbf{J_p}^T \\ \vdots & \vdots & & \vdots \\ \mathbf{J_p}+\mathbf{J_p}^T & \mathbf{J_p}+\mathbf{J_p}^T & \cdots & 2(\mathbf{J_p}+\mathbf{J_p}^T) \end{bmatrix}$$

$$+\sum_{v=1}^{M} \begin{bmatrix} 2x_1^{(v)}\mathbf{H}_{p_v} & (x_1^{(v)}+x_2^{(v)})\mathbf{H}_{p_v} & \cdots & (x_1^{(v)}+x_N^{(v)})\mathbf{H}_{p_v} \\ (x_2^{(v)}+x_1^{(v)})\mathbf{H}_{p_v} & 2x_2^{(v)}\mathbf{H}_{p_v} & \cdots & (x_2^{(v)}+x_N^{(v)})\mathbf{H}_{p_v} \\ \vdots & \vdots & \ddots & \vdots \\ (x_N^{(v)}+x_1^{(v)})\mathbf{H}_{p_v} & (x_N^{(v)}+x_2^{(v)})\mathbf{H}_{p_v} & \cdots & 2x_N^{(v)}\mathbf{H}_{p_v} \end{bmatrix}$$

$$-2\begin{bmatrix} \mathbf{H}_{C_1} & & & \\ & \mathbf{H}_{C_2} & & 0 \\ 0 & & \ddots & \\ & & & \mathbf{H}_{C_N} \end{bmatrix}. \quad (6.4.6)$$

We know that the equilibrium is globally asymptotically stable if this matrix is negative definite for all $\mathbf{x} \in X^*$. Assume that $\mathbf{J}_p + \mathbf{J}_p^T$ is negative semidefinite. We know that this condition is equivalent to the assumption that $-\mathbf{p}(s)$ is monotone. Assume furthermore that functions C_k are all convex. Note, that the same conditions were assumed in Theorem 3.1.2.

The first term of (6.4.6) can be rewritten as

$$\left(\mathbf{J}_p + \mathbf{J}_p^T\right) \otimes (\mathbf{1} + \mathbf{I}),$$

where $\mathbf{1}$ is the matrix, the elements of which are all equal to one. From Section 4.1 we know that the eigenvalues of this matrix are $\gamma_i \cdot 1$ and $\gamma_i \cdot (N+1)$, where γ_i denotes the eigenvalues of $\mathbf{J}_\mathbf{p} + \mathbf{J}_\mathbf{p}^T$. Thus the first term is negative semidefinite. Since for all k, C_k is convex, $\mathbf{H}_{C_k}$ is positive semidefinite, and therefore the third term of (6.4.3) is also negative semidefinite. One may easily verify that no definiteness property can be established in general for the second term. If the Hessians $\mathbf{H}_{\mathbf{p}_\nu}$ $(\nu = 1,2,...,M)$ are all zero, that is $\mathbf{p}(\mathbf{s})$ is linear, and either $\mathbf{J}_\mathbf{p} + \mathbf{J}_\mathbf{p}^T$ is negative definite or all Hessians $\mathbf{H}_{C_k}$ are positive definite, then matrix (6.4.6) is negative definite. Hence the equilibrium is globally asymptotically stable.

Assume next that the price function $\mathbf{p}(\mathbf{s})$ is nonlinear. Then for at least one $\mathbf{H}_{p_\nu} \neq \mathbf{0}$. Observe that the νth term in the middle term of (6.4.6) can be rewritten as a Kronecker product of matrices $\mathbf{H}_{p_\nu}$ and

$$\mathbf{X}^{(\nu)} = \begin{bmatrix} 2x_1^{(\nu)} & x_1^{(\nu)} + x_2^{(\nu)} & \cdots & x_1^{(\nu)} + x_N^{(\nu)} \\ x_2^{(\nu)} + x_1^{(\nu)} & 2x_2^{(\nu)} & \cdots & x_2^{(\nu)} + x_N^{(\nu)} \\ \vdots & \vdots & \ddots & \vdots \\ x_N^{(\nu)} + x_1^{(\nu)} & x_N^{(\nu)} + x_2^{(\nu)} & \cdots & 2x_N^{(\nu)} \end{bmatrix},$$

therefore the eigenvalues of this term equal $\alpha_i^{(\nu)}\beta_j^{(\nu)}$ where $\alpha_i^{(\nu)}$ and $\beta_j^{(\nu)}$ are the eigenvalues of $\mathbf{H}_{p_\nu}$ and $\mathbf{X}^{(\nu)}$, respectively. The eigenvalues of $\mathbf{X}^{(\nu)}$ will be determined next.

The eigenvalue equation of $\mathbf{X}^{(\nu)}$ has the form

$$\sum_{l\neq k}\left(x_k^{(\nu)}+x_l^{(\nu)}\right)v_l^{(\nu)}+2x_k^{(\nu)}v_k^{(\nu)}=\beta v_k^{(\nu)}\quad(k=1,2,...,N),$$

that is, with notation $\mathbf{x}^{(\nu)}=\left(x_k^{(\nu)}\right)$,

$$\mathbf{x}^{(\nu)T}\mathbf{v}^{(\nu)}+x_k^{(\nu)}\sum_{l=1}^{N}v_l^{(\nu)}=\beta v_k^{(\nu)}\ (k=1,2,...,N). \tag{6.4.7}$$

By adding these equations for k=1,2,...,N,

$$N\mathbf{x}^{(\nu)T}\mathbf{v}^{(\nu)}+\left(\sum_{k=1}^{N}x_k^{(\nu)}\right)\left(\sum_{l=1}^{N}v_l^{(\nu)}\right)=\beta\left(\sum_{k=1}^{N}v_k^{(\nu)}\right). \tag{6.4.8}$$

Assume first that $\sum_{k=1}^{N}v_k^{(\nu)}=0$. Then $\mathbf{x}^{(\nu)T}\mathbf{v}^{(\nu)}=0$, and from (6.4.7), $\beta_1^{(\nu)}=0$.

Assume next that $\sum_{k=1}^{N}v_k^{(\nu)}\neq 0$. Then we may assume that $\sum_{k=1}^{N}v_k^{(\nu)}=1$. Then (6.4.7) and (6.4.8) imply that

$$\begin{aligned}&\mathbf{x}^{(\nu)T}\mathbf{v}^{(\nu)}+x_k^{(\nu)}=\beta v_k^{(\nu)}\ (k=1,2,...,N)\\&N\mathbf{x}^{(\nu)T}\mathbf{v}^{(\nu)}+M_1=\beta,\end{aligned} \tag{6.4.9}$$

where $M_1=\sum_{k=1}^{N}x_k^{(\nu)}$. Multiply the first equation of (6.4.9) by $x_k^{(\nu)}$ and add the resulting equations for k=1,...,N to obtain

$$M_1\cdot\mathbf{x}^{(\nu)T}\mathbf{v}^{(\nu)}+M_2=\beta\mathbf{x}^{(\nu)T}\mathbf{v}^{(\nu)},$$

where $M_2=\sum_{k=1}^{N}x_k^{(\nu)2}$. By combining this equation with the second equation of (6.4.9) we conclude that

$$\beta_2^{(\nu)}=M_1+\sqrt{NM_2}(\geq 0),\ \beta_3^{(\nu)}=M_1-\sqrt{NM_2}(\leq 0).$$

Define

$$A(\mathbf{x}) = \sum_{\nu=1}^{M} \left[\max_i \left\{ \alpha_i^{(\nu)}(\mathbf{x}) \beta_2^{(\nu)}(\mathbf{x});\ \alpha_i^{(\nu)}(\mathbf{x}) \beta_3^{(\nu)}(\mathbf{x}) \right\} \right],$$
$$B(\mathbf{x}) = \max_i \max\left\{ \gamma_i(\mathbf{x});\ (N+1)\gamma_i(x) \right\},$$

and

$$C(\mathbf{x}) = -2 \min_{k,j} \left\{ \delta_j^{(k)}(\mathbf{x}) \right\},$$

where $\gamma_i(\mathbf{x})$, $\delta_j^{(k)}(\mathbf{x})$ and $\alpha_i^{(\nu)}(\mathbf{x})$ are the eigenvalues of $\mathbf{J_p}(\mathbf{x}) + \mathbf{J_p}(\mathbf{x})^T$, $\mathbf{H}_{C_k}(\mathbf{x})$ and $\mathbf{H}_{p_\nu}(\mathbf{x})$, respectively.

Assume that for all $\mathbf{x} \in X^*$,

$$A(\mathbf{x}) + B(\mathbf{x}) + C(\mathbf{x}) < 0. \tag{6.4.10}$$

Let $\mathbf{T}_1$, $\mathbf{T}_2$ and $\mathbf{T}_3$ denote the first, second and third term of (6.4.6), then for all $\mathbf{u} \neq \mathbf{0}$,

$$\mathbf{u}^T(\mathbf{T}_1 + \mathbf{T}_2 + \mathbf{T}_3)\mathbf{u} = \mathbf{u}^T\mathbf{T}_1\mathbf{u} + \mathbf{u}^T\mathbf{T}_2\mathbf{u} + \mathbf{u}^T\mathbf{T}_3\mathbf{u} \le \left(A(\mathbf{x}) + B(\mathbf{x}) + C(\mathbf{x})\right)\mathbf{u}^T\mathbf{u} < 0.$$

Thus we have verified the following

Theorem 6.4.3. Assume that (6.4.10) holds and $\mathbf{x}(t, \mathbf{x}_0) \in X^*$ for $t \ge 0$. Then the unique equilibrium is globally asymptotically stable with respect to the dynamic process (6.4.1).

Consider next the case of the classical Cournot model. In this special case $M=1$,

$$\mathbf{J_p} = p', \ \mathbf{H}_{p_\nu} = p'' \text{ and } \mathbf{H}_{C_k} = C_k''.$$

Hence

$$A(\mathbf{x}) = \max\left\{ p'' \cdot \left(M_1 + \sqrt{NM_2}\right); p'' \cdot \left(M_1 - \sqrt{NM_2}\right) \right\};$$
$$B(\mathbf{x}) = \max\left\{ 2p'; 2(N+1)p' \right\};$$
$$C(\mathbf{x}) = -2 \min_k C_k'',$$

and therefore the stability condition (6.4.10) reduces to

$$\max\{p''\cdot(M_1+\sqrt{NM_2});p''\cdot(M_1-\sqrt{NM_2})\}+\max\{2p';2(N+1)p'\}-2\min_k C_k''<0. \tag{6.4.11}$$

To interpret this condition, special cases will be examined.

(a) Assume first that $p'<0, p''\leq 0$. Then (6.4.11) can be rewritten as

$$p''\cdot(M_1-\sqrt{NM_2})+2p'-2C_k''<0 \text{ (for all } k).$$

The first term is nonnegative and the second term is negative. Therefore for fixed p' and p'' the left hand side becomes negative if C_k'' is large enough for all k.

(b) Assume next that $p'<0, p''\geq 0$, then we have the condition

$$p''(M_1+\sqrt{NM_2})+2p'-2C_k''<0 \text{ (for all } k).$$

Observe that the first term is nonnegative again and the second term is negative, so this condition holds, if C_k'' is large enough for all k.

An alternative approach is to find sufficient conditions which guarantee that matrix (6.4.6) is strictly diagonally dominant with negative diagonal elements. Without discussing the details we mention that in the case of the classical Cournot model this condition is equivalent to the inequalities

$$2p'+x_kp''-C_k''<0$$

and (6.4.12)

$$2|2p'+x_kp''-C_k''|>|2(N-1)p'+\left[(N-1)x_k+\sum_{l\neq k}\mathbf{x}_l\right]p''|.$$

If relations (6.4.12) hold, then the well known theorem of Gerschgorin (see Szidarovszky and Yakowitz, 1978) implies that all eigenvalues of (6.4.6) are negative, and therefore the matrix is negative definite.

2. Consider next the more general Lyapunov function

$$\phi(\mathbf{x})=(\mathbf{x}-\mathbf{x}^*)^T\mathbf{G}(\mathbf{x})(\mathbf{x}-\mathbf{x}^*)$$

where it is assumed that $\mathbf{G}(\mathbf{x})$ is symmetric and depends on $\mathbf{x}$. Since

$$\phi(\mathbf{x})=\sum_i\sum_j g_{ij}(\mathbf{x})(x_i-x_i^*)(x_j-x_j^*),$$

we conclude that

$$\frac{d}{dt}\phi(\mathbf{x}(t,\mathbf{x}_0)) = \sum_i \sum_j \left[\nabla g_{ij}(\mathbf{x}) \cdot \mathbf{f}(\mathbf{x})(x_i - x_i^*)(x_j - x_j^*) \right.$$
$$\left. + g_{ij}(\mathbf{x}) f_i(\mathbf{x})(x_j - x_j^*) + g_{ij}(\mathbf{x})(x_i - x_i^*) f_j(\mathbf{x}) \right],$$

where ∇ denotes gradient with respect to $\mathbf{x}$. Simple calculation shows that

$$\frac{d}{dt}\phi(\mathbf{x}(t,\mathbf{x}_0)) = 2(\mathbf{x}-\mathbf{x}^*)\mathbf{G}(\mathbf{x})\mathbf{f}(\mathbf{x}) + (\mathbf{x}-\mathbf{x}^*)^T \boldsymbol{\gamma}(\mathbf{x})(\mathbf{x}-\mathbf{x}^*), \tag{6.4.13}$$

where $\boldsymbol{\gamma}(\mathbf{x}) = (\gamma_{ij}(\mathbf{x}))$ with

$$\gamma_{ij}(\mathbf{x}) = \frac{1}{2}\left(\nabla g_{ij}(\mathbf{x}) + \nabla g_{ji}(\mathbf{x})\right)\mathbf{f}(\mathbf{x}).$$

We can guarantee the stability of the equilibrium if the first term of (6.4.13) is negative and the second term is nonpositive. Similarly to the proof of Theorem 6.4.2 we can easily verify that the first term is negative for $\mathbf{x} \neq \mathbf{x}^*$, if $\mathbf{J}_{Gf}(\mathbf{x}) + \mathbf{J}_{Gf}(x)^T$ is negative definite for all $\mathbf{x} \in T$, where $\mathbf{J}_{Gf}$ is the Jacobian of $\mathbf{G}(\mathbf{x})\mathbf{f}(\mathbf{x})$. The second term is nonpositive if $\boldsymbol{\gamma}(\mathbf{x})$ is negative semidefinite, that is, for arbitrary $\mathbf{u}\neq\mathbf{0}$,

$$0 \geq \mathbf{u}^T \boldsymbol{\gamma}(\mathbf{x})\mathbf{u} = \sum_i \sum_j \frac{1}{2}\left(\nabla g_{ij}(\mathbf{x}) + \nabla g_{ji}(\mathbf{x})\right) u_i u_j \mathbf{f}(\mathbf{x})$$
$$= \frac{1}{2}\left(\nabla \sum_i \sum_j \left(g_{ij}(\mathbf{x}) + g_{ji}(\mathbf{x})\right) u_i u_j \right)\mathbf{f}(\mathbf{x})$$
$$= \nabla\left(\mathbf{u}^T \mathbf{G}(\mathbf{x})\mathbf{u}\right)\mathbf{f}(\mathbf{x}) = \frac{d}{dt}\left(\mathbf{u}^T \mathbf{G}(\mathbf{x})\mathbf{u}\right).$$

Thus we have proved the following

Theorem 6.4.4. Assume that for all $t \geq 0$ and $\mathbf{x}_0 \in T$, $\mathbf{x}(t,\mathbf{x}_0) \in T$, and set T is compact. Furthermore there exists a continuously differentiable symmetric matrix $\mathbf{G}(\mathbf{x})$ such that $\mathbf{J}_{Gf}(\mathbf{x}) + \mathbf{G}_{Gf}(\mathbf{x})^T$ is negative definite for all $\mathbf{x} \in T$ and for all $\mathbf{u} \neq \mathbf{0}$ function $\mathbf{u}^T \mathbf{G}(\mathbf{x}(t,\mathbf{x}_0))\mathbf{u}$ is (not necessarily strictly) decreasing in t. Then the unique equilibrium is globally asymptotically stable with respect to dynamic process (6.5.1).

Remark. Note that in the special case, when $\mathbf{G}(\mathbf{x})$ is constant, the Jacobian of $\mathbf{Gf}$ equals $\mathbf{G} \cdot \mathbf{J}_{\mathbf{f}}$ and $\mathbf{u}^T \mathbf{G}(\mathbf{x}(t,\mathbf{x}_0))\mathbf{u}$ is a constant. Hence, this theorem generalizes the assertion of Theorem 6.4.2.

3. Define next

$$\phi(\mathbf{x}) = (\mathbf{x} - \mathbf{x}^*)^T \mathbf{f}(\mathbf{x}).$$

In this case

$$\begin{aligned}
\frac{d}{dt}\phi(\mathbf{x}(t,\mathbf{x}_0)) &= \frac{d}{dt}\sum_i (x_i - x_i^*) f_i(\mathbf{x}) \\
&= \sum_i \left[\left(\frac{d}{dt}x_i\right) f_i(\mathbf{x}) + (x_i - x_i^*)\nabla f_i(\mathbf{x}) \cdot \frac{d}{dt}\mathbf{x}\right] \\
&= \sum_i \left[f_i^2(\mathbf{x}) + (x_i - x_i^*)\nabla f_i(\mathbf{x})\mathbf{f}(\mathbf{x})\right] = \mathbf{f}^T(\mathbf{x})\mathbf{f}(\mathbf{x}) + (\mathbf{x} - \mathbf{x}^*)^T \mathbf{J}_\mathbf{f}(\mathbf{x})\mathbf{f}(\mathbf{x}) \\
&= \left(\mathbf{f}(\mathbf{x}) + (\mathbf{x} - \mathbf{x}^*)^T \mathbf{J}_\mathbf{f}(\mathbf{x})\right)\mathbf{f}(\mathbf{x}),
\end{aligned}$$

which leads to the following

Theorem 6.4.5. Assume that for all $\mathbf{x}_0 \in T$ and $t \geq 0$, $\mathbf{x}(t,\mathbf{x}_0) \in T$, T is compact and $\mathbf{f}$ is continuously differentiable on T, furthermore for all $\mathbf{x} \in T$,

$$\left(\mathbf{f}(\mathbf{x}) + (\mathbf{x} - \mathbf{x}^*)^T \mathbf{J}_\mathbf{f}(\mathbf{x})\right)\mathbf{f}(\mathbf{x}) < 0.$$

Then the unique equilibrium is globally asymptotically stable.

4. Select the Lyapunov function as

$$\phi(\mathbf{x}) = \mathbf{x}^T \mathbf{f}(\mathbf{x}),$$

then similarly to the previous case we can verify that

$$\begin{aligned}
\frac{d}{dt}\phi(\mathbf{x}(t,\mathbf{x}_0)) &= \frac{d}{dt}\sum_i x_i f_i(\mathbf{x}) = \sum_i \left[\left(\frac{d}{dt}x_i\right) f_i(\mathbf{x}) + x_i \nabla f_i(\mathbf{x}) \frac{d}{dt}\mathbf{x}\right] \\
&= \sum_i \left[f_i^2(\mathbf{x}) + x_i \nabla f_i(\mathbf{x})\mathbf{f}(\mathbf{x})\right] = \left(\mathbf{f}^T(\mathbf{x}) + x^T \mathbf{J}_\mathbf{f}(\mathbf{x})\right)\mathbf{f}(\mathbf{x}).
\end{aligned}$$

Hence, if this expression is negative for all $\mathbf{x} \in T$, the equilibrium is globally asymptotically stable.

5. Define

$$\phi(\mathbf{x}) = \mathbf{x}^T \mathbf{x},$$

then

$$\frac{d}{dt}\phi(\mathbf{x}(t,\mathbf{x}_0)) = \frac{d}{dt}\sum_i x_i^2 = \sum_i 2x_i \frac{d}{dt}x_i = 2\sum_i x_i f_i = 2\mathbf{x}^T\mathbf{f}(\mathbf{x}).$$

Consequently, if $\mathbf{x}^T\mathbf{f}(\mathbf{x}) < 0$ for all $\mathbf{x} \in T$, then the equilibrium is globally asymptotically stable.

Cases 2-5 and any other form of the Lyapunov function can be applied to the multiproduct oligopoly game in the same way as case 1. The details are omitted.

Consider next the case of *adaptive expectations* on vectors $\mathbf{s}_k^E(t)$ $(k = 1,2,...,N)$. It is assumed that the output vectors are adjusted according to differential equation (6.4.1), and vectors $\mathbf{s}_k^E(t)$ are adjusted according to the differential equation

$$\frac{d\mathbf{s}_k^E}{dt} = \mathbf{e}_k\left(\mathbf{s}_k - \mathbf{s}_k^E\right), \tag{6.4.14}$$

where $\mathbf{e}_k$ is a sign preserving function which increases in each component. By combining equations (6.4.1) and (6.4.14) the following differential equations are obtained:

$$\begin{aligned} \frac{d\mathbf{x}_k}{dt} &= \mathbf{g}_k\left(\mathbf{J}_p^T\left(\mathbf{x}_k + \mathbf{s}_k^E\right)\mathbf{x}_k + \mathbf{p}\left(\mathbf{x}_k + \mathbf{s}_k^E\right) - \nabla C_k(\mathbf{x}_k)\right) \\ \frac{d\mathbf{s}_k^E}{dt} &= \mathbf{e}_k\left(\sum_{l \neq k}\mathbf{x}_l - \mathbf{s}_k^E\right) \quad (k = 1,2,...N). \end{aligned} \tag{6.4.15}$$

The Jacobian of the right hand sides can be given as

$$\mathbf{Q}_A = \begin{bmatrix} \mathbf{Q}_{11} & \cdots & \mathbf{Q}_{1N} & \mathbf{S}_{11} & \cdots & \mathbf{S}_{1N} \\ \vdots & & \vdots & \vdots & & \vdots \\ \mathbf{Q}_{N1} & \cdots & \mathbf{Q}_{NN} & \mathbf{S}_{N1} & \cdots & \mathbf{S}_{NN} \\ \mathbf{R}_{11} & \cdots & \mathbf{R}_{1N} & \mathbf{T}_{11} & \cdots & \mathbf{T}_{1N} \\ \vdots & & \vdots & \vdots & & \vdots \\ \mathbf{R}_{N1} & \cdots & \mathbf{R}_{NN} & \mathbf{T}_{N1} & \cdots & \mathbf{T}_{NN} \end{bmatrix}; \tag{6.4.16}$$

where

$$\mathbf{Q}_{kl} = \begin{cases} \mathbf{J}_{\mathbf{g}_k} \cdot \left[\mathbf{J}_\mathbf{p} + \mathbf{J}_\mathbf{p}^T + \sum_{v=1}^{M} \mathbf{H}_{p_v} x_k^{(v)} - \mathbf{H}_{C_k}\right], & \text{if } l = k \\ \mathbf{0}, & \text{if } l \neq k; \end{cases}$$

$$\mathbf{S}_{kl} = \begin{cases} \mathbf{J}_{\mathbf{g}_k} \cdot \left[\mathbf{J}_{\mathbf{p}} + \sum_{\nu=1}^{M} \mathbf{H}_{p_\nu} x_k^{(\nu)} \right], & \text{if } l = k \\ \mathbf{0}, & \text{if } l \neq k; \end{cases}$$

$$\mathbf{R}_{kl} = \begin{cases} \mathbf{0}, & \text{if } l = k \\ \mathbf{J}_{\mathbf{e}_k}, & \text{if } k \neq l; \end{cases}$$

and

$$\mathbf{T}_{kl} = \begin{cases} -\mathbf{J}_{\mathbf{e}_k}, & \text{if } k = l \\ \mathbf{0}, & \text{if } k \neq l. \end{cases}$$

Consider the special case of

$$\mathbf{p}(\mathbf{s}) = \mathbf{A}\mathbf{s} + \mathbf{b},$$
$$C_k(\mathbf{x}_k) = \mathbf{x}_k^T \mathbf{B}_k \mathbf{x}_k + \mathbf{b}_k^T \mathbf{x}_k + c_k, \quad (\forall k)$$
$$\mathbf{g}_k(\mathbf{t}) = \mathbf{K}_k \mathbf{t} \text{ and } \mathbf{e}_k(\mathbf{t}) = \mathbf{M}_k \mathbf{t}.$$

Then

$$\mathbf{J}_{\mathbf{g}_k} = \mathbf{K}_k, \ \mathbf{J}_p = \mathbf{A}, \ \mathbf{H}_{p_\nu} = \mathbf{0},$$
$$\mathbf{H}_{C_k} = \mathbf{B}_k + \mathbf{B}_k^T \text{ and } \mathbf{J}_{\mathbf{e}_k} = \mathbf{M}_k.$$

Therefore it is easy to verify that in this case equations (6.4.15) coincide with equation (5.4.3), which was examined earlier in Chapter 5.

In the remaining part of this section the application of the Lyapunov function

$$\phi(\mathbf{x}) = (\mathbf{x} - \mathbf{x}^*)^T \mathbf{G} (\mathbf{x} - \mathbf{x}^*)$$

will be presented, where $\mathbf{G}$ is a constant symmetric matrix. Assume that $\mathbf{g}_k(\mathbf{t}) = \mathbf{K}_k \mathbf{t}$ and $\mathbf{e}_k(\mathbf{t}) = \mathbf{M}_k \mathbf{t}$, where $\mathbf{K}_k$ and $\mathbf{M}_k$ are constant symmetric matrices. The general case can be examined by selecting $\mathbf{x}$-dependent matrix $\mathbf{G}$. The details of this case and also of other types of Lyapunov functions can be discussed in a similar manner. By selecting

$$\mathbf{G} = \text{diag}(\mathbf{K}_1, \ldots, \mathbf{K}_N, \mathbf{M}_1, \ldots, \mathbf{M}_N)^{-1},$$

where we assume that matrices $\mathbf{K}_k$ and $\mathbf{M}_k$ are nonsingular for all k, matrix $\mathbf{G}\mathbf{Q} + \mathbf{Q}^T \mathbf{G}$ can be written as

$$
\left[\begin{array}{cccc|cccc}
2(\mathbf{J}_p+\mathbf{J}_p^T)+2\sum_{v=1}^{M}\mathbf{H}_{p_v}x_1^{(v)}-2\mathbf{H}_{C_1} & & & \mathbf{0} & \mathbf{J}_p+\sum_{v=1}^{M}\mathbf{H}_{p_v}x_1^{(v)} & \mathbf{I} & \cdots & \mathbf{I} \\
 & \ddots & & & \mathbf{I} & \mathbf{J}_p+\sum_{v=1}^{M}\mathbf{H}_{p_v}x_2^{(v)} & \cdots & \mathbf{I} \\
 & & & & \vdots & \vdots & \ddots & \vdots \\
\mathbf{0} & & & 2(\mathbf{J}_p+\mathbf{J}_p^T)+2\sum_{v=1}^{M}\mathbf{H}_{p_v}x_N^{(v)}-2\mathbf{H}_{C_N} & \mathbf{I} & \mathbf{I} & \cdots & \mathbf{J}_p+\sum_{v=1}^{M}\mathbf{H}_{p_v}x_N^{(v)} \\
\hline
\mathbf{J}_p^T+\sum_{v=1}^{M}\mathbf{H}_{p_v}x_1^{(v)} & \mathbf{I} & \cdots & \mathbf{I} & -2\mathbf{I} & & & \mathbf{0} \\
\mathbf{I} & \mathbf{J}_p^T+\sum_{v=1}^{M}\mathbf{H}_{p_v}x_2^{(v)} & \cdots & \mathbf{I} & & -2\mathbf{I} & & \\
\vdots & \vdots & \ddots & \vdots & & & \ddots & \\
\mathbf{I} & \mathbf{I} & \cdots & \mathbf{J}_p^T+\sum_{v=1}^{M}\mathbf{H}_{p_v}x_N^{(v)} & \mathbf{0} & & & -2\mathbf{I}
\end{array}\right]
\qquad (6.4.17)
$$

Sufficient conditions will be derived next which guarantee that matrix (6.4.17) is negative definite. First of all observe that this matrix can be rewritten as

$$\begin{bmatrix} 2\mathbf{F} & \mathbf{A}_0^T \\ \mathbf{A}_0 & -2\mathbf{I} \end{bmatrix},$$

where

$$\mathbf{F} = \mathrm{diag}(\mathbf{A}_1, \ldots, \mathbf{A}_N)$$

with

$$\mathbf{A}_k = \mathbf{J}_\mathbf{p} + \mathbf{J}_\mathbf{p}^T + \sum_{\nu=1}^{M} \mathbf{H}_{p_\nu} x_k^{(\nu)} - \mathbf{H}_{C_k};$$

and

$$\mathbf{A}_0 = \begin{bmatrix} \mathbf{J}_\mathbf{p}^T + \sum_{\nu=1}^{M} \mathbf{H}_{p_\nu} x_1^{(\nu)} & \mathbf{I} & \cdots & \mathbf{I} \\ \mathbf{I} & \mathbf{J}_\mathbf{p}^T + \sum_{\nu=1}^{M} \mathbf{H}_{p_\nu} x_2^{(\nu)} & \cdots & \mathbf{I} \\ \vdots & \vdots & \ddots & \vdots \\ \mathbf{I} & \mathbf{I} & \cdots & \mathbf{J}_\mathbf{p}^T + \sum_{\nu=1}^{M} \mathbf{H}_{p_\nu} x_N^{(\nu)} \end{bmatrix}.$$

Then Theorem 5.2.3 implies that if matrix $4\mathbf{F} + \mathbf{A}_0^T \mathbf{A}_0$ is negative definite, the equilibrium is globally asymptotically stable. The main advantage of this assertion is the fact that the dimension of this matrix is smaller than that of matrix (6.4.17).

An alternative approach is similar to the case of expectations á la Cournot. By rewriting matrix (6.4.17) in an additive form, the eigenvalues of the terms can be easily determined or at least estimated. In order to apply this idea we shall use the following decomposition:

$$\mathbf{T}_1 + \mathbf{T}_2 + \mathbf{T}_3,$$

where

$$\mathbf{T}_1 = 2 \ \mathrm{diag}(\mathbf{A}_1, \ldots, \mathbf{A}_N; -\mathbf{I}, \ldots, -\mathbf{I});$$

$$\mathbf{T}_2 = \left[\begin{array}{ccc|ccc} & & & \mathbf{B}_1 & & \\ & 0 & & & \ddots & \\ & & & & & \mathbf{B}_N \\ \hline \mathbf{B}_1^T & & & & & \\ & \ddots & & & 0 & \\ & & \mathbf{B}_N^T & & & \end{array}\right]$$

with

$$\mathbf{B}_k = \mathbf{J}_p + \sum_{v=1}^{M} \mathbf{H}_{p_v} x_k^{(v)};$$

and

$$\mathbf{T}_3 = \left[\begin{array}{cccc|cccc} & & & & \mathbf{0} & \mathbf{I} & \cdots & \mathbf{I} \\ & & & & \mathbf{I} & \mathbf{0} & \cdots & \mathbf{I} \\ & 0 & & & \vdots & \vdots & \ddots & \vdots \\ & & & & \mathbf{I} & \mathbf{I} & \cdots & \mathbf{0} \\ \hline \mathbf{0} & \mathbf{I} & \cdots & \mathbf{I} & & & & \\ \mathbf{I} & \mathbf{0} & \cdots & \mathbf{I} & & 0 & & \\ \vdots & \vdots & \ddots & \vdots & & & & \\ \mathbf{I} & \mathbf{I} & \cdots & \mathbf{0} & & & & \end{array}\right].$$

Let $\alpha_i^{(k)}$ denote the eigenvalues of matrix $\mathbf{A}_k$, then the largest eigenvalue of $\mathbf{T}_1$ equals

$$A(\mathbf{x}) = 2 \max\left\{-1; \ \max_{k,i}\left\{\alpha_i^{(k)}\right\}\right\}. \tag{6.4.18}$$

The eigenvalues of $\mathbf{T}_2$ will be determined next. Its eigenvalue equation can be written as

$$\begin{matrix} \mathbf{B}_k \mathbf{v}_k = \lambda \mathbf{u}_k \\ \mathbf{B}_k^T \mathbf{u}_k = \lambda \mathbf{v}_k \end{matrix} \quad (k = 1, 2, \ldots, N).$$

If matrix $\mathbf{T}_2$ is singular, then $\lambda = 0$ is an eigenvalue. If $\lambda \neq 0$, then from the first equation we know that

$$\mathbf{u}_k = \frac{1}{\lambda}\mathbf{B}_k\mathbf{v}_k,$$

and by substituting this relation into the second equation we conclude that

$$\mathbf{B}_k^T\mathbf{B}_k\mathbf{v}_k = \lambda^2\mathbf{v}_k.$$

That is, $\lambda = \pm\sqrt{\beta_i^{(k)}}$, where $\beta_i^{(k)}$ denotes the (nonnegative) eigenvalues of matrix $\mathbf{B}_k^T\mathbf{B}_k$. Hence the largest eigenvalue of $\mathbf{T}_2$ is given as

$$B(\mathbf{x}) = \max_{k,i}\left\{\sqrt{\beta_i^{(k)}}\right\}. \tag{6.4.19}$$

Finally, we determine the eigenvalues of matrix $\mathbf{T}_3$. Note first that its eigenvalue equation has the form

$$\left.\begin{aligned}\sum_{l\neq k}\mathbf{v}_l &= \lambda\mathbf{u}_k\\ \sum_{l\neq k}\mathbf{u}_l &= \lambda\mathbf{v}_k\end{aligned}\right.\quad (k=1,2,\ldots,N),$$

which imply that

$$\sum_{l=1}^{N}\mathbf{v}_l = \lambda\mathbf{u}_k + \mathbf{v}_k$$

and

$$\sum_{l=1}^{N}\mathbf{u}_l = \lambda\mathbf{v}_k + \mathbf{u}_k. \tag{6.4.20}$$

Hence for all k,l,

$$\begin{aligned}\lambda\mathbf{u}_k + \mathbf{v}_k &= \lambda\mathbf{u}_l + \mathbf{v}_l\\ \lambda\mathbf{v}_k + \mathbf{u}_k &= \lambda\mathbf{v}_l + \mathbf{u}_l\end{aligned}$$

that is,

$$\begin{aligned}\lambda(\mathbf{u}_k - \mathbf{u}_l) + (\mathbf{v}_k - \mathbf{v}_l) &= \mathbf{0}\\ (\mathbf{u}_k - \mathbf{u}_l) + \lambda(\mathbf{v}_k - \mathbf{v}_l) &= \mathbf{0}.\end{aligned}$$

These relations hold if and only if either $\lambda = \pm 1$, or $\mathbf{u}_k \equiv \mathbf{u}$ and $\mathbf{v}_k \equiv \mathbf{v}$. In the first case the eigenvalues are recovered. In the second case equations (6.4.20) imply that

$$(N-1)\mathbf{v} = \lambda \mathbf{u}$$
$$(N-1)\mathbf{u} = \lambda \mathbf{v}.$$

Since eigenvectors are nonzero, $\lambda \neq 0$. The first equation implies that

$$\mathbf{u} = \frac{1}{\lambda}(N-1)\mathbf{v},$$

and by substituting this relation into the second equation we observe that

$$(N-1)^2 \mathbf{v} = \lambda^2 \mathbf{v},$$

that is, $\lambda = \pm(N-1)$. Therefore the largest eigenvalue of matrix $\mathbf{T}_3$ equals

$$C(\mathbf{x}) = N-1. \tag{6.4.21}$$

In a manner similar to that used in proving Theorem 6.4.3 we can prove the following result:

Theorem 6.4.6. Assume that for all $\mathbf{x}_0 \in X^*$ and $t \geq 0$, $\mathbf{x}(t, \mathbf{x}_0) \in X^*$, and for all $\mathbf{x} \in X^*$, $A(\mathbf{x}) + B(\mathbf{x}) + C(\mathbf{x}) < 0$, and also that the equilibrium is unique. If for all k, $\mathbf{g}_k(\mathbf{t}) = \mathbf{K}_k \mathbf{t}$ and $\mathbf{e}_k(\mathbf{t}) = \mathbf{M}_k \mathbf{t}$ with constant symmetric matrices $\mathbf{K}_k$ and $\mathbf{M}_k$, then the equilibrium is globally asymptotically stable with respect to dynamic process (6.4.15).

Consider next the case of the classical Cournot model. In this special case M=1,

$$\mathbf{J}_p = p', \ \mathbf{H}_{p_v} = p'', \text{ and } \mathbf{H}_{C_k} = C_k''.$$

Hence

$$A(\mathbf{x}) = 2\max\left\{-1; \max_k \left\{2p' + x_k p'' - C_k''\right\}\right\}$$
$$B(\mathbf{x}) = \max_k \left\{\left|p' + x_k p''\right|\right\},$$

and

$$C(\mathbf{x}) = N-1,$$

and the stability condition has the form

$$2\max\left\{-1;\max_k\{2p'+x_kp''-C_k''\}\right\}+\max_k\{|p'+x_kp''|\}+N-1<0 \tag{6.4.22}$$

for all $\mathbf{x}\in X^*$.

To interpret this condition special cases will be examined.

(a) Assume first that $p'<0, p''\leq 0$. If for all k, $2p'+x_kp''-C_k''\leq -1$, then (6.4.22) reduces to relation

$$\max_k\{-p'-x_kp''\}+N-3<0;$$

which holds only if $N=2$, both $-p'$ and $-p''$ are small enough, and C_k'' is sufficiently large for all k. Otherwise (6.4.22) can be rewritten as

$$2\max_k\{2p'+x_kp''-C_k''\}+\max_k\{-p'-x_kp''\}+N-1<0,$$

which holds if C_k'' is large enough for fixed N, p', and p''.

(b) Assume that $p'<0$ and $p''\equiv C_k''\equiv 0$ $(\forall k)$. Then (6.4.22) holds if

$$2\max\{-1;2p'\}+|p'|+N-1<0.$$

That is,

(i) if $p'\leq -\frac{1}{2}$, then

$$-2-p'+N-1<0,$$

which holds if and only if

$$p'>N-3.$$

Note that these conditions are contradictory if $N>2$.

(ii) If $-\frac{1}{2}<p'\leq 0$, then (6.4.22) holds for

$$4p'-p'+N-1<0,$$

that is, if $3p' + N - 1 < 0$, which contradicts the initial assumption on p' for $N > 2$.

(c) Positive values for p' do not have an economic justification.

Note that the case of Lyapunov functions of other forms can be similarly discussed. The alternative approach, which guarantees that matrix (6.4.17) is negatively strictly diagonally dominant, also can be applied. While the details are not discussed here, they are analogous to those which were shown in the case of the model under expectations á la Cournot.

6.5 Supplementary Notes and Discussions

6.1 The main ideas for this section were taken from Szidarovszky and Okuguchi (1987b), where model (6.1.7), and Theorems 6.1.1 and 6.1.4 can be found.

6.2 The model and all results of this section are presented in Szidarovszky and Okuguchi (1987e).

6.3 The stability of the classical Cournot model was previously investigated by several authors (see Okuguchi, 1964, 1976; Seade, 1980; Al-Nowaihi and Levine, 1985; and Furth, 1986). Our analysis is based on the theory of contraction mappings (see for example Ortega and Rheinboldt, 1970; Szidarovszky and Yakowitz, 1978). Analogous results to our Theorems 6.3.2, 6.3.3 can be found in Conlinsk (1973) and Okuguchi (1978). Some generalizations are given in Szidarovszky (1989).

6.4 Our stability analysis under continuous time scale is based on the theory of Uzawa (1961), which is an alternative approach to Lyapunov's second method (Brauer and Nohel, 1969; Hartman, 1982). The particular Lyapunov functions which were discussed in this section were earlier analyzed by Okuguchi (1976) for the classical Cournot model.

In the last two sections only the classical oligopoly model was examined. The different variants such as labor-managed, or rent seeking games can be analyzed in a similar manner. The details are left as exercises for the readers.

7 Applications

Some applications of the oligopoly models will be outlined briefly in this chapter. The first two sections will discuss some additional variants and modifications of the Cournot model, and the next two sections will show real-life applications in natural resources management and fishery. The fifth section will discuss the elements of the controllability of oligopoly models.

7.1 Network Oligopolies

Consider a directed network, where the supply nodes represent the producers, the demand nodes represent the different markets, and the different paths between supplies and demands are the transportation possibilities. For the sake of simplicity it is assumed that only one product is produced and sold. This assumption serves only notational convenience, the general case can be formulated and discussed in a similar way. Introduce the following notation:

$m =$ number of supply nodes

$n =$ number of demand nodes

$x_{ij} =$ amount of output of producer i sold in market j

$K(i,j) =$ number of transportation routes between producer i and market j

$C_i =$ cost function of producer i

$\gamma_{ijk} =$ transportation cost function on route k between producer i and market j

$L_i =$ production capacity of producer i

$\Lambda_{ijk} =$ transportation capacity on route k between producer i and market j

$P_j =$ inverse demand function in market j.

The decision variables for each producer are the x_{ij} output values. It is assumed that each producer uses minimum transportation cost to deliver its products to the different markets and there is no conflict between producers in using the transportation network. Therefore it is assumed that for each i and j, and all feasible x_{ij}, the following optimization problem is solved:

Minimize

$$\sum_{k=1}^{K(i,j)} \gamma_{ijk}(t_{ijk})$$

subject to

$$\sum_{k=1}^{K(i,j)} t_{ijk} = x_{ij}$$
$$0 \le t_{ijk} \le \Lambda_{ijk}. \tag{7.1.1}$$

Let $\overline{C}_{ij}(x_{ij})$ denote the optimal objective function value with fixed x_{ij}. Then the profit of producer i can be written in the following form:

$$\sum_{j=1}^{n} x_{ij} P_j\left(\sum_{l=1}^{m} x_{lj}\right) - C_i\left(\sum_{j=1}^{n} x_{ij}\right) - \sum_{j=1}^{n} \overline{C}_{ij}\left(x_{ij}\right). \tag{7.1.2}$$

The strategy set of producer i is given as

$$X_i = \left\{(x_{i1},\dots,x_{in}) \middle| x_{ij} \ge 0 \text{ for all } j, \sum_{j=1}^{n} x_{ij} \le L_i\right\}. \tag{7.1.3}$$

Notice that payoff functions (7.1.2) are special cases of those introduced earlier for multi-product oligopolies. Therefore all results on multi-product oligopolies can be directly applied.

In the previous model we did not consider the transportation sector as an active participant. In the following part of this section a modified version of the above model will be introduced in which both the producers and the transporters are active players. Assume that there are T transporters. Let $T(i,j,k)$ denote the owner of route k between supply i and demand j. We mention here that several routes can be owned by the same owner. The strategy of each transporter is the selection of the transportation prices. Let P_{ijk} be the unit transportation price on route k between supply i and market j. Then

$$\gamma_{ijk}(t_{ijk}) = t_{ijk} P_{ijk}. \tag{7.1.4}$$

If Λ_{ijk} denotes again the transportation capacity limit on this route, then problem (7.1.4) can be solved in closed form. Assume that the routes are numbered such that

$$P_{ij1} \leq P_{ij2} \leq \ldots \leq P_{ijK(i,j)}. \tag{7.1.5}$$

If $x_{ij} \leq \Lambda_{ij1}$, then $t_{ij1} = x_{ij}$ and $t_{ijk} = 0$ for $k > 1$. Assume next that in general,

$$\Lambda_{ij1} + \ldots + \Lambda_{ijk-1} < x_{ij} \leq \Lambda_{ij1} + \ldots + \Lambda_{ijk-1} + \Lambda_{ijk}. \tag{7.1.6}$$

Then the optimal solution is:

$$\begin{aligned} &t_{ijl} = \Lambda_{ijl} \text{ for } l = 1,2,\ldots,k-1, \\ &t_{ijk} = x_{ij} - \sum_{l=1}^{k-1} \Lambda_{ijl}, \\ &\text{and} \\ &t_{ijl} = 0 \text{ for } l > k. \end{aligned} \tag{7.1.7}$$

Here we assume that

$$x_{ij} \leq \sum_{l=1}^{K(i,j)} \Lambda_{ijl}. \tag{7.1.8}$$

Therefore,

$$\overline{C}_{ij}(x_{ij}) = \begin{cases} P_{ij1} x_{ij} \text{ if } x_{ij} \leq \Lambda_{ij1} \\ \sum_{l=1}^{k-1} P_{ijl} \Lambda_{ijl} + P_{ijk}\left(x_{ij} - \sum_{l=1}^{k-1} \Lambda_{ijl}\right) \end{cases} \tag{7.1.9}$$

if (7.1.6) holds, which is a convex function. The payoff function of transporter q can be obtained in the following form:

$$\sum_{i=1}^{m} \sum_{j=1}^{n} \sum_{\{k | q = T(i,j,k)\}} P_{ijk} t_{ijk} - \overline{\overline{C}}_q(\mathbf{t}_q) \tag{7.1.10}$$

where $\mathbf{t}_q = \{(t_{ijk}) | q = T(i,j,k)\}$, and $\overline{\overline{C}}_q$ is the cost function of transportation route owner q. Notice that the t_{ijk} values depend on the selection of x_{ij} and the order (7.1.5) of the prices. Let f_{ijk} denote this function relation, then the payoff of transporter q has the form:

$$\sum_{i=1}^{m}\sum_{j=1}^{n}\sum_{\{k|q=T(i,j,k)\}} P_{ijk}f_{ijk}\left(P_{ij1},\ldots,P_{ijK(i,j)},x_{ij}\right)-\overline{\overline{C}}_q(\mathbf{f}_q) \tag{7.1.11}$$

where

$$\mathbf{f}_q=\left\{(f_{ijk})|q=T(i,j,k)\right\}.$$

Observe that this payoff has the form of multiproduct oligopolies, when P_{ijk} plays mathematically the role of the output, f_{ijk} plays the role of the corresponding price, furthermore $\overline{\overline{C}}_q$ is the cost function of transporter q.

There are however two major differences between this model and multiproduct oligopolies discussed earlier in this book. First, function f_{ijk} depends on the individual strategies $P_{ijk}(1\le k\le K(i,j))$ and x_{ij}, and not on the sums of these strategies with respect to all players. Second, the cost function $\overline{\overline{C}}_q$ depends also on the strategies of other players. In this case it depends on the outputs x_{ij} of the producers who use routes owned by transporter q. The existence of the equilibrium points can be discussed similarly to multiproduct oligopolies, the conditions must guarantee that the Nikaido-Isoda theorem is applicable. The details are left as an easy exercise.

7.2 Taxation

Let there be n firms in a Cournot oligopoly. The inverse demand function is $p=f(Q), f'<0$, where if x_i is firm i's output, $Q\equiv\sum_j x_j$ is the industry output and p is the price of the product. Let $C_i=C_i(x_i)$ be firm i's cost function. Then firm i's profit φ_i is given by

$$\varphi_i\equiv x_i\{(1-t_v)f(Q)-t_s\}-C_i(x_i),\ i=1,2,\ldots,n, \tag{7.2.1}$$

where t_v is the parameter for ad valorem tax, and t_s is the specific tax rate. Note that the ad valorem tax rate τ and t_v are related by $t_v=\tau/(1+\tau)$, where τ increases if and only if t_v increases. Given t_v and t_s, assuming an interior maximum, the first and second order conditions for firm i's profit maximization are given as

$$\partial\varphi_i/\partial x_i=(1-t_v)f(Q)-t_s+x_i(1-t_v)f'(Q)-C_i'(x_i)=0,\ i=1,2,\ldots,n. \tag{7.2.2}$$

$$\partial^2\varphi_i/\partial x_i^2 = (1-t_v)\{f'(Q)+x_i f''(Q)\}+(1-t_v)f'(Q)-C_i''(x_i)<0,\ i=1,2,...,n. \tag{7.2.3}$$

We now introduce the following two assumptions:

(A.1) $f' + x_i f'' < 0,\ i = 1,2,...,n.$

(A.2) $a_i \equiv (1-t_v)f' - C_i'' < 0,\ i = 1,2,...,n.$

If (A.1) and (A.2) hold, the second order condition is satisfied.

Expressing x_i in (7.2.2) as a function of Q, t_v and t_s, we have

$$x_i = \varphi^i(Q,t_v,t_s),\ i=1,2,...,n, \tag{7.2.4}$$

where the partial derivatives have the following signs:

$$\begin{cases} \varphi_Q^i \equiv \partial x_i/\partial Q = -(1-t_v)(f' + x_i f'')/a_i < 0 \\ \varphi_{t_v}^i \equiv \partial x_i/\partial t_v = (f + x_i f')/a_i < 0, \qquad i=1,2,...,n. \\ \varphi_{t_s}^i \equiv \partial x_i/\partial t_s = 1/a_i < 0, \end{cases} \tag{7.2.5}$$

where the second inequality is the consequence of (7.2.2).

Given t_v and t_s, the Cournot equilibrium industry output is characterized as a solution of equation

$$Q = \sum_j \varphi^j(Q,t_v,t_s) \equiv \varphi(Q,t_v,t_s), \tag{7.2.6}$$

where

$$\varphi_Q < 0,\ \varphi_{t_v} < 0,\ \varphi_{t_s} < 0. \tag{7.2.7}$$

The left-most expression in (7.2.6) is depicted as a 45 degree line and the right-most one as a downwards-sloping curve. Hence, if we assume $\varphi(0,t_v,t_s) > 0$ we can assert the existence of a unique solution, which is the following:

$$Q^* \equiv Q^*(t_v,t_s), \tag{7.2.8}$$

where

$$\begin{cases} \partial Q^*/\partial t_v = \varphi_{t_v}/(1-\varphi_Q) < 0, \\ \partial Q^*/\partial t_s = \varphi_{t_s}/(1-\varphi_Q) < 0. \end{cases} \tag{7.2.9}$$

Hence, the unique Cournot equilibrium industry output decreases and the corresponding equilibrium price increases in the event of an increase in both ad valorem and specific tax rates.

Taking into account the second and last expressions in (7.2.5), $\partial Q^*/\partial t_v$ and $\partial Q^*/\partial t_s$ are shown to be related in the following fashion:

$$\partial Q^*/\partial t_v = f\,\partial Q^*/\partial t_s + f' \sum x_i \varphi^i_{t_s}/(1-\varphi_Q). \tag{7.2.10}$$

The equilibrium tax revenue T is given by

$$T \equiv t_s Q^* + t_v f(Q^*)Q^*, \tag{7.2.11}$$

with

$$\begin{cases} T_v \equiv \partial T/\partial t_v = f(Q^*)Q^* + \{t_s + t_v(f + Q^* f')\}\partial Q^*/\partial t_v \\ T_s \equiv \partial T/\partial t_s = Q^* + \{t_s + t_v(f + Q^* f')\}\partial Q^*/\partial t_s. \end{cases} \tag{7.2.12}$$

Hence,

$$\begin{cases} T_s\big|_{t_v=t_s=0} = Q^*(0,0) > 0, \\ T_v\big|_{t_v=t_s=0} = f(Q^*)Q^* > 0. \end{cases} \tag{7.2.13}$$

Hence, $T_v > 0$ and $T_s > 0$ if (t_v, t_s) is in the neighborhood of (0,0). However, their signs are, in general, indeterminate. In order to avoid this indeterminacy, we assume that

(A.3) $\quad T_v > 0,\ T_s > 0.$

Therefore, if T is held constant,

$$dt_s/dt_v\big|_{dT=0} = -T_v/T_s < 0. \tag{7.2.14}$$

A little calculation based on (7.2.10) and (7.2.12) shows that

$$\begin{aligned} dQ^*/dt_v\big|_{dT=0} &= Q_v^* + Q_s^*\, dt_s/dt_v\big|_{dT=0} \\ &= \left\{f'(Q^*)Q^*\sum x_i\,\varphi_{t_s}^i/(1-\varphi_Q)\right\}/T_s > 0. \end{aligned} \qquad (7.2.15)$$

Hence the equilibrium industry output and price increases and decreases, respectively, in the event of a shift from specific to ad valorem taxation if the tax revenue is not affected by it. However, if the inequalities in (A.3) are reversed, the equilibrium industry output decreases, as a consequence of which the equilibrium price increases in the event of the same shift.

The social welfare at the equilibrium is defined by

$$\begin{aligned} W &= \int_0^{Q^*} f(q)dq - f(Q^*)Q^* + \sum\left[x_i^*\left\{(1-t_v)f(Q^*) - t_s\right\} - C_i(x_i^*)\right] + T \\ &= \int_0^{Q^*} f(q)dq - \sum C_i(x_i^*), \end{aligned} \qquad (7.2.16)$$

where x_i^* is firm i's equilibrium output. Hence,

$$\begin{aligned} dW/dt_v\big|_{dT=0} &= dW/dQ^* \cdot dQ^*/dt_v\big|_{dT=0} \\ &= \left\{f(Q^*) - \sum C_i'(x_i^*)dx_i^*/dQ^*\right\}dQ^*/dt_v\big|_{dT=0}. \end{aligned} \qquad (7.2.17)$$

The sign of dx_i^*/dQ^* is, in general, indeterminate. However, in the symmetric case where all firms' cost functions are identical, $dx_i^*/dQ^* = 1/n > 0$. Hence, taking into account $f(Q^*) - C_i'(x_i^*) > 0$, which is a consequence of the first order condition (7.2.2), we have $dW/dt_v\big|_{dT=0} > 0$ under (A.3). Even if firms' cost functions are not identical, the same conclusion holds provided $dx_i^*/dQ^* > 0$ for all i, or more generally, provided that the expression between the brace in (7.2.17) is positive.

We will next derive a formula for the optimal Pigouvian tax for controlling externalities within Cournot oligopoly. Let γ_i be emission of pollution per unit of firm i's output, and let t be the Pigouvian tax per unit of emission of pollution. Firm i's profit is

$$\pi_i \equiv px_i - C_i(x_i) - t\gamma_i x_i, \quad i = 1,2,\ldots,n. \qquad (7.2.18)$$

The first order condition for firm i's profit maximization is

$$f(Q) + x_i f'(Q) - C_i'(x_i) - t\gamma_i = 0, \quad i = 1,2,\ldots,n. \qquad (7.2.19)$$

We assume that condition (A.1) and

(A.4) $\quad f' < C_i'', \ i = 1,2,\ldots,n$

hold. Under (A.1) and (A.4), the second order condition is satisfied. Solving (7.2.19) with respect to x_i, we have

$$x_i \equiv \psi^i(Q,t,\gamma_i),\ i=1,2,...,n, \tag{7.2.20}$$

where

$$\begin{cases} \psi_Q^i \equiv \partial\psi^i/\partial Q = -(f' + x_i f'')/(f' - C_i'') < 0, \\ \psi_t^i \equiv \partial\psi^i/\partial t = \gamma_i/(f' - C_i'') < 0, \\ \psi_i^i \equiv \partial\psi^i/\partial\gamma_i = t/(f' - C_i'') < 0. \end{cases} \quad i=1,2,...,n. \tag{7.2.21}$$

The Cournot equilibrium industry output $Q^* \equiv Q^*(t,\gamma_1,...,\gamma_n)$ is the unique solution of equation

$$Q \equiv \sum_i \psi^i(Q,t,\gamma_i) \equiv \psi(Q,t,\gamma_1,...,\gamma_n). \tag{7.2.22}$$

The partial derivatives of Q^* are given as

$$\begin{cases} \partial Q^*/dt = \sum \psi_t^i/(1-\psi_Q) < 0, \\ \partial Q^*/\partial\gamma_i = \psi_i^i/(1-\psi_Q) < 0. \end{cases} \quad i=1,2,...,n. \tag{7.2.23}$$

The partial derivatives of the firms' outputs with respect to changes in t, γ_i and $\gamma_k (k \neq i)$ are as follows:

$$\begin{aligned} \partial x_i/\partial t = \psi_Q^i \partial Q/\partial t + \psi_t^i &= -(f' + x_i f'')/(f' - C_i'') \\ &\times \left\{ \sum_j \gamma_j \Big/ (f' - C_j'') \Big/ \left(1 - \sum_j (f' + x_j f'')/(f' - C_j'') \right) \right\} \\ &+ \gamma_i/(f' - C_i''), \quad i=1,2,...,n; \end{aligned} \tag{7.2.24}$$

$$\begin{aligned} \partial x_i/\partial\gamma_i &= \psi_Q^i \partial Q/\partial\gamma_i + \psi_i^i \\ &= \psi_i^i \left(1 - \sum_{j \neq i} \psi_Q^j \right) \Big/ (1-\psi_Q) < 0, \quad i=1,2,...,n; \end{aligned} \tag{7.2.25}$$

and

$$\partial x_i/\partial\gamma_k = \psi_Q^i \partial Q/\partial\gamma_k > 0, \quad i \neq k,\ i,k=1,2,...,n. \tag{7.2.26}$$

If the inverse demand function is linear and the firms have identical, constant marginal cost, then

$$\partial x_i/\partial t = \left\{\gamma_i + \sum \gamma_j/(n-1)\right\}/f' < 0, \quad i = 1,2,\ldots,n.$$

Otherwise, the sign of $\partial x_i/\partial t$ is, in general, indeterminate. However, in the case of symmetric firms having identical costs functions, we have $\partial x_i/\partial t < 0$.

Before proceeding further, let $D\left(\sum \gamma_i x_i\right)$ with $D' < 0$ be the damage function. Then the social welfare is defined by

$$\begin{aligned} W(\mathbf{x}(t)) = &\left\{\int_0^Q f(q)dq - f(Q)Q\right\} + \sum\left\{f(Q)x_i - C_i(x_i) - t\gamma_i x_i\right\} \\ &-D\left(\sum \gamma_i x_i\right) + t\sum \gamma_i x_i, \end{aligned} \tag{7.2.27}$$

where $\mathbf{x}$ is a vector of firms' outputs. The first order condition for maximization of W with respect to t yields

$$\begin{aligned} \sum \partial W/\partial x_i \, \partial x_i/\partial t &= \sum\Big\{f(Q) - f(Q) - f'(Q)Q + \left(f(Q) + x_i f'(Q) - C_i'(x_i) - t\gamma_i\right) \\ &\qquad + \sum_{j \neq i} x_j f'(Q) - D'\gamma_i + t\gamma_i\Big\}\partial x_i/\partial t \\ &= \sum\left(t\gamma_i - x_i f'(Q) - D'\gamma_i\right)\partial x_i/\partial t \\ &= 0, \end{aligned} \tag{7.2.28}$$

where we have made use of the first order condition (7.2.19). Hence, the optimal Pigouvian tax is determined by

$$t = D' + f' \sum x_i \, \partial x_i/\partial t \Big/ \sum \gamma_i \, \partial x_i/\partial t. \tag{7.2.29}$$

The sign of $\partial x_i/\partial t$ as well as that of the coefficient of f' is indeterminate. Two special cases are finally discussed:

Case a: $\partial x_i/\partial t = \partial x_j/\partial t$, $i \neq j$, $\gamma_i = 1$, $i, j = 1,2,\ldots,n$.

In this case (7.2.29) reads

$$t = D' + f' Q/n. \tag{7.2.30}$$

If all firms are symmetric, $\partial x_i/\partial t = \partial x_j/\partial t$ for $i \neq j$.

Case b: $\gamma_i = 1, i = 1,2,\ldots,n.$

In this case (7.2.29) reads

$$t = D' + f' \sum x_i \, \partial x_i / \partial t / \partial Q / \partial t. \tag{7.2.31}$$

The coefficient of f' is a weighted average of the x_is. If the inverse demand function is linear and if, in addition, the marginal costs *which may differ among firms* are constant, we have

$$\partial x_i / \partial t / \partial Q / \partial t = 1/n.$$

Hence, in this case (7.2.31) is identical to (7.2.30).

7.3 Water Resources Applications

Four particular models will be briefly outlined in this section.

The first model gives the description of a special problem in *environmental protection.* To prevent further deterioration of water quality polluters (industrial, urban, agricultural) within a region are willing to construct a regional waste treatment plant.

Denote by x_k the amount of pollution (to be treated) of polluter k. Denote $K\left(\sum x_i\right)$ the cost function of the treatment plant and $L_k(x_k)$ the benefit (e.g. economic value of better water quality, or savings in pollution fee) of treating x_k for polluter k. In this case each polluter endeavors to maximize his net benefit:

$$L_k(x_k) - \frac{x_k}{\sum x_i} K\left(\sum x_i\right) \quad (k \geq 1).$$

If one selects $p(s) = \frac{-1}{s} K(s)$ and $C_k = -L_k$, then the payoff function of the classical Cournot model is formally obtained. Hence this problem can be mathematically examined as a special N-person game, and all results on oligopoly theory can be readily applied.

An *irrigation system* can be modeled as follows. When considering irrigation systems it is important to harmonize the various interests of the irrigated farms. The question is: How is it possible to determine an equilibrium?

Define x_k to be the water volume for irrigation required by farm k, $K\left(\sum x_i\right)$ the capital cost of the irrigation system and $L_k(x_k)$ the irrigation benefit of farm k. The interest of each farm can then be expressed by the objective function:

$$L_k(x_k) - \frac{x_k}{\sum x_i} K\left(\sum x_i\right) \quad (k \geq 1).$$

This is formally the same objective function that was obtained in the previous example.

A model of a *multipurpose water management system* can be formulated in the following way. Various demands must usually be met in the development of water resources in a given system encompassed by a drainage basin or other areal unit. Some of the most common demands are: water supply, flood protection, irrigation, water quality control, recreation, etc. Development costs of the system should be allocated among the various beneficiaries. A reservoir system has a storage volume of $\sum x_i$, where x_k denotes the storage volume utilized by user k. Let $K\left(\sum x_i\right)$ be the development cost of the system and let $L_k(x_k)$ denote the benefit of user k as a result of the stored water x_k. Then the net benefit of each user can be presented according to the objective function

$$L_k(x_k) - \frac{x_k}{\sum x_i} K\left(\sum x_i\right) \quad (k \geq 1),$$

which has exactly the same form as in the previous cases.

A *water quality management problem* will be formulated as the last water resources example. Water authorities often employ economic incentives to maintain a standard level of water quality. Consider a city that has a central waste treatment plant. Industrial firms of the city may use the treatment plant if they pay for it. How much should this charge be if the objective of the water authority is to have all wastes treated by the central plant. Let x_k be the amount of wastes from firm k treated by the central plant and assume that $\phi\left(\sum x_i\right)$ is the unit treatment charge and $L_k(x_k)$ is the benefit of firm k, i.e. the amount saved by not treating it themselves. The objective function of firm k is

$$L_k(x_k) - x_k \phi\left(\sum x_i\right) \quad (k \geq 1).$$

Define $p = -\phi$ and $C_k = -L_k$ then this function formally agrees with the payoff function of the classical Cournot model.

7.4 An Oligopoly Model of Commercial Fishing

Population dynamics and N-person oligopolies are combined in this section to formulate international fishery models under imperfect competition. It is assumed that the fish harvesting countries behave as oligopolists, but their costs depend on the total level of available fish stock, which is governed by the biological growth law. We will first show that the number of nonextinct equilibria is 0, 1 or 2, and then we will characterize the dynamic behavior of the fish stock in terms of model parameters and initial value of the fish stock.

Assume that N countries are involved in an international fishing industry. Let x_{ki} denote the amount of fish harvested by country k and sold in country i (k=1,2,...,N; i=1,2,...,N). The inverse demand function in country i is assumed to be linear:

$$p_i = a_i - b_i Y_i, \tag{7.4.1}$$

where a_i and b_i are positive, and $Y_i = x_{1i} + x_{2i} + ... + x_{Ni}$ is the amount of fish being sold there. The fishing cost of country k is given by

$$C_k = c_k + \gamma_k X_k^2 / X, \tag{7.4.2}$$

where c_k and γ_k are positive, $X_k = x_{k1} + x_{k2} + ... + x_{kN}$, and X is the total level of fish stock. Therefore the profit of country k can be written as

$$\pi_k = \sum_{i=1}^{N} p_i x_{ki} - \left(c_k + \gamma_k X_k^2 / X\right), \tag{7.4.3}$$

which is a concave function of vector $(x_{k1}, x_{k2}, ..., x_{kN})$.

We assume that the N countries behave as Cournot oligopolists. Given X, the first order conditions for country k's profit maximization are given by equation

$$\frac{\partial \pi_k}{\partial x_{ki}} = -b_i x_{ki} + a_i - b_i Y_i - 2\gamma_k X_k / X = 0.$$

Excluding corner solutions, this equation holds for all k and i. Solving for x_{ki} we have

$$x_{ki} = \frac{a_i}{b_i} - Y_i - \frac{2\gamma_k}{b_i X} X_k.$$

Adding these equations for all values of i leads to the following:

$$X_k = A - S - B\frac{2\gamma_k}{X}X_k, \tag{7.4.4}$$

where S is the total amount of fish harvested,

$$A = \sum_{i=1}^{N}\frac{a_i}{b_i}, \qquad B = \sum_{i=1}^{N}\frac{1}{b_i}.$$

Solving equation (7.4.4) for X_k we have

$$X_k = \frac{A - S}{1 + 2B\frac{\gamma_k}{X}},$$

and by adding this equation for all values of k we get one equation for the single unknown S:

$$S = (A - S)\sum_{k=1}^{N}\frac{1}{1 + 2B\frac{\gamma_k}{X}},$$

from which we see that

$$S = \frac{Af(X)}{1 + f(X)} \tag{7.4.5}$$

with

$$f(X) = \sum_{k=1}^{N}\frac{1}{1 + 2B\frac{\gamma_k}{X}}.$$

We assume that the fish stock changes according to the well-known population dynamics rule

$$\dot{X} = X(\alpha - \beta X)$$

in the absence of fishing. Therefore it changes according to equation

$$\dot{X} = X\left(\alpha - \beta X - \frac{Af(X)}{(1 + f(X))X}\right) \tag{7.4.6}$$

in the presence of international commercial fishing, where α and β are positive constants, α being the intrinsic growth rate.

Introduce next the notation

$$g(X)=\frac{Af(X)}{(1+f(X))X}. \tag{7.4.7}$$

Simple differentiation shows that

$$f'(X)=\sum_{k=1}^{N}\frac{\frac{2B\gamma_k}{X^2}}{\left(1+2B\frac{\gamma_k}{X}\right)^2},$$

which implies that

$$Xf'(X)-f(X)=\sum_{k=1}^{N}\frac{-1}{\left(1+2B\frac{\gamma_k}{X}\right)^2}<0. \tag{7.4.8}$$

Therefore

$$g'(X)=\frac{A\left(f'(X)X-f(X)-f(X)^2\right)}{X^2(1+f(X))^2}<0.$$

Hence, g is strictly decreasing in X. Notice next that

$$f''(X)=\sum_{k=1}^{N}\frac{-\frac{4B\gamma_k}{X^3}}{\left(1+2B\frac{\gamma_k}{X}\right)^3},$$

which implies inequality

$$\begin{aligned}-f''(X)\cdot\frac{X^2}{2}&=\sum_{k=1}^{N}\frac{\frac{2B\gamma_k}{X}}{\left(1+2B\frac{\gamma_k}{X}\right)^3}<\sum_{k=1}^{N}\frac{1}{\left(1+2B\frac{\gamma_k}{X}\right)^2}\\&=f(X)-Xf'(X),\end{aligned} \tag{7.4.9}$$

where we used relation (7.4.8) in the last step. Finally, differentiation and simple calculation show that the numerator of $g''(X)$ (which determines its sign) can be written as

$$A(f''X+f'-f'-2ff')X^2(1+f)^2 - A(f'X-f-f^2)\left[2X(1+f)^2+X^2 2(1+f)f'\right]=$$
$$AX(1+f)\left[(f''X-2ff')X(1+f)-(f'X-f-f^2)(2+2f+2Xf')\right].$$

The sign of g'' coincides with the sign of the bracketed term, which can be simplified and bounded as follows:

$$\begin{aligned} & f''X^2(1+f)-2f'X(1+f)+2f+4f^2+2f^3-2(Xf')^2 \\ & > -2(f-Xf')(1+f)-2f'X(1+f)+2f+4f^2+2f^3-2f^2 \\ & = 2f^3 > 0 \end{aligned}$$

where we used relations (7.4.8) and (7.4.9). Hence g is strictly convex in X.

The nonextinct steady state or the bionomic equilibrium is the solution of equation

$$\alpha - \beta X = g(X). \tag{7.4.10}$$

The left hand side is strictly decreasing and linear, the right hand side is strictly decreasing and strictly convex, furthermore $g(0)=\frac{A}{2B}\sum_{k=1}^{N}\frac{1}{\gamma_k}>0$ and $\lim_{X\to\infty} g(X)=0$. Therefore we have the following possibilities:

Case 1. There is no positive root of equation (7.4.10). This case is illustrated in Figure 7.4.1, and occurs when $\alpha-\beta X<g(X)$ for all $X>0$;

Case 2. Equation (7.4.10) has only one positive root; and $g(0)>\alpha$, which case is shown in Figure 7.4.2;

Case 3. There is only one positive root and $g(0)\le\alpha$, which case is shown in Figure 7.4.3;

Case 4. There are two positive roots as illustrated in Figure 7.4.4.

Let $X_0=X(0)$ denote the initial total level of fish stock. In Case 1, $\dot{X}$ is always negative, therefore $X(t)$ is strictly decreasing. Since $X^*=0$ is the only equilibrium, $X(t)$ converges to zero as $t\to\infty$, resulting in extinction of fish stock. In Case 2, $\dot{X}$ is always negative, unless $X(t)=X^*$. Therefore, if

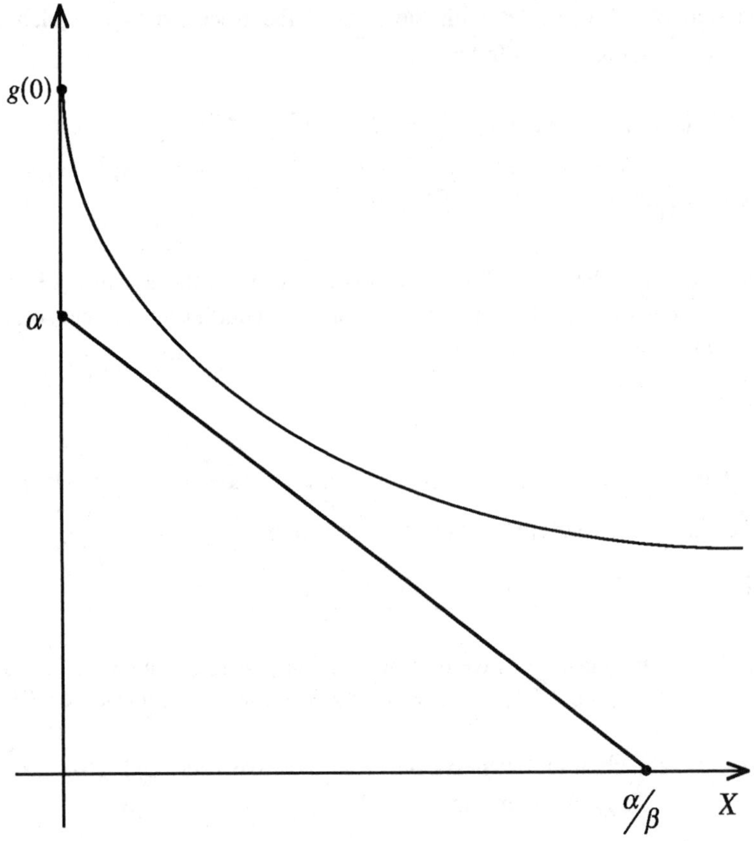

Figure 7.4.1 Case 1 without positive root

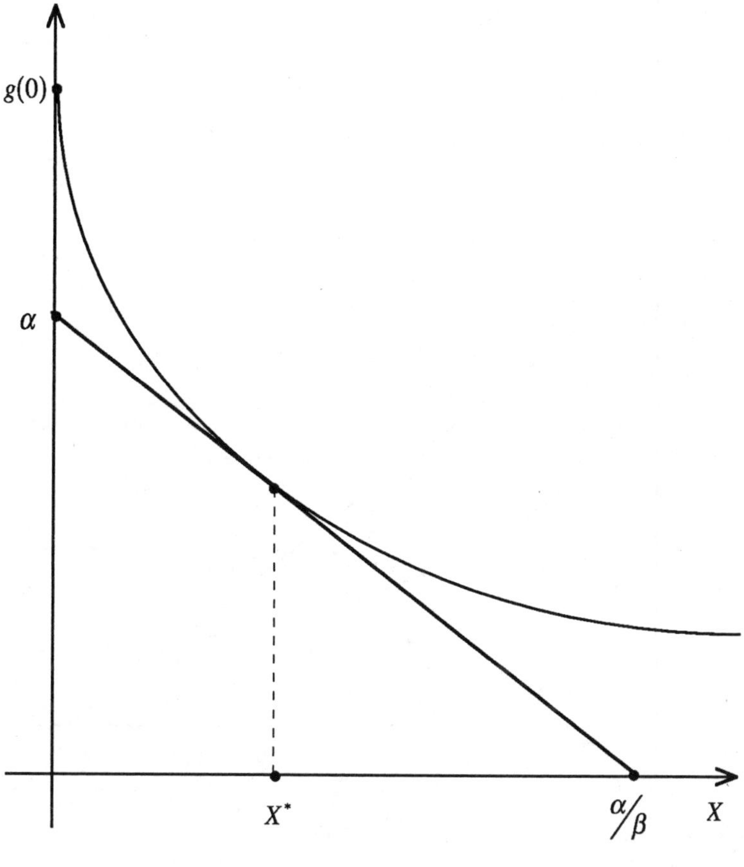

Figure 7.4.2 Case 2 with a single root

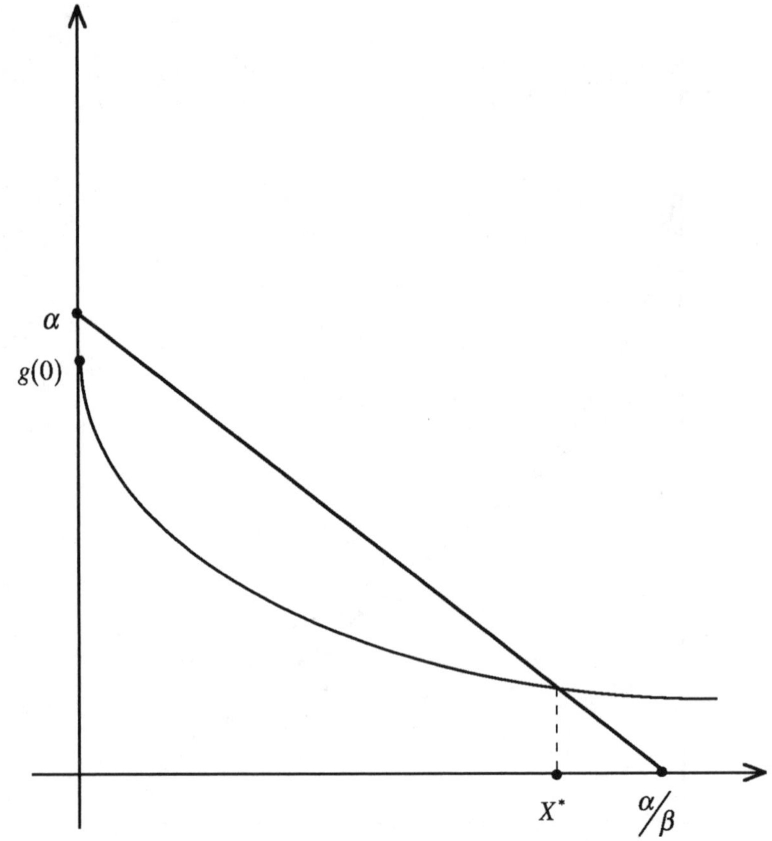

Figure 7.4.3 Case 3 with a single root

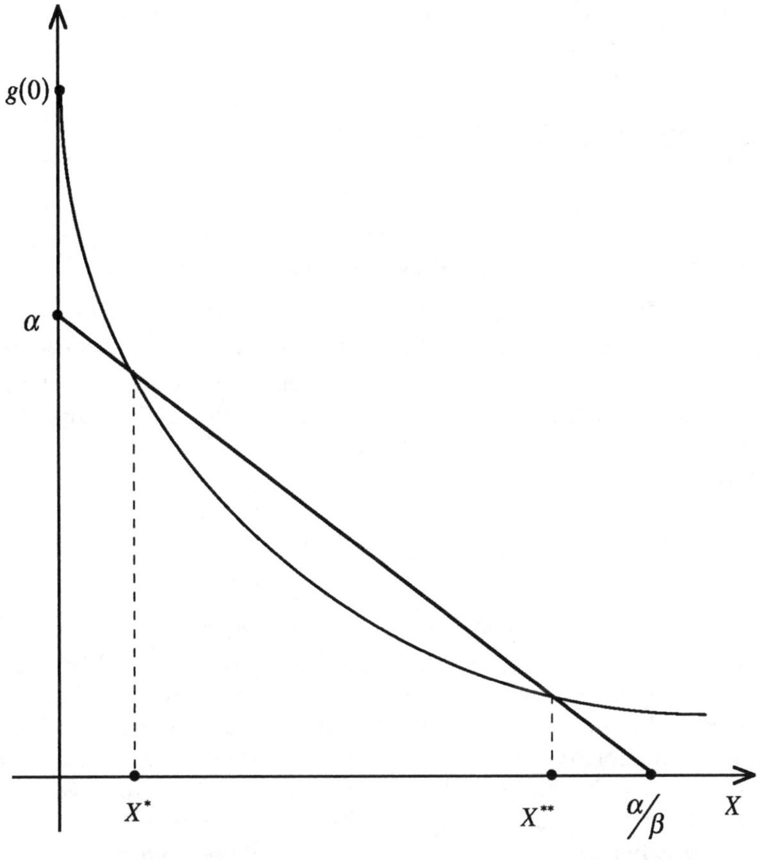

Figure 7.4.4 Case 4 with two positive roots

$X(0) > X^*$, then $X(t)$ converges to X^*, and if $X(0) < X^*$, then $X(t)$ converges to zero. In Case 3, $\dot{X} < 0$ for $X > X^*$, and $\dot{X} > 0$ for $X < X^*$. In the first case X decreases, and in the second case X increases. Therefore $X(t)$ converges to X^* regardless of the value of $X(0)$. In case 4, we have the following subcases. If $X(0) = 0$, then $X(t) = 0$ for all future times. If $0 < X(0) < X^*$, then $X(t)$ decreases and converges to zero; if $X(0) = X^*$, then $X(t)$ remains constant; if $X^* < X(0) < X^{**}$, then $X(t)$ increases, therefore $X(t) \to X^{**}$. If $X(0) = X^{**}$, then $X(t)$ remains constant; and if $X(0) > X^{**}$, then $X(t)$ decreases and $X(t) \to X^{**}$.

7.5 Controllability in Oligopolies

In this section, for the sake of simplicity, only single-product oligopolies will be examined. As earlier, let N denote the number of firms, let $P(s) = b - As$ $(A, b > 0)$ be the price function and for $k = 1,2,\ldots,N$, let $C_k(x_k) = c_k x_k + d_k$ $(c_k, d_k > 0)$ denote the cost function of firm k. Assume furthermore that the market is controlled with the cost function of the firms, which can be interpreted as subsidies, tax rates, etc. Under this assumption the profit of firm k can be expressed as

$$\varphi_k(x_1,\ldots,x_N) = x_k\left(b - A\sum_{l=1}^{N} x_l\right) - u(c_k x_k + d_k), \tag{7.5.1}$$

where u is the control variable. Before proceeding any further some remarks are in order. Notice first, that having the same control variable for all firms indicates that the firms are controlled in the same way. The case of different control variables will be discussed later. Notice also that it is sufficient to multiply only the cost by the control variable, since in the more general case of combined price and cost control the price control variable always can be normalized to one by introducing new monetary units. Price subsidies can be modelled by a multiplier of the price function, and for example, tax rates by multipliers of the cost functions. If tax and subsidy are imposed on unit output, then equation (7.5.1) has to be modified as follows:

$$\varphi_k(x_1,\ldots,x_N) = x_k\left(b - A\sum_{l=1}^{N} x_l\right) - (c_k x_k u + d_k). \tag{7.5.2}$$

We mention here, that in both discrete and continuous cases the forms of the resulting dynamic models will be the same regardless which of the controls

(7.5.1) or (7.5.2) is assumed. So, in the following discussion, only the control (7.5.1) will be considered.

Assuming discrete time scales and Cournot expectations first, at each time period $t \geq 1$, each firm maximizes its expected profit

$$x_k\left(b - Ax_k - A\sum_{l\neq k} x_l(t-1)\right) - (c_k x_k + d_k)u(t-1).$$

Excluding corner optimum, simple differentiation shows that

$$x_k(t) = -\frac{1}{2}\sum_{l\neq k} x_l(t-1) + \frac{b - u(t-1)c_k}{2A} \quad (k = 1,2,\ldots,N).$$

Introduce the new state variables

$$z_k(t) = x_k(t) - \frac{b}{(N+1)A}$$

to have a discrete control system

$$z_k(t) = -\frac{1}{2}\sum_{l\neq k} z_l(t-1) - \frac{c_k}{2A}u(t-1) \tag{7.5.3}$$

for k=1,2,...,N. Notice that this system can be written as

$$\mathbf{z}(t) = \mathbf{A}\mathbf{z}(t-1) + \mathbf{b}u(t-1) \tag{7.5.4}$$

with

$$\mathbf{z} = \begin{pmatrix} z_1 \\ z_2 \\ \vdots \\ z_N \end{pmatrix}, \mathbf{A} = \begin{pmatrix} 0 & -\frac{1}{2} & \cdots & -\frac{1}{2} \\ -\frac{1}{2} & 0 & \cdots & -\frac{1}{2} \\ \vdots & \vdots & & \vdots \\ -\frac{1}{2} & -\frac{1}{2} & \cdots & 0 \end{pmatrix}, \text{ and } \mathbf{b} = \begin{pmatrix} -\frac{c_1}{2A} \\ -\frac{c_2}{2A} \\ \vdots \\ -\frac{c_N}{2A} \end{pmatrix}.$$

It is well known from the theory of linear systems that system (7.5.3) is completely controllable if and only if the rank of the Kalman-matrix

$$\mathbf{K} = \left(\mathbf{b}, \mathbf{A}\mathbf{b}, \mathbf{A}^2\mathbf{b}, \ldots, \mathbf{A}^{N-1}\mathbf{b}\right)$$

is N.

Consider first the special case of a duopoly (that is, when N=2). In this case

$$\mathbf{K} = (\mathbf{b}, \mathbf{Ab}) = \begin{pmatrix} -\frac{c_1}{2A} & \frac{c_2}{4A} \\ -\frac{c_2}{2A} & \frac{c_1}{4A} \end{pmatrix}$$

which has full rank if and only if $c_1 \neq c_2$.

Assume next that $N \geq 3$. We will now verify that always $\text{rank}(\mathbf{K}) < N$, that is the system is not controllable. Observe first that

$$\mathbf{A} = \frac{1}{2}(\mathbf{I} - \mathbf{E})$$

where $\mathbf{I}$ is the $N \times N$ identity matrix and $\mathbf{E}$ is the $N \times N$ real matrix with all elements equal one. Since $\mathbf{E}^2 = N\mathbf{E}$,

$$\begin{aligned} \mathbf{A}^2 &= \frac{1}{4}\left(\mathbf{I} - 2\mathbf{E} + \mathbf{E}^2\right) = \frac{1}{4}\left(\mathbf{I} + (-2+N)\mathbf{E}\right) \\ &= \frac{N-1}{4}\mathbf{I} + \frac{2-N}{2}\mathbf{A} \end{aligned}$$

and

$$\mathbf{A}^2\mathbf{b} = \frac{N-1}{4}\mathbf{b} + \frac{2-N}{2}\mathbf{Ab}$$

showing that the columns of $\mathbf{K}$ are linearly dependent.

Let us modify the above model by assuming that different firms are controlled by different control variables. The modified model can be written as

$$\mathbf{z}(t) = \mathbf{Az}(t-1) + \mathbf{Bu}(t-1) \tag{7.5.5}$$

where $\mathbf{A}$ is as before,

$$\mathbf{B} = \text{diag}\left(-\frac{c_1}{2A}, -\frac{c_2}{2A}, \ldots, -\frac{c_N}{2A}\right),$$

and $\mathbf{u}$ is an N-element vector. Since $\mathbf{B}$ itself is nonsingular, the first N columns of the Kalman matrix $\mathbf{K}$ are linearly independent. Therefore $\text{rank}(\mathbf{K}) = N$ showing that the system is completely controllable.

Assume next that the time scale is continuous. The marginal profit of firm k is given as

$$\frac{\partial\varphi_k(x_1,\ldots,x_N)}{\partial x_k} = b - A\sum_{l=1}^{N} x_l - Ax_k - c_k u,$$

and by assuming that each firm adjusts its output proportionally to the marginal profit we get the adjustment equations:

$$\dot{x}_k(t) = K_k\left(-2Ax_k - A\sum_{l\neq k} x_l + b - c_k u\right) \quad (k = 1,2,\ldots,N)$$

where K_k is a positive constant for all k. Introduce the new state variables $z_k(t) = x_k(t) - \dfrac{b}{(N+1)A}$ to have the continuous control system

$$\dot{\mathbf{z}}(t) = \mathbf{A}\mathbf{z}(t) + \mathbf{b}u(t) \tag{7.5.6}$$

where

$$\mathbf{A} = \mathbf{K}\cdot\begin{pmatrix} -2A & -A & \cdots & -A \\ -A & -2A & \cdots & -A \\ \vdots & \vdots & & \vdots \\ -A & -A & \cdots & -2A \end{pmatrix}, \mathbf{b} = \mathbf{K}\cdot\begin{pmatrix} -c_1 \\ -c_2 \\ \vdots \\ -c_N \end{pmatrix}$$

with

$$\mathbf{K} = \mathrm{diag}(K_1, K_2, \ldots, K_N).$$

Consider first the special case of a duopoly (that is, when N=2). Then

$$\mathbf{K} = (\mathbf{b}, \mathbf{Ab}) = \begin{pmatrix} -K_1c_1 & A(2K_1^2c_1 + K_1K_2c_2) \\ -K_2c_2 & A(K_1K_2c_1 + 2K_2^2c_2) \end{pmatrix},$$

which has full rank if and only if

$$K_1c_1^2 + 2(K_2 - K_1)c_1c_2 - K_2c_2^2 \neq 0.$$

For example, if $K_1 = K_2$, then this condition is equivalent to the assumption that $c_1 \neq c_2$.

If $N \geq 3$, then the sufficient and necessary controllability conditions are even more complicated. However, if $K_1 = K_2 = \ldots = K_N$, then

$$\mathbf{A} = -AK(\mathbf{I} + \mathbf{E})$$

and

$$\mathbf{A}^2 = A^2K^2(\mathbf{I}+2\mathbf{E}+\mathbf{E}^2) = A^2K^2(\mathbf{I}+(N+2)\mathbf{E})$$
$$= A^2K^2\left(\mathbf{I}+(N+2)\left(-\mathbf{I}-\frac{1}{AK}\mathbf{A}\right)\right)$$
$$= -(N+1)A^2K^2\cdot\mathbf{I}-(N+2)AK\cdot\mathbf{A}$$

showing that the columns of matrix **K** are linearly dependent.

The case of different control for different firms can be discussed analogously to the discrete case. The details are left as an exercise as well as the cases of adaptive and extrapolative expectations.

7.6 Supplementary Notes and Discussions

7.1 The models being discussed in this section have been earlier examined by Szidarovszky (1998), where particular existence results for the equilibrium point in the slightly more general case are also presented.

7.2 The results of this section are taken from Okuguchi and Yamazaki (1994). Assuming *quadratic* cost functions, Dierickx, Matutes and Nevin (1988) have analyzed the effects of indirect taxation within Cournot oligopoly without product differentiation. Earlier Levin (1982, 1985), Katz and Rosen (1985), and later Besley (1989) have taken up the same problem for specific tax. The control of the industry by taxation can be discussed in the way as it will be demonstrated in Section 7.5.

7.3 The models discussed in this section have been studied and illustrated by numerical examples in Bogárdi and Szidarovszky (1976).

7.4 An early two-person version of the model and stability conditions were presented in Okuguchi (1996c). The version given in this section is taken from Szidarovszky and Okuguchi (1997c).

7.5 The discrete model has been earlier examined in Szidarovszky and Yen (1993). The continuous case contains new results.

References

Al-Nowaihi, A. and P.L. Levine (1985): The Stability of the Cournot Oligopoly Model: A Reassessment. *J. of Econ. Theory*, Vol. 35, 307-321.

Arrow, K.J. and M. McManus (1958): A Note on Dynamic Stability. *Econometrica*, Vol. 26, 448-454.

Basar, T. and G.J. Olsder (1982): Dynamic Noncooperative Game Theory. Academic Press, New York/London.

Bellman, R. (1969): Stability Theory of Differential Equations. Dover Publ. Inc., New York.

Bellman, R. (1970): Introduction to Matrix Analysis, 2nd edition. McGraw-Hill, New York.

Besley, T. (1989): Commodity Taxation and Imperfect Competition. A Note on the Effect of Entry. *Journal of Public Economics*, Vol. 40, 359-367.

Bogardi, I. and F. Szidarovszky (1976): Application of Game Theory in Water Management. *Appl. Math. Modeling*, Vol. 1, 16-20.

Brauer, F. and J.A. Nohel (1969): The Qualitative Theory of Ordinary Differential Equations. W.A. Benjamin Inc., New York/Amsterdam.

Brock, W.A. and J.A. Scheinkman (1975): Some Results on Global Asymptotical Stability of Difference Equations. *Journal of Econ. Theory*, Vol. 10, 265-268.

Burger, E. (1959): Einfuhrung in die Theorie der Spiele. De Gruyter, Berlin, Germany.

Carlson, D. (1968): A New Criterion for H-Stability of Complex Matrices. *Lin. Alg. and Appl.*, Vol. 1, 59-64.

Cheng, L. (1985): Comparing Bertrand and Cournot Equilibria: A Geometric Approach. *Rand J. of Economics*, Vol. 16, 146-152.

Chiarella, C. and K. Okuguchi (1996): A Dynamic Analysis of Cournot Duopoly in Imperfectly Competitive Product and Factor Markets, *Mimeo*, University of Technology, Sydney and Nanzan University, and *Keio Econ. Studies*, XXXIV (1997), 21-33.

Conlinsk, J. (1973): Quick Stability Checks and Matrix Norms. *Economica*, Vol. 40, 402-409.

Cournot, A. (1838): Recherches sur les Principles Mathématiques de la Théorie des Richesses. Hachette, Paris. (English translation (1960): Researches into the Mathematical Principles of the Theory of Wealth. Kelley, New York).

Dafermos, S. (1983): An Iterative Scheme for Variational Inequalities. *Math. Programming*, Vol. 26, 40-47.

Debreu, G. (1952): A Social Equilibrium Existence Theorem. *Proc. of the Nat. Acad. of Sci.*, Vol. 38, 886-893.

Dierickx, I., C. Matutes, and D. Nevin (1988): Indirect Taxation and Cournot Equilibrium. *Intern. J. of Industrial Organization*, Vol. 4, 385-399.

Dixit, A. (1986): Comparative Statics of Oligopoly. *Intern. Econ. Review*, Vol. 27, 107-121.

Eichhorn, W. (1971a): Zur Statischen Theorie des Mehrprodukten-Oligopols. *Operations Research Verfahren*, Vol. 10, 16-33.

Eichhorn, W. (1971b): Zur Dynamischen Theorie des Mehrprodukten-oligopols. *Jahrbücher für Nationalökonomie und Statistik*, Vol. 186, 498-515.

Fisher, F.M. (1961): The Stability of the Cournot Oligopoly Solution: The Effects of Speeds of Adjustment and Increasing Marginal Costs. *Review of Econ. Studies*, Vol. 28, 125-135.

Frank, C.R., Jr. and R.E. Quandt (1963): On the Existence of Cournot Equilibrium. *Intern. Econ. Review*, Vol. 5, 192-196.

Friedman, J.W. (1977): The Theory of Games and Oligopoly. North Holland Publ. Co., Amsterdam/New York/Oxford.

Friedman, J.W. and A.C. Hoggatt (1980): An Experiment in Noncooperative Oligopoly. JAI Press, Greenwich, Conn.

Friedman, J.W. (1981): Oligopoly Theory. Chapter 11 in K.J. Arrow and M.D. Intriligator (eds.), *Handbook of Mathematical Economics*. North Holland Publ. Co., Amsterdam, 491-534.

Friedman, J.W. (1986): Game Theory with Applications to Economics. Oxford Univ. Press, New York/Oxford.

Funke, H. (1985): Eine Allgemeine Theorie der Polypol- und Oligopolpreisbilding. Springer Verlag, Berlin/Heidelberg/New York.

Furth, D. (1986): Stability and Instability in Oligopoly. *J. of Econ. Theory*, Vol. 40, 197-228.

Gabay, D. and H. Moulin (1980): On the Uniqueness and Stability of Nash-Equilibria in Noncooperative Games. In Bensoussan *et al.* (eds.) *Applied Stochastic Control in Econometrics and Management Science*. North Holland, Amsterdam.

Gale, D. and H. Nikaido (1965): The Jacobian Matrix and the Global Univalence of Mappings. *Math. Ann.*, Vol. 159, 81-93.

Hadar, J. (1966): Stability of Oligopoly with Product Differentiation. *Review of Econ. Studies*, Vol. 33, 57-60.

Hadley, G. (1964): Nonlinear and Dynamic Programming. Addison-Wesley, Reading, MA.

Harker, P.T. (1984): A Variational Inequality Approach for the Determination of Oligopolistic Market Equilibrium. *Math. Programming*, Vol. 30, 105-111.

Hartman, P. (1982): Ordinary Differential Equations, 2nd edition. Birkhauser, Boston/Basel/Stuttgart.

Henderson, J.M. and R.E. Quandt (1958): Microeconomic Theory. McGraw-Hill, New York.

Hill, M. and M. Waterson (1983): Labor-Managed Cournot Oligopoly and Industry Output. *J. of Comparative Economics*, Vol. 7, 43-51.

Inada, K. (1971): The Production Coefficient Matrix and Stolper-Samuelson Condition. *Econometrica*, Vol. 39, 219-240.

Johnson, C.R. (1974): Sufficient Conditions for D-Stability. *J. of Econ. Theory*, Vol. 9, 53-62.

Karamardian, S. (1969): The Nonlinear Complementarity Problems with Applications. Part I and Part II, *J. of Optimization Theory and Appl.*, Vol. 4, 87-98 and 167-181.

Katz, M. and H. Rosen (1985): Tax Analysis of an Oligopoly Model. *Public Finance Quarterly*, Vol. 13, 3-19.

Krelle, W. (1976): Preistheorie I, 2nd edition. Tubingen, J.C.B. Mohr (Paul Siebeck).

Lancaster, P. (1969): Theory of Matrices. Academic Press, New York/London.

Levin, D. (1982): Cournot Oligopoly and Government Regulation. Second Essay in Ph.D. Thesis, MIT, 68-101.

Levin, D. (1985): Taxation within Cournot Oligopoly. *Journal of Public Economics*, Vol. 27, 281-290.

Li, W. and F. Szidarovszky (1997): An Elementary Result in the Stability Theory of Time-Invariant Nonlinear Discrete Dynamical Systems. *Appl. Math. and Comp.*, to appear.

Mañas, M. (1972): A Linear Oligopoly Game. *Econometrica*, Vol. 40, 917-922.

Miller, R.K. and A.N. Michel (1982): Ordinary Differential Equations. Academic Press, New York/London.

Murphy, F.H., H.D. Sherali, and A.L. Soyster (1982): A Mathematical Programming Approach for Determining Oligopolistic Market Equilibrium. *Math. Programming*, Vol. 24, 92-106.

Neary, H. M. (1984): Labor-Managed Cournot Oligopoly and Industry Output: A Comment. *J. of Comparative Economics*, Vol. 8, 322-327.

Nerlove, M. (1958): The Dynamics of Supply. Johns Hopkins Press, Baltimore, MD.

Neumann, J. von(1928): Zur Theorie der Gesellschaftsspiele. *Math. Annalen*, Vol. 100, 295-320. (English translation (1959): On the Theory of Games of Strategy. In A.W. Tucker and R.D. Luce (eds.), Contributions to the Theory of Games IV. Princeton University Press, Princeton, N.J.)

Neumann, J. von and O. Morgenstern (1944): Theory of Games and Economic Behavior. Princeton University Press, Princeton, N.J.

Nikaido, H. and K. Isoda (1955): Note on Noncooperative Convex Games. *Pac. J. of Math.*, Vol. 5, 807-815.

Okuguchi, K. (1964): The Stability of the Cournot Solution: A Further Generalization. *Review of Econ. Studies*, Vol. 31, 143-146.

Okuguchi, K. (1968): The Stability of Price Adjusting Oligopoly: The Effects of Adaptive Expectations. *Southern Econ. J.*,Vol. 35, 34-36.

Okuguchi, K. (1969): On the Stability of Price Adjusting Oligopoly Equilibrium Under Product Differentiation. *Southern Econ. J.*, Vol. 35, 244-246.

Okuguchi, K. (1970): Adaptive Expectations in an Oligopoly Model. *Review of Econ. Studies*, Vol. 36, 233-237.

Okuguchi, K. (1976): Expectations and Stability in Oligopoly Models. Springer Verlag, Berlin/Heidelberg/New York.

Okuguchi, K. (1978): Matrices with Dominant Diagonal Blocks and Economic Theory. *J. of Math. Econ.*, Vol. 5, 43-52.

Okuguchi, K. (1983): The Cournot Oligopoly and Competitive Equilibria as Solutions to Non-Linear Complementarity Problems. *Economics Letters*, Vol. 12, 127-133.

Okuguchi, K. (1984): Equilibrium Prices in the Bertrand and Cournot Oligopolies. Sonderforschungsbereich 303, Bonn University, Bonn, and *Journal of Econ. Theory*, Vol. 42 (1987), 128-139.

Okuguchi, K. and F. Szidarovszky (1985a): On the Existence and Computation of Equilibrium Points for an Oligopoly Game with Multi-Product Firms. *Annales*, Univ. Sci.Bud.Rol.Eotvos Nom., Sectio Computatorica, Vol. 6, 131-137.

Okuguchi, K. and F. Szidarovszky (1985b): The Equilibrium Problem for a Linear Model of Oligopoly with Multi-Product Firms. *Annales*, Univ. Sci.Bud.Rol.Eotvos Nom., Sectio Computatorica, Vol. 6, 139-144.

Okuguchi, K. (1986a): Adaptive Expectations and Stability of the Oligopoly Equilibrium in a Model where Outputs are Adjusted in Proportional to the Marginal Profit. *Mimeo*, Department of Economics , Tokyo Metropolitan University, Tokyo, Japan, and Bonn University, Germany.

Okuguchi, K. (1986b): Labor-Managed Bertrand and Cournot Oligopolies. *Journal of Economics*, Vol. 46, 115-122.

Okuguchi, K. and F. Szidarovszky (1987a): Stability of the Linear Cournot Oligopoly with Multi-Product Firms. *Econ. Studies Quarterly* (now *Japanese Economic Review*), Vol. 38, 184-187.

Okuguchi, K. and F. Szidarovszky (1987b): Dynamics of the Cournot Oligopoly with Multi-Product Firms. *Mimeo*, Department of Economics, Tokyo Metropolitan University, Tokyo, Japan, and Bonn University, Germany, and *J. of Math. Soc. Sci.*, Vol. 16 (1988), 159-169.

Okuguchi, K. and F. Szidarovszky (1987c): A Note on Sequential Adjustment in a Multiproduct Oligopoly Market. *Mimeo*, Department of Economics, Tokyo Metropolitan University, Tokyo, Japan.

Okuguchi, K. and F. Szidarovszky (1987d): An Adaptive Model of Oligopoly with Multi-Product Firms. *Mimeo*, Department of Economics, Tokyo Metropolitan, University, Tokyo, Japan, and *Econ. Studies Quarterly*, Vol. 40 (1989), 48-52.

Okuguchi, K. and F. Szidarovszky (1990): The Theory of Oligopoly with Multi-Product Firms. Springer Verlag, Berlin/Heidelberg/New York.

Okuguchi, K. (1991a): Existence of an Equilibrium for Labor-Managed Cournot Oligopoly. *Mimeo*, Department of Economics, Tokyo Metropolitan University, Tokyo, Japan.

Okuguchi, K. (1991b): Labor-Managed and Capitalistic Firms in International Duopoly: The Effects of Export Subsidy. *Journal of Comparative Economics*, Vol. 15, 476-484.

Okuguchi, K. (1993a): Cournot Oligopoly with Product-Maximizing and Labor-Managed Firms. *Keio Econ. Studies*, Vol. XXX, 27-38.

Okuguchi, K. (1993b): Unified Approach to Cournot Models: Oligopoly, Taxation and Aggregate Provision of a Pure Public Good. *European J. of Political Economy*, Vol. 9, 233-245.

Okuguchi, K. and T. Yamazaki (1994): Bertrand and Hierarchical Stackelberg Oligopolies with Product Differentiation. *Keio Econ. Studies*, Vol. XXXI, 75-80.

Okuguchi, K. (1995): Decreasing Returns and Existence of Nash Equilibrium in Rent-Seeking Games. *Mimeo*, Department of Economics, Nanzan University, Nagoya, Japan.

Okuguchi, K. (1996a): Cournot Oligopoly-Oligopsony. *Mimeo*, Department of Economics, Nanzan University, Nagoya, Japan.

Okuguchi, K. (1996b): Existence of Equilibrium for Labor-Managed Cournot Oligopoly. *Nanzan J. of Econ. Studies*, Vol. XI, No. 2, 111-119.

Okuguchi, K. (1996c): Long-run Fish Stock and Imperfectly Competitive International Commercial Fishing. Series No. 19, Nanzan University, Nagoya, Japan and *Keio Econ. Studies*, Vol. XXXV (1998).

Okuguchi, K. and T. Yamazaki (1996): Two-Stage Cournot Oligopolies with Industry-Wide Externalities. *Seoul J. of Economics*, Vol. 9, No. 1, 1-15.

Ortega, J.M. and W.C. Rheinboldt (1970): Iterative Solutions of Nonlinear Equations in Several Variables. Academic Press, New York/London.

Ostrowski, A.M. (1973): Solutions of Equations in Euclidean and Banach Spaces. Academic Press, New York/London.

Pérez-Castrillo, J.D. and T. Verdier (1992): A General Analysis of Rent-Seeking Games. *Public Choice*, Vol. 73, 335-350.

Rives, N.W., Jr. (1975): On the History of the Mathematical Theory of Games. *History of Political Economy*, Vol. 7, 549-565.

Rosen, J.B. (1965): Existence and Uniqueness of Equilibrium Points for Concave *n*-Person Games. *Econometrica*, Vol. 33, 520-534.

Rózsa, P. (1974): Lineáris algebra alkalmazásokkal (Linear Algebra with Applications). Müszaki Könyvkiadó, Budapest.

Scarf, H. (1973): The Computation of Economic Equilibria. Yale University Press, New Haven, CT.

Seade J. (1980): The Stability of Cournot Revisited. *J. of Econ. Theory*, Vol. 23, 15-27.

Selten, R. (1970): Preispolitik der Mehrproduktenunternehmung in der Statischen Theorie. Springer-Verlag, Berlin/Heidelberg/New York.

Simmons, D.M. (1975): Nonlinear Programming for Operations Research. Prentice Hall, Englewood Cliffs, N.J.

Stackelberg, H. von (1934): Markform und Gleichgewicht. Springer-Verlag, Berlin.

Szép, J. and F. Forgó (1972): Bevezetés a játékelméletbe. (Introduction to Game Theory). Közg. es Jogi Könyvkiadó, Budapest.

Szép, J. and F. Forgó (1985): Introduction to the Theory of Games. Akadémiai Kiadó, Budapest.

Szidarovszky, F. (1970): On the Oligopoly Game. DM-70-1, K. Marx Univ. of Economics, Budapest.

Szidarovszky, F. (1975): Az oligopol játék csoportegyensuly-problémája. (Group-Equilibrium Problem for the Oligopoly Game). Kandidátusi Értekezés, MTA, Budapest (Thesis for degree Cand. in Math., Hung. Academy of Sciences, Budapest).

Szidarovszky, F. and S. Yakowitz (1977): A New Proof of the Existence and Uniqueness of the Cournot Equilibrium. *Intern. Econ. Review*, Vol. 18, 787-789.

Szidarovszky, F. (1978): Játékelmélet (Game Theory). Textbook for Eötvös University, Tankönyvkiadó, Budapest.

Szidarovszky, F. and S. Yakowitz (1978): Principles and Procedures of Numerical Analysis. Plenum Press, New York.

Szidarovszky, F. and S. Yakowitz (1982): Contributions to Cournot Oligopoly Theory. *J. of Econ. Theory*, Vol. 28, 51-70.

Szidarovszky, F. and S. Molnar (1986): Játékelmélet müszaki alkalmazásokkal (Game Theory with Engineering Applications). Müszaki Könyvkiadó, Budapest.

Szidarovszky, F. and K. Okuguchi (1986): Stability of the Cournot Equilibrium for an Oligopoly with Multi-Product firms. *Proceedings*, 5th IFAC/IFORS Conf. on Dynamic Modelling and Control of National Economies, 17-20 June, 1986, Budapest, 165-167, Pergamon Press, New York/London.

Szidarovszky, F., M. Gershon, and L. Duckstein (1986): Techniques for Multicriteria Decision Making in Systems Management. Elsevier, Amsterdam.

Szidarovszky, F. and K. Okuguchi (1987a): A Note on the Existence of the Cournot Equilibrium for a Multiproduct Oligopoly. *Mimeo*, Department of Economics, Tokyo Metropolitan University, Tokyo, Japan.

Szidarovszky, F. and K. Okuguchi (1987b): Notes on the Stability of Quadratic Games. *Mimeo*, Department of Economics, Tokyo Metropolitan University, Tokyo, Japan, and *Keio Econ. Studies*, Vol. XXIV (1987), 33-45.

Szidarovszky, F. and K. Okuguchi (1987c): A Note on the Stability of Quadratic Games under Combined Expectations. *Mimeo*, Department of Economics, Tokyo Metropolitan University, Tokyo, Japan.

Szidarovszky, F. and K. Okuguchi (1987d): Stability of the Nash Equilibrium for a Non-Cooperative Quadratic Game. *Mimeo*, Department of Economics, Tokyo Metropolitan University, Tokyo, Japan.

Szidarovszky, F. and K. Okuguchi (1987e): Egy adaptiv kvadratikus játék stabilitásáról. (On the Stability of an Adaptive Quadratic Game). *SZIGMA*, Vol. 20 (1987-88), 79-82.

Szidarovszky, F. and K. Okuguchi (1987f): Adaptive Expectations in a Multi-Product Oligopoly Model. *Mimeo*, Department of Economics, Tokyo Metropolitan University, Tokyo, Japan.

Szidarovszky, F. and K. Okuguchi (1987g): On the Stability of Games with Time-Dependent Pay-off Functions. *Mimeo*, Department of Economics, Tokyo Metropolitan University, Tokyo, Japan.

Szidarovszky, F. and K. Okuguchi (1987h): On Multistep and Monotone Stability of Equilibria in a Multiproduct Oligopoly. *Mimeo*, Department of Economics, Tokyo Metropolitan University, Tokyo, Japan.

Szidarovszky, F. and K. Okuguchi (1987i): Some Notes on Multistep Iteration Methods. Working Paper, Dept. of Mathematical Sciences, University of Texas at El Paso, El Paso, TX, and *Annales*, Univ. Sci. Bud. Rol. Eotvos Nom., Sectio Computatorica, Vol. 13 (1992), 35-46.

Szidarovszky, F. and K. Okuguchi (1987j): On a General Stackelberg-type Leader-Follower Oligopoly Market. *Mimeo*, Department of Economics, Tokyo Metropolitan University, Tokyo, Japan.

Szidarovszky, F. and K. Okuguchi (1987k): A Note on Global Asymptotical Stability of Nonlinear Difference Equations. *Mimeo*, Department of Economics, Tokyo Metropolitan University, Tokyo, Japan, and *Economics Letters*, Vol. 26 (1988), 349-352.

Szidarovszky, F., J. Szép, and K. Okuguchi (1987): On a Stable Dynamic Model of Oligopoly. *Mimeo*, Department of Economics, Tokyo Metropolitan University, Tokyo, Japan.

Szidarovszky, F. and K. Okuguchi (1988a): On the Existence and Uniqueness in an Oligopoly with Product Differentiation. *Mimeo*, Department of Economics, Tokyo Metropolitan University, Tokyo, Japan.

Szidarovszky, F. and K. Okuguchi (1988b): On the Uniqueness of Equilibrium in a Multiproduct Oligopoly Model. *Mimeo*, Department of Economics, Tokyo Metropolitan University, Tokyo, Japan.

Szidarovszky, F and K. Okuguchi (1988c): A Linear Oligopoly Model with Adaptive Expectations: Stability Reconsidered. *Journal of Economics*, Vol. 48, 79-82.

Szidarovszky, F. (1989): On Time Dependent Multistep Dynamic Processes with Set-Valued Iteration Function. Working Paper, Dept. of Systems and Industrial Eng., University of Arizona, Tucson, AZ.

Szidarovszky, F. and K. Okuguchi (1989a): Dynamic Oligopoly. Part 1: Discrete Time-Scale Models. *Mimeo*, Department of Economics, Tokyo Metropolitan University, Tokyo, Japan.

Szidarovszky, F. and K. Okuguchi (1989b): Dynamic Oligopoly. Part 2: Continuous Time-Scale Models. *Mimeo*, Department of Economics, Tokyo Metropolitan University, Tokyo, Japan.

Szidarovszky, F. and K. Okuguchi (1989c): Dynamic Oligopoly. Part 3: Models with Incomplete Informations. *Mimeo*, Department of Economics, Tokyo Metropolitan University, Tokyo, Japan.

Szidarovszky, F. (1990): Multiproduct Cournot Oligopolies with Market Saturation. *Pure Math. and Appl.*, Series B, Vol. 1, No. 1, 3-15.

Szidarovszky, F and K. Okuguchi (1990): Dynamic Oligopoly: Models with Incomplete Information. *Appl. Math. and Comp.*, Vol. 38, No. 2, 161-177.

Szidarovszky, F. and J. Yen (1991): Stability of a Special Oligopoly Market. *Pure Math. and Appl.*, Series B, Vol. 2, No. 2-3, 93-100.

Szidarovszky, F. and A.T. Bahill (1992): *Linear Systems Theory.* CRC Press, Boca Raton/London.

Szidarovszky, F., S. Rassenti, and J. Yen (1992): Modified Cournot Expectations in Dynamic Oligopolies. *Pure Math. and Appl.*, Series B, Vol. 3, No. 2-3-4, 143-150.

Szidarovszky, F and K. Okuguchi (1993): Dynamic Oligopoly with Complete Information. *Belgian J. of Operational Research, Stat. and Comp. Sci.*, Vol. 33, 13-44.

Szidarovszky, F. and J. Yen (1993): Cournot Expectations Revisited. *Keio Econ. Studies*, Vol. XXX, 39-41.

Szidarovszky, F., S. Rassenti, and J. Yen (1994): The Stability of the Cournot Solution Under Adaptive Expectation: A Further Generalization. *International Review of Econ. and Finance*, Vol. 3, No. 2, 173-181.

Szidarovszky, F. and J. Yen (1995): Dynamic Cournot Oligopolies with Production Adjustment Costs. *J. of Math. Econ.*, Vol. 24, 95-101.

Szidarovszky, F. and K. Okuguchi (1996): Oligopoly-Oligopsony Equilibrium as a Solution of a Complementarity Problem. *Mimeo*, Department of Economics, Nanzan University, Nagoya, Japan.

Szidarovszky, F. and K. Okuguchi (1997a): On the Existence and Uniqueness of Pure Nash Equilibrium in Rent-Seeking Games. *Games and Econ. Behavior*, Vol. 18, 135-140.

Szidarovszky, F. and K. Okuguchi (1997b): Dynamic Analysis of Oligopsony Under Adaptive Expectations. *Mimeo*, Systems and Industrial Engineering Department, University of Arizona, Tucson, AZ.

Szidarovszky, F. and K. Okuguchi (1997c): An Oligopoly Model of Commercial Fishing. *Mimeo*, Gifu Shotokugakuen University and University of Arizona, and *Seoul J. Of Econ*, Vol. 11 (1998), forthcoming.

Szidarovszky, F. (1998): Network Oligopolies. *Pure Math and Appl.*, (to appear).

Theocharis, R.D. (1959): On the Stability of the Cournot Solution on the Oligopoly Problem. *Review of Economic Studies*, Vol. 27, 133-134.

Tullock, G. (1980): Efficient Rent-Seeking. In M. Buchanan, R. D. Tollison and G. Tullock (eds.), Toward a Theory of the Rent-Seeking Society, Texas A & M Press, College Station.

Uzawa, H. (1961): The Stability of Dynamic Processes. *Econometrica*, Vol. 29, 617-631.

Vives, X. (1984): On the Efficiency of Bertrand and Cournot Equilibria with Product Differentiation. *J. of Econ. Theory*, Vol. 36, 166-175.

Ward, B. (1958): The Firm in Illyria: Market Syndicalism. *American Econ. Review*, Vol. 48, 566-589.

Yakowitz, S. and F. Szidarovszky (1986): Introduction to Numerical Computations, 2nd edition, 1989. Macmillan, New York.

Index

Druck: Strauss Offsetdruck, Mörlenbach
Verarbeitung: Schäffer, Grünstadt